TERRORISM AND COUNTER-TERRORISM IN CHINA

MICHAEL CLARKE
(*Editor*)

Terrorism and Counter-Terrorism in China

Domestic and Foreign Policy Dimensions

HURST & COMPANY, LONDON

First published in the United Kingdom in 2018 by
C. Hurst & Co. (Publishers) Ltd.,
41 Great Russell Street, London, WC1B 3PL
© Michael Clarke and the Contributors, 2017
All rights reserved.
Printed in India

The right of Michael Clarke and the Contributors to be identified as the authors of this publication is asserted by them in accordance with the Copyright, Designs and Patents Act, 1988.

A Cataloguing-in-Publication data record for this book is available from the British Library.

ISBN: 9781849048774

This book is printed using paper from registered sustainable and managed sources.

www.hurstpublishers.com

This book is dedicated to my wife, Kelli, and our daughters, Grace and Lydia, for all their love and patience

CONTENTS

Acknowledgements ix
Notes on Contributors xi
Abbreviations xv

Introduction: Terrorism and Counter-Terrorism in China
  Michael Clarke 1

1. China's 'War on Terrorism': Confronting the Dilemmas of the 'Internal–External' Security Nexus *Michael Clarke* 17
2. 'Fighting the Enemy with Fists and Daggers': The Chinese Communist Party's Counter-Terrorism Policy in the Xinjiang Uyghur Autonomous Region (XUAR) *Julia Famularo* 39
3. 'Fighting Terrorism According to Law': China's Legal Efforts against Terrorism *Zunyou Zhou* 75
4. The Narrative of Uyghur Terrorism and the Self-Fulfilling Prophecy of Uyghur Militancy *Sean Roberts* 99
5. China and Counter-Terrorism: Beyond Pakistan? *Andrew Small* 129
6. China's Counter-Terrorism Policy in the Middle East *Mordechai Chaziza* 141
7. Uyghur Terrorism in a Fractured Middle East *Raffaello Pantucci* 157
8. Uyghur Cross-Border Movement into South East Asia: Between Resistance and Survival *Stefanie Kam Li Yee* 173

Notes 187
Index 269

ACKNOWLEDGEMENTS

This book derives from a two-day conference organised and hosted by the National Security College (NSC), Crawford School of Public Policy, Australian National University on 16-17 August 2016.

I would therefore first like to thank Director of the NSC, Professor Rory Medcalf, for the generous funding provided for the conference which enabled us to bring together a leading group of international experts on Xinjiang and China's approach towards terrorism and counter-terrorism. Additionally, a great vote of thanks is also due to other NSC staff who assisted in the organisation, logistics and hosting of the event including Christopher Farnham, James Mortensen, and Tom Chen.

Secondly, I would also like to express my gratitude to the following academic colleagues who kindly gave of their time to attend the conference and act as discussants for each of the participants' presentations: Matthew Sussex, David Brewster, Kirill Nourzhanov, David Brophy, Anna Hayes, James Leibold, and Jian Zhang.

Last, but certainly not least, I would like to thank all of the contributors for their efforts to revise and sharpen their papers in light of comments received from the discussants and other attendees at the conference.

Michael Clarke   Canberra, May 2018

CONTRIBUTORS

Mordechai Chaziza is currently a Lecturer in the Department of Politics and Governance, Ashkelon Academic College, Israel. He holds a PhD from Bar-Ilan University, Israel. His doctoral dissertation focused on China's post-Cold War foreign policy in the Middle East, Iraq, Iran, and the Arab-Israeli Peace Process. His academic publications on these issues have appeared in *Middle East Policy*, *Middle East Review of International Affairs*, *China Report*, *Contemporary Review of the Middle East*, *Israel Journal of Foreign Affairs*, *Asian Journal of Political Science* and *Chinese Journal of International Politics*.

Michael Clarke is Associate Professor at the National Security College, Crawford School of Public Policy, Australian National University (ANU), and Co-Director of the ANU–Indiana University Pan-Asia Institute. He is an internationally recognized expert on the history and politics of the Xinjiang Uyghur Autonomous Region, the People's Republic of China, Chinese foreign policy in Central Asia, Central Asian geopolitics, and nuclear proliferation and non-proliferation. His academic articles have been published in *Orbis*, *Asian Security*, *Terrorism and Political Violence*, *Australian Journal of International Affairs* and *Global Policy* amongst others, while his opinion and commentary pieces have appeared in *Foreign Policy*, *Wall Street Journal*, *CNN*, *The National Interest* and *The Diplomat*. He is the author of *Xinjiang and China's Rise in Central Asia: A History* (Routledge, 2011), co-editor (with Anna Hayes) of *Inside Xinjiang: Space, Place and Power in China's Muslim Far Northwest* (Routledge, 2016) and co-editor (with Douglas Smith) of *China's Frontier Regions: Ethnicity, Economic Integration and Foreign Relations* (I. B. Tauris, 2016).

Julia Famularo is a research affiliate at the Project 2049 Institute in Arlington, Virginia (USA). She is also preparing to defend her doctoral dissertation at

Georgetown University. Ms Famularo specializes in China's ethno-religious and counter-terrorism policies in Tibet and Xinjiang, as well as in Taiwan politics and cross-Strait relations. In 2014–15 she was a Smith Richardson Foundation International Security Studies pre-doctoral fellow at Yale University. She is the Vice-Chairperson of the Board of Directors for the Uyghur Human Rights Project. Ms Famularo has received a number of research grants, including the United States NSEP Boren Fellowship (People's Republic of China, 2012–13); Smith Richardson Foundation World Politics and Statecraft Fellowship (Nepal and India, 2013); United States Fulbright Fellowship (Taiwan, 2007–8); Columbia University Weatherhead East Asian Institute Training Grant (Tibet, 2005); and China Scholarship Council Chinese Cultural Scholarship (China, 2002–3). She previously served as editor-in-chief of the *Georgetown Journal of International Affairs*; she managed both the International Engagement with Cyber 2013 special issue and also the 2009–10 bi-annual publication. She has written articles for *The Diplomat*, *The National Interest*, *ChinaFile*, *Reuters*, *inFocus Quarterly* and the Project 2049 Institute. Ms Famularo earned an MA in History from Georgetown University; an MA in East Asian Studies from Columbia University; and a BA in East Asian Studies and Spanish Literature from Haverford College. She has lived and travelled extensively in the People's Republic of China, ethnographic Tibet, Xinjiang and Taiwan.

Stefanie Kam Li Yee is a doctoral student at the National Security College, ANU. Prior to commencing her doctoral research, Stefanie was a Research Associate with the International Centre for Political Violence and Terrorism Research at the S. Rajaratnam School of International Studies (RSIS), Nanyang Technological University. Her primary research focus lies in the history of terrorism in the Asia-Pacific region, particularly in South East Asia. Ms Li Yee graduated from Reed College, Portland, OR with a BA in English Literature (2009). She graduated from the University of Chicago (2010) with an MA in English Literature, and has an MSc in International Relations from RSIS (2014). She is co-editor (with Rohan Gunaratna) of the *Handbook of Terrorism in the Asia-Pacific* (Imperial College Press, 2016).

Raffaello Pantucci is Director of International Security Studies at the Royal United Services Institute (RUSI), London. His research focuses on counter-terrorism as well as China's relations with its Western neighbours. Prior to RUSI, Raffaello lived for over three years in Shanghai, where he was a visiting scholar at the Shanghai Academy of Social Sciences (SASS). Before that he

CONTRIBUTORS

worked in London at the International Institute for Strategic Studies (IISS), and the Center for Strategic and International Studies (CSIS) in Washington. He has also held positions at the European Council of Foreign Relations (ECFR) and is an associate fellow at the International Centre for the Study of Radicalisation (ICSR) at King's College, London. He is author of *We Love Death as You Love Life: Britain's Suburban Terrorists* (Hurst/Oxford University Press, 2015). His journal articles have also appeared in *Survival*, *The National Interest*, *Studies in Conflict and Terrorism*, *Terrorism and Political Violence*, and *RUSI Journal*, amongst others, and his journalistic writing has appeared in the *New York Times*, *Financial Times*, *Wall Street Journal*, *Sunday Times*, CNN, *Guardian*, *Foreign Policy*, and *South China Morning Post*.

Sean Roberts is Associate Professor of the Practice of International Affairs and Director of the International Development Studies Program at George Washington University, Washington, DC. He has conducted extensive ethnographic fieldwork among the Uyghur people of Central Asia and China and has published extensively on this community in scholarly journals and in collected volumes. In addition, he produced a documentary film on the Uyghur community entitled *Waiting for Uighurstan* (1996). In 1998–2000 and 2002–6 he worked at the United States Agency for International Development (USAID) in Central Asia on democracy programmes, designing and managing projects in civil society development, political party assistance, community development, independent media strengthening and elections assistance. Recent publications include: '"Imaginary Terrorism"? The Global War on Terror and the Narrative of the Uyghur Terrorist Threat', *PONARS Eurasia Working Paper* (Elliott School of International Affairs, George Washington University, 2012) and 'Development with Chinese Characteristics in Xinjiang: A Solution to Ethnic Tension or Part of the Problem?', in Michael Clarke and Douglas Smith (eds), *China's Frontier Regions: Ethnicity, Economic Integration and Foreign Relations* (I. B. Tauris, 2016).

Andrew Small is a transatlantic fellow with the German Marshall Fund's Asia programme, which he established in 2006. His research focuses on US–China relations, Europe–China relations, Chinese policy in South Asia, and broader developments in China's foreign and economic policy. He was based in GMF's Brussels office for five years, and worked before that as the director of the Foreign Policy Centre's Beijing office, as a visiting fellow at the Chinese Academy of Social Sciences, and as an ESU scholar in the office of Senator Edward M. Kennedy. His articles and papers have been published in the *New*

CONTRIBUTORS

York Times, *Foreign Affairs*, *Foreign Policy* and *Washington Quarterly*, as well as many other journals, magazines and newspapers. He is author of *The China–Pakistan Axis: Asia's New Geopolitics* (Hurst/Oxford University Press, 2015).

Zunyou Zhou is a senior researcher and head of the China section at Germany's Max Planck Institute for Foreign and International Criminal Law. His main research interests include criminal justice and counter-terrorism, with a focus on China. He is the author of *Balancing Security and Liberty: Counter-Terrorism Legislation in Germany and China* (Duncker & Humblot, 2014). In addition to academic articles, he has also frequently contributed to *South China Morning Post*, *Wall Street Journal*, *The Diplomat*, *China Brief*, *China Daily* and *Global Times*.

ABBREVIATIONS

ALMAC	Anti-Money Laundering Monitoring and Analysis Center
AMLB	Anti-Money Laundering Bureau
AML	Anti-Money Laundering Law
APEC	Asia-Pacific Economic Cooperation
ASEAN	Association of South East Asian Nations
ASEAN+3	Association of South East Asian Nations Plus Three
ASG	Abu Sayyaf Group
BIFF	Bangsamoro Islamic Freedom Fighters
CAC	Cyberspace Administration of China
CCP	Chinese Communist Party
CIA	Central Intelligence Agency
CMC	Central Military Commission
CPL	Criminal Procedure Law
CSL	Cyber Security Law
CTD	Counter-Terrorism Decision
CTF	Combating Terrorist Financing
CTL	Comprehensive Terrorism Law
DRS	Designated Residential Surveillance
ETIC	East Turkestan Information Center
ETIM	East Turkestan Islamic Movement
ETLO	East Turkestan Liberation Organisation
EU	European Union
FATF	Financial Action Task Force
GDP	Gross Domestic Product
GWOT	Global War on Terror
IDD	International Direct Dialling

ABBREVIATIONS

IJU	Islamic Jihad Union
IMU	Islamic Movement of Uzbekistan
IRCTL	Implementing Rules on the Counter-Terrorism Law
ISIS	Islamic State of Iraq and al Sham
MFA	Ministry of Foreign Affairs
MIT	Mujahidin Indonesia Timur
MPS	Ministry of Public Security
MSS	Ministry of State Security
NCTLG	National Counter-Terrorism Leading Group
NGO	Non-Governmental Organization
NPC	National People's Congress
NSC	National Security Commission
OBOR	One Belt One Road
ORS	Ordinary Residential Surveillance
PAP	People's Armed Police
PBC	People's Bank of China
PLA	People's Liberation Army
PLAAF	People's Liberation Army Air Force
PRC	People's Republic of China
RATS	Regional Anti-Terrorism Structure
RMB	Renminbi
RRA	Regulation on Religious Affairs
RTL	Re-education Through Labour
SCO	Shanghai Cooperation Organization
SMS	Short Messaging Service
SREB	Silk Road Economic Belt
S-5	Shanghai Five
SWAT	Special Weapons And Tactics
TIM	Technical Investigation Measures
TIP	Turkestan Islamic Party
UN	United Nations
US	United States
VPN	Virtual Private Network
WUC	World Uyghur Congress
WUYC	World Uyghur Youth Conference
XPCC	Xinjiang Production and Construction Corps
XUAR	Xinjiang Uyghur Autonomous Region

INTRODUCTION

TERRORISM AND COUNTER-TERRORISM IN CHINA

Michael Clarke

The events of 9/11 proved to be catalytic, generating a 'legislative wildfire' amongst governments the world over to enact legislation to help detect, prevent, prosecute and eradicate terrorism. Much scholarly attention has been paid to the implications of this for the protection of human rights in the context of the US, Europe and Australia, but relatively little to the strength, scope and implications of this consequence of 9/11 throughout Asia. One particular lacuna in this context continues to be the relationship between anti-terror laws and human rights in the People's Republic of China (PRC). This failure has arguably been due to a general perception that China has no 'real' threat posed to it by terrorism and that its authoritarian government ultimately has little practical need to enact legislation to confront and suppress terrorism.

Yet, this dynamic is beginning to change. Domestic extremism leading to violence in China is a growing problem, and there has been evidence that the problem has some links—both physical and online—abroad. And China has not been entirely immune from the 'legislative wildfire' generated by 9/11, nor from the core tension between national security and human rights protection that has been evident across the world. The key criticism levelled at governments in the West post-9/11, particularly in the US and UK, has been that national security or anti-terror laws have tended to erode standards of human rights protection. This concern has been even greater in relation to non-democratic states such as China, with various Western governments and non-governmental organizations accusing Beijing of utilizing post-9/11 international concern over terrorism as an excuse to tighten controls on society and clamp down on dissent. While this privileging of security concerns over the protection of human rights is prevalent in China, it is one that is acutely felt in a *specific* regional context that has broad implications for how China conceives of the threat of terrorism and how it has structured its counter-terrorism architecture. China's problem with terrorism has been largely isolated to the Xinjiang Uyghur Autonomous Region (XUAR) in the far north-west of the country. The central charge levelled against prominent Western governments—i.e. that national security and counter-terrorism legislation have eroded the protection of individual human rights—is one that needs to be tempered in the context of Xinjiang by noting that the impact of such measures there has been to widen the scope for the state's suppression of real and imagined threats to national security.

This has ultimately resulted in problematic community–government relations, not only within Xinjiang but also across the border in the neighbouring Central Asian states in which significant numbers of Uyghurs reside. But the effects of Xinjiang-linked terrorist violence have also begun to be felt not only in other provinces but beyond China's borders in Central Asia and the Middle East. This problem now appears to be spreading into South East Asia, where growing numbers of Uyghurs appear to head when trying to flee China. The growing community of Uyghurs outside Xinjiang appears to be clashing with the Chinese state, as well as becoming a growing source of international concern and activity for Chinese authorities. Relations with neighbouring countries are becoming increasingly complicated as China looks at these flows solely through the lens of counter-terrorism, rather than the possibility that some cases might be economic or political refugees.

China's response to the issue of terrorism post-9/11 thus operates at two levels. Internationally, Beijing has reconfigured its discourse regarding Xinjiang and the Uyghurs to reflect the contemporary international focus on Islamist-inspired terrorism and extremism in order to gain international recognition of what it regards as a legitimate struggle against Uyghur terrorism. China's efforts in this regard should be seen as a continuation of a long-term struggle (begun with the region's 'peaceful liberation' by the PLA in 1949) to

INTRODUCTION

integrate this ethnically diverse region.[1] But at the same time, and as demonstrated by a number of contributions to this volume, China's global posture has evolved and China is now facing a terrorist threat at home that has links abroad. Furthermore, China is now operating in a world with an evolving threat picture of terrorist groups and networks around the world. Not only does China find itself in a situation where it sees possible links to groups and networks at home and abroad, but it also finds its nationals and interests caught in foreign terrorist incidents. Such a challenge is of increasing importance for Beijing as it embarks on President Xi Jinping's signature foreign policy initiative, the Belt and Road Initiative (BRI). BRI seeks to stimulate trans-Eurasian 'connectivity' through the development of six 'economic corridors' (three of which are centred on Xinjiang) and multilateral financial institutions such as the Silk Road Fund (SRF) and Asian Infrastructure and Investment Bank (AIIB).[2]

Domestically, the 'war on terror' has permitted China not only to deploy significant repressive force, in political, legal and police/military terms, to confront the perceived threat to Xinjiang's security posed by Uyghur terrorism, but also to establish the political and legal framework through which to confront any future challenges to state power. This latter aspect can be seen in Beijing's increasing tendency to label not only dissenting Uyghurs but also Tibetans, Falun Gong members and even protesting workers/peasants as 'terrorists'. Further, as the perceived terrorist threat at home has increased, Beijing has increasingly tried to cast a wider net in an attempt to stop a problem that appears to be developing. Heavy security measures are matched with heavy investment in local economies, including the development of the domestic side of BRI.[3] This economic push largely reflects the traditional Chinese response to security problems: heavy security and heavy economic investment. China has moved towards the achievement of these goals through four main avenues: amendments to China's criminal law; the deployment of an expansive definition of 'terrorism'; security and counter-terror cooperation globally and rhetorical support for the US 'war on terror'; and increased economic relationships around the world to counter either local terrorist problems or links to Xinjiang-connected groups.

The core issue here is thus a contextual one: to embed the analysis of China's efforts to combat terrorism in the domestic and international political, economic and social milieu in which they have arisen, rather than view them in isolation. As noted above, exploration of China's approach to terrorism and counter-terrorism should operate at two levels: the domestic and the international. Domestically, four major domains of investigation present themselves: (i) the historical and contemporary nature of Chinese rule in Xinjiang; (ii) the evolution of China's legislative measures to combat terrorism (including how relevant bodies have defined 'terrorism'); (iii) the evolution of China's counter-terrorism bureaucracy; and (iv) the evolving threat picture within Xinjiang.

Despite the significant attention given in the scholarly literature to exploring the strength, scope and implications of counter-terrorism policy since 9/11, there has been no systematic analysis of China's approach to terrorism and counter-terrorism. This is a major lacuna given China's increasing power and influence in international affairs and the increasing incidence of violent extremism in Xinjiang. Prior to the events of 9/11, the issue of terrorism was very rarely raised in either popular or scholarly discourse in connection to China. This has been especially true with respect to scholarly writing on terrorism and political violence. For instance, a search of two prominent journals in the field, *Terrorism and Political Violence* and *Studies in Conflict and Terrorism*, yields no significant results for the search terms 'China and terrorism' between 1980 and 2001. Meanwhile a prominent and often prescribed reading for undergraduate and graduate courses on terrorism, *Inside Terrorism* by Bruce Hoffman, contains no reference at all to China in its 432 pages.[4]

This lack of consideration of the potential for terrorism to be a national security concern for China was also mirrored in emerging Chinese scholarship on the issue across a similar period. Much of the literature published by Chinese scholars on terrorism between 1978 and 1991, as Jeffrey Reeves has recently documented, 'treated terrorism as an external threat to which China was more or less immune'. This resulted in 'clinical, detached accounts of international terrorism as if China were an outside observer to terrorism, not a potential victim'.[5] Chinese scholarly literature in this period also viewed terrorism as a traditional security challenge to be combated primarily through police and military instruments. However, this began to change as a result of the Soviet Union's collapse, which was perceived to have (re)introduced phenomena into the international security environment that had long been constrained by the tight bipolar and state-centric environment of the Cold War, such as ethnic nationalism and religious conflict. From the early 1990s until 2001, much Chinese scholarship often framed terrorism as a constituent element of a raft of 'non-traditional' security challenges that were perceived to be affecting China's peripheries.[6]

As a number of scholars have detailed, such concerns also informed the development of Beijing's so-called 'new security diplomacy' (NSD) in the

INTRODUCTION

1990s, which was focused on dampening tensions in China's periphery in order 'to focus on domestic, political and social reform challenges'.[7] A direct outgrowth of this approach was China's role in establishing the 'Shanghai Five' (S-5) process in 1996 and its transformation into the Shanghai Cooperation Organization (SCO) in 2000. This multilateral forum, comprising China, Russia, Kazakhstan, Kyrgyzstan, Tajikistan and Uzbekistan, while initially concerned with resolving Soviet-era border disputes, evolved to focus on combating what the organization would term the 'three evils' of 'separatism, extremism and terrorism'.[8] This reflected the centrality of China's concerns with the security of Xinjiang in framing its engagement with the Central Asian states.[9] After the events of 9/11, Chinese perceptions of terrorism as a security threat underwent a further transformation, with analysts now conceiving it as a threat of global nature and ultimately transnational in scope.[10]

The evolution of Chinese thinking about terrorism as a security challenge tracked by Reeves—from treatment of it as a largely external phenomenon in the 1980s to the post-9/11 conception of it as a global threat—is also revealing when placed in parallel with an account of how Chinese authorities framed unrest or violence in Xinjiang over the same period (i.e. the late 1970s to the present). For the majority of this period China consistently framed violent incidents in Xinjiang as manifestations of 'splittism' and 'separatism', either aided or inspired by 'hostile external forces' comprised of 'reactionary', 'pan-Turkist' elements in the Uyghur diaspora in Central Asia or Turkey.[11] Even in the midst of a spike in violent incidents in the 1990s which, as James Millward has pointedly noted, stimulated journalistic interest in 'Islam-inspired separatism' in Xinjiang, Chinese authorities steadfastly maintained the 'splittist' or 'separatist' narrative.[12] This narrative also, as noted above, permeated China's relations with the Central Asian republics and became embedded within the agenda of the S-5 and SCO processes.

It was only the events of 9/11 that provided Beijing with the stimulus for fundamentally reframing its struggle with Uyghur 'separatists' as a counter-terrorist one. Here, China has constructed a discourse that documents what it perceives to be the terrorist threat posed not only by Uyghur militants within Xinjiang but also their connections to prominent regional and global terrorist organizations such as al-Qaeda. A number of contributors to this volume explore different aspects of this dynamic. In my own contribution to the volume, I argue that this identification of 'Uyghur terrorism' as a transnational threat has acted as a 'cognitive threat amplifier' upon Beijing's domestic policy approaches within Xinjiang and its foreign policy. Not only has it contributed to the securitization of the Uyghur issue in China's domestic and foreign policy, but it has also stimulated the development of new institutional structures (such as the 27 December 2016 Counter-Terrorism Law) to combat the perceived threats that are redolent of an emergent 'national security state' in China.

Julia Famularo's contribution explores the conception and implementation of counter-terrorism measures within Xinjiang itself. Famularo provides a detailed 'on the ground' perspective of the CCP's 'ideological struggle' against religion in Xinjiang and the expansion of the surveillance apparatuses of the state into Uyghur society. Zunyou Zhou's contribution then provides a detailed perspective on the evolution and rationale of the legal architecture supporting China's counter-terrorism strategy—which he characterizes as an attempt to 'fight terrorism according to law'. Zhou identifies the core drivers of this legislative emphasis as being motivated by the CCP's perception that: (i) counter-terrorism decisions and arrangements needed to be incorporated into law; (ii) relevant laws and penalties pertaining to terrorism needed to be integrated into a cohesive whole; and (iii) organizations in charge of combating terrorism required a clear framework delineating their responsibilities and various powers to act. Zhou also notes that, in practice, China's counter-terrorism approach has clearly been framed by the CCP's perception of terrorism as, in the first instance, emanating from both Xinjiang and Islam. Thus, China has focused part of its strategy on efforts to deter or prevent 'religious extremism' through censorship of information, detecting terrorist financing and greater cooperation with international partners.

Sean Roberts then dissects the origins of claims about the Uyghur terrorist threat by providing a history of how Uyghur terrorism has evolved out of a long-standing conflict between Uyghurs and China through a combination of PRC policies to stifle dissent in the XUAR and the state's opportunistic use of the US-led global war on terror. He examines how the narrative of a Uyghur terrorist threat evolved in the wake of the 9/11 attacks on the US and argues that the use of this narrative to brand and suppress Uyghur dissent since has made Uyghur militancy, and perhaps terrorism, a self-fulfilling prophecy for Beijing.

Significantly, the contributions of Famularo, Zhou and Roberts provide further area-specific evidence for debates within the terrorism studies literature concerning correlations between domestic regime type, terrorism and effectiveness of counter-terrorism measures. One major stream of this debate argues that authoritarian regimes, unconstrained by civil society and

INTRODUCTION

democratic processes, make it harder for terrorist groups to organize and operate.[13] However, another stream building on the work of Ted Gurr holds that authoritarian regimes, while often holding tactical advantages in the pursuit of counter-terrorism via their willingness to deploy outright repression and overt instruments of political and social control, are in fact more likely to provide fertile conditions for terrorism.[14] This is particularly the case in the context of multiethnic states where the disadvantage of particular minorities—combined with state repression—acts to solidify group identities. James Piazza argues that:

> collective or social status disadvantages—when accompanied by repression on the part of the state—help to produce cohesive minority group identities within countries that differentiate group members from larger society. These collective disadvantages, the sense of 'otherness' vis-à-vis the majority, and alienation from the state and mainstream society facilitate the creation of long-term grievances within afflicted subgroups.[15]

In fact, as long-term observers of Xinjiang have documented, the Chinese state's approach to the region has engendered just such a dynamic vis-à-vis the Uyghurs. China's approach to Xinjiang has been shaped not only by the authoritarian nature of the one-party state since 1949, but also by the region's history as a liminal geographic zone. Xinjiang, as Owen Lattimore once famously argued, constituted the 'marginal Inner Asian zone' of Chinese expansion that was more often than not ruled by polities other than those based in the Chinese heartland.[16] To overcome this marginality, the Chinese Communist Party (CCP) has pursued a muscular strategy of integration defined by tight political, social and cultural control (including via Han Chinese domination of the regional government, regulation of religion and outright suppression of dissent), and encouragement of Han Chinese settlement.[17] Over the past two decades this integrationist agenda has been augmented by a state-led economic modernization programme designed to re-make Xinjiang into a major hub of trans-Eurasian economic connectivity.[18] Indeed, under President Xi Jinping's ambitious 'One Belt, One Road' initiative, Beijing seeks to exploit Xinjiang's 'geographic advantages' to facilitate China's 'westward opening-up'.[19] A core assumption underpinning this approach has been that economic development and modernization will ultimately overcome Uyghur aspirations for greater political autonomy.[20]

However, the state's integrationist agenda has done little to ameliorate long-standing Uyghur grievances. Although yielding economic development, this strategy has stimulated opposition from the Uyghur population, who bridle against demographic dilution, political marginalization and continued state interference in the practice of religion. Such a dynamic, as Piazza argues, 'reinforces social exclusion' and 'leaves aggrieved minority populations alienated from the mainstream economic system, distrustful of state institutions and authority and, thereby, more susceptible to radicalization and fertile ground for terrorist movements to recruit cadres, raise money, and plan and execute attacks'.[21] Moreover, he suggests that in such contexts, terrorist organizations 'as small organized actors led by elites that draw recruits from aggrieved subnational communities' can act as 'instruments of mobilization that allow group grievances to be channeled into violent activity'.[22] This now appears to be occurring in Xinjiang, where there has been a marked increase in violent incidents that most observers would define as acts of terrorism.

It is important to note here that contributors to this volume are cognizant of the ongoing debates regarding the definition of terrorism.[23] Since the events of 9/11 and the war on terror prosecuted by the administration of President George W. Bush, many governments across the world adopted legislation to counter terrorism that often contains attempts to define the act itself. This issue is of major significance in contexts such as Xinjiang, where the state often conflates a wide variety of actions as constituting terrorism. Article III of China's 27 December 2015 counter-terrorism legislation, for example, defines terrorism as any 'propositions and actions that create social panic, endanger public safety, violate person and property, or coerce national organs or international organizations, through methods such as violence, destruction, intimidation, so as to achieve their political, ideological, or other objectives'.[24] Article III then proceeds to define 'terrorist activities' as:

(1) Activities that seriously harm society such as organizing, planning, preparing for, or carrying out any of the following conduct so as to cause injuries to persons, major property damage, damage to public facilities, or havoc in public order;
(2) Advocating terrorism, inciting others to commit terrorist activities, unlawfully possessing items that advocate terrorism, or compelling others to wear or bear clothes or symbols that advocate terrorism in a public place;
(3) Organizing, leading, or participating in a terrorist organization;
(4) Providing information, capital, funding, labor, technology, venues or other support, assistance or facilitation for terrorist organizations, terrorist activity personnel, or the commission of terrorist activities;
(5) Other terrorist activities.[25]

INTRODUCTION

The use of problematic definitions of terrorism in national legislation is, of course, not isolated to China. In the US context, as Sean Roberts notes in his contribution, Title 22 of the United States Code, Section 2656f(d), provides a problematic definition of terrorism whereby 'the term terrorism means premeditated, politically motivated violence perpetrated against noncombatant targets by subnational groups or clandestine agents, usually intended to influence an audience'.[26] Such definitions are broadly consistent with the summary by prominent terrorism studies expert Bruce Hoffman in four core elements: (i) political in aims and motivation; (ii) violent (or threatens violence); (iii) designed to have psychological impact beyond immediate victims/targets; and (iv) perpetrated by sub-national groups or non-state entities.[27]

These examples are symptomatic of a long-standing tendency to define terrorism as an act primarily committed by non-state or sub-state groups or individuals against the state and its institutions. This of course does not permit consideration of the agency of non-state actors or groups that may understand their use of violence in pursuit of political objectives as 'legitimate' resistance to perceived oppression by state actors. This, as many contributors to this volume acknowledge, is often intrinsic to discussion of the historical evolution of Uyghur separatism and terrorism. Major insights from the perspective of critical terrorism studies however permit us to avoid the 'one person's freedom fighter is another person's terrorist' cliché. Critical terrorism studies have sought to move beyond the predominant 'problem-solving' and 'essentialist' approach to the study of terrorism within international security studies. The 'problem-solving', 'orthodox' approach, Lee Jarvis argues, has not only been primarily concerned with 'quests' for defining terrorism, determining causation and prescribing effective responses to terrorism, but also presumes it 'to exist not as social construction, performance or representation, but, rather, as an objective entity that is given, not made'.[28] This orthodoxy is problematic as it 'offers very limited space for reflecting on the historical and social processes through which this identity, behaviour or threat has been constituted', resulting in an understanding of the phenomenon that 'remains consistently and artificially detached from the processes of its construction'.[29]

Critical terrorism studies, in contrast, offer 'broadening' and 'interpretivist' approaches. The former builds on earlier work in the critical security studies sub-field of international security/relations to extend the meaning of security beyond the state-centric and militarized understandings of the Cold War, and has sought to extend our understanding of terrorism beyond one confined principally to the violence of non-state actors against civilian populations.

This has resulted in avenues of research that seek to move terrorism studies away from an 'actor-based' analysis towards an 'action-based analysis' that conceptualizes terrorism not as the action of particular *types* of actors but rather 'as a method, strategy or tool that can be deployed by any actor'.[30] The interpretivist approach, in turn, offers critical explorations of the discursive construction of terrorism and how such constructions shape our understandings of the phenomenon itself and those that perpetrate it. This stream of critical terrorism studies has drawn attention to the manner in which particular discursive constructions of terrorism serve, for instance, to stifle domestic dissent and opposition or accentuate the 'barbarism' of terrorists in order to normalize recourse to 'extra-legal' responses to them. It is these themes—i.e. exploration of historical and social processes through which this identity, behaviour or threat of terrorism has been constituted and critical appraisals of discursive strategies deployed by the state to frame the threat—which have animated the analysis of many of the contributors to this volume.

With such considerations in mind, our discussions in this volume are also framed by an understanding that terrorism be defined, following Israeli scholar Boaz Ganor, by three core characteristics: (i) the essence of the activity must be violent; (ii) the aims must be deliberately political (violence perpetrated for personal reasons not representing a political aim for a larger group would not be considered terrorism); and (iii) the act of violence deliberately targets citizens as victims (attacks on military, militarized groups and state institutions would not be considered terrorism, whether or not they are engaged in combat during the attack).[31]

When assessed by these 'action-based' rather than 'actor-based' criteria, it is apparent that while China has experienced a number of terrorist attacks in or connected to Xinjiang in recent years, there also often remains uncertainty around key aspects of such attacks. Indeed, as Murray Scott Tanner has remarked, a number of key questions—including assessments of premeditation, identification of individual or group perpetrators, level of organization in a specific attack, and connections with internationally recognized terrorist organizations—are often left unaddressed in official Chinese statements and descriptions of alleged terrorist attacks in Xinjiang.[32]

The 1 March 2014 mass knife attack at Kunming's main train station, for instance, where eight masked Uyghur assailants attacked commuters, killing 31 and injuring 141, was clearly a violent act, indiscriminately targeting civilians.[33] The ethnicity of the attackers resulted in a presumption that the motive was connected to Chinese policy in Xinjiang, although the exact nature of that

INTRODUCTION

connection remained unclear. Indeed, two conflicting narratives emerged here. One, carried by Chinese state media and repeated by some international media, asserted that the attackers had been attempting to leave China, bent on joining 'global jihad' in the Middle East. After they were prevented from crossing into Laos, this narrative continues, the Uyghurs decided to 'wage jihad' in Yunnan.[34] The other narrative, reported by Radio Free Asia, suggested that the group, who came from Hanerik township in Khotan prefecture in Xinjiang's far south, had sought to leave after a Chinese 'crackdown' in the area following a violent incident in June 2013 when police had fired on Uyghurs protesting against the arrest of a religious leader in the township. The group was subsequently prevented from crossing the Yunnan–Laos border and in an act of 'desperation' carried out the attack in Kunming.[35] As a number of contributions to this volume suggest, however, both narratives are not mutually exclusive, but rather appear to have interacted to stimulate terrorist violence.

The events surrounding the Kunming attack also highlight the expansion of China's terrorism problem beyond the geographic confines of Xinjiang. The practice of China's counter-terrorism strategy within Xinjiang has provided stimulus for an increasing number of Uyghurs to attempt to leave China, while externally its focus on developing cooperative security relationships with the SCO states has effectively prevented Uyghurs from using traditional migration routes out of Xinjiang via Central Asia. In fact since 2009 there has been evidence that Uyghur migration has as a result been redirected through China's south-eastern provinces, especially Yunnan, and into South East Asia.[36] This dynamic, as Raffaello Pantucci and Stefanie Kam's contributions detail, has also been stimulated in part by the outbreak of the crises in Syria and Iraq. In this context, the recruiting efforts of a variety of jihadist groups have converged with the desire of significant numbers of Uyghurs to flee China, resulting in the involvement of some in jihadi groups in South East Asia, such as MIT in Indonesia and TIP or Islamic State of Iraq and al-Sham (ISIS) in Syria and Iraq.[37]

Coupled with this Uyghur-specific problem for China are broader dynamics connected to its growing power, strategic weight and economic presence in international affairs. China's deeper engagement in nearly every major region of the globe, including regions both long beset by terrorist violence and central to Beijing's BRI agenda, such as Central Asia, South Asia and the Middle East, has increased its exposure to the risk of terrorism. Over the 2004 to 2016 period, for example, forty Chinese nationals have been killed in terrorist attacks in twelve different countries.[38] In 2015 alone, Chinese nationals were victims of a number of high-profile terrorist attacks across a wide geographical reach spanning from Africa to South East Asia: seven Chinese nationals were killed in the 17 August 2015 bombing of the Erawan Shrine in Bangkok, Thailand;[39] on 18 November ISIS publicized its execution of Chinese hostage Fan Jinghui;[40] and three Chinese nationals were killed during an attack by the al-Qaeda in the Islamic Maghreb (AQIM) affiliate, al-Murabitoun, on the Radisson Blu Hotel in Bamako, Mali.[41]

Some observers have seen this as simply an outgrowth of China's growing economic and strategic footprint. Paul J. Smith, for instance, has suggested that 'terrorists—whether domestic or international—may target Chinese interests because China increasingly matters on the world stage'.[42] In this reading, China, much like the United States before it, is finding that the increase in both its power and strategic and economic reach around the globe, and particularly in the Middle East, has incurred increased risk of its becoming the target of terrorism. This line of argumentation has also been heightened with increasing debates in the West about the apparent waning of American primacy and its prospective replacement by a situation in which China may be much more prominent.[43]

The implications of such a power shift in international affairs for the dynamics of jihadist terrorism has been most perceptively explored by Brian Fishman.[44] Fishman argued in 2011 that globally-oriented jihadist groups, such as al-Qaeda, had in fact begun to consider how they should adapt in the event that China overturned 'the US-led system that has been its [al-Qaeda's] primary boogeyman for nearly 15 years'.[45] While noting that the Uyghur issue had been of marginal concern for al-Qaeda since the late 1990s, his analysis suggested that in time China's continued penetration of the Middle East—including its close relationships with a variety of regimes there that al-Qaeda views to be 'worthy of overthrowing'—could make it a replacement for the American 'boogeyman'.[46] More immediately, Fishman also noted that al-Qaeda and its various affiliates had begun to link 'China's local insurrection' in Xinjiang to global jihadist goals, citing al-Qaeda in the Islamic Maghreb's (AQIM) threats to China in the wake of the July 2009 inter-ethnic violence in Xinjiang's capital, Urumqi.[47]

This, as Andrew Small and Mordechai Chaziza's chapters demonstrate, has proven to be a prescient observation. Small demonstrates how the shifting centre of gravity of Uyghur militancy from Afghanistan and Pakistan to Syria is likely to require China to embed counter-terrorism more directly within its diplomatic relations and foreign policy. The net effect of this, he argues, is that

INTRODUCTION

after many years of Beijing being able to mediate major elements of its counter-terrorism policy through its closest security partner, Pakistan, it is now finally required to countenance a more direct role in addressing the threat across virtually all dimensions of policy—politically, economically and potentially even militarily. Chaziza complements Small's analysis through an examination of the dilemmas posed to Beijing by the interaction of its increasing engagement in the Middle East with the rising profile of the Uyghur issue amongst jihadi groups there. He notes that China will likely suffer an increasing number of terrorist attacks at home and abroad perpetrated either by Uyghur extremists or by Islamist extremist organizations that assist each other. However, he concludes that, in the Middle East context at least, the question of whether such developments will prompt Beijing to re-evaluate its low-profile diplomatic policy of 'non-interference' remains to be seen.[48]

Prominent terrorism studies scholar Martha Crenshaw argued over two decades ago that 'Both the phenomenon of terrorism and our conception of it depend on historical context—political, social and economic—and on how the groups and individuals who participate in or respond to the actions we call terrorism relate to the world in which they act.'[49] This volume has been guided by this exhortation to contextualize the study of terrorism appropriately. As such the contributions to this volume constitute a sustained attempt: (i) to map and understand the nature of the threat posed to China by terrorism; (ii) to provide an up-to-date account of how that threat is perceived, understood and responded to by China; and (iii) to provide insights into the effects of terrorism on China's domestic and foreign policy. We believe that this volume makes a major contribution to our understanding in each of these areas and takes appropriate account of 'how the groups and individuals who participate in or respond to the actions we call terrorism relate to the world in which they act'.

* * *

Taken as a whole, the analyses presented in this book suggest a number of important implications for both Beijing's approach to the issue of Uyghur militancy and terrorism and the international community's engagement with China on counter-terrorism issues. With respect to central issues of the causes and consequences of Uyghur terrorism and militancy, a number of contributors make it clear that there is something of a self-fulfilling prophecy at play here. Beijing's instrumentalization of the threat of Uyghur terrorism within its domestic governance of Xinjiang *and* its foreign policy has correlated with an increase both in terrorist attacks in Xinjiang itself and in the threat posed to Chinese interests abroad. The repressive and surveillance instruments of the emergent 'security state' in Xinjiang—including a militarized police presence, use of facial recognition scanners, regular scanning of electronic devices and social media for 'suspect' content[50] and detention of thousands of Uyghurs in 're-education camps'[51]—have reinforced long-standing perceptions of marginalization amongst Uyghurs in Xinjiang. As detailed in a number of chapters, such marginalization and repression have prompted significant numbers of Uyghurs to migrate abroad, often via insecure and illicit channels. This has created not only a flow of unregulated migration with adverse consequences for the migrants themselves, but also security challenges for both China and transit countries as migrants become targets of people smugglers and/or jihadi recruitment efforts.

BRI's focus on enhancing trans-Eurasian 'connectivity' promises to make China's foreign policy interests truly global in scope. It will do so by enmeshing them in regions and security dilemmas—such as those in the Middle East and South Asia—in which China has historically had both a limited role and a limited capability to influence events. This, as detailed by a number of contributors, holds the potential to take Beijing into uncharted territory, including but not limited to consideration of greater intervention abroad in pursuit of key security goals and greater engagement in counter-terrorism cooperation with a variety of partners throughout Central Asia, South Asia and the Middle East. While some may view this as a potentially fertile avenue through which to socialize China into prevailing international treaties, conventions and norms of counter-terrorism cooperation, such a view fails to take due consideration of China's instrumentalization of the issue of Uyghur militancy and terrorism in its domestic and foreign policy. Uncritical international cooperation with Beijing on counter-terrorism runs the risk of facilitating not only the expansion of the 'security state' in Xinjiang, but also the pressuring of Uyghur individuals and organizations in third countries.[52]

President Xi Jinping has proclaimed that BRI will 'benefit people across the whole world' as it will be based on the 'Silk Road spirit' of 'peace and cooperation, openness and inclusiveness'.[53] Although this rhetoric may enhance Beijing's diplomatic position, it is one that the contributors to this volume strongly believe rings hollow for Uyghurs in Xinjiang, where BRI has coincided with the imposition of new and intrusive forms of political and social control. The contributions in this volume make clear that China has endured acts of terrorism in or connected to Xinjiang. However, we judge that the heavy-handed response forthcoming from Beijing is not only disproportionate

INTRODUCTION

with the scale and scope of the threat, but is also a potential contributor to the radicalization of Uyghurs that Beijing so evidently fears. This dynamic is damaging to the security of *all* the peoples of Xinjiang, and China more broadly, and we hope that the insights of this volume may contribute to the development of greater understanding, at the levels of both scholarship and policy, of the complexities and consequences of this issue.

1

CHINA'S 'WAR ON TERRORISM'

CONFRONTING THE DILEMMAS OF THE 'INTERNAL–EXTERNAL' SECURITY NEXUS

Michael Clarke

China's problem with terrorism has until recently been largely isolated to the Xinjiang Uyghur Autonomous Region (XUAR) in the far north-west of the country. However, as a number of contributors to this volume demonstrate, this is now changing as Uyghur militancy and terrorism increasingly impinge upon Chinese interests in Central Asia, the Middle East and South East Asia. China's response to the issue of terrorism is thus increasingly operating at two levels. Internationally, Beijing has reconfigured its discourse regarding Xinjiang and the Uyghurs to reflect the contemporary international focus on Islamist-inspired terrorism and extremism in order to gain international recognition of its 'legitimate' struggle against Uyghur terrorism. China's efforts in this regard should be seen as a continuation of a long-term struggle (begun with the region's 'peaceful liberation' by the PLA in 1949) to integrate this ethnically diverse region. But at the same time, China's global posture has evolved and China is now facing a terrorist threat at home that has links abroad, particularly to Central and South Asia (especially Pakistan and Afghanistan). Furthermore, China is now operating in a world with an evolving threat picture of terrorist groups and networks around the world stemming from the growth and mutation of al-Qaeda and its various affiliates and offshoots such as Islamic State of Iraq and al-Sham (ISIS). Not only does China find itself in a situation where it sees possible links to groups and networks at home and abroad, but it also finds its nationals and interests caught in foreign terrorist incidents such as ISIS's execution of Chinese hostage Fan Jinghui in Iraq in 2015 and the participation of Uyghur militants in the fighting in Syria and Iraq.

China's dilemmas with respect to terrorism are thus increasingly transnational in nature, compelling China to come to terms with what Johan Eriksson and Mark Rhinard have termed the 'internal–external security nexus'.[1] For Eriksson and Rhinard, the post-Cold War era (and the post-9/11 period especially) has come to be defined in the security sphere by the interpenetration of 'internal' and 'external' issues and threats. They argue that it is this '"nexus", or critical connections, between the internal and external security domains' that has increasingly conditioned government responses to security-related problems.[2] They construct a framework for the analysis of security issues/threats arising from this nexus organized around five dimensions—problems, perceptions, policies, politics and polity—that seeks to 'unpack the complexity' of transnational security issues. This chapter will provide an account of each of these dimensions and then map them onto the discrete case of Xinjiang (and the Uyghurs). This discussion suggests that Uyghur separatism and terrorism has: (i) become more transnational in nature; (ii) been securitized by the Chinese state, a process reflected in Chinese domestic policy within Xinjiang and in China's foreign policy (particularly in Central Asia); and (iii) stimulated the development of new institutional structures to combat the perceived threat. The application of this framework will also help us to place China's experience of and response to terrorism into comparative perspective. In this latter regard, China's responses to the threat of terrorism, while bearing individual and context-specific characteristics, nonetheless display some parallels with global trends or dynamics post-9/11 with respect to counter-terrorism.

As noted in the introductory chapter, in this volume we understand terrorism to be defined by three characteristics: (i) the essence of the activity must be violent; (ii) the aims must be deliberately political (violence perpetrated for personal reasons not representing a political aim for a larger group would not be considered terrorism); and (iii) the act of violence deliberately targets citizens as victims (attacks on military, militarized groups and state institutions would not be considered terrorism, whether or not they are engaged in combat during the attack).[3] Given such a definition, it is possible to distinguish between the activities of the small groups of Uyghur militants connected to Afghanistan and Pakistan (and, more recently, Syria) and those of the non-violent Uyghur diaspora that have engaged in what some have termed non-violent 'cyber' or 'virtual' separatism.[4]

The transnationalization of Uyghur separatism and terrorism

Simply put, 'Problems are the security issues confronting the world today and illustrate the most obvious nexus between internal and external domains.'[5] Such problems are not self-evident, however, but must be 'understood and problematized as a precursor to studying their effects on policies, politics, perceptions and polity'. Only by exploring the nature of the problem in question can we hope to negotiate effectively the extremes of contemporary security studies between traditional realist paradigms, on the one hand, which continue to perceive internal and external security as inherently separate domains; and various strands of critical theory, on the other, that see such a distinction as irrelevant.[6] As Eriksson and Rhinard argue, a pragmatic approach here is critical as 'not all security problems or governmental responses to them have a transboundary reach, but some do, and there is a complex pattern of problems and responses which partially implies a nexus or a divide between the external and internal domains of security'.[7] We thus need to problematize, and not assume, that a given security issue is indeed transnational in nature.

Additionally, Eriksson and Rhinard argue that we must distinguish between 'transnational security issues', which have 'objective content', and 'transnational security threats', which are 'subjectively constructed'. 'Transnational security issues' in this context are understood as an outgrowth of the forces unleashed by the collapse of the tight bipolar, and state-centric, international security environment of the Cold War era and by the 'open-ended global flows' of information, capital and people that have been characteristic of the phenomena of globalization.[8] These very broad forces have arguably stimulated a similarly broad range of security-related issues that have been catalogued in the post-Cold War era as transcending the 'internal–external' divide, such as international crime, terrorism, migration flows, disease and pandemics, global environmental degradation and climate change. What links such variegated threats is the fact that, first, 'transnational security challenges do not have a crisis "focal point" where policymakers and government leaders can direct their attention,'[9] and second, they are often driven by 'sovereignty-free' actors (e.g. non-state terrorist groups) or phenomena (e.g. disease).[10]

Critically, however, such forces do not necessarily affect all states equally. Rather, the manner in which such forces may impact on the security of a particular state is likely to be dependent upon such factors as its history, politics, social cohesion and national power. This is an important consideration during the impact of terrorism in the post-9/11 period, when the archetypical transnational security threat has been one that no one state, no matter how wealthy and powerful, may hope to combat by its individual efforts alone; but also this is the harbinger of a fundamentally new international order.[11] Representative of these latter views was Joseph Nye's early characterization of the 9/11 attacks as 'a terrible symptom of the deeper changes that were already occurring in the world', wrought by the forces of globalization that were 'diffusing power away from governments, and empowering individuals and groups to play roles in world politics—including wreaking massive destruction—which were once reserved to governments'.[12] Others conceptualize international terrorism as symptomatic of a pervasive 'insecurity from below' that was undermining the Westphalian state's capacity to provide security in the internal domain ('Weber's "monopoly of legitimate violence" in the domestic sphere') and in the external domain ('the capacity for Clausewitz's "pursuit of politics by other means" in the international sphere').[13] Moreover, measures taken by states to forestall this challenge and provide domestic and international security were increasingly problematic, as they 'create severe backlashes at both local and transnational levels' which 'interact with economic and social processes of complex globalisation to create overlapping and competing cross-border networks of power, shifting loyalties and identities, and new sources of endemic low-level conflict'.[14]

Such a description of the major 'backlash' elements of this new world order—overlapping and competing cross-border networks of power, shifting loyalties and identities, and new sources of endemic low-level conflict—fits the consensus that has emerged since the end of the Cold War regarding the core stimulants for, and characteristics of, the 'new' or 'fourth wave' of terrorism.[15] Central to the conceptualization of the 'new' or 'fourth wave' of terrorism is that it has been characterized by the return of religious ideologies as a motivating factor and has utilized the forces of globalization to become truly transnational in scope.[16] Thus, in contrast to previous manifestations of terrorism that deployed (often localized) violence in the service of bounded political goals, 'fourth wave' variants have tended to globalize their violence in the service of often localized or regionalized causes, a dynamic facilitated by the fact that 'modern communication systems and globalized travel networks' permit terrorist groups to operate across and between political boundaries.[17] This places contemporary terrorism in the same category as other archetypical transnational threats, such as disease pandemics that 'originate from opaque locations, cross political and functional boundaries with ease and can affect a wide variety of referent objects'.[18]

We have noted that China's dilemmas with Uyghur separatism and terrorism appear to fit within such broad conceptualizations of 'transnational threats'. Yet Eriksson and Rhinard's approach exhorts us to problematize such a conceptualization, as it is only by 'coming to grips with the nature of the issue' that we can then hope to examine its effects and 'assess the nexus, or critical connections, between internal and external security rather than simply assuming a "dissolving" or "blurring" line'.[19] As I shall detail below, the issues of Uyghur separatism and terrorism have arguably become *more* transnational in nature since the end of the Cold War, due to the convergence of a number of key factors including: the collapse of the Soviet Union; the rise of radical Islamism in Central and South Asia (especially Afghanistan); the events of 9/11; the nature of Chinese governance in Xinjiang; and China's increased openness to and integration with the global political and economic order. These factors have contributed to the rise not only of Uyghur militancy based in, or connected to, Afghanistan and Pakistan, but also to what a number of scholars have variously described as Uyghur 'long distance nationalism', 'virtual transnationalism' or 'cyber-separatism'.[20]

Crucially, both of these phenomena (i.e. Uyghur militancy/terrorism and transnational diasporic activism) have been generated by the 'pull' factors of globalization (defined as greater mobility of people, capital, and information) and the 'push' factors stemming from the (perceived) declining political and economic opportunities for the Uyghur population within Xinjiang itself. Both violent Uyghur militant groups and non-violent Uyghur diaspora advocacy organizations (e.g. the World Uyghur Congress) have, in very different ways, harnessed the dynamics of globalization consistent with Fiona Adamson's notion of 'transnational political mobilisation networks' that 'attempt to market their political cause abroad, engaging in framing activities that will link their local political concerns with existing discourses that can bring them both political and material support'.²¹ The key factor that links these violent and non-violent groups, I argue, is their desire to bypass the 'blocked' institutions of the Chinese state in order to pursue their political project or cause.²²

Historically, the region now defined as Xinjiang has been characterized by intermittent periods of Chinese control, due primarily to the region's geopolitical liminality between the civilizational zones of East, South and Central and the ethno-cultural dominance of Turkic and Mongol peoples.²³ However, since 1949, Beijing has sought to negate such qualities through encouragement of Han Chinese settlement and extension of the institutions of state power and control. Significantly, the means utilized by the CCP towards this end—such as tight state control of religious or cultural practices and encouragement of Han settlement or colonization—have often played a significant role in generating ethnic minority discontent and separatism/terrorism and impacted negatively on China's foreign relations.²⁴

As Enze Han has noted, however, other traditional frontier regions such as Inner Mongolia have also experienced similar dynamics, yet have not produced increased separatist sentiment nor experienced terrorism. The determining factor vis-à-vis Xinjiang has arguably been the interaction of dynamics and forces at the international level: in particular, 'big power support, external cultural ties, and Uighur diaspora community activism'.²⁵ Developments in China's foreign relations have certainly played a role in fuelling ethnic minority discontent in Xinjiang since 1949. Most notable in impact in this regard have been Sino-US and Sino-Soviet enmity during the Cold War, the Soviet Union's disintegration in 1991, the events of 11 September 2001 and their aftermath (including the US invasion of Afghanistan) and the enduring linkages between Turkey and the Uyghur diaspora.

China's enmity with the superpowers during the Cold War proved conducive to the development of proxy conflicts, whereby the US and Soviet Union provided support to and sympathy for Tibetan, Uyghur and Mongol discontent and separatism in Tibet, Xinjiang and Inner Mongolia. With respect to Xinjiang, as the Sino-Soviet alliance soured in the late 1950s, the Soviet Union provided succour to Uyghur separatist aspirations through a range of activities, including underscoring 'the Central Asian and non-Chinese origins of the Uyghurs', direct criticism of Chinese 'nationality policy', and permitting the creation of a variety of separatist organizations amongst the significant Uyghur diaspora population in Soviet Central Asia (especially Kazakhstan).²⁶ This dynamic was however fundamentally weakened by the Sino-US rapprochement by the mid-1970s and the thawing of Sino-Soviet relations in the 1980s, where other security-pertinent issues altered the perception in Washington and Moscow as to the utility of their support for Tibetan, Uyghur and Mongol proxies.[27] An additional element of external support for Uyghur separatist aspirations during the Cold War was the existence of strong links between the Uyghur diaspora and Turkey.[28] Turkey had become a haven for Uyghur nationalists fleeing Xinjiang after its incorporation into the PRC in 1949. Prominent among these was Isa Yusuf Alptekin, who sought to raise the profile of the Uyghur cause by cultivating links to Turkish political and military leaders with pan-Turkist leanings, most notably Süleyman Demirel and Turgut Özal, and publicizing the Uyghur cause throughout the Muslim and non-aligned world.[29] These efforts bore little fruit due to Beijing's limited ties with Turkey; its ideological offensives in the Third World; and its ability to paint Uyghur nationalists as aided and abetted by both 'Soviet revisionism' and 'reactionaries', and NATO member Turkey.[30]

The collapse of the Soviet Union and the simultaneous emergence of a variety of new independent states in Central Asia and the return of ethnic conflict suggested a global recrudescence of nationalism that could threaten other multi-ethnic states, including China. China paid particular attention to the ethnic conflicts in the Balkans and the international interventions that followed them, as Beijing feared that they would establish dangerous precedents for China's own simmering ethnic conflicts in Xinjiang and Tibet.[31] The sources of external support for Uyghur separatism and terrorism in the post-Cold War era, consistent with Cerny's notion of globalization's encouragement of a 'pervasive insecurity from below', would come from non-state or sub-state spheres.

For much of the 1990s, the major fear of authorities in Xinjiang was that the independence of the Central Asian states and the ascent of various *mujahideen* factions in Afghanistan would stimulate either a resurgence in Turkic nationalism or radical Islam in Xinjiang. The first of these fears was to some degree borne out during the 1990s, when Kazakhstan and Kyrgyzstan, in particular, emerged as major sites of largely non-violent Uyghur diaspora political and cultural activism.[32] Groups established (or re-established) at this time included the legal political parties in Kazakhstan, such as the 'Uyghur Liberation Organization' and 'Free Uyghurstan', and the 'International Uyghur Union', formed in Almaty in January 1992, which sought to be an umbrella organization for the Uyghur population of the five Central Asian republics.[33] Turkey's activism in Central Asia[34] in the mid-1990s was also coupled with more overt rhetorical support for Uyghur aspirations, raising fears in China about a nascent revival of 'pan-Turkism' in Central Asia.[35]

The likelihood of the second scenario (i.e. of radical Islamism taking root in Xinjiang) was also underlined for Chinese authorities by a number of incidents in the early 1990s. The 'Baren Incident' of April 1990 was particularly alarming for the authorities. In this incident a group of Uyghur men conducted an armed uprising against Chinese police and security forces in a small township near Kashgar with the aim of establishing an 'East Turkestan Republic'. While the rebellion was swiftly and forcibly quelled, the authorities subsequently claimed that the leader of the rebellion, Zahideen Yusuf, had not only been the leader of an 'Islamic Party of East Turkestan' that was bent on launching a *jihad* against Chinese rule, but also that he had links to *mujahideen* groups in Afghanistan.[36] Throughout the remainder of the 1990s, Xinjiang experienced sporadic episodes of violence, such as:

- *5 February 1992:* bombing of two buses in the provincial capital Urumqi, killing three and injuring over twenty.
- *Summer 1993*: a number of bombings in Kashgar, which killed two and injured six.
- *July 1995*: a riot in the city of Hotan in July, sparked by the detention of two imams.
- *February 1997*: rioting in Yining, sparked by the detention of two Uyghur religious students. Protests involved several hundred people and turned violent, continuing for several days and forcing PRC authorities to seal off the city.
- *25 February 1997*: three bus bombings in Urumqi coinciding with the funeral of Deng Xiaoping.
- *February–April 1998*: a series of bombings aimed at economic targets and local public security officials in Kargilik County.[37]

Such incidents were blamed by the authorities on the malign influence of 'pan-Turkist' 'splittists' such as Isa Yusuf Alptekin[38] and, by the mid-1990s, on the infiltration of Islamist influences from Central Asia, Afghanistan and Pakistan.[39]

It was the 9/11 attacks, and the US-led 'War on Terror', that irrevocably shifted Chinese perceptions regarding the locus of external threat vis-à-vis Xinjiang.[40] From 2001 onwards, incidents of violence in Xinjiang were inevitably linked to 'international terrorism'. Beijing's first detailed document cataloguing 'terrorist incidents' in, or connected to, Xinjiang, published in January

2002, claimed that a heretofore unknown organization, the East Turkestan Islamic Movement (ETIM), based in Taliban-controlled Afghanistan, and 'supported and funded' by Osama bin Laden's al-Qaeda, had been responsible for many terrorist attacks in Xinjiang.[41] In December 2003, the Ministry of Public Security (MPS) also released its first list of officially designated terrorist organizations: ETIM, East Turkestan Liberation Organization (ETLO), World Uyghur Congress (WUC) and East Turkestan Information Center (ETIC). Significantly, each of these organizations was based outside China amongst the Uyghur diaspora.[42]

For the rest of the decade, Beijing repeated the charge of strong connections between terrorist incidents in Xinjiang and ETIM and what many see as its successor organization, the Turkestan Islamic Party (TIP). While the claim of al-Qaeda's direct support of ETIM has been widely disputed,[43] the group appears to have functioned from 1998 to the early 2000s and had a presence in Taliban-controlled Afghanistan. With the US invasion of Afghanistan, however, the group shifted its base operations into the Af-Pak tribal areas. ETIM was dealt a substantial blow when its leader, Hasan Mahsum, was killed during a Pakistani military operation in South Waziristan in October 2003. TIP emerged as a successor organization sometime between 2006 and 2008; it is believed to consist of hundreds of militants based near Mir Ali in North Waziristan and allied with the Pakistani Taliban and the Islamic Movement of Uzbekistan (IMU), one of Central Asia's most resilient Islamist movements.[44]

As with ETIM, TIP's operational capabilities remain unclear. Chinese authorities have however attributed a variety of terrorist attacks since 2011 either directly to TIP or to its influence. These have included:

- *29 June 2012 (Xinjiang)*: six Uyghurs reportedly attempted to hijack a Tianjin Airlines flight from Hotan to Urumqi.
- *26 June 2013 (Xinjiang)*: 35 people were reportedly killed in an altercation between Uyghurs and police in the town of Lukqun. The Xinjiang regional government blamed the incident on a 17-member 'terrorist cell'.
- *28 October 2013 (Beijing)*: an SUV ploughed into a group of tourists and burst into flames at Beijing's historic Tiananmen Square, killing the three occupants as well as two pedestrians.
- *1 March 2014 (Yunnan)*: eight individuals armed with knives attacked passengers at the Kunming train station, killing 31 and injuring 141.
- *30 April 2014 (Xinjiang)*: two assailants attacked bystanders with knives and detonated explosives at Urumqi's train station.

- *22 May 2014 (Xinjiang)*: five assailants reportedly threw up to a dozen explosives into a crowded street market in Urumqi, killing 39 and wounding another 89.
- *28 July 2014 (Xinjiang)*: 100 people were killed and over 200 arrested following a 'premeditated terrorist attack' on a police station in Shache County.
- *6 March 2015 (Guangdong)*: two assailants armed with knives wounded ten individuals at Guangzhou's main train station.
- *18 September 2015 (Xinjiang)*: at least 50 people, most of them Han Chinese, were killed in an attack on a coal mine in Aksu County by knife-wielding assailants. Local officials described the assailants as 'separatists'.[45]

Such incidents arguably represent a major shift in the nature of the threat posed by Uyghur terrorism. In particular, recent high-profile incidents such as the October 2013 SUV attack in Beijing, the March 2014 Kunming attack and the April 2014 attacks in Urumqi suggest an expanding geographic reach, increasing sophistication and, perhaps most troubling of all, a shift to more indiscriminate attacks.[46]

In parallel with these developments, the core external locus of such Uyghur militancy has gradually shifted from Af-Pak to the wider Middle East, particularly with the outbreak of the Syrian crisis and the rise of Islamic State. In October 2012, in the first public utterance connecting Uyghur terrorism with these crises, Chinese Major General Jin Yinan was quoted in state media saying, 'East Turkistan organizations are taking advantage of the Syrian civil war to obtain experience and raise the profile of Xinjiang among jihadists from other theatres'.[47] Imad Moustapha, Syria's foreign minister, asserted in July 2013 that at least thirty Uyghurs had travelled from 'jihadist' training camps in Pakistan to Syria via Turkey and that the Syrian government was sharing its intelligence on the Uyghurs with Beijing.[48]

Reports of linkages between Uyghurs and the fighting in Syria has only increased since that time. *Al-Monitor* columnist Metin Gurcan reported in September 2014 that an 'Ankara intelligence source' estimated that '1500 recruits from Central Asia', including Uyghurs, were already fighting ISIS in Syria and Iraq.[49] Lebanon-based Al Mayadeen TV also aired a report on 3 September 2015 that purported to show not only Uyghur fighters of the TIP engaged in the 'conquest' of the town of Jisr Al-Shughur, but the settlement of Uyghur militants and their families in nearby villages.[50] It is important to note, however, that some of the reports do not accurately distinguish between Uyghur and other Central Asian militants. The Al Mayadeen TV report, for instance, at 1 minute 36 seconds uses footage that purports to show a 'Uyghur' child soldier, 'Abdallah al Turkistani', in the service of ISIS executing two alleged Russian 'spies'. The same footage, however, was taken from an ISIS propaganda video that was reported on widely by international media as an ISIS-recruited Kazakh child soldier executing Russian 'spies'.[51] Analysis of jihadist social media by Caleb Weiss of the *Long War Journal* has also provided photographic evidence of TIP participation in al-Nusra Front-led offensives against Syrian regime forces in Idlib province, including TIP's alleged key role in capturing a regime-held airbase at Abu Duhour.[52] Finally, *Al-Masdar News* reported on 26 October 2015 that a 'Uyghur terrorist', identified as 'Abbas Al-Turkistani', had been killed by the Syrian Army in north-west Hama.[53]

There are therefore a number of troubling implications for Beijing flowing from these developments. The apparent linkage of Uyghur militants not only to long-standing sanctuaries in the 'Af-Pak' frontier region but also to the jihadist 'witches' brew' of Syria points to an unprecedented transnationalization of Uyghur terrorism. While the number of Uyghurs involved would appear to be small, the danger for Beijing is that some may either return to Xinjiang or seek to influence or recruit others. As well as the direct threat to security within Xinjiang posed by such links, this transnationalization holds potential to complicate China's foreign policy in key regions. The well-documented cases of significant Uyghur trans-migration through South East Asia since 2009, in which Uyghurs detained by authorities in transit countries such as Malaysia, Indonesia and Thailand have been travelling on either forged Turkish passports or have claimed Turkish citizenship, have already created controversy in this context.[54] This issue achieved prominence in the aftermath of the bombing of the Erawan Shrine in Bangkok on 18 August 2015, which some reports speculated was perpetrated by Uyghurs in retaliation against Thailand's earlier deportation of 109 Uyghurs discovered by Thai authorities in a camp run by people-smugglers in southern Thailand.[55]

Beyond South East Asia, the Sino-Turkish relationship appears to be the most troubled by the Uyghur terrorism issue. Here, Turkey's long-standing sympathy for the cause of Uyghur separatism has combined since 2011 with the geopolitical dynamics of the Syrian crisis to produce some potentially troubling issues for Beijing. Seymour Hersh, for instance, asserted in an article for the *London Review of Books* in 2015 that Turkey's National Intelligence Agency (MIT) had facilitated a 'rat line' to funnel Uyghurs 'from China into Kazakhstan for eventual relay to Turkey, and then to Islamic State territory in Syria'.[56] Media reporting from the Middle East has also asserted that Turkey has supplied fake Turkish passports to ISIS and other jihadist groups to facilitate recruitment of militants.[57] This charge has also been echoed in China, with Chinese media reporting on cases of prospective Uyghur recruits being supplied with forged Turkish documents and directed to seek the assistance of Turkish embassies if apprehended in South East Asia.[58] Lending further weight to such claims, Chinese authorities reported uncovering a people-smuggling ring comprising ten Turkish citizens and a number of Uyghurs in Shanghai in January 2015.[59] According to *Global Times*, the ring was orchestrated by a 'Uyghur living in Turkey and a Turkish suspect' who 'charged 60,000 yuan ($9,680) per person' and also procured Turkish passports for their prospective clients.[60]

The securitization of Uyghur terrorism in China's domestic and foreign policy

How, then, has China reacted to the transnationalization of Uyghur separatism and terrorism since the end of the Cold War? What is important to note in framing this discussion is that categorizing a security issue as 'internal', 'external' or 'transnational' has particular cognitive effects. Indeed, as Eriksson and Rhinard argue, one effect 'is to perpetuate a distinction between the known/controllable versus the unknown/uncontrollable'.[61] However, acceptance of a security issue as 'transnational' in nature (i.e. that it perforates sovereign boundaries) can act as a 'cognitive threat amplifier', as 'one is essentially admitting loss of governmental control, which in turn implies a threat to national security'.[62] This section suggests that Uyghur separatism and terrorism, and their increasing transnational dimensions, have acted as just such a 'cognitive threat amplifier' to inform both Chinese policies within Xinjiang and the framing of their diplomacy in Central Asia and South Asia.

With respect to the first aspect (i.e. policy within Xinjiang), the perception of linkages between internal unrest/violence and external sources of material or rhetorical support for Uyghur separatism and terrorism has amplified long-standing concerns regarding the political consequences of Uyghur identity and socio-economic under-development. This twin concern has prompted the Chinese state to couple increased state-led economic development strategies with ongoing campaigns against aspects of Uyghur identity—such as religious practice—that are perceived to maintain or even accentuate the distinctions between the Uyghur population and the dominant Han Chinese culture. In the latter context (i.e. China's foreign policy), Beijing since the mid-1990s has deployed the issue of Uyghur separatism and terrorism first to structure its relationship with independent Central Asia, and second to legitimate both domestically and internationally the implementation of repression of Uyghur opposition in Xinjiang. In effect, China has arguably securitized the issue of Uyghur separatism and terrorism in the pursuit of key domestic and foreign policy goals.[63]

Domestic dimensions

As previously noted, Chinese policy in Xinjiang since 1949 has been focused on achieving the territorial, political, economic and cultural integration of Xinjiang and its non-Han ethnic groups into the Chinese state.[64] However, China's concerns vis-à-vis the security of Xinjiang were not resolved with the collapse of the Soviet Union. Rather, the focus of these concerns shifted from state-based threats to largely non-state ones driven by the convergence of the Islamic revival in neighbouring Central Asia and Afghanistan and the relative weakness of the post-Soviet states. A factor which compounded these concerns was the internal dynamics associated with China's post-1978 reform era. In Xinjiang, these internal dynamics stemmed from an initial liberalization of the state's approach to the region, particularly towards ethnic minority religious and cultural practices. Ultimately, such liberalization generated increasing demands by ethnic minorities for greater political autonomy and contributed to a wave of ethnic unrest in Xinjiang towards the end of the 1980s. China's strategy to manage it has rested upon the development of a 'double-opening' approach: simultaneously integrating Xinjiang with Central Asia and China proper in economic terms while establishing security and cooperation with China's Central Asian neighbours.[65]

Since the institution of 'reform and opening' under Deng Xiaoping, the core assumption of Chinese policy has been that the delivery of economic development and modernization will ultimately 'buy' the loyalty of such ethnic groups as the Uyghurs. The question of Xinjiang's economic development assumed national importance under the Great Western Development campaign, formally launched by President Jiang Zemin in 2000. The region was envisaged as becoming an industrial and agricultural base and a trade and energy corridor for the national economy.[66] While this campaign was nationwide, its operation in Xinjiang reflected the intensification of long-standing state-building policies in the region. The goal of transforming Xinjiang into a trade and energy corridor could only be achieved with the development of greater interaction and cooperation between China and the Central Asian states. This point has been underlined by a Chinese policy that seeks to transform Xinjiang into a new 'Continental Eurasian land bridge', not only linking the major economies of Europe and East and South Asia, but also enmeshing Xinjiang with China.[67] This imperative has been reinforced under President Xi Jinping, who has proposed the deepening of Sino-Central Asian economic cooperation to create a 'Silk Road Economic Belt'.[68]

China's strategy to ameliorate ethnic minority discontent with continued rule from Beijing has since the late 1990s almost entirely rested on the delivery of state-led modernization. This approach has been embodied in a variety of mega-projects, such as massive oil and natural gas pipelines and infrastructure developments linking Xinjiang with Central and South Asia.[69] While undoubtedly bringing economic development, such projects have also created new socio-economic pressures (e.g. encouraging further Han Chinese settlement), exacerbating inter-ethnic tensions and complicating Uyghur relations with the state.[70] Indeed, while Xinjiang's GDP has surpassed the national average since 2003, many Uyghurs feel that they have not benefited from it due to a variety of factors, including: the concentration of Xinjiang's urban centres and industry in the north of the province; targeting of state investment in large infrastructure projects in which companies have tended to employ Han Chinese; and rural–urban disparities (the rural population is overwhelmingly Uyghur).[71]

In parallel with this state-led modernization strategy, the authorities have also implemented yearly 'Strike Hard' campaigns against those that it defines as 'splittists' and, since 9/11, as terrorists and extremists. Uyghur religious expression has always been closely managed by the state, but in the past two decades the authorities have tended to rely increasingly on such campaigns against religious education, 'illegal' mosque construction, mosque attendance by persons under eighteen years of age, and the 're-education' of religious leaders in order to manage the perceived threat from Uyghur religious identity. Since the upswing in terrorist attacks in 2013 and 2014, the state has intensified its implementation of restrictions on religious dress, with some localities in Xinjiang banning *burqas*, *niqabs* or *hijabs*, Islamic symbols such as 'crescent and stars' and even 'long beards' on public transport in some cities.[72] In December 2014 some county-level authorities in Xinjiang had begun disseminating a brochure that identified seventy-five forms of 'religious extremism' for local officials to be aware of. Some of the behaviours identified as religious extremism included referring to local officials or party members as 'heretics', placing pressure on others to stop smoking or drinking alcohol, and the 'boycotting of normal commercial activities as "not halal"'.[73]

For the state, it is heightened elements of ethnic identity (such as Islamic consciousness with respect to the Uyghurs) and economic under-development that are judged to be at the root of outbreaks of Uyghur opposition and violence (including terrorism). It was the violence in Lhasa in May 2008 and Urumqi in July 2009 when Tibetans and Uyghurs attacked ordinary Han citizens rather than representatives of the state (e.g. police officers and party officials) that particularly underscored this connection. These events provided those who have advocated change in the state's approach to ethnic issues with ample 'proof' of the failure of existing policy. For critics, the so-called 'first generation' of ethnic minority policy based on the concept of 'national regional autonomy' (modelled on the Soviet Union's approach to the 'nationalities question') has politicized and institutionalized ethnic identity, as it connects 'each ethnic minority to a certain geographic area, provides these groups with political status, administrative power in their "autonomous territory", and guarantees ethnic minorities the potential to develop at a higher speed'.[74] This policy framework, it has been argued, emphasizes 'equality between ethnic groups' rather than 'equality between citizens', and as such it has strengthened ethnic consciousness and entrenched inter-ethnic barriers.[75] In contrast, as James Leibold has detailed, Ma Rong advocates a reformist agenda that draws upon classical Western liberal thought: stressing the importance of individual over group rights and, in brief, seeking to take the 'ethnic minority' out of ethnic minority policy. Thus for Ma Rong, 'The growing economic and social gap between Han and minority communities means that the Chinese state must continue to play a leading role in subsidizing marginalized communities—but these programs should be *minzu*-blind [i.e. ethnically-blind] and instead target localities and individuals in need.'[76]

These core themes have recently converged, with regional authorities' renewed efforts to combat Islamic veiling and head-coverings. While, as James Leibold and Timothy Grose have recently noted, 'Minority and Han cultures have long been at odds in modern China with the former symbolizing "backwardness" and "tradition", and the latter "modernity" and "progress" in China's civilizing project', the state's recent 'sartorial engineering campaign' in Xinjiang is emblematic of the extent of the securitization of core elements of Uyghur identity.[77] The authorities have increasingly framed particular forms of veiling not only as expressions of 'religious extremism and cultural backwardness', but also as a 'pernicious' outcome of 'foreign' (i.e. Middle Eastern) influences. 'In the current environment', Leibold and Grose argue, 'issues once deemed purely ethnic, cultural or even personal are being reinterpreted as overtly political and ideological acts that warrant closer Party scrutiny and intervention.' They demonstrate the dynamics of this process via a discussion of the US$ 8 million, five-year 'Project Beauty' campaign (begun in 2011), which aimed to 'counter "this regressive fad" [i.e. veiling] and promote a "modern lifestyle"'.[78] An editorial promoting the rationale of the campaign asserted that:

> veils and long robes block a woman's splendor and beauty. Without a doubt this is a backward and regressive trend that deviates from modern development and thus is incompatible with the vast beauty of Xinjiang. Women represent the love and beauty of the world and they should personify beauty and serve as emissaries of love. Wrapping oneself up is not only un-pretty, it can also destroy one's body and mind. One's heart and soul can wither due to long periods in the dark.[79]

However, such campaigns, Leibold and Grose note, are arguably counter-productive as 'Ironically ... many Uyghur women now view headcovering as part of a modern and global Islamic public, rather than anything particularly "traditional" or "backward", let alone unique to Uyghur culture.' They conclude that 'local authorities have adopted a far heavier hand' in prosecuting such campaigns and have targeted '"outward manifestation" of religious extremism, equating certain types of veiling with extremist thoughts and activities. Attempts to maintain security and stability now entail blatant ethnic profiling and maladroit policing tactics that are fueling a dangerous cycle of ethnic and religious bloodshed.'[80]

Foreign dimensions

As detailed above, Beijing has long claimed that Uyghur separatism and terrorism have been inspired and supported by external sources, with Beijing directing such charges during the Cold War, for instance, at the largely secular Uyghur nationalist 'pan-Turkist' exiles based in Turkey and the Soviet Central Asian republics. However, post-9/11 the narrative shifted, with Beijing appropriating the lexicon of the 'war on terror' to label Uyghur opposition as 'religious extremism' linked to the influence of regional and transnational jihadist organizations such as al-Qaeda in order to generate diplomatic capital for the ongoing repression of Uyghur autonomist aspirations.[81] According to some, this framing of China's Uyghur problem through the discourse of the 'war on terror', 'imbued with the fear of an evil and irrational Other', has furthered a 'perception of disorder and chaos' in the region that justifies the more forceful intrusion of the state's security apparatus.[82] This dynamic has not been felt in

China alone, of course, as evidenced by the securitization of Islam and immigration from predominantly Muslim societies, for instance in the United States, the United Kingdom or Australia since 9/11. What is of interest here, rather, is how China has utilized its own concerns with Uyghur terrorism in its foreign policy, especially in Central and South Asia.

As noted earlier, China's strategy after the fall of the Soviet Union was to open Xinjiang to Central Asia in order to achieve economic growth and ensure the stability and security of the region. The opening to Central Asia also resulted in Uyghur communities in the now-independent Central Asian republics re-establishing links with the Uyghurs of Xinjiang and, more concerning for Beijing, the emergence of Uyghur advocacy organizations in the Central Asian republics, particularly Kazakhstan and Kyrgyzstan. These two factors combined with a third—concern to resolve border disputes left over from Sino-Soviet acrimony—to spur China to establish relationships rapidly with the independent Central Asian states. All three major Chinese interests—economic ties, separatism and border demarcation—were, for example, explicitly raised by Chinese premier Li Peng on his diplomatic tour of Central Asian capitals in April 1994. They were central to the establishment in 1996 of the multilateral talks between China, Russia, Kazakhstan, Kyrgyzstan and Tajikistan, thereafter called the 'Shanghai Five' (S-5).[83]

The inclusion and ongoing importance of the issue of 'separatism' within the multilateral framework of the S-5 reflected solely Chinese interests, as none of its partners in these groupings themselves face serious separatist challenges. From 1996 to 2000, China succeeded through the S-5 process and its increasingly close bilateral relations with Kazakhstan and Kyrgyzstan in effectively neutralizing Uyghur advocacy organizations in Central Asia. Indeed, the 1998 S-5 joint statement, in a clear reference to such organizations, stated that the member states would not 'allow their territories to be used for the activities undermining the national sovereignty, security and social order of any of the five countries'. Over the course of the next two years, regional developments, including the consolidation of the Taliban in Afghanistan and the intensification of the insurgency of the Islamic Movement of Uzbekistan in the Ferghana Valley, assisted China in its ability to persuade its S-5 partners to take a stronger stance on what it increasingly termed the 'three evils' of 'separatism, extremism and terrorism'.[84] These issues became a foundational concern for the S-5's successor organization, the SCO, when it was inaugurated on 14 June 2001 in Shanghai. One of the SCO's first acts was to adopt the Shanghai Covenant on the Suppression of Terrorism, Separatism and

Religious Extremism, declaring the organization's intent to establish a regional response to the perceived threat of radical Islam.[85] As one observer put it: 'Agreement on "the three evils" indicated that the member states were ready to move beyond the initial phase of merely removing obstacles to peaceful co-existence and to work instead to develop new areas of co-operation (or, to put it differently, to move from negative to positive security co-operation).'[86]

Despite this, the impact of 9/11 on Beijing's foreign policy in Central Asia was contradictory for them. On the one hand, the 'tilt' of the majority of Central Asian republics towards the United States after the invasion of Afghanistan undermined China's diplomatic gains in the region since the mid-1990s, particularly the SCO. For example, in 2001 and 2002 all of the Central Asian states except Turkmenistan signed military cooperation and base-access agreements with the United States, and received significant economic aid packages.[87] Since that time, however, Beijing has been able to reassert its role in the region, both bilaterally and multilaterally, through the SCO. A key element in this process has been its promotion of a normative framework for inter-state relations in Central Asia, particularly via the SCO, which privileges the maintenance of 'stability' and non-interference in the 'internal affairs' of member states.[88] This has been reflected in the establishment and operation of the SCO's 'Regional Anti-Terrorism' center in Tashkent (Uzbekistan), the SCO's joint annual military exercises since 2003, and the organization's response to the Tulip Revolution in Kyrgyzstan and the Andijan Incident in Uzbekistan in March and May 2005, respectively. China's success in embedding the normative values of 'stability' and 'non-interference' within the SCO was best illustrated by the fact that, at the August 2008 summit meeting in Dushanbe, Tajikistan, Russian President Dmitry Medvedev attempted (but ultimately failed) to get the SCO's unconditional support for Russia's incursion into Georgia.[89] Moreover, since 2001, China, by virtue of bilateral security agreements with key Central Asian states (Kazakhstan and Kyrgyzstan) and police/security cooperation through the SCO, has successfully extradited a significant number of alleged Uyghur 'separatists and terrorists' from Kazakhstan, Kyrgyzstan and Uzbekistan.[90]

In the post 9/11 decade, the SCO has developed a number of further initiatives, such as the Regional Anti-Terrorism Structure (RATS) in Tashkent in 2004, that have served to stifle Uyghur opposition in Central Asia. RATS, according to prominent Chinese scholar, Zhao Huasheng:

> conducts routine work related to anti-terrorist activities, such as giving advice and proposals on combating the 'three forces'; gathering, analyzing, and sharing

among member states relevant information; creating a data bank of terrorist organizations and personnel; organizing seminars on the topic of anti-terrorism; providing help in training experts; and maintaining contacts with other international security organizations, among other responsibilities.[91]

Other SCO-related initiatives in this context have included:

- *July 2005*: SCO governments formally pledged not to extend asylum to any individual designated as a terrorist or extremist by an SCO member
- *March 2008*: the RATS council approved agreements to combat weapons smuggling and train the counter-terrorist personnel of the member states
- *2009*: RATS adopted a draft action plan to combat terrorism, separatism and extremism during the 2010–12 period
- *16 June 2009*: summit in Yekaterinburg, where the SCO heads of state signed a Counter-Terrorism Convention that established a more comprehensive legal foundation for greater cooperation among SCO governments.[92]

In this fashion the SCO, in Zhao Huasheng's words, 'expands the fight against "East Turkistan" from China to the SCO itself, particularly the Central Asian member states directly bordering Xinjiang'.[93] Such processes however are also arguably emblematic of China's (and its SCO partners') development of a 'shared discourse about trans-regional security threats' (e.g. the 'three evils') that has fostered a 'statist multilateralism'. By framing their responses to such 'trans-regional security threats' by the prioritization of 'sovereignty, the protection of state borders and regime security', SCO member states can 'cooperate on issues of "high politics" while safeguarding (and legitimising) their specific political institutions, (state-sponsored) domestic identities and interests'.[94]

Uyghur terrorism and the evolution of a Chinese 'national security state'?

The question remains, however, as to how these processes have impacted on the Chinese polity—defined in Eriksson and Rhinard's terms as those 'institutional structures that shape how governments act'? Such institutional structures are found at the domestic level, such as different elements of the national bureaucracy, and at the international level, such as various forms of cooperative bilateral or multilateral security arrangements. Has the increasing transnationalization of Uyghur separatism and terrorism, and its securitization in both domestic and foreign policy, had an identifiable impact on China's relevant institutional structures?

35

At the most basic level, China's increasing concern with, and identification of, Uyghur terrorism as a transnational security threat has resulted in a rapid increase in the Xinjiang government's counter-terrorism budget. From an annual budget of 1.54 billion yuan (US$ 241 million) in 2009, the counter-terrorism budget increased to an annual figure of approximately 6 billion yuan ($938 million) by 2014.[95] As Julia Famularo has documented, a major component of this increased spending on public security in Xinjiang has included investment in the extension of China's electronic surveillance system, Skynet, into the region. Authorities have 'installed high-definition video surveillance cameras on public buses and at bus stops; on roads and in alleys; in markets and shopping centers; and in schools'; police monitor them 'constantly, searching for actionable intelligence'.[96] Adrian Zenz and James Leibold have also mapped in detail the exponential growth in the recruitment of public security officers—numbering some 90,000 new personnel since 2009—to staff what they describe as a rapidly evolving 'security state' in Xinjiang.[97]

Yet, the most potent symbols of Beijing's instrumentalization of terrorism have come with the establishment of China's National Security Commission (NSC) in 2014 and the passing of the country's first counter-terrorism legislation on 27 December 2015. The establishment of the NSC and the identification of eleven broad areas of focus for the commission—ranging from 'political' to 'ecological' security—reflects President Xi's effort to articulate a 'holistic' approach to national security that encompasses traditional and non-traditional threats to security.[98] Significantly, of the eleven areas of security concern identified, 'political' and 'homeland' security top the bill. Prominent Chinese analyst Shen Dingli has noted here that 'political security has been long phrased as institutional security or ideological security', while 'homeland security ... refers to anti-terror related security, which is different from national defense against foreign aggression'.[99] Here, then, 'national security' becomes synonymous with state or regime security. This, David Lampton argues, betrays the intensification of the long-standing linkage between 'external and internal security in Chinese thinking' under President Xi's leadership.[100]

The new law has been hailed by some Chinese commentators as an 'unambiguous legal document' that 'conforms to the new developments in the global fight against terrorism' and as a tool to 'help fight terrorism at home and help maintain global security'.[101] From this perspective, China is simply following in the footsteps of many other states in establishing a clear legal basis for the counter-terrorism activities of its national security agencies.

The law formalizes counter-terrorism as a national security priority for Beijing through the establishment of a 'national leading institution for counter-terrorism efforts' and provides a legal basis for the country's various counter-terrorism organs, such as the People's Liberation Army (PLA) and People's Armed Police (PAP), to identify and suppress individuals or groups deemed to be 'terrorists'.[102] It also requires internet providers to provide technical assistance and information, including encryption keys, during counter-terror operations, and includes a provision by which the PLA or PAP may seek approval from the Central Military Commission (CMC) to engage in counter-terrorism operations abroad.[103]

While official pronouncements may thus stress that the law's primary purpose is to strengthen Beijing's ability to ensure the security and safety of the country's citizenry and interests both at home and abroad, a closer examination suggests that ensuring the security of the state lies at its heart. Since coming to power, President Xi Jinping has expended considerable energy on two core domestic security issues: Xinjiang and *wenwei* or 'stability maintenance' campaigns.[104] The former has been driven by nationally and internationally prominent terrorist attacks by Uyghur militants, such as the March 2014 Kunming railway station attack; and the latter by rising numbers of violent incidents by 'ordinary' Han Chinese related to personal gripes, local political grievances or corruption.[105]

The new law's definition of 'terrorism' as 'propositions and actions that create social panic, endanger public safety, violate person and property, or coerce national organs or international organizations, through methods such as violence, destruction, intimidation, so as to achieve their political, ideological, or other objectives'[106] would appear to be broad enough to apply to events as distinct as the Kunming attack and the series of mail bomb attacks in Liucheng County in Guangxi in September 2015 that killed ten people.[107] Yet, acts such as those in Guangxi, in stark contrast to those in Kunming, have been labelled 'criminal' rather than 'terrorist' in nature by the authorities.

Under Xi Jinping, the threat of terrorism in Xinjiang has now been instrumentalized nationwide to assist the CCP's efforts to maintain 'stability'. Tom Cliff has argued:

> The mobilization of the Uyghur terror threat is not simply about preventing terror attacks on Han civilians—it is primarily about rapidly or even pre-emptively 'harmonising' potentially unstable elements of the Han population itself. People feel less uncomfortable when they are told that the police on the streets are there to protect them from dangerous 'others,' rather than to protect the state from them or other Han.[108]

Such measures as the creation of China's NSC and new counter-terrorism legislation have thus been taken by some observers to be concrete manifestations of Beijing's conflation of state security (ensuring the functioning of state institutions, processes and structures) and regime security (protection of an existing political leadership). Yet, China's privileging of its 'national security'—defined in its own terms—is not surprising, given the long history of separatism (and more recently terrorism) in or linked to Xinjiang, and the post-9/11 securitization of this issue in China's domestic governance and its foreign policy.

What has passed largely unremarked in discussions of China's response to terrorism, and other transnational threats, are similarities with some Western experiences of and responses to similar challenges. In this respect, the concept of the 'national security state', popularized with reference to the privileging and politicization of 'national security' in the United States during the Cold War, would seem to have some resonance. Norrin Ripsman and T. V. Paul suggest that the term has been deployed in three major ways to refer to/describe: (i) the so-called 'real-state' of the Cold War era in which primacy was afforded to the protection of borders, physical assets and core values through military means; (ii) the institutionalized provision of security and prioritization of it over other functions of the state (e.g. US 1947 National Security Act); and (iii) the collection of institutions, structures and processes within an individual state responsible for the conduct of foreign policy.[109]

In China's case, each of these understandings of the 'national security state' appears to have purchase. The threat of transnational terrorism at the global level has been seen by some as fundamentally weakening the concept of the 'real-state'. Such transnational threats, while undoubtedly posing challenges to the second and third understandings, have also presented opportunities for their expansion and adaptation. The Chinese case detailed above, and explored in a number of subsequent chapters, suggests some affinity with the second understanding, i.e. the institutionalized provision of security and its prioritization over other functions of the state.

2

'FIGHTING THE ENEMY WITH FISTS AND DAGGERS'

THE CHINESE COMMUNIST PARTY'S COUNTER-TERRORISM POLICY IN THE XINJIANG UYGHUR AUTONOMOUS REGION

Julia Famularo

非我族類 其心必異

If he is not one of us, he is surely of a different mind.
Commentary of Zuo on the Spring and Summer Annals (Cheng 4.4), fourth century BCE[1]

China's counter-terrorism policy in Xinjiang represents an evolving, complex and controversial approach to managing ethno-religious tensions. Chinese Communist Party (CCP) General Secretary Xi Jinping is using a spectrum of tactics to combat the 'three evil forces' of ethnic separatism, religious extremism and violent terrorism, ranging from heavy police actions against violent elements to inducements for minorities to enjoy the purported fruits of CCP rule and assimilate into Chinese society. Xi's vision is to grasp the present 'period of strategic opportunity' to make progress towards achieving the nation's centenary goals.[2] Prior to the one hundredth anniversary of the founding of the CCP in 2021, he has pledged to transform China into a 'moderately well-off society'.[3] Xi furthermore aspires to 'secure the success of socialism with Chinese characteristics for a new era' as well as realize the 'Chinese Dream' of 'national rejuvenation' prior to 2049, which marks the one hundredth anniversary of the founding of the People's Republic of China (PRC).[4]

The Xinjiang Uyghur Autonomous Region (XUAR)—also referred to as the occupied country of East Turkestan—is home to the Uyghurs and other Turkic Muslims, who practise a moderate, syncretic form of Islam.[5] The XUAR is rich in energy resources and comprises roughly 1/6 of the total land area of the People's Republic of China. According to the 2010 census, Turkic Muslims represent nearly 60 per cent of the XUAR population: Uyghurs accounted for approximately 46 per cent of that total, while Kazakhs, Hui and other minorities accounted for the other 14 per cent.[6] Chinese comprised roughly 40 per cent of the population, a tenfold increase since 1949, when they accounted for only 4 per cent. As the number of Chinese immigrants continues to grow, tensions are also on the rise.[7] According to Thomas Cliff, one can describe 'the massive project of cultural, economic, physical, and personal transformation' in which 'these migrants are involved' as a 'colonial endeavour'.[8]

Convincing ethno-religious minorities that they stand to reap significant benefits by embracing these goals would consequently also yield benefits for China's counter-terrorism strategy: a local population that wholeheartedly supports the regime is less likely to subvert the nation through violent means. The Party thus seeks to strengthen and deepen its ongoing campaign to assimilate Turkic Muslims into mainstream Chinese society through a combination of hard and soft power. An increase in interventionist policies concurrently facilitates political, economic, cultural and linguistic integration. Following the controversial arrest of Uyghur scholar Ilham Tohti and a series of politically embarrassing attacks committed by Uyghurs, authorities launched a 'strike hard' counter-terrorism campaign in May 2014.[9] Former XUAR Party Secretary Zhang Chunxian stated that Xinjiang would 'promote the eradication of extremism, further expose and criticize the "reactionary nature" of the "three [evil] forces," enhance schools' capacity to resist ideological infiltration by religious extremism, and resolutely win the ideological battle against separation [separatism] and infiltration'.[10] In line with Xi's vision, he pledged a full implementation of the CCP's ethnic policies as well as improvement of people's lives through development.[11] Yet it is his successor, Party Secretary Chen Quanguo, who has radically transformed the security landscape in both the Xinjiang Uyghur Autonomous Region and also the Tibet Autonomous Region.[12]

This chapter will examine some of the core aspects of the Xi administration's counter-terrorism policy in Xinjiang. First, it will discuss how ideological imperatives influence Beijing's approach to combating terrorism. Second, it will reflect upon the management of religious affairs in the XUAR. Third, the chapter will describe other manifestations of hard power, including the use of militarized policing and a deepening system of surveillance, patrols and restrictions on movement. Finally, the author will consider the potential impact of recent national and regional legislation on ethno-religious instability in the XUAR.

A renewed focus on ideological struggle in the People's Republic of China

China formulated its 'three evil forces' terminology prior to the 11 September attacks, but the consequent global focus on fighting a 'war on terror' provided China with a new platform for its political and security agenda in Xinjiang.[13] More recently, General Secretary Xi's ideological imperatives have influenced the development of China's long-term strategy for combating the root causes of terrorism.

As part of his efforts to support the PRC's centenary goals, including the 'Chinese Dream', Xi stresses the need to 'actively guide people of all ethnic groups to enhance their sense of identification with our great country, and to help them further identify with the Chinese nation, Chinese culture, and the path of socialism with Chinese characteristics'.[14] In practical terms, Xi Jinping's ethnic policy actively seeks to accelerate 'interethnic contact, exchange, and mingling' by providing incentives for mixed marriages and enhancing opportunities for social and cultural exposure.[15] During the 24–25 August 2015 Tibetan Work Forum, Xi added support for the Chinese Communist Party as a fifth 'identification'.[16] The unspoken understanding is that Xi's remarks are actually directed at PRC ethnic minorities—particularly Turkic Muslims and Tibetans—who have hitherto resisted full integration into the Chinese nation-state. Former Tibet Autonomous Region Chairman Losang Gyaltsen pled Xi's case more directly by stating that ethnic minorities will have nothing but 'bright prospects for the future if they bind their destiny to that of the entire Chinese nation'.[17] PRC leaders thus contend that the 'Chinese Dream' is achievable only if all citizens unite to participate actively in the process of national renewal and rejuvenation.

In order to understand the types of policy choices that CCP leaders have made at the state, regional and local levels, one must first comprehend the contemporary ideological framework in which leaders operate. In April 2013, the General Office of the Chinese Communist Party released an internal communiqué. As it was the ninth dispatch disseminated that year, observers refer to it as 'Document 9'.[18] Meant for absorption and implementation at all levels of society—from the centre down to the grassroots—it has already shaped the official public discourse in the western PRC. The communiqué identifies 'disseminating thought on the cultural front as the most important political task' facing the current regime. It advocates the study and implementation of Eighteenth Party Congress goals; support for socialism with Chinese characteristics as well as the 'Chinese Dream'; the promotion of ideological purity and unification of thought; and strengthening the role of Party propaganda and official guidance within Chinese society.[19]

Specifically, Document 9 focuses upon what it identifies as key problems that threaten the CCP ideological sphere. These 'false ideological trends, positions, and activities' aim to weaken the Party-state by calling for the implementation of Western thought and practices, such as a constitutional democracy; 'universal values'; neoliberal economic thought; a free and open press; and a strong, independent civil society. The Party also condemns those who seek to undermine the state through revisionist criticisms of Party history; the Reform and Opening policy; or socialism with Chinese characteristics.[20]

These measures, argues the document, are necessary due to the grave threat of ideological infiltration. China must confront 'Western anti-China forces and their attempt at carrying out Westernization, splitting [separatism], and Color Revolutions' at 'all levels of Party and Government'.[21] Leaders must therefore 'strengthen leadership in the ideological sphere; guide our party member[s] and leaders to distinguish between true and false theories; [demonstrate] unwavering adherence to the principle of the Party's control of [the] media; and conscientiously strengthen management of the ideological battlefield'.[22] The directives appear to represent deep anxieties within the central leadership regarding China's external and internal security environment, and have arguably shaped China's foreign policy imperatives, such as the launch of the 'Belt and Road Initiative'.[23] An increasing number of articles in the official media and academic journals consequently contend that China must fight against foreign ideological infiltration. Just as a nation might respond to a perceived military threat along its border by rallying its troops and preparing for battle, the Chinese Communist Party is committing itself to an ideological self-strengthening movement. Through the rectification, unification and fortification of thought, the Party hopes to guard against corrosive 'foreign' ideas that potentially threaten its rule.

Growing official frustration with perceived Western 'interference' in China's 'internal affairs' means that more journal and newspaper articles echo CCP criticisms of Western—and especially American—policies. For example, a number of official XUAR publications excoriate not only the United States executive and legislative branches of government, but also quasi-government organizations—such as the National Endowment for Democracy—for allegedly attempting to destabilize the Chinese Communist Party, either directly or through proxies such as the Uyghur American Association.

Consider two articles from the *Journal of Xinjiang Police Officers' Academy*. Gu Liyan asserts that the United States, 'as leader of the Western antagonist powers, will not abandon its strategy to Westernize and split up China'.[24] Meanwhile, Wang Xiuli argues:

> Western nations slander the Chinese government's legal management of the Internet, claiming that China infringes upon 'Internet freedom' and asserting that its management of online news limits the free distribution of information as well as freedom of speech. They actively cultivate 'three evil forces' organizations both within and outside [Chinese] borders, supply support and funding, and make abundant use of the Internet to permeate Xinjiang's cultural sphere and create serious violent terrorist movements, for example. [Western nations have thus] gravely influenced Xinjiang cultural security and social stability.[25]

In other words, such work endeavours to draw a direct link between extremism and Western liberalism.

Similarly, Chen Quancheng contends in the *Journal of Kashgar University* that 'western hostile forces are using human rights, democracy, ethnicity, religion, and other issues to intensify' their efforts to 'split apart' China. Xinjiang secondary school students, the author notes, are particularly susceptible to the influence of ideological infiltration. Embracing the 'three evil forces' negatively impacts the safety and stability of Xinjiang schools by causing the breakdown of ethnic unity and fostering ethnic separatism.[26] Given that Chinese newspaper and journal articles undergo review by Party censors, it is unlikely that authors could publish such statements without at least tacit government approval. It is equally likely that the current administration encourages such statements.

The XUAR Department of Culture made one of the only comprehensive public statements in Xinjiang regarding Document 9.[27] During a study session on 20 May 2013, party leaders extolled the 'great importance of doing meticulous cultural and ideological work'.[28] Cadres endeavoured to 'unify their thinking and increase their awareness' of the situation at hand, as they 'must possess a sober understanding of the grim situation and challenges confronting the ideological sphere'. They 'must fully recognize the urgency and necessity of doing meticulous ideological work and effectively enhance their political awareness'. Cadres must possess 'a sense of urgency' and a 'sense of responsibility'. This strong, consistent emphasis on consensus and ideological unity echoes imperatives articulated in Document 9.[29] The report subsequently identifies five key areas of focus in the ideological realm. First, the Department of Culture must 'attach great importance to unifying [Party] thinking and completely implement its policies'. Earnestly studying and understanding the spirit of Document 9 will enable cadres to resist dangerous ideological infiltration and separatist sentiment. Second, the Party should 'strengthen its guidance' by helping the populace 'discern right from wrong' and 'improving its capability to perform meticulous cultural work'. There is an emphasis on infusing traditional culture with a 'modern spirit, modern ideas, modern technology, and modern means of integration [a likely reference to integrating ethnic minorities into mainstream Chinese culture]', which are key reccurring themes in the western PRC. Third, 'cultural workers of all ethnicities' must demonstrate leadership through 'strict political discipline, education, and guidance on sensitive problems'. They must consistently maintain a 'sober and vigilant' mindset so that they are not 'deceived by illusions or confused by rumors' or susceptible to 'erroneous communication channels' that promote 'incorrect thoughts or opinions on public affairs', which can play into the hands of criminals. Fourth, cadres should ensure that they maintain control over the direction of both traditional and modern culture. Among their responsibilities are promoting patriotism, the rule of law, and maintaining stability in the ideological and cultural realms. Fifth, the Party emphasizes the need to supervise and control effectively the implementation of cultural policies. Although it should 'firmly establish a pragmatic work style', at the same time the Party must strengthen policy execution without compromising its principles and goals.

Xi Jinping is strengthening the role of ideological education throughout China, down to the grassroots level of society. Ideological imperatives are inextricably linked with—and are arguably among the key factors driving—

Beijing's long-term counter-terrorism strategy, reflecting the official belief that only by successfully integrating ethnic minorities into the nation-state can China achieve the twin goals of thwarting ethno-religious terrorism and 'rejuvenating' China.

Management of religious affairs in the Xinjiang Uyghur Autonomous Region

Chinese leaders state that 'religious extremism' comprises one of the 'three evil forces' threatening China's national security. The effective regulation and management of religious affairs is consequently a critical component of China's counter-terrorism strategy. From the time when authorities promulgated the 1994 Xinjiang Uyghur Autonomous Region Regulations on the Management of Religious Affairs until the present, regional religious policies have grown increasingly strict. On the one hand, CCP cadres and government officials have defined the 'legal' parameters of religious faith and practice; on the other hand, they have placed an ideological emphasis on maintaining fidelity to the Party-state through patriotic re-education campaigns. Such policies are meant to frame and regulate the religious discourse in society and ultimately subordinate religion to the Party.

The XUAR regulations are ostensibly meant to protect religious freedom; maintain social and religious harmony among groups that practise various religions or none at all; and manage the administration of religious affairs in the PRC. Yet, although authorities have officially proclaimed that 'religious belief is a citizen's personal affair', the state increasingly controls all aspects of religious doctrine and practice.[30] China 'protects normal religious activities, and safeguards the lawful rights and interests of religious bodies, sites for religious activities and religious citizens… [which/who] shall abide by the Constitution, laws, regulations and rules, and safeguard unification of the country, unity of all nationalities and stability of society'.[31] Chinese citizens cannot engage in religious activities that 'disrupt public order', 'interfere with the educational system' or otherwise 'harm State or public interests'.[32] Foreign interests must not interfere with the independent functioning of religion in China, although exchanges based on amity and equality are permitted. Religious affairs departments at the county level of government and above must administer religious affairs in accordance with State laws and interests.[33]

XUAR religious regulations stress the primary importance of maintaining fidelity to the Party-state, a message that General Secretary Xi re-emphasized at the April 2016 Central Religious Affairs Conference.[34] The regulations state that 'Citizens who profess a religion must support the leadership of the Chinese Communist Party and the socialist system, love their country and abide by its laws, safeguard the unification of the motherland and national solidarity, and oppose national splittism [separatism] and illegal religious activities.'[35] Religious affairs officials must approve all religious seminaries, schools and scripture classes, as well as the clergy that teach therein. They shall also approve the appointment of clergy to places of worship. Furthermore, all clergy must 'love the country'; abide by all Chinese laws and regulations; and submit to routine supervision by religious affairs bureaus, religious organizations and 'democratic management committees' [supervisory bodies drawn from clergy and worshippers] at their places of worship or sites of religious activities.[36]

Under Chinese law, authorities thus have the power to determine which religious organizations and activities are deemed 'normal' and which are deemed 'abnormal' or 'unlawful'. They may similarly judge whether members of the clergy are sufficiently 'patriotic', as they are essentially state employees. Furthermore, CCP members, civil servants, members of the armed forces and students must officially adhere to atheism and refrain from participating in religious activities, which in practice include visiting mosques and fasting during Ramadan. The Party may expel members who have joined religious organizations.[37] Any religious activities which the state deems to undermine ethnic unity, national unity or social stability are likewise forbidden. Citizens who believe that their right to religious freedom has been violated may not take legal action against the state.[38] The atheist Party-state thus attempts to create new norms or re-establish previous norms to cement its authority over religious dogma and practice, while consequently creating a more docile, Sinicized version of Islam.[39]

Developments in 'Xinjiang Religious Work' under the Xi Jinping administration

An understanding of CCP ideological and security imperatives is essential to ascertaining the future direction of XUAR religious and consequently counter-terrorism policies. In addition to considering Document 9, one can also examine CCP General Secretary Xi Jinping's statements at the Second Xinjiang Work Forum in May 2014 and the Central Religious Affairs Conference in April 2016.[40] All Chinese Politburo members attended the work forum in Beijing, the second such event in four years.[41] The *People's Daily* published a front-page article entitled 'Do Religious Work Meticulously

Well: Three Theories on the Study and Implementation of General Secretary Xi Jinping's Important Speech at the Xinjiang Work Forum'.[42] While many previous official statements have discussed the importance of economic development in the XUAR, the content and prominent placement of this article in the Party's most prominent newspaper signifies official recognition of the urgent need to control and manage religion. James Leibold has argued that, in fact, Xi differs from his predecessor in making it clear that 'leap-frog development' alone is insufficient to address the 'minzu [ethnic] question' in China.[43]

According to Xi Jinping, the Chinese Communist Party 'must engage in meticulous religious work, actively guiding the adaptation of religion to socialist society and ensuring that religious figures and believers play a positive role in promoting economic development'.[44] He articulated that the nation should adopt particular principles, methods and paths to promote ethnic unity and religious harmony.[45] The article proceeded to discuss the dangers of 'extremist religious ideology', which 'is behind a series of violent terrorist incidents from Bachu [Kashgar Prefecture] to Shanshan [Turpan Prefecture], and from Kunming to Urumqi'. Perhaps echoing Mao's depiction of religion as the 'opiate of the masses', the *People's Daily* referred to extremist ideology as a 'powerful hallucinogen' that turns an 'average individual' into a 'killer' who seeks to commit 'violent terrorist crimes'.[46] The editorial argues that 'distorted' religious doctrines are used to foment ethnic separatism and terrorism. Party cadres and government officials must therefore support the basic principles of 'upholding that which is legal, suppressing that which is unlawful, containing extremism and resisting its penetration, and striking against crime. We must also safeguard religious harmony, ethnic unity, and social stability; herein lies the well-being of the 22 million people of Xinjiang'.[47] Here, Party leaders once again draw attention to the importance of suppressing the 'three evil forces'. They believe that the CCP has the right and the responsibility to determine which religious activities are considered legal. By 'delineating right from wrong' and guiding the development of religious policy in Xinjiang, it can resist destabilizing ideological penetration.

Media reports on high-level official visits to the western PRC often include accounts of leaders interacting with ethnic minority locals. Such encounters reflect the common historical tropes of Chinese cadres listening to and learning from the masses, as well as providing 'model minorities' for public consumption and emulation. During his 'inspection work' in Xinjiang, General Secretary Xi Jinping praised an old imam in Kashgar. The elderly man had told Xi that 'when expounding upon the Qur'an, he pays attention to preaching about the Party's good policies in order to make the masses understand them better'.⁴⁸ The article states that:

> the existence of religion in human society is an objective fact, so we must do religious work well. Legal protection for religious believers is a prerequisite for normal religious needs. We must comprehensively implement the Party's religious policies, respect the practices of religious adherents, broaden legal channels for religious people to accurately grasp religious knowledge, guide them to establish the right faith, reject extremism, keep their minds on developing the economy, and improve their lives.⁴⁹

In practice, this means that the Party, rather than religious leaders themselves, will determine which forms of religious knowledge and religious activities are permissible. CCP leaders nevertheless recognize that they must co-opt religious elites to implement their agenda effectively:

> In doing religious work well, we must focus on cultivating a team of patriotic clergy. We must take effective measures to improve the quality of religious figures, and mobilize them to carry forward the fine tradition of loving the country as well as the people. We must place more focus on refuting fallacies as well as preach the ideology of patriotism, peace, [and] ethnic unity.⁵⁰

The Party believes that in order to win over ethno-religious minorities, it must first target religious leaders. Chinese authorities can subsequently use these clerics as tools to support the state counter-terrorism campaign against religious extremism.

During the Central Religious Affairs Conference, General Secretary Xi furthermore stated that religions must adapt to socialism with Chinese characteristics, while religious leaders must guide the faithful masses to love their country, protect the unification of the motherland, and serve national interests. All religious groups must submit to Chinese Communist Party leadership and support the socialist system. According to Xi, they must 'merge religious doctrines with Chinese culture, abide by Chinese laws and regulations, and devote themselves to China's reform and opening up drive and socialist modernization in order to contribute to the realization of the Chinese dream of national rejuvenation'.⁵¹ He added that the Party-state should 'guide and educate' religious elites and their followers with 'socialist core values'. Religious groups should 'dig deep into doctrines and canons that are in line with social harmony and progress', 'interpret religious doctrines in a way that is conducive to modern China's progress' and hew to 'traditional' Chinese culture.⁵² Xi's underlying message was clear: the Party will continue to tighten its policies to shape effectively religious doctrine and the direction of religious practice in China.

To the Party, religion cannot supplant the Chinese Communist Party as the most powerful force in people's lives; it must remain subservient to as well as serve the Party. Muslims are thus instructed that they cannot place obedience to God over obedience to the CCP. The Party must therefore 'ensure that the leaders of religious organizations are firmly in the hands of people who love the country as well as religion. In this way we can exhort them to play a positive role in promoting economic and social development, as well as unite religious adherents to jointly promote better and faster development in Xinjiang.'[53] Thus, the Party is placing new emphasis on cultivating relationships with religious elites, who in turn can responsibly influence the direction of religious ideology and harness the energy of the people for further economic development.

The 2015 Xinjiang Religious Regulations and 2017 Anti-Extremist Regulations

The XUAR Religious Affairs Regulations came into effect on 1 January 2015. At the time, Xinjiang People's Congress Deputy Director and Legislative Affairs Committee Director Ma Mingcheng argued that religious problems in Xinjiang were increasingly widespread and complex. 'The old regulation, which was passed 20 years ago, just cannot handle new situations, such as the spreading of terrorist or extreme religious materials via the Internet or social media, and using religion to interfere in people's lives.'[54]

Many of the 66 articles comprising the law subsequently 'clarify the nature of illegal and extreme religious activities'. Keeping in line with China's post-9/11 focus on combating the 'three evil forces', the new regulations sought to address the threat of 'violent terrorism' in addition to 'ethnic separatism' and 'religious extremism'.[55] The regulations also emphasized the importance of preventing individuals and organizations from 'coercing' others to radicalize which reflects an official belief that extremism is on the rise throughout Xinjiang society.

In March 2017, the XUAR People's Congress passed anti-extremism legislation, better known in China as the Xinjiang Uyghur Autonomous Region Regulation on De-extremification. 'In Xinjiang, the root of terrorist activities is separatism, and its ideological foundation is extremism,' stated Nayim Yessen, director of the legislative standing committee.[56] The regulation defines extremism as 'speech and actions … that spread radical religious ideology' as well as 'reject and interfere with normal production and livelihood'.[57] The measure lists fifteen prohibited 'acts of extremism, proposes detailed measures to prevent, contain and purge them, and identifies responsibilities of government departments and the public'.⁵⁸ Although various localities had already placed curbs or even adopted outright prohibitions on certain behaviours—in December 2014, police issued a compilation of '75 specific signs of religious extremism'—these new anti-extremism regulations attempted to standardize and codify these prohibitions across the XUAR.⁵⁹

It appears that the Chinese Communist Party was using its new emphasis on strengthening established legal provisions and procedures to replace some government directives with written regulations.⁶⁰ Authorities seem to have incorporated some local regulations implemented in various parts of Xinjiang into this new, region-wide version. One can characterize such efforts as an attempt to further 'normalize' and 'standardize' the management of ethnic and religious affairs. As Carl Minzner has articulated, however, the Party-state did not embrace Western concepts of constitutional democracy or rule of law during the October 2014 Fourth Plenum. The CCP:

> continues to promote technocratic legal reforms in China, subject to one-party political control. But it also takes clear steps to redefine the concept of 'rule according to law' by neutering elements it deems dangerous, such as bottom-up participation and autonomous legal forces, in favor of a heavily top-down version, one increasingly being clad in classical Chinese garb.⁶¹

Although the continuing crackdown on freedom of religion is disturbing in itself, the XUAR Regulations on Religious Affairs and Anti-Extremist Regulations are ultimately symptomatic of a far larger problem. In an attempt to restrict civil society and stifle dissent, authorities are using the spectre of 'ethnic separatism, religious extremism and violent terrorism' to conflate many traditional, 'normal' religious activities with 'abnormal' and 'illegal' ones. The fact that all but the most serious of transgressions are ostensibly met with administrative penalties, rather than criminal ones, also suggests that the government is overstating its case regarding the extent to which minor violations 'threaten national security'.

Uyghurs online

The 2015 XUAR Religious Affairs Regulations also provide authorities with broader powers to stifle online dissent. Chinese analysts commonly argue that 'hostile anti-China Western forces' seek to control the internet to promote Western values and subvert socialist ideology; rhetoric regarding internet freedom is meant simply to deflect attention from the Western goal of undermining political stability, ethnic unity and economic development in minority regions of China. Beijing has espoused an alternative vision for a 'patriotic' nation of bloggers who promote the 'Chinese Dream' and eschew corrosive foreign influences.[62]

Government concerns over the dangers of 'foreign infiltration' in Xinjiang extend to the ability of radical elements to access and disseminate religious extremist materials and promote separatist ideology online.[63] Mirroring its response to the Hong Kong protests and the 2008 unrest in ethnographic Tibet, the regime blamed the 2009 Urumchi riots neither on its own counterproductive domestic policies nor its mishandling of Han–Uyghur relations in Guangzhou factories, but rather on outside agitators.[64]

Authorities in Xinjiang subsequently enacted the XUAR Informatization Promotion Regulation in December 2009 as well as updated regulations on 24 December 2014, which aim to 'strengthen the management of Internet information security'.[65] An overarching goal of the regulations is to 'crack down on and prevent the use of the Internet to manufacture, copy, disseminate, propagate, or store information relating to violent terrorist and other criminal activities, as well as safeguard national security and social stability'.[66] Chinese authorities believe that tightening internet controls will stem the flow of extremist materials into Xinjiang and help prevent future terrorist attacks.

In November 2016, the National People's Congress approved a sweeping, yet purposely ambiguous, cybersecurity law, which came into effect on 1 July 2017. The regulations strengthen central government control over the flow of online information as well as the nation's critical information infrastructure. Government agencies and businesses alike must not only defend against network intrusions and submit to security reviews, but also bear responsibility for failing to censor information appropriately online.[67] Network operators must provide authorities with 'technical support' during 'national security and criminal investigations'.[68] Furthermore, the law legally enshrines the government's ability to shut down the internet in response to 'major [public] security incidents', as authorities have already done in both Xinjiang and ethnically Tibetan regions of the PRC.[69] The national and regional laws—part of an evolving system of 'institutions, laws, regulations, and policies aimed at strengthening cyber governance'—mutually reinforce and strengthen cybersecurity controls in Xinjiang, providing authorities with tools not simply to buttress social stability, but rather to curb free speech and further isolate Turkic Muslims from the international community.[70]

Many foreign commentators argue that the CCP is fearful of online Uyghur communities that seek to highlight their own unique cultural, linguistic and religious identity.[71] Authorities believe that such netizens may secretly harbour separatist sentiments. Beijing has subsequently moved beyond monitoring online activity to a campaign of censoring and shutting down websites that it believes threaten national stability.[72] Prominent Uyghur economist Ilham Tohti was accused of inciting separatism and sentenced to life in prison for creating an online forum dedicated to exchange between the Chinese and Uyghur communities.[73] Authorities arrested and sentenced seven of his students as well.[74]

2018 Religious affairs regulations

The breadth and depth of state intervention in religious affairs continues unabated, at a rate not witnessed in decades. Authorities revised the 2005 religious affairs regulations following the 2016 Central Religious Affairs Conference. The resulting regulations—which were announced one month prior to the 19th Party Congress and more closely reflect CCP General Secretary Xi's national security and ideological imperatives—came into effect on 1 February 2018.[75] Chinese authorities furthermore stated that the State Administration for Religious Affairs, in cooperation with other relevant departments, will draft a regulation on the management of online religious information in 2018.[76]

An official statement called upon authorities at all levels of government 'to strengthen religious work' and 'improve the mechanism of religious affairs' by adhering 'to the principle of protecting legitimate religious activities while curbing and preventing illegal and extreme practices'.[77] The revised regulations explicitly prohibit 'religious groups, religious schools, religious activity sites, and religious citizens' from using 'religion as a tool to sabotage national security, social order, religious harmony, or the educational system'. Religion must not undermine ethnic or national unity. Promoting, supporting or undertaking extremist or terrorist activities is forbidden. Institutions and individuals alike must 'abide by the Constitution, laws, regulations, and rules' as well as 'practice core socialist values'.[78] While the State Administration for Religious Affairs continues to maintain 'responsibility for managing legal religious activity', new provisions explicitly codify the role of the Ministry of Public Security in responding to 'unapproved' or 'illegal religious activity'.[79]

'Compared to the previous version', stated the *Global Times*, 'the latest regulations are more specific and stricter.' The measures are meant to ensure 'ethnic unity' and 'social stability' by addressing 'contradictions' and 'conflict' among various groups of religious believers and non-believers as well as protecting domestic religious groups from falling under the control of foreign powers.[80] Religious groups are no longer allowed to receive foreign funding.[81] Chinese leaders have also vowed to strengthen 'the role of patriotic religious organizations', which are 'designed to pre-empt domestic believers' close connections with foreign religious groups'.[82] Regulations governing online religious content are also meant to ward against foreign infiltration.[83]

The revisions, with their enhanced emphasis on national security and adherence to 'core socialist values', reflect Xi Jinping's exhortations on religious affairs. On the one hand, religious institutions and believers must support the leadership of the Chinese Communist Party and uphold the system of socialism with Chinese characteristics. On the other hand, the Party-state must 'resolutely guard against overseas infiltrations via religious means and prevent ideological infringement by extremists, as well as focus on religious issues on the Internet and disseminate the Party's religious policies and theories online'.[84] The implementation of these measures may further isolate Turkic Muslims from the international Islamic community, as the Party-state exercises its authority to shape religious dogma and practice so that it hews more closely to socialist dogma and practice.[85]

Building a national framework to combat terrorism

Upon its formation, many observers speculated that the National Security Commission would play a prominent new role in the formulation and execution of the central leadership's overarching national security strategy, policies and legal infrastructure in Xinjiang.[86] Announced during the CCP Third Plenum in November 2013, the Commission places 'a highly empowered group of security experts' at Chairman Xi Jinping's disposal, to 'work the levers of the country's vast security apparatus'.[87] It leads and coordinates efforts among various domestic, intelligence and foreign affairs organs to respond more effectively to critical security and counter-terrorism challenges.[88] 'The maintenance of internal cohesion and stability is the indispensable core of Chinese national security', argues political scientist David Lampton.[89] To thwart internal or external acts of subversion in the cause of maintaining stability and perpetuating the longevity of the regime, the state 'requires a broadly conceived central foreign and security policy coordination mechanism of increasing sophistication, a mechanism that can provide top leaders with options, help establish priorities, evaluate costs and gains, and enforce implementation on a fractious bureaucracy and society'.[90] However, officials have grown increasingly loath to discuss the Commission. Extremely little has appeared in the state media on it since 2014, and it is thus difficult to know the full scope of its power and influence.[91]

Following a deadly bombing in an Urumqi market that left thirty-nine dead and eighty-nine injured, China launched a national counter-terrorism campaign on 25 May 2014. Vice Public Security Minister Yang Huanning stated that while Xinjiang is the 'main battlefield' in the fight against terrorism, security personnel should view 'the entire country as one chessboard'.[92] Authorities consequently began to accelerate the establishment of counter-terrorism working groups at the national, provincial/regional, local and district levels.[93] In many cases, it seems that local leaders of political and legal affairs commissions chair the working groups, but security officials also tend to hold prominent positions. The differences in the composition and configuration of these working groups suggests that while Beijing strongly adjures lower tiers of government to establish them, it may demonstrate some flexibility with regard to their development and implementation.[94] With regard to China's policies abroad, Beijing already cooperates internationally through the Shanghai Cooperation Organization and United Nations, and through bilateral and multinational dialogues.[95]

Beijing first established its national counter-terrorism leading group in August 2013, replacing an earlier coordination group. Minister of Public Security Guo Shengkun serves as chair of the powerful new body, while Liu Yuejin acts as counter-terrorism commissioner. Liu had previously served as an assistant minister of public security.[96] At the national level, the leading group consists of a variety of stakeholders. Regular attendees include those in diplomatic and security circles, but individuals with transportation, civil affairs or health portfolios, for example, may also play a supporting role.[97]

At the regional level, the newly promulgated 2016 XUAR counter-terrorism regulations provide greater clarity on the counter-terrorism coordination process.[98] Article 8 confirms the establishment of a leading group to direct regional counter-terrorism efforts as well as vertically linked groups at the prefectural/city and (as required) county level.[99] The paramilitary Xinjiang Production and Construction Corps (XPCC) has similarly established a counter-terrorism leading group, which is subordinate to the regional body but also coordinates with the Public Security Ministry.[100] Each leading group will establish a working group that handles day-to-day counter-terrorism work. Leading groups at each level report on their counter-terrorism work to the body directly above, unless an emergency requires a leading group to bypass the chain of command.[101]

By creating these vertically and horizontally linked groups, leaders hope to prevent or manage emergencies by enhancing coordination; implementing central directives more effectively; gathering and disseminating timely intelligence to thwart potential attacks; conducting drills and training exercises; and responding decisively to attacks through the rapid mobilization and deployment of counter-terrorism teams. During a national counter-terrorism work meeting on 12 April 2017, Guo stressed that China must continue to build a solid foundation for counter-terrorism work. Leaders must examine the symptoms and root causes of terrorism, deepen efforts to eradicate extremism, strictly implement the Party's ethnic and religious policies, and deepen efforts to eradicate extremism. He also emphasized the importance of actively mobilizing the masses to participate in the battle against terrorism.[102]

These institutions and mechanisms are also likely to serve to buttress General Secretary Xi's personal control over the direction of counter-terrorism work in Xinjiang. His August 2016 appointment of rising political star and acolyte Chen Quanguo as XUAR Party Chairman further reflects the priority he places on stability in Xinjiang. Chen had previously served as the hardline Party leader in Tibet, where he dramatically increased state surveillance capabilities as well as the reach of the Party and security apparatus into every level of Tibetan society.[103]

Hard(er) power: 'strike hard' campaigns, surveillance and restrictions on movement

XUAR authorities have caused a great deal of international controversy through their use of hard power tactics to combat the 'three evil forces'. Manifestations of hard power include ongoing 'strike hard' anti-terror campaigns, regular vehicular and foot patrols, and a deepening system of surveillance that enables authorities to monitor as well as restrict the movements of the populace. According to scholars James Leibold and Adrian Zenz, the 'Party-state's incremental securitization strategy in Xinjiang' occurred in stages over the course of the past decade. Stage one (2009–11) began directly following the 2009 unrest: authorities were not prepared to cope with the violence, and regained control only after Beijing dispatched 14,000 PAP forces as well as Special Police Units from thirty-one provinces to the XUAR. Regional authorities consequently responded by boosting personnel recruitment efforts across public security organs in the XUAR. The total number of security-related positions in the region rose from 6,876 (2006–8) to 15,841 (2009–11).[104]

During stage two (2012–13), authorities focused on increasing the number of security personnel in southern Xinjiang, as they believed that migrants south of the Tian Shan Mountains precipitated the 2009 unrest. Stage three (2014–15) began following a spate of terror attacks during 2013–14.[105] Officials recruited over 10,000 new security personnel and expanded the use of grid-style social management, which divides urban communities into smaller units. Security personnel use a mixture of traditional surveillance tactics and new technologies to monitor methodically any activities occurring in each portion of the 'grid'.[106] This period marked an 'evolution toward new surveillance-oriented, technology-focused security jobs'.[107]

Finally, observers have witnessed a significant expansion of surveillance and policing capabilities during stage four (2016–present). A massive recruitment drive enabled the Party-state to enhance dramatically its surveillance capabilities—and consequently the effectiveness of grid policing—throughout the XUAR. Out of the 31,687 security-related positions that regional authorities advertised in 2016, 89 per cent of all new hires manned 'convenience police stations'.[108] These small depots function as 'a series of forward operating bases for community policing and 24-hour patrols'.[109]

Authorities in Xinjiang and across China have deployed large numbers of armed police units to combat terrorist threats, including People's Armed Police (PAP) and Special Weapons and Tactics (SWAT) teams. Former PAP Deputy Commander Wang Yongsheng stated in March 2015 that while he feels that China's security situation is stable overall, the struggle against terrorism remains severely complicated.[110] Terrorist networks are simultaneously globalizing and localizing; attacks are more and more sophisticated; and there are growing numbers of 'lone wolves' who seek to commit atrocities.[111] Deputy Commander Wang also argued that extremists are abandoning 'cold weapons' such as knives and axes in favour of 'hot weapons' such as guns and explosives.[112] Reflecting official concerns that China must contend with increasingly organized, coordinated and deadly terrorist attacks, in 2015 authorities deployed members of the People's Armed Police in 300 cities across China, where they guarded 40 airports, 170 train stations, 130 entry and exit points, and 150 additional high-priority venues.[113]

Wang identified four critical goals for the People's Armed Police. First, strike hard against terrorism in Xinjiang. The former PAP deputy commander asserted that armed police now patrol the streets daily in every city, county, town and district. Second, redouble efforts to increase control over and protect Chinese society by deploying armed police at major events nationwide. Third, respond rapidly and efficiently to terrorist threats through the presence of armed police at national, provincial, regional and county levels. Fourth, provide enhanced opportunities for counter-terrorism combat training through live-fire exercises as well as participation in international exercises and competitions.[114] These security measures are far from inexpensive. Following the July 2009 riots, XUAR authorities dramatically increased the amount of money spent on public security. Official expenditure rose 87.9 per cent from 1.54 billion yuan (US$ 241 million) in 2009 to 2.89 billion yuan ($452 million) in 2010.[115] By 2014, the annual budget for public security expenditures had increased to approximately 6 billion yuan ($938 million). The figure represented an increase of 24 per cent over the 2013 budget. Officials expected spending to rise to 6.7 billion yuan ($1.05 billion) in 2015, an increase of 9.1 per cent.[116] It is difficult to find any current government data on counter-terrorism spending in the XUAR. However, it appears that during the first quarter of 2017 alone, Beijing invested more than US$ 1 billion into various security-related projects in the XUAR. Conversely, authorities spent a total of $27 million on security projects in 2015. At the same time, procurement orders reveal that the government has spent millions of dollars on 'unified combat platforms', which are computer systems meant to analyze surveillance data amassed by the police and various government organs.[117]

In comparison, the central government reported in January 2018 that it spent a total estimated 183.86 billion yuan (roughly US$ 29 billion) on 'public safety' in China in 2017, an increase of 9.67 billion yuan (roughly US$ 1.5 billion) or 5.5 per cent over the previous year. The 2017 budget included 139.76 billion yuan (roughly US$ 22 billion) for the People's Armed Police, an increase of 9.8 billion yuan (roughly US$ 1.5 billion) or 7.5 per cent over the 2016 figure. The 2017 public safety budget also allocated an estimated 20.15 billion yuan (roughly US$ 3.2 billion) to public security, an increase of 449 million yuan (roughly US$ 71 million) or 2.3 per cent over the 2016 figure.[118] In *China Goes Global: The Partial Power*, David Shambaugh notes that China's publicly disclosed domestic security budget expenditures do not include detailed breakdowns for the People's Armed Police, Ministry of State Security, People's Armed Militia, and local security force budgets. He estimates that the entire internal security budget might exceed $300 billion.[119]

Strengthening the surveillance state

Social instability remains a major concern for Beijing, which seeks to curb the outbreak of ethno-religious unrest and extremist attacks. China is consequently increasing surveillance of its citizens both online and offline.[120] Observers have reported widely on Party paranoia with regard to dissident activity, but the CCP is also continuously enhancing its capacity to monitor as well as disrupt potential or successful separatist, extremist and terrorist plots. Yet, because surveillance mechanisms ostensibly targeting criminal elements snare real and imagined regime critics as well, Beijing blurs the lines between legitimate counter-terrorism measures and crackdowns on any perceived opposition to state policies.

The Hu Jintao administration began constructing 'Skynet', China's nationwide surveillance system, back in 2005.[121] Officials argue that Skynet maintains the safety and security of the public by deterring and combating 'immoral' as well as 'illegal' behaviour.[122] Increasing numbers of cameras in Beijing and beyond monitor public transportation, roads, shopping centres, hospitals, public utilities, residential communities and schools.[123] Dissidents find themselves under constant watch.[124] The process has accelerated following the 2008–9 unrest in ethnographic Tibet and Xinjiang, where officials have blanketed the region with cameras.

By July 2010, XUAR authorities had installed high-definition video surveillance cameras on public buses and at bus stops; on roads and in alleys; in markets and shopping centres; and in schools.[125] Officials also placed mosques under video surveillance.[126] An official boasted that the region's 'Eagle Eye' cameras are capable of 'seamless' surveillance in all 'sensitive' parts of Urumqi, undoubtedly a reference to the Uyghur quarter. Unbreakable, fire-proof and 'riot-proof' shells encase the cameras, which can produce sharp, clear images, even at night. Police monitor the camera feeds constantly, searching for actionable intelligence.[127] Nevertheless, visitors to the region recognize that the system is not yet seamless.

XUAR officials are now combining surveillance tools with artificial intelligence, as well as other scientific and technological advancements, to make the process of monitoring and tracking individuals more automated and more effective. According to the *Wall Street Journal* journalists who travelled through Xinjiang in late 2017, authorities have transformed the region into a 'laboratory for high-tech social controls':

> Security checkpoints with identification scanners guard the train station and roads in and out of town. Facial scanners track comings and goings at hotels, shopping malls and banks. Police use hand-held devices to search smartphones for encrypted chat apps, politically charged videos and other suspect content. To fill up with gas, drivers must first swipe their ID cards and stare into a camera.[128]

An executive from a technology corporation that has 'sold facial-recognition algorithms to police and identity-verification systems to gas stations in Xinjiang' mused that the Turkic Muslim region is the 'world's most heavily guarded place'. He estimated that for every 100,000 individuals that Chinese security personnel wish to monitor, they would employ the 'same amount of surveillance equipment' that personnel elsewhere 'would use to monitor millions'.[129]

Localities in Xinjiang are currently testing a facial-recognition system that links to a police database. When individuals of concern venture more than 300 metres beyond certain areas deemed 'safe', such as their residences or workplaces, the so-called 'alert project' warns security personnel.[130] Chinese authorities also began 'collecting DNA samples, fingerprints, iris scans, and blood types of XUAR residents' in 2017 to build a population database. The aim of this programme is to facilitate the 'exchange of population information across government agencies' as well as 'achieve precise identification and real name registration management'.[131] One of the ways in which authorities are collecting citizen biodata is through a programme offering free annual physicals. Officials expect all residents between the ages of 12 and 65 to participate in the programme, with the exception of 'focus personnel' (i.e. those deemed threatening to social stability) and their family members, who must provide biometrics 'regardless of age'.[132] Health workers can input DNA and blood type information directly into a specially-designed mobile app, which is subsequently provided to security personnel and linked to national identification numbers. Although participation is nominally voluntary, one Uyghur told Human Rights Watch that his neighbourhood committee demanded that everyone must comply. He relented, believing that failing to provide biometric data would cause authorities to deem him politically disloyal.[133]

Chinese leaders pledge to cover all crucial public spaces, nationwide, with video surveillance cameras by 2020. According to the National Development and Reform Commission, 'Building a public security surveillance net is an important measure ... to maintain national security and social stability as well as prevent and combat violent terrorist crimes.' Leaders furthermore stress the need to 'improve social management', a euphemism for tightening security.[134]

China is using its surveillance network to develop an advanced crime detection system. The Ministry of Public Security has constructed 'big data policing platforms that aggregate and analyze massive amounts of civilians' personal data' regarding individuals' online activities, financial records, travel history, and work history, as well as data from police and government records, private enterprises and surveillance footage.[135] Through the national

'Police Cloud' system, security officials can buttress current counter-terrorism efforts by tracking the 'activities of activists, dissidents, and ethnic minorities'—including those with 'extreme thoughts'—and 'predict' when and where incidents are likely to occur.[136] The same Chinese company behind the 'alert project' is developing software in support of 'predictive policing' efforts.[137] China is also adopting its *dang'an*—personal dossiers dating back to the Maoist era—for the digital era.[138] As part of Xi Jinping's ongoing campaign to enhance 'social management', the Party-state is developing a new 'social credit' system. By aggregating and analyzing public and private data on the financial and socio-political behaviour of individuals as well as institutions, authorities seek to 'monitor, shape, and rate' behaviour.[139] Individuals and entities deemed 'trustworthy' will receive greater access to financial as well as public goods and services.[140]

Meanwhile, authorities continue to buttress electronic surveillance measures in the XUAR. Following the November 2015 Paris attacks, telecom providers have shut down mobile services for individuals who have avoided use of the real-name registration system; use virtual private networks (VPNs) to surmount China's Great Firewall; or download foreign messaging software. Affected individuals in Urumqi have received text messages stating that 'due to police notice, we will shut down your cellphone number within the next two hours in accordance with the law. If you have any questions, please consult the cyberpolice affiliated with the police station in your vicinity as soon as possible.'[141] In October 2016, security personnel arrested a teenager in Changji City for downloading VPN software, which the police report described as a 'violent and terrorist circumvention tool'.[142] The Ministry of Industry and Information Technology subsequently announced a nationwide crackdown on VPN usage in January 2017.[143]

On 27 June 2017, a notice issued to residents of Urumqi's Baoshan district—but reportedly applicable to all residents and business owners in the capital—indicated that the community would carry out 'stability maintenance measures' to comply with an 'anti-terrorist videos operation'. The instructions required all parties to submit national ID cards, mobile phones, external and portable hard drives, laptops, tablets, USB drives and media storage cards to their local police stations by 1 August for 'registration and scanning'. According to a police officer, the order applied to everyone born in Xinjiang, regardless of ethnicity. He stated that even those who lived elsewhere in China or in one of 26 unspecified countries abroad should report to local police stations upon their return home.[144]

Tianshan district authorities in Urumqi subsequently issued a directive on 10 July, ordering residents to install an app called 'CleanWebGuard':

> In order to achieve city-wide coverage in the antiterrorist video and audio clean-up, and to target people, materials, and thinking for clean-up work, management, and crackdowns, a technology company affiliated with the municipal police department has developed an app for Android smartphones that can filter out terrorist video and audio content.[145]

Authorities stipulated that all residents, regardless of ethnicity, must download and use the app to carry out 'self-surveillance'. The app reportedly scans the mobile device for 'video or audio containing terrorist content or illegal religious content, images, e-books, or documents' and purges them. The product website advertises that the app provides 'mobile phone remote control and other security services'. Those who attempt to save flagged content or hinder the app from deleting it 'will be pursued according to law'.[146] Authorities warned residents that they must install the app within ten days. Security personnel began random inspections of phones at checkpoints; anyone found in violation of the order potentially faced a ten-day detention period.[147]

Reports emerged in early 2018 that residents in Ili Kazakh Autonomous Prefecture and Bortala Mongol Autonomous Prefecture were experiencing difficulties making calls on iPhones. Moreover, security personnel inspecting mobile phones for banned content have reportedly detained individuals for days or weeks when they were found in possession of an iPhone. A local official stated that while there is no formal directive prohibiting the use of iPhones, in reality their usage is now forbidden.[148] The origin and extent of the ban is unclear. However, it is apparent that while Chinese companies will readily bend to national security imperatives, authorities are not likely to believe that foreign firms will provide Beijing with the knowledge and access it desires to monitor the use of foreign technologies, and their users, in China.[149] It is thus possible that XUAR authorities are deciding to allow only Chinese 'national champions' access to the regional market.[150]

In late January 2018, Minister of Industry and Information Technology Zhang Feng announced that in order to maintain a 'fair and orderly market' and 'promote the healthy development of the industry', China would 'regulate VPNs which unlawfully conduct cross-border operational activities'. Authorities intend to begin blocking overseas providers of VPNs on 31 March 2018, leaving only licensed domestic providers.[151]

As authorities gain the tools necessary to 'trace and monitor content and individual phones', netizens will increasingly censor themselves rather than risk detection.[152] According to Amnesty International's Nicholas Bequelin,

Xinjiang is 'the frontier for Internet surveillance in China' due to the critical importance of ongoing counter-terrorism campaigns.¹⁵³ XUAR authorities famously shut off the internet for ten months following the 2009 riots. When the region came back online in May 2010, nearly 80 per cent of Uyghur-run websites had disappeared from the internet.¹⁵⁴

The PRC is also buttressing its surveillance programmes through the use of advanced technologies, such as border control video monitoring systems, radars and unmanned aerial vehicles (UAVs) along its western and southwestern borders.¹⁵⁵ Border defence units in locales such as Xinjiang have stated that they employ such tools to conduct border patrols, curb illegal border crossings, support counter-terrorism operations and combat trafficking of drugs or contraband.¹⁵⁶ In comparison with the closed-circuit video surveillance previously in use in Xinjiang, the new systems reportedly include electro-optic devices and use advanced communications gear and image analysis equipment. They can operate continuously, regardless of weather conditions, and send real-time information to border control officers.¹⁵⁷

Since the early days of its 2014 'strike hard' anti-terror campaign, China has deployed UAVs in Xinjiang to hunt down 'suspected terrorists'.¹⁵⁸ During a Shanghai Cooperation Organization anti-terror drill in August 2014, Chinese drones fired several live missiles. People's Liberation Army Air Force (PLAAF) spokesman Shen Jinke remarked that PLA drones, which are 'tasked with surveillance, reconnaissance and ground attacks, will play a vital role in fighting against terrorism'.¹⁵⁹ Western observers have consequently asked whether authorities will eventually begin to deploy armed drones against terror suspects in Xinjiang, raising fears of an increase in the extrajudicial use of lethal force.¹⁶⁰

Observers increasingly believe that tools, techniques and technologies developed for use in Xinjiang are unlikely to remain there. Authorities 'constantly take lessons' learned from operating in the 'high-pressure' security environment in Xinjiang and implement them in eastern China, asserted Zhu Shengwu, a human rights defender who has experience with surveillance cases. 'What happens in Xinjiang has bearing on the fate of all Chinese people.'¹⁶¹

Monitoring citizen movements

Foot and vehicular patrols are a common sight in Xinjiang, particularly in Turkic Muslim communities. Although some patrols reflect sensitive anniversaries or events, others are in response to specific incidents or reflect a heightened overall security posture.¹⁶² Authorities in the XUAR and beyond regularly deploy significant numbers of PAP and SWAT to patrol local train stations, public squares, tourist spots, downtown areas and other crowded places.[163] Such forces have also set up both temporary as well as hardened security checkpoints throughout Xinjiang.

Just as the security presence grew increasingly visible, so did the political presence. In 2014, Chinese authorities dispatched over 200,000 officials to over 8,000 Xinjiang villages as part of the 'Visit, Benefit, Come Together' campaign, a quest to 'win people's hearts and to improve the local economy and people's lives'.[164] Communist cadres consider this programme an important part of their soft power strategy towards Turkic Muslims—as well as a mechanism to maintain 'social stability and long-term peace' in the region—and have consequently devoted a great deal of resources towards promoting and implementing the campaign.[165] In 2017, 76,000 cadres took part in the campaign.[166] Cadres preparing to be 'sent down' to Turkic Muslim communities are trained to use the 'mass line' approach to 'sincerely listen to opinions and recommendations, earnestly find ways to solve problems, and make every effort to ensure social stability. Through the "Visit, Benefit, Come Together" campaign, they can make sincere efforts to serve people of all ethnicities.'[167]

However, their presence also further buttresses the Communist Party's ability to 'gather intelligence on the lives of villagers and create a vast community surveillance network'.[168] Following his appointment, Xinjiang Party Secretary Chen Quanguo has launched initiatives similar to ones he implemented in Tibet, with the goal of closely monitoring local ethno-religious minorities and fostering integration. The 'Becoming Family' programme requires 110,000 officials to meet with local Turkic Muslims every two weeks to buttress 'ethnic harmony'.[169] Chen has also begun to embed officials in local mosques, a policy he previously implemented in Tibetan monasteries. Over the course of their three-year assignment in Hotan, 350 officials will manage the work of imams and conduct door-to-door visits with local residents.[170]

During Ramadan 2017 (26 May–24 June), in addition to conducting regular neighbourhood patrols and searches (particularly during *iftar*, the meal eaten after sunset during Ramadan), restricting access to mosques, and forcing eateries to remain open during fasting hours, Hotan authorities initiated a campaign whereby CCP cadres would reside in Uyghur households for up to fifteen days, enabling officials to grow 'close to the people'.[171] Officials assessed residents' ideological views and urged them not to fast or pray.[172]

In December 2017, over one million cadres participated in the XUAR 'unity week campaign'. They spent one week living, eating and studying with their 'relatives' in an effort to 'enhance ethnic unity and practice the spirit' of the 19th Party Congress. On the one hand, officials assisted their 'relatives' with farm work by shucking corn and herding sheep, assisted children with homework, offered employment opportunities to youth, donated clothes and funds, and accompanied ill 'relatives' to hospitals. On the other hand, the cadres performed United Front work: they organized Party meetings in the homes of local people, educated Uyghurs on state policies and the 19th Party Congress in the Uyghur language, and strove to make villagers realize that the Party and the government are responsible for 'the good changes in their lives'. They should thus 'work hard, listen to, and follow the Party'.[173]

Even after Turkic Muslim families have bid their 'relatives' a fond farewell, they are still expected to report on their participation in any religious activities—including circumcisions, weddings and funerals—to religious committees and residential communities that the government has established to 'manage religious practices'.[174] However, it appears that authorities are not taking any chances. Small, neighbourhood police depots—also known as 'convenience police service stations'—are an increasingly common sight across Urumqi and throughout Xinjiang.[175] Under the leadership of Party Secretary Chen, they proliferated throughout Tibet; he has accelerated their construction at the prefecture, city and county level in Xinjiang following his August 2016 appointment.[176] These 'grass-roots' service centres are meant to undertake '24-hour seamless patrols', effectively gather 'police intelligence', manage police cases, and provide emergency services to make people feel 'secure' and 'at ease'.[177] Authorities laud them as innovative social management tools that will promote ethnic harmony and help maintain long-term social stability in Xinjiang.[178] In an effort to win hearts and minds, convenience service stations are also offering free public services, ranging across phone charging stations, public WiFi, restrooms, tool and first aid kits, hot tea and free newspapers.[179] Their primary function is nevertheless clear: convenience police service stations act as 'forward operating bases' that conduct 'community policing' and round-the-clock patrols to strengthen Chinese 'grid-style social management'.[180]

Public security officials from Beijing to Urumqi increasingly rely on volunteers not only to assist these patrol teams, but also to inform them of any suspicious activities in their communities.[181] XUAR authorities now offer up to 5 million yuan (roughly US$ 800,000) for information regarding activities with potential links to religious extremism or terrorism.[182] Localities may also offer rewards in response to particular events: for example, following a knife attack outside Hotan, prefectural authorities announced that they set aside 100 million yuan (roughly US$ 16 million) to reward residents who provided tips on 'suspicious' activities or for individuals who 'attack or kill terrorists'.[183] The campaign also rewards residents reporting 'religious extremists' who meddle in judicial, governmental or educational affairs, or who seek to 'obstruct implementation of the constitution'. Authorities are furthermore calling for residents to support the campaign by informing on 'two-faced' Uyghur officials who neglect to follow official directives and fail to demonstrate loyalty to the regime by advocating 'extremist' ideas, offering succour to separatists, or publishing materials that 'harm the unity of the country' or 'distort the history of Xinjiang'.[184]

The Urumqi Public Security Bureau even released an Android app in April 2017—dubbed 'safety for the public' and available in both Chinese and Uyghur language interfaces—that enables residents to upload texts, photos and video clips if they witness 'suspicious activity that might pose a threat to social stability and security'. Users must submit their real name, national ID card number and occupational details to activate the app.[185] Four months later, a *Xinjiang Daily* report indicated that over 147,000 people had downloaded it. Individuals submitted more than 30,000 tips during that time period, although it appears that the majority of submissions pertained to everyday nuisances—such as ill-behaved canines—rather than tips on terrorists. A public security spokesperson stated that those providing valuable information are rewarded with 'WeChat red envelopes'.[186]

One could also argue that certain aspects of the XUAR's enhanced security posture are a response to demands from Chinese residents in Xinjiang who clamour for state protection from 'the Other' because they believe that their safety is in jeopardy. Policing the Turkic Muslim community may thus function just as much, if not more, to alleviate the fears of Chinese migrants.

The development of a complex and comprehensive security state enables authorities to monitor the movement of everyone in Xinjiang with increasing effectiveness. For example, village and township patrols and a system of checkpoints help police track local residents in Hotan, while visitors must provide their national identification number, place of origin and the length as well as purpose of their visit to local authorities. Those wishing to travel outside their township must similarly seek permission.[187] In February 2017, authorities began to implement a new 'stability maintenance' campaign across the XUAR to require all motor vehicle owners to install compulsory Chinese Beidou GPS tracking systems and use RFID (Radio Frequency Identification) license plates to ensure 'comprehensive supervision' of all vehicles. Drivers are required to pay an annual fee of 90 yuan (roughly US$ 1.40), but are not responsible for the cost of the equipment or installation. Those who fail to comply cannot access gasoline stations.[188]

In recent years, officials have further restricted the movement of Turkic Muslims by severely limiting their ability to leave the country. Xinjiang authorities began instructing residents to surrender their passports to local police for 'safekeeping'.[189] Authorities notified residents of Ili—a prefecture abutting Kazakhstan—on 30 April 2015 that they must relinquish their passports.[190] It appears that no new passports were issued for over a year, until officials issued a directive on 1 June 2016 which required residents to submit a 'DNA sample, fingerprints, a voice-print sample, and a 3D body scan image' in order to apply for passports or other travel documents. It was followed up on 1 June 2017 by a directive requiring all applicants for passports and other travel documents in Ili to supply a DNA sample, fingerprints, a voice-print sample and a 3D body scan image.[191]

Other local governments subsequently followed suit. According to at least four official directives from various locations in Xinjiang—all released in October 2016—and the online accounts of netizens from different towns and counties, authorities have variously stated that residents must relinquish their passports, or that no new passports will be issued.[192] Anyone wishing to travel abroad must apply for 'approval to leave the country' at their 'neighbourhood government offices' prior to submitting an official application to the Public Security Bureau.[193] Chinese state media attempted to argue that local governments may have 'misunderstood' new regulations, and that only those with suspected links to terrorism must hand over their passports.[194] However, in actuality, passport controls continue to grow stricter. Following the 19th Party Congress in Beijing, authorities are reportedly requiring Uyghurs throughout China to relinquish their passports.[195]

In May 2017, Chinese officials began notifying overseas Uyghur students—particularly those studying abroad in Muslim-majority countries—that they must return home. In many cases, their parents were detained in order to ensure compliance. Authorities meted out harsh punishments to those who nevertheless disobeyed. Egypt, presumably under pressure from Beijing, reportedly detained over 200 Turkic Muslim students that summer, many of whom were studying religion at Al-Azhar Islamic University in Cairo. Some students were subsequently deported to China, while others managed to flee to Turkey.[196] Four months after the Egyptian raids, the whereabouts of nearly twenty students remained unknown.[197]

At the same time, Xinjiang authorities started to detain those who had already returned from foreign travel; many individuals were subsequently sent to political re-education facilities. According to the director of public security in Korla's Qara Yulghun township, individuals must remain in so-called 'career development centres' until they confess their crime, namely that it was 'wrong' for them to leave China.[198] He explained that while citizens have the 'right' to travel abroad, those who do so are 'influenced by extremism'. Authorities must therefore educate them on Chinese laws and regulations so that they express 'remorse' for their actions. Detainees are asked to write self-criticisms; if authorities determine that their statement is inaccurate or inadequate, they must submit to further re-education until their self-criticism is deemed satisfactory. 'During the re-education [process], they will say… "Yes, it was a mistake to travel abroad, when the [ruling Communist] Party and government have created such a high living standard in our own country—we were ungrateful when we decided to go elsewhere."'[199] The director argued that 'If they don't study hard and cure their disease, we have no choice but to continue giving them medicine. When the disease is cured, they will feel it themselves, and we can also see it from their actions and behavior.'[200]

Following the passage of the 'de-extremification' regulation, authorities have sent a vast number of Turkic Muslims accused of harbouring 'extremist' and 'politically incorrect views' to political and ideological re-education camps.[201] A list of '75 signs of religious extremist activities', which first circulated in December 2014, is reportedly among the criteria police are using to identify and detain suspected 'extremists'.[202] The campaign appeared to intensify in early October, directly prior to the 19th Party Congress—a time when the central leadership seeks to minimize potential political 'distractions'. Authorities argued that it was necessary to put 'safety measures' into place to 'prevent violent incidents' from occurring during the event. Some local officials informed families affected by the campaign that they would cease making arrests and allow their loved ones to return home upon the conclusion of the Party Congress. Yet, months later, the re-education camps remain open and fully operational.[203]

The number of detainees is particularly high in southern Xinjiang, where the highest concentration of ethno-religious minorities live.[204] According to the relatives of detainees sent to camps in Kashgar City and Bortala Prefecture, authorities presented no 'warrant, evidence of a crime, or other documentation'.[205] While in detention, Turkic Muslims reportedly study Mandarin Chinese, learn national as well as regional laws and policies, view propaganda videos, and recite such shibboleths as 'religion is harmful' and 'learning Chinese is part of patriotism'.[206]

By the close of 2017, conditions at these facilities were extremely 'cramped and squalid', as they were already filled far beyond capacity.[207] Among those detained were reportedly children as young as fifteen years old, the elderly and individuals in desperate need of medical care.[208] Numerous reports from Korla indicated that officials were denying detainees admission to the re-education camps due to overcrowded conditions.[209] In one Bullaqsu township, Kashgar prefecture, a judiciary official reported that over 3,300 of the township's 36,000 residents were detained in prisons or re-education facilities.[210] By February 2018, pressure on Uyghurs in Kashgar was so great that there were already documented cases of distraught Uyghurs choosing suicide over continued harassment and re-education.[211]

The rapid rise in detainees appears to correlate with reports that officials must fulfill certain quotas as part of the campaign to combat extremism. In Qaraqash county, Hotan prefecture, authorities received orders to dispatch 40 per cent of residents to re-education facilities; the children left behind were brought to schools, nurseries or orphanages for care.[212] According to multiple police officers, their stations participated in 'online conferences' with higher authorities, who provided verbal directives on the campaign but no formal documentation.[213] Meanwhile, in Urumqi, police were reportedly instructed to detain 3,000 Turkic Muslims—mainly ethnic Uyghurs and Kazakhs—each week.[214]

Yasinahun, the chief of security in Chasa township, Kashgar, was uncertain when the re-education campaign would conclude. He recounted that during a meeting, a Chinese official stated that 'you can't uproot all of the weeds hidden among the crops in a field one by one—you need to spray chemicals to kill them all. Re-educating these people is like spraying chemicals on the crops. That is why it is a general re-education, not limited to a few people.'[215] 'The message I got from this,' said Yasinahun, 'was that the re-education will last a very long time.'[216]

Assessing contemporary counter-terrorism policy in the XUAR

Following the passage of China's first comprehensive national counter-terrorism law on 26 December 2015, the XUAR People's Congress Standing Committee responded by approving an even stricter regional law on 29 July 2016.[217] This XUAR legal interpretation defines what constitutes an act of terror and who constitutes terrorist actors; describes measures meant to combat terrorism; details security and prevention mechanisms; and provides insight into punishments for transgressors.[218] The regulations, which comprise

61 articles in 10 chapters, came into force on 1 August 2016.[219] Regional authorities formulated the measures by combining the national counter-terrorism law as well as other relevant laws and regulations with local policies and practices.[220] Nayim Yassen, Director of the Standing Committee, stated that the regulation 'can help Xinjiang tackle both the symptoms and root causes of terrorism', namely religious extremism, to prevent attacks in the region.[221]

Legal scholars have viewed China's recent counter-terrorism, national security and foreign NGO legislation with great skepticism. Rather than strengthen the rule of law in China, they argue that the measures serve primarily to buttress Chinese Communist Party rule and suppress dissenting voices at home and abroad.[222] Legal scholar Jerome Cohen opined that the laws collectively 'reflect the party's determination to create a garrison state' through the creation of 'an ideological platform' to guide 'domestic and foreign policies'.[223] Other scholars have expressed similar attitudes towards the regulations. 'The thrust of the new [foreign NGO] law is very clear,' said law professor Stanley Lubman.[224] 'It is consistent with a vigorous neo-Maoist campaign launched by President Xi Jinping against foreign ideologies and other influences on Chinese social and political development, and is intended to strengthen control by the Chinese Communist Party over Chinese society.'[225] Prominent Chinese human rights defender and Harvard Law School fellow Teng Biao asserted that the national security law would 'legitimize the abuse of power by state and public security bureaus'. To the Chinese Communist Party, enhancing 'the rule of law means using legislation as a tool of control'.[226]

The XUAR's counter-terrorism legislation likewise contains vague language that authorities can use to suppress dissent in the name of national security. Yet, it also incorporates puzzling punishments for offences that ostensibly have little to do with national security. Authorities can detain those who destroy national identification cards or Chinese banknotes for five to fifteen days or fine them up to 10,000 RMB (roughly US$ 1,500), for example.[227] Given nationwide civil society crackdowns and vitriolic state rhetoric warning against the spectre of religious extremism or colour revolutions on Chinese soil, authorities could plausibly use these regulations as justification to detain or arrest Uyghurs (or even target their family members) who pass information to the foreign media, download Arabic pop music onto their phones, or attempt to flee across the border to escape religious repression.[228]

Western scholars and officials tend to argue that counterproductive state policies have exacerbated ethno-religious tensions in the XUAR. However, it is not necessarily restrictive central state policies alone that explain tensions; regional and local policies as well as the haphazard implementation of central policies also appear directly or indirectly responsible for the growth of unrest. Furthermore, divisions and disagreements on policy matters among higher-ranking officials may also enable lower-level leaders to adopt a broad approach to interpreting or exploiting directives, regulations or laws, as they see fit.

Politburo members articulate specific goals and frame the debate over religious policy. Directives such as Document 9 that place an emphasis on defeating the 'three evil forces' provide the ideological framework within which authorities should act. PRC legislation such as the counter-terrorism, national security, cybersecurity and foreign NGO regulations provide the security apparatus with the legal backing to strike hard against real or perceived threats to state power.[229] CPP General Secretary Xi Jinping's statements on religious policy at the Xinjiang Work Forum provided state, regional and local officials with a set of guidelines regarding how the 'religious masses' can adapt Islam to the requirements of a modern, socialist society. During the Central Religious Affairs Conference, he went further by calling for the Sinicization of foreign faiths and explicitly linking the development and implementation of the Party's policies on religion to his vision of national rejuvenation and the achievement of the 'Chinese Dream'.[230] XUAR Party Secretary Chen echoed Xi's remarks at a meeting of regional representatives on 29 October 2016. Patriotic clergy have a key role to play in the pursuit of religious harmony and long-term stability. Authorities thus expect them to adhere firmly to the Party principles and policies by promoting legal religious activities while halting illegal ones; curbing extremism; and resisting infiltration (by hostile external actors).[231]

Such high-level pronouncements invariably stress patriotism, ethnic unity and religious harmony. They seek to create a framework under which 'patriotic' religious figures can safely instruct the masses on which 'legitimate' religious practices can meet their 'normal' needs. The state subsequently labels 'illegitimate' or 'illegal' religious activities as forms of 'religious extremism', which undermine social stability and endanger state security. The types of ideological and patriotic campaigns that leaders consequently champion provide increasingly shrinking discursive as well as physical space for ethno-religious minorities to challenge established or developing state norms. However, while leaders in Beijing emphasize that 'the nation should adopt particular principles, methods, and paths' to achieve these goals, the degree to which Beijing is directly or indirectly responsible for specific religious and counter-terrorism regulations implemented on the ground in the XUAR remains somewhat unclear.[232] Nevertheless, it appears likely that, as Party Secretary Xi Jinping continues to consolidate his power and deepen his influence, he and his allies are taking a more prominent role in shaping the trajectory of Xinjiang's counter-terrorism policies.

In years past, the Politburo likely exhorted the XUAR Party Committee to battle against the 'three evil forces' and create the conditions necessary to foster ethnic unity and religious harmony. It is also quite possible that Beijing provided specific clandestine directives or religious regulations to provincial officials for local implementation. Even the XUAR-spearheaded 'Project Beauty' is framed more as an economic development as well as a social and cultural campaign that merely 'encourages' Muslim women to embrace modernity and eschew extremism, rather than as a region-wide crackdown on 'Islamic' practices.[233] Yet, there is now undeniably a new emphasis upon legitimizing and standardizing a diverse set of local directives and regulations through an ostensibly more transparent legal framework.

China's Regional Ethnic Autonomy Law (REAL) acknowledges the need for flexibility in creating and implementing laws in ethnic minority regions of China. In times of uncertainty and unrest, however, officials at all levels of government have actually used this law to implement policies that are stricter than those in other regions of the People's Republic of China. This is arguably the case at present, as Chinese Muslims such as the Hui have not experienced the same degree of official scrutiny as Turkic Muslims.[234] However, James Leibold argues that as 'an increasing nationalist and xenophobic body politic in China continues to lash out against Islam', and the Party-state continues to move towards 'more uniform implementation of policies ... very likely this surveillance society that has been created in Tibet and Xinjiang will be extended into Hui areas'. Policies that 'isolate and severely restrict Hui culture and mobility' may furthermore have consequences for Xi Jinping's Belt and Road Initiative.[235] Providing guidelines and directives to provincial authorities, yet granting some flexibility to local leaders, may explain why observers have witnessed a diverse set of restrictions and regulations implemented in different prefectures, counties, townships and villages. If central or provincial authorities were issuing uniform instructions to all localities in the XUAR, then observers would not see so many discrepancies from one area to the next. The new national counter-terrorism law and XUAR-level interpretation, among others, may well represent an effort to address some of these inconsistencies.

As ancient Chinese rulers turned their gaze westwards, they encountered the wild and pugnacious *shengfan*, i.e. 'raw barbarians', whose purported savagery derived from their consumption of raw food. The state sought to subdue and transform them into docile and passive *shufan*, i.e. 'cooked barbarians', who would no longer pose a threat to China.²³⁶ Today, Chinese authorities are undertaking a long-term campaign of gradually erasing the unique cultural differences that separate Turkic minorities from the Chinese majority, with the goal of 'domesticating' them and assimilating them fully into the nation-state. The Chinese Communist Party is thus concerned by the marked increase in ethno-religious tensions since the 2009 unrest. Beijing has begun to shift its rhetoric and approach to the 'Xinjiang problem', even if its ultimate mission remains unchanged. During the [First] Work Forum on Xinjiang in May 2010, General Secretary Hu Jintao focused on creating 'leapfrog-style development' to stimulate the local economy.²³⁷ Yet, the Second Work Forum on Xinjiang in May 2014 focused far more on the challenges that ethno-religious tensions pose to society, with an ultimate goal of 'safeguarding social stability and achieving an enduring peace'.²³⁸ General Secretary Xi thus placed new emphasis on ideological imperatives, arguing consistently that development alone will not solve the 'minzu problem'.

As a multi-ethnic socialist state that purportedly upholds principles of unity and equality among all ethnic groups, Beijing is loath to admit that its policies are at the root of unrest. Instead, it continues to blame 'hostile anti-China Western forces'. The American-led 'war on terror' provided China with a more readily understandable and digestible global lexicon, but in reality one might view terms such as 'extremist' and 'terrorist' as placeholders for classic Chinese Communist Party terms such as 'counter-revolutionary'. In both cases, the CCP employs these terms to describe individuals or groups that hold ideas or commit acts which openly contradict state ideologies and policies. This is not to say that terrorism does not pose a threat to China. However, the problem is that China lacks effective mechanisms for ethnic and religious minorities to express legitimate grievances with the state. The state security apparatus threatens prominent ethnic minority intellectuals—such as Uyghur economist Ilham Tohti or Tibetan writer Tsering Woeser—with punishment when they publicly argue that CCP ethnic, religious and linguistic policies exacerbate social divisions and tensions. Under the 'three evils' framework, the discursive space for intellectual and civic dialogue is rapidly shrinking.

CCP General Secretary Xi Jinping has exhorted 'all ethnic groups to show mutual understanding, respect, tolerance and appreciation, and to learn and help each other, so they are tightly bound together like the seeds of a pomegranate'.²³⁹ Yet, prior to his eventual arrest, Professor Ilham Tohti wrote:

as a Uighur intellectual, I strongly sense that the great rift of distrust between the Uighur and Han [Chinese] societies is getting worse each day, especially within the younger generation. Unemployment and discrimination along ethnic lines have caused widespread animosity. The discord did not explode and dissipate along with the July 5 [2009] incident and during subsequent social interactions. Instead, it has started to build up once again. The situation is getting gradually worse. Yet, fewer and fewer people dare to speak out.[240]

If Chinese authorities wish to address the 'great rift of distrust' that exists between Uyghur and Chinese societies, then the Party-state should reconsider how it manages its ethno-religious and counter-terrorism policies. While China faces legitimate security concerns in the region, restricting or prohibiting traditional linguistic, cultural or religious norms is not the appropriate solution. Severely curbing freedoms in the name of combating separatism, extremism and terrorism will only increase inter-ethnic tension and enhance the prospects for societal turmoil.

3

'FIGHTING TERRORISM ACCORDING TO LAW'

CHINA'S LEGAL EFFORTS AGAINST TERRORISM

Zunyou Zhou

In the People's Republic of China (PRC), the problem of terrorism is almost exclusively linked to Uyghurs, a Muslim ethnic group concentrated in the far-western region of Xinjiang, officially known as the 'Xinjiang Uyghur Autonomous Region' (XUAR). For China, terrorism is just one of 'three forces', along with separatism and extremism, which collectively impose a serious threat to the country's national security and social stability. The Chinese government treats these forces with equal seriousness and determination, simply because they are inter-dependent: separatism is the ultimate goal; whereas terrorism is the instrument to achieve the goal; and extremism lays the ideological foundation for terrorism.[1]

Historically, Uyghur separatism may date back to an Islamic kingdom that existed between 1867 and 1877 in southern Xinjiang. This incident was followed by the establishment of two separate short-lived 'East Turkestan Republics', in 1933 and 1944 respectively, in parts of Xinjiang. In the subsequent decades up to the withdrawal of Soviet troops from Afghanistan in

1989, Xinjiang sporadically suffered from political unrest by Uyghur people.[2] Since the 1990s, the political resistance has gradually evolved into an ambitious movement striving to set up an Islamic state called 'East Turkestan' through violent means. In the wake of the 11 September 2001 attacks, China actively participated in the global anti-terror war led by the US. As an official Chinese report in 2002 claimed, between 1990 and 2001 in Xinjiang the 'East Turkestan' terrorist forces had been behind more than 200 terrorist attacks, resulting in 162 deaths and over 440 injuries.[3]

In the run-up to the Beijing 2008 Olympic Games, Xinjiang was rocked by a series of terrorist attacks. In July 2009, a riot broke out in Urumqi, the capital of Xinjiang, killing 197 people and wounding more than 1,700 others. In spite of subsequent increased measures by the authorities, China encountered another spike of terrorist violence in 2013 and 2014, which resulted in several hundred deaths. Since 28 October 2013, when a jeep crashed into a group of tourists in Beijing's Tiananmen Square, the violence has been spreading beyond Xinjiang. Cities in other provinces like Kunming and Guangzhou also became targets of Uyghur terrorists. Even worse, hundreds of Chinese Uyghurs have reportedly fled via Southeast Asia to Turkey and many of them have been fighting alongside the terror group Islamic State (IS) against the Syrian regime.[4] Such reports were corroborated by two US research institutions, which found in July 2016, on the basis of leaked IS data, that from mid-2013 to mid-2014 alone more than 100 Chinese Uyghurs had joined IS.[5] China has long feared that these battle-hardened Uyghurs might at some point in the future march home to conduct destructive attacks. In addition to domestic terrorism, Chinese nationals and commercial interests abroad have also come into the crosshairs of Uyghur jihadists, ISIS and other international terrorist groups.

In the face of the upsurge in domestic terrorism, China started in May 2014 to respond with draconian, iron-fisted actions. Since then, China has seen a clear decline in terrorist violence, except for a few high-profile attacks.

After the attacks of 9/11, China has given the fight against terrorism high priority and taken a comprehensive counter-terrorism approach that aims to mobilize all state organs and civil groups in order to reach the fabric of Uyghur society. For the regional government of Xinjiang, counter-terrorism is unquestionably a primary task. In implementing the Chinese Communist Party's (CCP) famous resolution on 'ruling the country according to law',[6] adopted in October 2014, Xinjiang pushes forward a slogan of 'ruling Xinjiang according to law'.[7] The proclamation of giving full play to the role of law is a welcome sign that may lead to greater human rights protection in Xinjiang's counter-terrorism efforts.

In China, the increasing threat of terrorism since the 9/11 attacks has generated an array of legislative instruments to address the problem. Counter-terrorism legislation as discussed in this chapter includes not just China's only anti-terror code, the Counter-Terrorism Law (CTL), but also specific anti-terror provisions in other laws such as the Criminal Law, the Criminal Procedure Law and the Cybersecurity Law. Below is a list of national anti-terror laws that China has adopted and implemented since 2001:

- Third Criminal Law Amendment, adopted on 29 December 2001;
- Anti-Money Laundering Law, adopted on 31 October 2006;
- 'Counter-Terrorism Decision', adopted on 29 October 2011;
- 'Decision on Amending the Criminal Procedure Law', adopted on 14 March 2012;
- Ninth Criminal Law Amendment, adopted on 29 August 2015;
- Counter-Terrorism Law, adopted on 27 December 2015.

In addition to the above-noted national laws, Xinjiang's legislatures adopted various local regulations, including:

- XUAR's Regulation on Religious Affairs, adopted on 28 November 2014;
- Urumqi's Regulation on Burqa Ban, adopted on 10 January 2015;
- XUAR's Implementing Rules on the Counter-Terrorism Law, adopted on 29 July 2016;
- XUAR's Regulation on De-Radicalization, adopted on 29 March 2017.

In order to develop the context for the subsequent discussion, it is necessary to provide a brief overview of the so-called 'Counter-Terrorism Decision' (CTD) and its successor, the CTL. The CTD refers to the 'Decision on Issues Related to Strengthening Counter-Terrorism Work' adopted in October 2011 by the National People's Congress (NPC) Standing Committee.[8] The CTD, made up of eight articles, created the first legal framework for China's general counter-terrorism efforts. According to the CTD's explanatory report as submitted to the legislature, a full-blown anti-terrorism law was, at that time, deemed premature, whereas a 'decision' was a more appropriate choice.[9] Among other things, the CTD sought to define terrorism, establish a national counter-terrorism body, maintain a terrorist watch list and create a procedure for freezing terrorist assets. In December 2015, the CTD was replaced by the CTL, passed by the NPC Standing Committee.

Debates on the necessity of a special anti-terror code emerged in the wake of the 9/11 attacks, but it was not until November 2014 that the first draft of the CTL was published for public consultation. Having taken into account international criticism and domestic suggestions, the second and third versions of the CTL brought significant changes to reflect the need for stronger human rights protection. The third—also the final—version[10] has been in effect since 1 January 2016.

The CTL is composed of ninety-seven articles in ten chapters. With the first and last chapters involving general and supplementary provisions, the other eight chapters cover the following major aspects, respectively: terrorist designation, prevention, intelligence, investigation, emergency response, international cooperation, safeguards and legal liabilities. The CTL entails a combination of administrative, judicial and military means, with the purpose of creating a synergy between various state organs. Given the diversified, multiple measures it has introduced, the CTL is genuinely 'a comprehensive law' as China claims.[11]

A high point of the law is to regulate the legal status of specialized counter-terrorism organs in the national, provincial and prefecture-level governments. Following 9/11, the Chinese government moved quickly to bolster its own counter-terrorism capabilities by, for example, setting up a National Counter-Terrorism Coordination Group. In August 2013, the 'Coordination Group' was upgraded to 'National Counter-Terrorism Leading Group' (National CTLG).[12] Currently, the National CTLG's office is housed in the Ministry of Public Security (MPS), China's highest police agency, and headed by Guo Shengkun, Minister of Public Security.[13]

This chapter will explore China's major legal measures that attempt to intensify the criminal justice response, blacklist terrorist organizations and individuals, censor terrorism-related information, combat terrorist financing, deter religious extremism and promote international cooperation.

Intensifying the criminal justice response against terrorism

As previously noted, the CTL is a comprehensive law but it does not cover all aspects of China's counter-terrorism effects. Rather, the Criminal Law contains significant provisions on terrorism offences and punishments for these offences. Although terrorism was rarely heard of in China prior to 9/11, Chinese lawmakers had anticipated the necessity of criminalizing terrorist activities. The Criminal Law as amended by a reform law in 1997 had the first provision establishing a terrorism offence, criminalizing founding, leading or participating in a terrorist organization (Article 120).[14]

After 9/11, China's first legal response to terrorism was to adopt the Third Criminal Law Amendment in December 2001 to increase the penalty for the existing terrorism offence and criminalize a further wide range of terrorism-related acts. The amendment is also known as the 'Counter-Terrorism Amendment' as it dealt specifically with terrorism. The reform law involved both totally new offences (Articles 120a and 291a) and revisions to some of the existing provisions in the section 'Offences Endangering Public Security',[15] with the intention to:[16]

- Intensify the crackdown on terrorist organizations, by increasing the penalty for a founder, a leader, or an active member of a terrorist group to a prison term of more than ten years or life imprisonment, whereas the penalty for other, ordinary members remains at less than three years (Article 120);
- Criminalize terrorist financing, including the providing of funds to any terrorist group or person who engages in terrorism (Article 120a) and the laundering of money generated from terrorist activities (Article 191);
- Criminalize the 'disseminating', the 'illegal manufacturing, trading, transporting or storing', or the 'stealing, seizing or plundering' of 'poisonous or radioactive substances or contagious-disease pathogens' (especially anthrax powder) (Articles 114, 115, 125, and 127);
- Criminalize the dissemination of false dangerous substances (especially false anthrax powder), as well as the fabrication or dissemination of false terror information (especially false bombing or anthrax threats) (Article 291a).

Partly owing to the escalation of terrorism in 2013 and 2014, China adopted the Ninth Criminal Law Amendment in August 2015.[17] By adding new offences (Articles 120c through 120f) and revising old provisions (Articles 120b and 311), this amendment was designed to criminalize the following terrorism-related activities:

- Financing terrorist training; recruiting or transporting people for joining a terrorist group, for committing a terrorist act or for participating in terrorist training (Article 120b);
- Propagating or inciting terrorism by producing, distributing or spreading information related to terrorism or extremism (Article 120c);
- Inciting or forcing people to violate China's legal systems on marriage, justice, education and social management, by using extremist ideology (Article 120d);

- Compelling other people to wear or adorn themselves with clothes or emblems that propagate terrorism or extremism, by force or coercion (Article 120e);
- Possessing illegally books, audio-visual materials or any other objects that propagate terrorism or extremism (Article 120f);
- Declining to provide investigating organs with information about terrorist or extremist offences committed by other people (Article 311).

Prior to the passage of the reform law, some of China's leading criminal law scholars raised their concerns about the over-criminalization of terrorism-related activities. In their opinion, some of these new provisions seem to contradict the basic principle that 'law must not punish thoughts' to the detriment of China's legal development.[18]

In March 2012, the NPC adopted another reform law, 'Decision on Amending the Criminal Procedure Law'. Among the large number of mainly progressive changes introduced by the reform law, there were seven terrorism-related revisions intended to:[19]

- Designate intermediate courts as first-instance courts for adjudicating terrorism cases (Article 20);
- Limit the access to counsel in terrorism cases (Article 37);
- Provide special protection for witnesses in terrorism cases (Articles 62 and 63);
- Allow the use of residential surveillance for terrorism cases (Article 73);
- Impose restraints on the right to notification in terrorism cases (Article 83);
- Legalize the use of 'technical investigation measures' (Articles 148 through 152);
- Create a procedure for confiscating illegal earnings in terrorism cases (Articles 280 through 283).

Although the current Criminal Procedure Law (CPL) of 2012 is hailed as a landmark of China's legal development, due to its advances regarding the protection of the accused, it also contains controversial provisions on measures such as 'secret detention' and 'secret investigation'. Both measures attract strong criticism for their serious infringements of the fundamental right to a fair trial.

The above-noted Articles 73 and 83, dubbed 'clauses of secret detention', have provoked strong criticism among legal experts and human rights advocates in China and throughout the world.[20] Article 73 regulates the use of 'residential surveillance', one of five coercive measures in the CPL. The measure is usually enforced at the domicile of the suspect or defendant ('ordinary residential surveillance' or 'ORS'), but if there is no permanent domicile, it may also be enforced at a designated place of residence ('designated residential surveillance' or 'DRS'). If ORS is likely to impede the investigation in cases involving state security, terrorism and serious bribery, DRS may be used instead. However, neither ORS nor DRS may be enforced at a detention facility or an investigating facility. In case of DRS, the family members of the person under surveillance should be notified within twenty-four hours of enforcement, except where notification is impossible.

Based on the provisions in Article 73, investigators have the power to detain a person suspected of terrorism in a designated location for up to six months, which is the maximum duration for residential surveillance. The investigators are required to notify relatives within twenty-four hours, but are not required to disclose the reasons for the detention and the whereabouts of the person. This enables the investigators to deny the detainee access to a lawyer during the six-month custody.[21]

Article 83 regulates the detainee's right of notification in case of detention. The investigators are required to send the detainee immediately, and within no more than twenty-four hours, to a detention facility. They must notify the detainee's family members within the twenty-four hours after he or she has been taken into custody, except in circumstances where the notification cannot be delivered or where state security crimes or terrorism crimes are suspected and the notification may impede the investigation. As soon as the circumstances impeding the investigation no longer apply, the family members must be notified immediately.

A close look at the provisions in Article 83 reveals that, in terrorism cases, the investigators may hold a suspect in formal detention centres for no more than thirty-seven days, the maximum duration as allowed elsewhere in the CPL, without notifying his or her family members. Even if the family members are notified of the detention within twenty-four hours, they are most likely not informed of the charges against the detainee or the location of the detainee. Even if the family members are notified of the charges and the location, defence lawyers cannot meet their detained clients without the investigators' permission. Thus, at the investigation stage, terrorist suspects are not in a position to have access to counsel for a long period of time.[22]

Another highlight of the 2012 CPL is the addition of a new section, entitled 'Technical Investigation Measures' (TIMs), which ranges from Articles 148 through 152. In fact, the TIMs refer to secret investigation measures, such as electronic surveillance and undercover investigation, which had been employed by law enforcement agencies for many years before they were actually brought into the CPL.[23] In theory, the use of TIMs must conform to the following substantive requirements and procedural safeguards:

- *Use of TIMs*: A police agency, if the investigation of a crime so requires and following a strict approval procedure, may use TIMs for terrorism and other cases (Article 148).
- *Approval*: The approval should provide the types of TIMs to be employed and the intended targets. The approval is in effect for three months from the date of issue. TIMs that are no longer necessary should be rescinded promptly. Where the effective period in a complicated or difficult case expires but the TIMs continue to be required, the effective period may be extended upon approval, but each extension may not exceed three months (Article 149).
- *Implementation*: When a TIM is taken, it must be executed strictly in keeping with the type of measure, the intended targets, and the approved duration. An investigator who becomes aware of a state secret, trade secret, or private personal information during the investigation must maintain confidentiality. Any information obtained through a TIM that is unrelated to the case must be promptly destroyed. Materials obtained through a TIM may be used only for the investigation, prosecution, and trial in the case, and may not be used for other purposes (Article 150).
- *Admissibility of evidence*: Materials obtained through a TIM may be used as evidence in criminal proceedings. If the use of evidence obtained through a TIM may pose a risk to the personal safety of relevant personnel or may cause other serious consequences, measures should be taken to withhold the real identities of the relevant personnel, and, where necessary, such evidence may be verified by judges outside the court (Article 152).

It is a positive step that the use of TIMs is regulated in the legal framework, but it remains questionable whether these requirements and safeguards can be truly respected in practice.

Indeed, the above-noted provisions would not be sufficient. It is equally necessary to know how they are implemented in practice. A striking feature of China's criminal justice system is its frequent use of 'strike hard' (in Chinese, *yanda*) anti-crime campaigns that are characterized by severe punishments and swift prosecutions. 'Strike hard' used to be a national criminal policy for fighting a variety of specific crimes considered a serious threat to the public order, within a specific period. Such nationwide campaigns invariably involved joint actions by police officers, prosecutors and judges, as well as being the result of mass arrests, prosecutions, trials and executions.[24] Considering its limited effect on the reduction of crime rates and its tough restrictions on fundamental human rights, the 'strike hard' strategy gradually gave way to a new criminal policy of 'balancing severity and leniency' (in Chinese, *kuan yan xiang ji*) that was recognized by the authorities in 2006.[25] Although the new policy has taken centre stage in other provincial regions, the old 'strike hard' practices remain active in Xinjiang. Owing to Xinjiang's strategic importance to national security, it appears that the regional government has sought to cling to the 'strike hard' approach to maintain control.

In the aftermath of the 2008 Beijing Olympic Games, Xinjiang authorities were widely reported to have taken increased measures to 'strike hard' against the 'three forces'. After the July 2009 unrest, Xinjiang authorities mounted a thorough 'strike hard' campaign to 'further consolidate the fruits of maintaining stability and eliminate security dangers', 'root out places where criminals breed' and 'change the face of the public security situation in these areas'.[26] Following a series of deadly attacks, including the explosion on 22 May 2014 that killed thirty-nine people and injured eighty-nine others in Urumqi, China's central government launched a one-year anti-terror campaign with Xinjiang as the major battleground.[27] In the first six months of the campaign, the government of Xinjiang alleged that it had destroyed 115 terrorist groups to prevent most of the potential terrorist attacks. Meanwhile, 171 religious training sites were shut down and 238 people were detained for arranging these sites.[28]

Such 'strike hard' campaigns often severely curtail or even ignore the due process rights of the accused. It is questionable whether such a heavy-handed approach is desirable, because an effective counter-terrorism strategy hinges to a large extent on a criminal justice system that is embedded in respect for human rights.

Defining and proscribing terrorism

China established an official definition of terrorism in October 2011, owing to the adoption of the CTD.[29] In December 2015, the CTL replaced the old definition with a new one in its Article 3. Thus, terrorism is defined as 'any advocacy or activity that, by means of violence, sabotage, or threat, aims to create social panic, undermine public safety, infringe on personal and property rights, or coerce a state organ or an international organization, in order to achieve political, ideological, or other objectives'.[30]

Admittedly, a universally accepted definition of terrorism does not exist. However, there has been a certain degree of international consensus in this regard, as evidenced by the UN's 'Draft Comprehensive Convention on International Terrorism' and the EU's 'Framework Decision of June 2, 2002 on Combating Terrorism'.[31] In terms of legal wording, the current Chinese definition is already quite close to the global consensus, except for its use of the term 'advocacy' (in Chinese, *zhuzhang*). It needs to be pointed out that the keyword 'advocacy' in the definition may be interpreted as 'thoughts' or 'speeches'. The lawmakers may have intended to punish the dissemination of terrorist thoughts or speeches, but the fact is that the keyword 'activity' in the definition already covers such terrorist propaganda.[32]

Based on the terrorism definition and the subsequent procedural provisions of the CTL, the Chinese government may in future blacklist terrorist organizations and individuals:

– Both the National CTLG and courts at an intermediate or higher level have the competence to blacklist terrorist groups and persons, but the right to announce listing results rests with the National CTLG (Articles 12 and 16);
– Ministries of Public Security (MPS), State Security (MSS), and Foreign Affairs (MFA) as well as provincial CTLGs may submit listing proposals to the National CTLG (Article 13);
– Financial institutions, as well as designated non-financial institutions, must freeze funds or other assets of the listed groups and persons and report this fact to the MPS, MSS, and the Anti-Money Laundering Bureau (AMLB) of China's central bank, the People's Bank of China (PBC) (Article 14);
– Listed groups and persons may request a final review of the listing by the National CTLG; if the listing is revoked, the affected assets must be unfrozen (Article 15).

It is clear that the CTL adopts a double-track approach towards the listing of terrorist organizations and individuals. The double tracks refer to the 'judicial track' and 'administrative track'. In terms of the judicial track, the court determines whether a criminal group is a terrorist organization when it adjudicates crimes committed by the group. As regards the administrative track, the government decides, as a stand-alone matter, whether an organization should be placed on a terror list.[33] Listing by the court usually results in criminal punishments such as a fine, a prison term or even a death sentence, whereas listing by the government often leads to non-criminal sanctions such as extradition, travel bans and asset freezing.

In view of the devastating consequences that the blacklisting entails for the fundamental right to property and freedom of movement, the listing regime is even described as a 'civil death penalty'.[34] The fact that the CTL provides for a mechanism for legal remedies may be a welcome step, but given the controversy of legitimacy surrounding the instrument of blacklisting,[35] China needs to put in place more meaningful legal rules to minimize potential negative effects of the regime on affected entities and people.

Before the CTL was adopted, the Chinese government, through its MPS, had made three listing announcements. While the first two announcements were based on the administrative discretion of the MPS, the third one had a solid legal basis provided by the then Counter-Terrorism Decision. Since the adoption of the CTL, there has however been no further refinement of the legal basis of the proscription of terrorist organizations.

The earliest terrorism list, as issued in December 2003, included four organizations: the East Turkestan Islamic Movement (ETIM), East Turkestan Liberation Organization (ETLO), World Uyghur Youth Congress (WUYC) and East Turkestan Information Centre (ETIC). These groups were allegedly connected to and supported by al-Qaeda networks and were responsible for a string of terrorist acts inside and outside Chinese territory. The list also named eleven individuals.[36] In October 2008, the terror list was expanded to include eight more individuals allegedly linked to the ETIM.[37] Six further alleged members of the ETIM were put on the list in April 2012, when the blacklist was expanded for a second time.[38]

On the list was the ETIM's founder, Hasan Mahsum. He was reportedly killed in October 2003 during a Pakistani military operation in South Waziristan.[39] Memetiming Memeti, allegedly the current leader of the ETIM's successor, the Turkestan Islamic Party (TIP), is also on the list. Memeti, also known as 'Abdul Haq', is a terrorist recognized by the UN and the US.[40] Another key person on the list is Dolkun Isa, who fled China in the 1990s and later became a German citizen. In November 2017, he was elected as president of the 'World Uyghur Congress' (WUC) based in Munich, Germany, while long-serving leader Rebiya Kadeer was elevated to the honorary post of paramount leader.[41] Partly stemming from the listed WUYC, the WUC claims to represent all Uyghur people at home and abroad.[42]

Although not all of the listed groups or persons have been deemed terrorist by Western countries, the blacklist does provide China with a powerful legal mechanism to crack down on terrorism and push for international cooperation. By relying on the list, China integrates its counter-terrorism actions into the global war on terrorism and urges other countries to ban the listed groups, hunt down the listed persons and extradite them back to China.[43]

Censoring terrorism-related information

China keeps tight reins on both traditional and new media for fear of their disruptive or subversive influence. Compared with the state-run traditional media, the Chinese government feels more uneasy about the new media based on internet use. The government is well aware that the internet has become a major platform for terrorist propaganda and recruitment, as well as for the preparation of terrorist activities.[44] In March 2014, then XUAR Party Secretary Zhang Chunxian told reporters that the previous spate of domestic terrorist attacks had mostly been linked to online videos that terrorists had obtained by using VPNs (virtual private networks) to bypass China's powerful 'Great Firewall' censorship system.[45] In 2016, the advocacy group Reporters without Borders ranked China 176th place out of 180 countries in its annual World Press Freedom Index. In 2016, Freedom House ranked China the worst abuser of internet freedom for the second consecutive year out of sixty-five countries that represent 88 per cent of the world's internet users.[46]

When it comes to the censorship of media reports, Article 63 of the CTL allows for a media blackout on the reporting of terrorist attacks and subsequent government responses as follows:

– A provincial CTLG is responsible for releasing information on terrorist incidents, their developments and the government's emergency responses;
– Except for the provincial CTLG, nobody is allowed to disseminate details of the incidents that may lead to copycat actions, nor may they spread cruel or inhuman images of the incidents;
– Except for news media with the permission of the provincial CTLG exclusively responsible for releasing such information, nobody is allowed to publish identifying information on response personnel or hostages, nor on emergency responses.

For Chinese and foreign journalists, these provisions are effectively a reaffirmation of China's usual censorship practices for media reports on countless sensitive topics. Terrorism is just one of these delicate subjects. A recent example of media censorship was imposed on a deadly terrorist assault on workers at a coal mine on 18 September 2015 in Baicheng county of Aksu prefecture in Xinjiang. Radio Free Asia, a US-funded broadcaster, was the first to report the massacre. It was not until 20 November 2015, however, that China's state-run media officially broke the silence, stating that Chinese security forces had killed twenty-eight members of a terrorist group in a fifty-six day hunt operation, and that this group had carried out the Baicheng attack resulting in sixteen deaths and eighteen other injuries.[47]

With regard to the censorship of terrorism-related internet information, the CSL deserves more attention than the CTL. A high point of the CSL is the leadership role awarded to the Cyberspace Administration of China (CAC). The agency has in fact become a powerful internet regulator, with responsibilities for administering, coordinating and supervising cyberspace affairs. On the one hand, the law imposes numerous obligations on internet and telecommunication companies and internet users, and grants almost unbridled powers to government departments. On the other hand, it contains few provisions on restraining censorship powers and protecting civil liberties.[48]

The sweeping counter-terrorism measures provided by the CSL include the following:

- Internet (and telecommunication) companies are required to provide police or intelligence agencies with technical support, including backdoor access and decryption, for the government's efforts to prevent and investigate terrorist activities ('backdoor provisions') (Article 18);
- These companies are required to take monitoring measures as provided by other laws in order to preclude the dissemination of terrorist information (Article 19);
- They are also required to block the dissemination of terrorist information, record and delete it, and report the recorded information to the authorities (Article 19);
- Internet users are required to provide their real identities to receive internet services ('real-name registration') (Article 24);[49]
- The government may order internet companies to stop the dissemination of such information, delete it, shut down related websites or terminate related services (Article 19);
- It may also adopt technical measures to interrupt the transnational dissemination of such information (Article 19).[50]

Article 61 of the CTL also gives a green light to internet and telecommunication blackouts by providing that local CTLGs, in the wake of a terrorist attack, may decide to impose control over internet and telecommunication services in designated areas. The measure of internet blackout is also regulated by the Cybersecurity Law (CSL) adopted on 7 November 2016.[51] Pursuant to Article 58 of the CSL, when a serious, sudden mass incident is deemed to threaten national security and public order, local governments, with the permission of the central government, may take temporary measures in certain regions with regard to internet communication, such as temporarily controlling it. It is not clear, however, to what extent the control may be imposed, how long the control may last at a maximum, how serious an attack needs to be to justify the control, and under what circumstances the control may be extended or discontinued. In authorizing tough measures such as these, the CTL fails to lay down any substantive requirements or procedural safeguards.

These vague catch-all provisions on internet (and telecommunication) blackout are actually the Chinese step for legalizing tactics that had already been deployed in Xinjiang following the 5 July 2009 riot.[52] The internet ban in Xinjiang lasted ten months before it was lifted. In addition to internet access, short message service (SMS) and international direct dialling (IDD) was also blocked, albeit for a shorter period.[53] The Chinese government blamed the Germany-based WUC, led by the then president Rebiya Kadeer, a Uyghur political activist living in the US, for using these communication channels to incite and organize the riot.[54]

Combating terrorist financing

With regard to the combating of terrorist financing (CFT), the CTL includes several general provisions:

- The People's Bank of China (PBC) is the primary agency for supervising CFT efforts by financial institutions and designated non-financial institutions (Article 24);
- The PBC's Anti-Money Laundering Bureau (AML Bureau) has the capacity to investigate suspected terrorist financing activities and freeze related assets (Article 24);
- Other governmental departments such as those for auditing, finance, and taxation may report suspected terrorist financing to police authorities (Article 25);
- Customs authorities are required to report such activities to both the AML Bureau and related police agencies (Article 26).

In fact, these provisions are not altogether new. Prior to the adoption of the CTL, numerous laws had been put in place to suppress money laundering and terrorist financing activities. These instruments had also been part of China's efforts to meet its international anti-terrorism obligations, as well as the requirements of the Financial Action Task Force (FATF), a Paris-based intergovernmental body that promotes the global operation against money laundering and terrorist financing.

A major instrument is the Anti-Money Laundering Law (hereinafter referred to as 'the AML Law'), adopted on 31 October 2006. The AML Law, consisting of 37 articles, serves as a framework to impose a wide range of duties and liabilities on financial institutions, to expand the powers of the PBC, and to facilitate cooperation between financial institutions and police departments in anti-money laundering activities. Major points of this law include:

- Financial institutions and certain designated non-financial institutions are required to set up internal control systems to prevent, monitor, and report money laundering, such as identification of customers, recording of customers' identities and transactions, and reporting of large and suspicious transactions (Article 3);
- The PBC and its provincial branches are empowered to investigate any suspicious transactions and compel financial institutions to cooperate and provide truthful information (Article 23);
- Temporary freezing with a maximum period of forty-eight hours is permitted if the suspected funds are requested to be transferred overseas (Article 26);
- The PBC is authorized to represent China in international cooperation regarding the combating of money laundering and the exchange of information, whereas judicial organs take the lead in judicial assistance in money laundering cases (Articles 28 and 29).

Specific CFT regulations include 'Administrative Measures for Financial Institutions on Reporting Suspicious Transactions for Terrorist Financing' ('Reporting Regulation') promulgated by the PBC on 11 June 2007, and 'Administrative Measures on the Freezing of Terrorism-Related Assets' ('Asset Freezing Regulation'), adopted jointly by the PBC, the MPS and the MSS on 10 January 2014.[55]

Significant provisions of the Reporting Regulation include:

- 'Terrorist financing' is defined as: '(1) raising, possessing, utilizing funds or other forms of assets by terrorist organizations or individuals; (2) providing assistance to terrorist organizations or individuals, terrorism, or terrorist crimes with funds or other forms of assets; (3) possessing, utilizing, or rais-

ing funds or other forms of assets for terrorism, or carrying out terrorist crimes; (4) possessing, utilizing, or raising funds or other forms of assets for terrorist organizations or individuals' (Article 2);
- The PBC and its branch offices are authorized to supervise and examine the reports of suspicious transactions for terrorist financing by financial institutions (Article 4);
- The China Anti-Money Laundering Monitoring and Analysis Centre (China ALMAC), a special arm of the PBC, is responsible for receiving and analysing reports of suspicious transactions for terrorist financing (Article 5);
- If financial institutions suspect that their clients' transactions are linked to terrorism, they are obliged to report them regardless of the amount of money or value of assets involved (Article 8);
- Financial institutions are also required to report immediately if they believe their clients or the clients' counterparties are on the terror lists announced by the Chinese government or courts, and the UN Security Council (Article 9).

Highlights of the Asset Freezing Regulation include:

- Financial institutions and designated non-financial institutions have an obligation to freeze the assets of persons on the terror list released by the MPS (Article 3);
- Freezing measures must be taken promptly after these institutions discover any such assets owned or controlled by the listed entities or persons (Article 5);
- These institutions are required to cooperate and provide relevant information in AML investigations by police or intelligence agencies, as well by the PBC or its major local offices (Article 7);
- If these institutions have reasonable grounds to suspect that their clients, the transaction partners of these clients, and related assets are connected with terrorism, they are required to report the suspicious transactions to the PBC or its local offices responsible for anti-money laundering and report their suspicions to Public Security and State Security authorities (Article 9).

Deterring 'religious extremism'

China remains vigilant about the danger posed by religion. China's Constitution promises to protect the basic right to religious belief, but the protection only applies to 'normal religious activities'. Another Chinese law, the Regulation on Religious Affairs (RRA), requires all religious groups, religious sites and religious citizens to abide by the law and safeguard national unity, ethnic unity and social stability. Relying on the Constitution, the RRA and other laws, the Chinese government exercises tight control over religious affairs, including the recognition of religious groups, the appointment of religious personnel, the contents of religious publications, the operation of religious sites and the use of religious property.

Due to the surge in terrorist violence, China has been intensifying its legal campaign against religious extremism, which is viewed by the authorities as a driving force of terrorism. As part of this campaign, China amended the RRA in June 2017. The newly amended law incorporates five basic principles for strengthening the 'management'—a euphemism for 'control'—of religious affairs: protecting legal religious activities, stopping illegal ones, deterring religious extremism, guarding against its infiltration, and cracking down on related crimes (Article 3 of the RRA).[56] These principles were proposed by Xi Jinping at the CCP Central's Second Work Conference on Xinjiang in May 2014.[57]

In Xinjiang, the regional legislature had taken a legislative step, as early as November 2014, by amending a two-decades-old law, 'Xinjiang's Regulation on Religious Affairs' (Xinjiang RRA). This regional law, consisting of sixty-six articles in eight chapters, legalizes a number of previous governmental directives implemented by region-wide local authorities, thereby granting the authorities more power to restrict religious practices, to censor terrorism-related speeches, and to ban attire or beards perceived to be extremist.[58] With particular regard to the wearing of specific attire, the legislature of Urumqi passed 'Urumqi's Regulation on Banning the Wearing of Burqas in Public Places' in January 2015. The title appears to suggest that the ban applies only to the wearing of burqas, but the regulation itself indicates that the ban also applies to other clothes, badges, utensils, souvenirs, symbols and signs that might propagate religious extremism.[59]

Xinjiang pursues a strategy of de-radicalization to prevent and combat religious extremism. The concept of de-radicalization may date back to 2010 or 2011, when Xinjiang authorities realized the importance of addressing religious extremism by promoting the role of modern culture and tightening control over religious affairs.[60] However, counter-extremism measures at that time were not based on laws but on unofficial CCP or governmental directives. In 2013, the concept of de-radicalization materialized in an official policy document entitled 'Several Guiding Opinions on Further Suppressing

Illegal Religious Activities and Combating the Infiltration of Religious Extremism in Accordance with Law' ('Counter-Extremism Document'), issued by the CCP leadership in Xinjiang. In 2014, the policy document was followed by another Xinjiang CCP policy guideline entitled 'Several Opinions on Further Strengthening and Improving the Work with regard to Islam' ('Islamic Religion Management Document').

Despite being often lauded as key de-radicalization guidelines, both documents are actually internal CCP regulations and remain out of public view. Based on these internal, confidential regulations, the legislature of Xinjiang, in addition to revising the above-mentioned 'Xinjiang RRA', adopted a new regional law called 'XUAR's Implementing Rules on the "Counter-Terrorism Law"' (Xinjiang IRCTL) in July 2016.

The CTL is the earliest Chinese legal instrument with specific provisions on de-radicalization. Articles 29 and 30 of the law regulate three types of de-radicalization:

– *Custodial de-radicalization*. Custodial facilities such as prisons are not only incubators of radicalization, but also stations for reforming radicalized people. Therefore, prisons and detention centres are required to supervise, educate and correct terrorist or extremist criminals.

– *Post-imprisonment de-radicalization*. As released prisoners may return to terrorism, it is necessary to continue with de-radicalization efforts even after former terrorists are out of prison. There is a new form of administrative detention called 'placement and education' (in Chinese, *anzhi jiaoyu*) to meet this need.

– *Social de-radicalization*. For those who have engaged in terrorism or extremism but are not criminally punishable, the responsibility lies with the police agencies to help and educate them, in cooperation with relevant authorities, the villages or communities from which they come, their employers, the schools where they study, and their family members.

Of the above-mentioned three types, the post-imprisonment de-radicalization is a particular cause of concern. According to the CTL, the 'placement and education' measure is implemented as follows:

– *Risk assessment*: Before terrorist inmates are released, custodial facilities should assess their risks to society. During the assessment, the assessors need to listen to the opinions of the villages or communities where the inmates originally came from, as well as the opinions of the investigators, prosecutors and judges involved in the cases. If the inmates are considered danger-

ous, the custodial facilities should submit a recommendation for 'placement and education'.
- *Judicial order*: It is up to an intermediate court to decide whether such a measure is necessary. If those subject to the measure object to the decision, they may apply to the court for reconsideration at a higher level.
- *De-radicalization facilities*: The 'placement and education' measure is implemented by facilities administered by provincial governments.
- *Reassessment(s) and release*: The facilities should assess the inmates on an annual basis. If they are found to be genuinely repentant, the facilities are required to submit promptly a release recommendation to the court that issued the original judicial order. The court decides whether to release them. The inmates may also apply for release from the facilities.
- *Prosecutorial supervision*: The prosecution office supervises the decision-making of the court and the implementation of the measure.

The Xinjiang IRCTL designates a competent body and specifies tasks for post-imprisonment de-radicalization:

- The Xinjiang government's Department of Justice is responsible for 'placement and education' affairs and for the planning, construction and daily management of such facilities (Article 42);
- Related governmental organs are obliged to organize educational activities in law, ethics, mental health, modern culture, scientific knowledge, religious faith, and occupational skills (Article 43).

In justifying the measure, the Chinese scholar Liu Hangying argues that there is a dynamic balance between the use of state power and the protection of human rights. The main reasons given for the justification are that the right to liberty is not absolute and that the measure is associated with good intentions. Good intentions include, for example, the maintenance of public security and the elimination of the terrorist ideology deeply ingrained in the recipient's heart.[61]

It is obvious that 'placement and education' involves the denial of liberty without trial, a measure similar to the 're-education through labour' (RTL) system that China abolished in 2013.[62] Although the deprivation of freedom is based on a judicial order, the decision-making process lacks the usual safeguards available under ordinary criminal procedure. Due to the fact that no time limit is provided for its duration, this measure sounds especially alarming.

In addition, when we speak of de-radicalization efforts in Xinjiang, we should never forget the XUAR's Regulation on De-Radicalisation (Xinjiang RDR), which is China's first-ever specific law against 'religious extremism'. This regional law prohibits a wide range of behaviours deemed extremist, including wearing face-covering veils and growing unusual beards. More importantly, it requires relevant governmental agencies and various social groups to assume specific responsibilities for the de-radicalization campaign.

Promoting international counter-terrorism cooperation

International cooperation is also undoubtedly a major component in China's counter-terrorism efforts. Pursuant to the CTL, China's cooperation with individual nations and regional and global organizations is based on international treaties that it recognizes, as well as the principles of equality and reciprocity (Article 68). In general, areas of international cooperation include policy dialogues, data exchange, law enforcement, and financial monitoring (Article 69); in case of terrorist crimes, they may include judicial assistance, extradition and transfer of convicted persons (Article 70).

Following the 9/11 attacks, Chinese participation in international anti-terror cooperation has become wider and stronger at global, regional and bilateral levels. At the global level, China is actively involved in the counter-terrorism campaign within the framework of the UN. At the regional level, China promotes its cooperation through mechanisms such as SCO, APEC, and ASEAN Plus Three. Among these mechanisms, a pivotal role is played by the Shanghai Cooperation Organization (SCO), a regional security-oriented organization established by six countries (China, Russia, Kazakhstan, Kyrgyzstan, Tajikistan and Uzbekistan) on 15 June 2001.[63] The SCO focuses particularly on countering the 'three forces'. In fighting terrorism, China cooperates with its SCO allies mainly through a permanent body, the 'Regional Anti-Terrorist Structure' (RATS SCO). In individual cooperation cases, China's bilateral relationship with related nations is of utmost importance.

Among the above-noted areas of international cooperation, the extradition of Chinese nationals suspected of terrorism and the repatriation of illegal migrants suspected of being terrorist recruits are particularly important in legal practice. For reasons of space, this chapter will only use selected examples of extradition and repatriation to illustrate China's bilateral counter-terrorism cooperation.

In terms of extradition, China had signed extradition treaties with thirty-nine countries by March 2015.[64] These countries do not include notable nations such as the US, Germany, Canada and Turkey. The Chinese government is trying to convince Western countries to sign such treaties to facilitate the transfer of suspected terrorists, but most of them are reluctant to do so because of their concerns about China's active use of the death penalty and their doubts about the fairness of criminal trials in China.[65] Reportedly this is also the reason why the US refused to repatriate to China twenty-two Uyghurs held in the US detention camp at Guantanamo Bay after their capture during the US invasion of Afghanistan in 2001.[66]

China attaches great importance to its bilateral cooperation with the US, but the effect of the cooperation seems to be limited, largely due to their marked differences in perspective on what constitutes terrorism and how it should be countered. China views terrorism as an existential threat, whereas the US tends to view it as a human rights issue.[67] For example, the US shows sympathy towards and provides support to the East Turkestan independence movement by shielding the Uyghur activist Rebiya Kadeer, whom China blames for inciting terrorism in and against China. From the Chinese perspective, the operation of the camp at Guantanamo and the CIA's use of torture against terror suspects are telling examples of the US's 'double standard' in human rights.[68] In the eyes of many American politicians, political violence may be called terrorism only when it is perpetrated by those they do not like.[69]

Although China's cooperation with the US is fraught with difficulties, its cooperation with countries in Central Asia and Southeast Asia has been fruitful.[70] Owing to the large size of the Uyghur population in Central Asia, the support of China's SCO allies is crucial. China has been very successful in obtaining the extradition of suspected Uyghurs from these countries for prosecution in China. In the past several years, Southeast Asian countries such as Cambodia, Malaysia, Burma, Laos and Vietnam emerged as a major transit route for Uyghurs seeking asylum in Turkey.[71] China claims that, many of these 'illegal migrants' were radicalized and were prepared to join the Syrian conflict. Despite criticism by rights groups and the UN Refuge Agency, Thailand deported 109 Uyghurs to China. In defending the deportation, China's state-run media argued that it was 'normal cooperation' between nations[72] and this would act as 'effective deterrence' to other prospective terrorists.[73]

A topic attracting great media attention is the CTL's authorization to send security forces, including military troops, for overseas operations.[74] The decision to send such personnel must be based on an agreement with the country in question. While China's central government decides whether to dispatch police or intelligence officers, its Central Military Commission decides on the sending of military or semi-military troops (Article 71). With its ascendancy to the status of a great power, China is facing the formidable task of protecting its growing expatriate population and commercial interests.[75] The legalization of sending military forces abroad for counter-terrorism purposes is potentially a game changer for China's foreign policy.[76] Due to worldwide concerns about the brutal IS, China watchers have often voiced the view that China should join the US-led global anti-IS military coalition if it wants to be respected as a responsible power. This view is countered by the notion represented by Human Rights Watch claiming that such overseas interventions may violate 'China's extra-territorial obligations to respect international human rights law'.[77]

The prominent counter-terrorism expert Zhang Jinping at China's Northwest University of Political Science and Law anticipates three likely scenarios under which China may send troops abroad for anti-terrorism operations. The first scenario is a direct attack on Chinese citizens or vital institutions abroad. The second is the establishment of states by international terrorists within China's neighbouring countries, such as Afghanistan and Pakistan. The third is the infiltration of Chinese territory by large numbers of international terrorists.[78] It is interesting to note that Zhang seems to leave out the possibility of China's sending forces to participate in the global coalition against ISIS or to destroy a stronghold of the Turkestan Islamic Party (TIP) in North Syria.[79]

Conclusion

The 9/11 incident is remembered as the worst terrorist attack in modern history and is viewed as a watershed for the global fight against terrorism, largely because the US and some other powerful countries have overreacted to the scourge of terrorism by privileging public security over civil liberties.[80] As this chapter has demonstrated, China too has followed this global trend. Given rising domestic terrorism and the grim nature of contemporary global jihadism, it is perhaps understandable that China, like many other countries, is taking extraordinary measures to prevent and suppress terrorism. Compared with Western democracies, China generally enjoys much greater legal discretion in its fight against terrorism. In the post-9/11 period, China keeps giving additional discretionary powers to its government. Indeed, there is no denying that the CTL and other related laws as discussed in this chapter have significantly enhanced China's counter-terrorism capabilities. Since

2014, Chinese authorities seem to be more confident, decisive and relentless in using these laws to cope with terrorism. At the end of 2016, China's most prominent counter-terrorism expert, Li Wei, used the recent obvious drop in numbers of terrorist attacks to conclude that China's counter-terrorism measures had been 'effective'.[81]

Yet, this effectiveness is not achieved without a high price. The legal instruments outlined in this chapter touch on many fundamental rights and individual freedoms, such as the right to liberty, the right to privacy, the right to a fair trial, and the freedoms of movement, religion and expression. China's legal efforts against terrorism are clearly not fully compatible with international human rights standards.

China's pledge to respect the rule of law in its counter-terrorism campaign is important.[82] Even more important are China's real actions to honour this pledge. For China, striking a proper balance between security and liberty in its legal campaign against terrorism is not only a formidable task but also an urgent obligation. This is especially so given the fact that China has embarked on the arduous voyage of 'ruling the country according to law'. In order to achieve the right balance, China must ensure that sufficient legal safeguards are introduced to prevent or reduce human rights violations.

4

THE NARRATIVE OF UYGHUR TERRORISM AND THE SELF-FULFILLING PROPHECY OF UYGHUR MILITANCY

Sean Roberts

On 28 October 2013, an SUV crashed into a stone bridge on Beijing's Tiananmen Square and exploded into flames, killing the three people inside the car as well as two bystanders visiting the square. The car was driven by a Uyghur man from the Xinjiang Uyghur Autonomous Region (XUAR), and his passengers were his wife and mother-in-law. In the days following the attack, the Chinese government announced that this had been a terrorist attack and blamed the East Turkestan Islamic Movement (ETIM) for carrying it out. A spokesperson for the foreign ministry noted about the ETIM that 'members of the organization have for a long time engaged in terrorist acts in South Asia, Central Asia, West Asia and other regions; it has links to many international extremist terrorist groups; it is China's most direct and realistic security threat.'[1] Several weeks later, an organization called the Turkestan Islamic Party (TIP), thought to be the successor organization to ETIM, praised the attack as a sign that the Uyghur people were ready to take up arms to fight the Chinese state.² Subsequently, the PRC arrested and eventually executed three other Uyghurs for allegedly masterminding the attack on behalf of ETIM.³

The People's Republic of China (PRC) had long claimed that it faced a serious terrorist threat from Uyghur militants, but it had never before claimed that violence in China outside the XUAR was a premeditated attack by Uyghurs. However, before assuming that these events represent an escalation in a Uyghur terrorist threat that had spread from the XUAR to the heart of China's capital, there is a fundamental question that should be asked: was this, in fact, a terrorist attack? After all, the litany of violent incidents and political dissent among Uyghurs that the PRC had to date characterized as terrorism included many actions that were quite obviously not terrorism, as well as others where the details were murky at best. Trying to analyse these various incidents to determine whether or not they should be categorized as terrorism brings up an inconvenient truth: despite the fact that much of the world today is engaged in a 'global war on terror' (GWOT), there still exists no universally accepted definition of what constitutes terrorism.

Walter Laqueur's famous historical examination of 'terrorism' suggested that the phenomenon defied definition because any attempt to achieve international consensus on the subject 'would lead to endless controversies'.⁴ Implied in Laqueur's statement is that many international actors seek to maintain a vague definition of the phenomenon because such imprecision allows them more latitude both in shielding those non-state militant movements they support and in condemning those they do not. This political manipulation of the characterization of 'terrorists' is frequently evoked via a quote from Gerald Seymour's 1975 novel, *Harry's Game*: 'One man's terrorist is another man's freedom fighter.'⁵ While geopolitical powers may find the absence of a definition for terrorism politically expedient, such politically motivated relativism only makes it more difficult to address the root problem of terrorism— its targeting of innocent civilians. The Israeli scholar Boaz Ganor points this out in his work and, along with others, has argued forcibly for the need for a normative and concrete definition of terrorism.⁶ The need for such a definition is all the more important in the context of the global war on terror, under the banner of which many countries around the world are using the threat of terrorism as a means to suppress legitimate opposition.

Many countries in recent years have adopted laws to combat terrorism, and most of these laws provide some guidance on recognizing when an act of violence qualifies as terrorism. On the basis of title 22 of the United States

Code, Section 2656f(d), for example, US law provides one such definition: 'the term terrorism means premeditated, politically motivated violence perpetrated against noncombatant targets by subnational groups or clandestine agents, usually intended to influence an audience.'[7] However, this definition's focus on 'noncombatant targets' is problematic in the context of many grassroots groups engaged in armed conflicts with what they believe to be either occupying forces or oppressive states. According to Ganor, for example, the US definition 'designates attacks on noncombatant military personnel as terrorism'.[8] In the context of a war, international law does not condemn surprise attacks on military forces or state institutions of strategic importance, yet such targets would be considered 'noncombatant' under US law. Thus, it would appear equitable to afford the same rights to non-state insurgencies that are reserved for sovereign states in conflicts. In lieu of the definition provided by US law, this chapter will adopt a definition of terrorism proposed by Ganor, which is based on international law's protection of civilians in war.

Ganor presents three criteria to help determine normatively what should and should not be considered terrorism:

1) The essence of the activity must be violent (non-violent resistance would not be considered terrorism).
2) The aims must be deliberately political (violence perpetrated for personal reasons not representing a political aim for a larger group would not be considered terrorism).
3) The act of violence deliberately targets citizens as victims (attacks on military, militarized groups and state institutions would not be considered terrorism, whether or not they are engaged in combat during the attack).[9]

Implicit in these three points is that the violent act must be premeditated and that the intent of targeting civilians is, at least partially, to evoke fear in a wider population. This provides a useful, de-politicized and normative definition of terrorism that returns us to the roots of what the international community decided to condemn in the wake of the 2001 attacks on the United States. It also allows the analyst to distinguish who should and should not be considered the terrorists being targeted in the global war on terror.

With this working definition of terrorism, it is useful to return to the incident that occurred in Beijing on 28 October 2013. This indeed was a violent act, and it appeared to target citizens. However, the motives of the Uyghurs who died in the car crash remains unclear. The PRC claims that the family that drove the 4x4 vehicle into Tiananmen Square was motivated by Islamic extremism and allegiance to ETIM, but others have claimed that the motive for the attack related to local disputes with authorities in the village where the family had lived, including the destruction of a mosque built by the local community.[10] In this alternative explanation of the motives behind the incident, there has been some speculation that the people who drove the large car into the square were in fact killing themselves as a means of protest akin to self-immolation and had no intention to harm civilians, thus also bringing into question the target of the attack.[11]

While it may be impossible to uncover fully the details behind this incident and to determine whether it was merely an act of suicide in protest or a suicide attack on innocent civilians, it did represent a serious turning point in a long-standing conflict between Uyghurs and states based in China that goes back to the mid-eighteenth-century Qing conquest of the territory that is today the XUAR.[12] If nothing else, the incident in Tiananmen Square suggested that at least some Uyghurs were willing to take their own lives to make a political statement about their discontent in China, a sentiment that could certainly make them capable of terrorism.

Thus, it is not entirely surprising that violent incidents involving Uyghurs that look very much like terrorism have increased since. In March 2014, a group of Uyghurs allegedly killed thirty-one people at a train station in Kunming.[13] In April 2014, there was a bomb explosion and several knife killings at the Urumqi train station, which were also praised by TIP.[14] In September 2015, a group of men allegedly killed fifty people at the Sogan coal mine in the north of the XUAR.[15] Although the details of these subsequent acts of violence, like others that have both preceded and followed them, remain mostly unclear, the attacks were both more brutal and more likely terrorist in nature than anything witnessed prior to the incident in Tiananmen Square. In this sense, these events taken together may be the first concrete evidence that the PRC faces a Uyghur terrorist threat, despite the fact that the state has claimed to be struggling with one for over a decade.

Although the PRC had previously claimed that various acts of violence within the XUAR were terrorism perpetrated by ETIM, most of these violent incidents could not be conclusively characterized as terrorism. Some had been riots that evolved out of clashes between protesters and security organs; others were assassinations that could have been either politically motivated or personal but generally targeted military, police and other state figures, and some involved clashes with the police that could have merely reflected resisting arrest or retribution for arrests of family members. Furthermore, there was little evidence that ETIM or TIP was capable of organizing attacks inside China, let alone that this organization had long been 'engaged in terrorist acts' outside the PRC as the foreign ministry claimed after the Tiananmen Square incident. Yet, since 2002, the PRC had been aggressively implementing counter-terrorism policies in the XUAR to mitigate what it perceived as a grave terrorist threat.

To understand how a Uyghur terrorist threat and a state-led counter-terrorism campaign could pre-date any conclusive evidence of terrorist acts perpetrated by Uyghurs by over ten years, it is important to dissect the origins of claims about the Uyghur terrorist threat and to highlight what threat of Uyghur terrorism actually existed prior to October 2013 and exists today. This chapter seeks to do just that by providing a brief history of how Uyghur terrorism evolved out of a long-standing conflict between Uyghurs and states based in China through a combination of PRC policies to stifle dissent in the XUAR and the state's opportunistic use of the US-led global war on terror. In doing so, it examines how the narrative of a Uyghur terrorist threat evolved in the wake of the 11 September 2001 attacks on the US and discusses how the use of this narrative to brand and suppress Uyghur dissent since has made Uyghur militancy, and perhaps terrorism, a self-fulfilling prophecy for the PRC, which may well turn into a lengthy struggle. In many ways, this is a cautionary story about how the global war on terror has helped both to bolster the authoritarian regime's suppression of opposition or dissent and to drive marginalized Muslim peoples in such states to militancy. This is an argument that I expand on in much more depth in a forthcoming book manuscript about the self-fulfilling prophecy of Uyghur militancy and terrorism.[16]

The global war on terror and the narrative of Uyghur terrorism

Nine days after the 11 September 2001 terrorist attacks on the United States, US President George W. Bush declared a broad war on 'terror' that would begin with al-Qaeda, but 'not end until every terrorist group of global reach has been found, stopped and defeated'.[17] Warning that this war would be protracted, George W. Bush also called upon the rest of the world to join in a coalition against global terror, noting that 'you are either with us, or you are with the terrorists'.[18] This rather ill-defined declaration of war was to change the world order dramatically and quickly established new and unlikely allies internationally. It has also served over time to embolden international terrorist groups and substantially increase their recruiting capacities, while empowering many authoritarian regimes to repress opposition among Muslim populations in the name of counter-terrorism. While a dramatic change in US policy was at the centre of this transformation, it has also involved the efforts of many other countries who seized on the opportunity to use the US global war on terror (GWOT) as a means to suppress sources of dissent within their own countries. This manipulation of the GWOT narrative by authoritarian states was, of course, greatly assisted by the war's seemingly intentional decision not to define 'terrorism' or, by extension, GWOT's ultimate enemy. One of the countries that has manipulated the GWOT narrative most for its own domestic security agenda is China.

Although the PRC initially was not overtly supportive of the US-led GWOT, it was quick to find parallels between the threat faced by the US and their own situation with the Muslim Uyghurs of the XUAR. Previously, the PRC had primarily used a narrative of separatism or 'splittism' to describe Uyghur activities that it identified as a security risk. While the state had linked religious practices with separatism after the Baren incident, they appeared less concerned about religion as a vehicle for separatism than about religious gatherings as an opportunity to organize. Furthermore, while Central Asian states had used accusations of Islamic extremist terrorism to dismantle Uyghur political movements and other local forms of dissent during the 1990s, the PRC had not generally used such terminology in describing its Uyghur threat. Rather, the Chinese state was most fearful of a secular nationalist movement among Uyghurs that could promote national liberation. However, about six weeks after the 11 September attacks on the US, the PRC's narrative about Uyghur separatism dramatically transitioned to one about Uyghur terrorism.

On 29 November 2001, the PRC released a document entitled 'Terrorist Activities Perpetrated by "Eastern Turkistan" Organizations and their Links with Osama bin Laden and the Taliban'. In this document, the government first outlined its case that it faced a terrorist threat linked with global jihadism from Uyghurs. It listed a number of Uyghur organizations which it accused of carrying out terrorist attacks, but it also noted that the Uyghur terrorist threat came from 'a total of over 40 organizations'.[19] Additionally, the document listed a number of alleged terrorist attacks perpetrated by these groups both in China and outside. Finally, it made a case that Osama bin Laden and the Taliban were supporting these organizations financially and with training, and, in turn, that a Uyghur battalion of about 320 soldiers was fighting in support of the Taliban against the United States in Afghanistan.[20]

The credibility of the claims in the document were questionable, particularly given that the PRC was seeking to link over forty Uyghur organizations around the world to an alleged terrorist movement that had previously been unknown; but some of the claims it outlined were plausible. Indeed, given Uyghurs' access to the outside world and the oppressive policies inside the XUAR during the 1990s, there could be Uyghur militants in Afghanistan, and they could have been radicalized and aligned with al-Qaeda and the Taliban. Furthermore, all of the acts listed as terrorist attacks in the document were reported as having occurred, but whether or not they were actually terrorist attacks or carried out by the groups claimed in the document was open to question. Using the working definition of terrorism employed in this chapter, for example, most of the events did not qualify as terrorism, and those that might be classified as terrorism could not be conclusively determined as such given the lack of information about the incidents in question. Furthermore, none of the organizations accused of carrying out these attacks had ever claimed responsibility for them. Although the document garnered some international attention in these early weeks of the US-led GWOT, few if any countries were immediately ready to include Uyghurs in a list of the most dangerous international terrorists.

Shortly after the release of this first document, in January 2002 the PRC published a second, more extensive paper on the Uyghur terrorist threat, entitled '"East Turkistan" Terrorist Forces Cannot Get Away with Impunity'. This paper went into far more detail in making the case for the Uyghur terrorist threat faced by the PRC, linking virtually all Uyghur organizations around the world to this threat, and establishing its ties to al-Qaeda and the Taliban. Furthermore, it clearly made the argument that, despite claims by international Uyghur organizations that they are working under the banner of protecting 'human rights, religious freedom and the interests of ethnic minorities', they are in fact terrorists no different from those who had attacked the United States on 11 September.[21] As the document notes, 'While they [i.e. Uyghur advocacy/terrorist groups] are distressed by the destruction of the bin Laden terrorist forces and Taliban terrorist training bases by US missiles, they cannot but "take the initiative" to express their support for the US military retaliation, attempting to distance themselves from the bin Laden terrorist forces.'[22]

Like the initial document published by the government in 2001, this more detailed paper's acknowledgement of the terrorist threat faced by the PRC vastly exaggerated both the militancy of most of the organizations it accused of being terrorists and the number of potential terrorist attacks carried out during the 1990s. However, also like the first document, it provided plausible information about Uyghurs being active in terrorist networks in Afghanistan. In particular, it named ETIM, led by Hasan Mahsum, as an organization with close ties to the Taliban and al-Qaeda.

The tone of this second document and its attempts to draw parallels to the 11 September attacks on the US appeared to be an obvious plea for Western support in the PRC's struggle with Uyghur separatism.[23] Whether or not this was the intent, it appears to have been the result, since eight months after the publication of the aforementioned White Paper, both the United Nations and the United States officially recognized the alleged terrorist threat that ETIM posed to China and the world. In September 2002, the United States' Executive Order 13224 and the United Nations' Security Council Resolutions 1267 and 1390 recognized ETIM as a 'terrorist organization', subsequently subjecting it to international sanctions and raising concerns about Uyghurs as an international terrorist threat.[24]

The US government's recognition of ETIM as a terrorist organization was highly controversial. Given that no scholars studying the Uyghurs, the XUAR or China more generally had ever mentioned this organization in their work; that there was little evidence proving that any premeditated violence in the XUAR over the last two decades was actually carried out by organized terrorists; and that no concrete evidence of the organization's capacity or even its existence was publicly available beyond the claims of the Chinese government, some analysts questioned whether the recognition of ETIM was a *quid pro quo* action aimed at involving the PRC more substantively in GWOT. While the United States probably wanted more Chinese involvement in Afghanistan at this time, a more cynical analysis of the situation suggests that first and foremost the US sought China's tacit support for the invasion of Iraq, which took place a mere six months after the American recognition of ETIM as a terrorist organization.

Perhaps the most damning accusation against the US government in support of such analysis is that it relied exclusively on biased Chinese and Central Asian intelligence in determining whether to recognize this group as a terrorist organization. Although State Department officials who had been involved in the decision insisted in a congressional hearing that there was additional non-Chinese intelligence proving that ETIM was indeed a terrorist threat, they also did not elaborate on what that information detailed, noting that it was still classified.[25]

Whether or not the US recognition of ETIM as a terrorist group was a *quid pro quo* action, over the last fifteen years it has been the single most important act lending validity to China's claims that it faces a substantial Uyghur terrorist threat. It has served to deflect international criticism of the political repression that has ensued in the XUAR in the name of counter-terrorism, and it has allowed the PRC to get numerous Uyghur political activists internationally on global terrorism watch-lists. It has also provided the justification for the production of a long chain of knowledge about ETIM produced by thinktank experts, policy analysts, security experts and academics around the world. Although this chain of knowledge has been mostly based on dubious evidence at best, it has established a convincing narrative about the Uyghur terrorist threat that has spread both in the US and globally. Despite frequent doubts raised by regional experts, this narrative has become particularly influential in policy and security circles in the United States and has resulted in grave consequences affecting the lives of Uyghurs both inside and outside China.

One of the most critical links in the chain of knowledge reproducing this narrative has been the reports of various reputable 'expert organizations' in international affairs and security that have provided thumbnail sketches of ETIM. Although these reports are, for the most part, merely web-based descriptions of global terrorist organizations, they represent the endorsement by credible institutions of the questionable assumption that ETIM is a capable and long-established terrorist organization that presents a global threat.

On the Council of Foreign Relations' (CFR) website, for example, ETIM is identified as 'one of the more extreme groups founded by Uighurs [*sic*] ... seeking an independent state called East Turkestan', noting that 'China's communist regime ... has long called ETIM a terrorist group'.[26] Although CFR's characterization of the organization offers a fairly balanced view of debates surrounding the extent of ETIM's threat and its links to al-Qaeda, it takes as fact the disputed assertions that ETIM has long existed as a source of terrorism focused against the government of China, which first publicly referred to the organization only in 2001.

Similarly, the Center for Defense Information (CDI), in addition to suggesting that China has long accused the organization of terrorism, notes that ETIM 'is a separatist Muslim group operating in China's western Xinjiang province' and 'is the most militant of various groups operating in the Xinjiang region'.[27] In reality, however, there is no conclusive evidence that ETIM or any organized and capable terrorist or separatist group has ever been able to establish sophisticated operations within the XUAR during the Communist period.

Further down this chain of knowledge, assumptions made about ETIM by reputable organizations that analyse foreign affairs have allowed less established 'terrorism trackers' to assert even more suspect characterizations of the organization. One such 'terrorism-tracking' organization, IntelCenter (which says that its 'primary client base is comprised of military, law enforcement, and intelligence agencies in the U.S. and other allied countries around the world), markets a 'Turkistan Islamic Party (TIP) Threat Awareness Wall Chart' that outlines the organizational structure and history of ETIM.[28] Not surprisingly, this chart is based completely on Chinese government documents and questionable internet-based sources. Similarly, an organization called the Investigative Project on Terrorism (IPT) (which claims to possess 'the world's most comprehensive data center on radical Islamic terrorist groups') asserts that ETIM 'is a small Islamic extremist group linked to al-Qaida [sic] and the international jihadist movement ... pursuing an independent "Eastern Turkistan," an area that would include Turkey, Kazakhstan, Kyrgyzstan, Uzbekistan, Pakistan, Afghanistan, and Western China's Xinjiang Uighur [sic] Autonomous Region'.[29] Obviously, anybody familiar with the region and the goals of Uyghur political organizations would recognize that such an expansive geographic conception of 'Eastern Turkistan' is erroneous.

These organizations offer no specific evidence for their characterizations, save some suspect internet-based sources and the publicly available statements by the US and Chinese governments. Furthermore, they probably have no staff doing analysis of Uyghur language documentation, despite the fact that they regularly comment on videos released by ETIM and TIP. They have adopted a clear position that, regardless of its immediate threat, ETIM is aligned with America's enemy in GWOT, is highly organized and is ready to carry out random acts of violence.[30]

Although scholarly experts on China and Central Asia have generally adopted a more nuanced view of the problem of Uyghur terrorism by questioning, yet not denying the possibility of, its existence and capacity, many in the field of security studies have taken at face value the assertion that the Uyghurs pose a substantial terrorist threat to China and possibly to the West. This has been at least partially propelled by the work of one prolific self-fashioned academic 'terrorism expert', Rohan Gunaratna of Singapore. Although Gunaratna has an impressive list of affiliations in the security studies field, as well as with government security agencies around the world, media watchdog groups and commentators have questioned his non-evidence-based assertions about a variety of terrorist groups, including ETIM.[31] In a series of articles and policy briefings, as well as in his book on al-Qaeda's global network, Gunaratna suggests that ETIM is closely associated with al-Qaeda, is supported by 'covert funding from the Uighur [*sic*] diaspora population' and possesses a 'sophisticated capability to access financing and a logistics network'.³² His sources for this information once again are limited to publicly available Chinese and US government documents as well as internet-based sources of questionable origin.

Drawing on the work of Gunaratna, whose book on al-Qaeda has the academic legitimacy of being published by Columbia University Press, others in the field of security studies who are not specialists in Central Asia or the Uyghurs have tended to reproduce many of his assertions as fact. Consequently, the portrayal of ETIM as a capable terrorist organization and a credible threat to China, and perhaps the world, has been reproduced uncritically throughout the academic literature related to terrorism, including in journal articles, monographs and doctoral dissertations.³³ In the chain of reproduced knowledge, the authors of these academic works on the Uyghur terrorist threat have, in turn, frequently crossed back into the policy community and into popular media through punditry.

In general, this chain of knowledge has become self-perpetuating as the literature that fuels it grows and increasingly cross-references itself. In fact, the literature on ETIM has grown to such an extent that enough information can be compiled from secondary sources to fill an entire manuscript. As a testament to this phenomenon, two journalists/terrorist experts in 2010 published *The ETIM: China's Islamic Militants and the Global Terrorist Threat*, which proudly characterizes itself as 'the first book to focus specifically on the East Turkistan Islamic Movement'.³⁴ The book exhaustively documents the narrative that has grown around ETIM, using secondary sources to provide a thorough list of alleged terrorist acts undertaken by the organization, as well as brief biographies of eighty Uyghurs who are alleged to be or have been members of ETIM. Although the authors admit that they are not scholars and that their sources are primarily 'media accounts and government documentation', they obviously have aspirations of influencing policy, since they cite their intended audience as being 'particularly members of the U.S. defense and intelligence communities'.³⁵

This chapter does not intend to suggest that the self-perpetuating literature on ETIM is completely and intentionally fabricated. Rather, it argues that this literature is based on sloppy research and unreliable sources and that it has come together to create a dangerous and unsubstantiated narrative about Uyghur terrorism. Among other things, this narrative has helped to facilitate the draconian counter-terrorism measures that the PRC has adopted in the

XUAR over the last fourteen years, which are documented more fully elsewhere in this volume, ensuring that these polices receive no substantial or credible push-back from other governments. Furthermore, as I will argue below, the increased oppression of Uyghurs inside the XUAR due to these measures has actually driven more of them to leave the PRC and join militant groups based elsewhere, particularly the Turkestan Islamic Party (TIP) in Syria. As a result, it has breathed new life into ETIM's alleged successor organization, when it looked as if the organization had all but disappeared.

In this context, it is important to make a critical assemblage of what information we do know about the ETIM and TIP to try to piece together a more reliable narrative about these organizations, what they represented in 2001 and what they represent today. Such a narrative offers a more nuanced picture of the evolution of Uyghur militancy and the ways that GWOT has perhaps created more new terrorists than it has obliterated.

The evolution of ETIM/TIP: an alternative narrative

Spurred by my doubts about the accuracy of the prevalent narrative on Uyghur terrorism that has been developed by the government of China and perpetuated by the counter-terrorism industry in the United States and elsewhere, I have been researching ETIM, TIP and the Uyghur terrorist threat for several years. In doing so, I examined documents from the hearings of the Combatant Status Review and Administrative Review Boards regarding Uyghurs who were interned at Guantánamo Bay detention facilities and conducted interviews with four former detainees who were released to Albania in 2006. I have also researched more intensively several events that are alleged to have been Uyghur-led terrorist attacks, and I have spoken with several Uyghurs accused of being members of Uyghur terrorist organizations both by the PRC and in the aforementioned book published about the organization.[36] More recently, I interviewed a group of Uyghur refugees in Turkey, one of whom claimed to have fought with TIP in Syria and all of whom knew Uyghurs who had fought in Syria.

My research has demonstrated that it is very difficult to determine the full truth about these organizations, given the unreliability of the sources that discuss them. That being said, by reviewing these sources with a knowledge of the history and local context of Uyghurs and by bolstering them with interviews with accused and self-proclaimed Uyghur militants, it is possible to provide a more nuanced and more reliable account of how these organizations have evolved. While such an account is inevitably incomplete and involves conjecture, given the sources available, it should provide some insight into the degree to which the PRC has faced a terrorist threat in the past, does today or is likely to do in the future. In order to examine the evolution of these organizations, it is important to consider three time periods in their short history: the origins and early years of ETIM under Hasan Mahsum, TIP in Pakistan under Abdul Haq after 2003, and TIP in Syria since 2013.

Hasan Mahsum and the origins of ETIM in Afghanistan

According to Chinese sources, Hasan Mahsum was born in 1964 in a rural region near the XUAR city of Kashgar.[37] Thus, he would have experienced the chaos of the Cultural Revolution as a child, but he came of age in the relatively liberal atmosphere of the 1980s. The same Chinese sources note that he was arrested in October 1993 for terrorism, but it is more likely he was charged with 'splittism' given the year of the arrest, and he was sentenced to three years of re-education by labor.[38] In 1997, apparently shortly after completion of his imprisonment, he left the PRC. Beyond his departure from the PRC, little is known about his whereabouts until he was identified in the initial 2001 document mentioned above as leading a group called ETIM in Afghanistan. According to one PRC document, he organized the ETIM in an unidentified location upon leaving China, but only established a base in Afghanistan in September 1998.[39]

Chinese sources make numerous grand claims regarding the terrorist activities of Mahsum and ETIM inside the XUAR during the period prior to 2001, but it is difficult to substantiate any of them. Furthermore, it is striking that the PRC only publicly blamed the ETIM and Mahsum for masterminding these attacks after 2001 and that the ETIM never publicly claimed responsibility for them. A careful reading of the sparse sources on the subject suggests that ETIM was not an active militant organization which had the capacity to carry out attacks. Rather, it was at least initially created as a training organization that could give aspiring Uyghur militants experience with weapons. The self-proclaimed deputy chairman of the organization, Abudula Kariaji, claimed in a brief 2004 *Wall Street Journal* interview that the organization had three training camps in Afghanistan prior to 2001, which allegedly prepared several hundred Uyghurs to carry out militant acts within China.[40] However, in the same interview Kariaji notes that none of those who were trained in these camps and had returned to China had carried out actual terrorist attacks.

Testimonies of Uyghur former detainees at Guantánamo Bay offer more insight into these alleged ETIM camps in Afghanistan and their capacity to train militants. In essence, the accounts of these former detainees are the closest thing we have to raw eyewitness accounts of ETIM and its operations, at least for 2001. The majority of these prisoners appear to have passed through some sort of Uyghur 'training camp' in the Jalalabad area of Afghanistan which was intended to help Uyghurs prepare to fight against the Chinese state, and the people they identified as running this camp are the same as those usually associated with the initial leadership of ETIM: Hasan Mahsum and Abdul Haq.[41]

Although all of the Uyghur detainees who were in this camp were forthcoming in their statements at various Guantánamo hearings about their distaste for Chinese rule in their homeland, they all denied belonging to ETIM, and most suggested that they had never heard of the group until they were brought to the detention facilities. Interestingly, most of them also said that they had not heard of Osama bin Laden, al-Qaeda or even the Taliban until coming to Guantánamo, and those who had heard of them demonstrated no interest in the global jihad ideology of these groups. Finally, all of them made a point of refuting any allegations that they saw the United States as an enemy. As one detainee noted in making this point, 'A billion Chinese enemies, that is enough for me; why would I get more enemies?'[42]

Perhaps most importantly, the detainees' testimony about the 'training camp' where they spent time does not fit the profile of a professional, organized and resource-rich organization. They describe a small, old and decrepit building in need of dire repair, and they note that their primary activities while at the location were to repair it and bring it back to livable condition. When asked about the training received at this camp, the detainees discuss running in the mornings and a one-time opportunity to fire a few bullets with the only Kalashnikov rifle that was available at the camp. In short, their description of this 'training camp' suggests that it provided them with very little training and that it had virtually no resources to support any kind of militant operation. In fact, most of the detainees did not recognize this location as a 'training camp' at all, and the majority suggested that they went there as a temporary refuge while seeking ways to get to Turkey, where they hoped to settle as refugees. As one detainee answered interrogators asking about the 'camp': 'it was a little Uigher [sic] community where Uighers [sic] went; I do not know what you mean about the place called camp.'[43]

Although one can justifiably question the accuracy of the statements of Uyghur detainees at Guantánamo concerning their activities in Afghanistan, it is notable that their statements generally do not contradict each other: they offer a cohesive story about their associations, or lack thereof, with al-Qaeda and the Taliban, as well as about the relatively benign nature of the alleged ETIM camp in which they lived. Nonetheless, in an effort to get a clearer picture of how and why these individuals went to Afghanistan in the first place, I went to Albania during the summer of 2009 to interview four former detainees who had been released in 2006. These interviews generally reconfirmed the accounts from Guantánamo hearings and provided me with a richer understanding of how these individuals came to be in Afghanistan when the US military entered the country in 2001.

As I began to interview the men, who had mostly become apprentice pizza cooks in Albania's capital city of Tirana, their stories sounded very familiar. Their lives prior to being taken captive were reminiscent of the accounts of the many Uyghur traders from China whom I had interviewed in Kazakhstan during the mid-1990s.[44] Most of them were born in rural areas and had become involved in trading because few other career opportunities existed. Once engaged in trading, they realized that to make a living beyond subsistence they needed to become part of the transnational trade that joins the XUAR to its western neighbours.[45] As a result, they travelled westwards, trying to sell Chinese manufactured goods in bordering states. Among the former detainees in Albania, those who had lived in the southern regions of the XUAR had gone directly to Pakistan; and those who were from the north had first gone to Kazakhstan and Kyrgyzstan before coming to Pakistan.

If the stories of these former detainees were similar to those of the men I had interviewed in Central Asia during the 1990s, there were also some important differences. Unlike in the 1990s, by 2000 it had become increasingly difficult for Uyghurs from the XUAR to make a living trading in bordering states. Larger Chinese companies dominated the trade in Chinese goods in both Central Asia and Pakistan by this time, making such small-time Uyghur middlemen traders nearly obsolete.[46] At the same time, the Chinese state was increasingly putting pressure on the Central Asian and Pakistani security organs for close scrutiny, and frequent extradition, of Uyghurs living in their states.[47] As a result, the former detainees living in Albania all told me that they eventually needed to flee Central Asia and Pakistan, either due to a lack of commercial success or because of visa problems. In this situation, the easiest destination for them was the relatively lawless state of Afghanistan, where they did not need visas to enter the country or even to work.

The four Uyghurs in Albania with whom I spoke all suggested that their move to Afghanistan was temporary. Most said that they were destined for

Turkey, hearing that Turkey frequently provided refuge to Chinese Uyghurs. They also claimed that people in Pakistan had told them that the safest passageway to Turkey for undocumented Uyghurs was via Afghanistan and Iran. Furthermore, they were told that there was a small Uyghur community near Jalalabad in Afghanistan, which could assist them in making such a journey. Although the former detainees arrived in Afghanistan at different times, they all found themselves in the same town near Jalalabad when the American bombing of the region began shortly after 9/11. The youngest in the group, who was eighteen when taken captive, said he had arrived in the country on 12 September 2001 without any knowledge of the previous day's events.

When US bombing began in Afghanistan, the Uyghurs with whom I spoke all fled to northern Pakistan. By their accounts, a Pakistani community gave them shelter upon arrival, but almost immediately turned them over to bounty hunters, who sold them to the US military for $5,000 each. Subsequently, they found themselves in Guantánamo Bay accused of being 'enemy combatants' of the United States in the GWOT.

None of the former detainees I met in Albania refuted that they are adamantly opposed to Chinese rule in their homeland, and it is certainly possible that they would have been willing to partake in violence targeting the Chinese state. They were quite clear, however, that they have never had any negative attitudes towards America. As one said to me, 'We were never enemies of America; we have only seen America in films and on television; what do we know about America?' Furthermore, none of the Uyghurs with whom I spoke in Tirana blamed the United States directly for their fate. They continually characterized their incarceration as a 'mistake' of the Bush administration, which they now hoped Obama was correcting. However, the youngest of the group, who had only turned twenty-one on his arrival in Afghanistan, did note that he wished somebody in the United States would apologize for what had happened to him.

As one of the former detainees with whom I spoke, Abu Bakker Qassim, wrote in a 2006 opinion piece for the *New York Times* after he was released, he and his fellow Uyghurs in Guantánamo had ended up there for 'being in the wrong place at the wrong time in America's war in Afghanistan'.[48] Given the more general fate of all of the Uyghur detainees in Guantánamo, it appears that the US military eventually agreed with this assessment. Since the first five Uyghur detainees were cleared of charges against them and were transferred to Albania in 2006, a series of litigations on behalf of the remaining Uyghur detainees was initiated. One participating judge characterized their cases as

'Kafkaesque', and relieved the remaining seventeen of their 'enemy combatant' status.[49] Fearful that their extradition to China would result in further internment and perhaps execution, the United States found refuge for all of the remaining Uyghur detainees in a variety of countries around the world by the end of 2013.

An analysis of the statements of Uyghur detainees from Guantánamo hearings and my own interviews conducted in Albania suggest a very different narrative of ETIM and its threat to the PRC during the 1990s than the one that has been cultivated by China and perpetuated by international 'terrorism experts'. Information from the detainees does suggest that ETIM, or an organization like it, existed in 2001. This organization, apparently led by Mahsum and Haq, probably tried to recruit young Uyghur men and train them for militant activity against the Chinese state, using the camp in Jalalabad described by the detainees as well as perhaps other training locations.

That being said, the statements of Guantánamo detainees also suggest that this effort was mostly informal, highly disorganized and deprived of both weapons and financial resources. Aside from the poor conditions at the abandoned encampment that was reclaimed by Uyghurs in Jalalabad, the detainees were unanimous in noting that 'weapons training' in the camp was limited to brief access to a single automatic rifle. Furthermore, while some of the detainees did note that they had gone to Jalalabad in the hope of receiving combat training, most had ended up there through a variety of benign circumstances. While all of the detainees clearly articulated their animosity towards the Chinese state, those who had not come to Jalalabad explicitly for combat training were ambivalent at best about the prospect of participating in armed struggle. In terms of the support enjoyed by ETIM and its capacity to carry out organized terrorist acts prior to 2001, almost all of the detainees suggested that they did not even view their participation in the 'camp' as indicative of belonging to an organization, and they further suggested that they had never even heard of ETIM.

In general, the statements of Uyghur detainees from Guantánamo also suggest that this organization had little, if any, contact with the Taliban or al-Qaeda. Most detainees actually said that they had never heard of either group prior to their detention, and they all suggested that they had no interest in these groups' pan-Islamic political aims, but were only concerned about the fate of their own people within China. Perhaps more importantly, it is unlikely that a 'camp' supported financially by either the Taliban or al-Qaeda would be as poorly equipped as that described by the detainees. Given statements provided to the *Wall Street Journal* by Kariaji in 2004, it is likely that ETIM leaders, such as Mahsum, had interactions with both the Taliban and al-Qaeda, at least prior to 2001. Kariaji noted that Mahsum had gained permission from the Taliban and al-Qaeda to establish ETIM camps in Afghanistan, but he also suggests that ETIM did not receive financing from these organizations and had tense relations with them due to the Uyghurs' disinterest in global jihad and their exclusive focus on China.[50]

However, none of the sources of information about ETIM, its capacity and support base provided thus far shed any light on the organization's activities after 2001. Indeed, there is little reliable information available about the organization post-2001. Even the above-cited *Wall Street Journal* article from 2004 that cites Kariaji provides no updated information about ETIM's activities in the post-9/11 context.

The main information on the period from 2001 until the Pakistani army killed Hasan Mahsum in the north-west region of that country in October 2003 comes from the words of Mahsum himself.[51] In a January 2002 telephone interview with Radio Free Asia, Mahsum forcefully asserted that 'The East Turkestan Islamic Party hasn't received any financial assistance from Osama Bin Laden or his Al-Qaeda organization. We don't have any kind of organizational links with Al-Qaeda or the Taliban; we have enough problems of our own.'[52] These comments are further substantiated by video clips of Mahsum in which he accuses the Chinese state of trying to brand ETIM as a terrorist organization opposed to Western states as a means of destroying them.[53] It is noteworthy, however, that he calls in the same video for the Uyghur people to continue to wage a struggle for independence.[54] In all likelihood, the presumably already weak organization he had established in Afghanistan was even weaker in its site of refuge in north-west Pakistan and virtually dissolved with his death. We do know that ETIM's self-proclaimed deputy chairman, Kariaji, had left the organization and was in hiding when he gave his interview in 2004 to the *Wall Street Journal*.[55]

TIP in Pakistan and Abdul Haq

It was not until 2005 that any concrete evidence of ETIM's existence appeared again, now allegedly led by Abdul Haq and renamed the Turkestan Islamic Party (TIP). Little is known about Haq beyond his association with Mahsum and ETIM's training operations. Numerous detainees at Guantánamo Bay who had been in the Jalalabad training camp noted that Adbul Haq had been one of the organizers. According to a 2008 PRC source, Haq was born in 1971 near the town of Khotan and left China illegally in 1998 to join ETIM in a 'south Asian country', presumably Afghanistan.[56] The same report claims that Haq, who had previously been the head of ETIM's training, upon Mahsum's death became the leader of the organization and was actively involved in recruiting new members.[57]

In 2005, videos about the martyrdom of Mahsum and the importance of jihad to the Uyghur people began to appear on YouTube using the new name, the Turkestan Islamic Party (TIP). Temporarily enjoying its own channel on YouTube and constructing its own public website, TIP began to publicize its existence and to make bold statements about its threat to the Chinese state. Most notably, TIP issued a video on the internet in the run-up to the 2008 Beijing Olympics, boasting that the organization was poised to disrupt the international event through violent acts of terrorism.[58] While two bombs did go off in buses in the Chinese city of Kunming prior to the Olympics, and TIP issued a video praising the act, PRC authorities officially denied any link between the bombings and Uyghur terrorism.[59] However, authorities did blame TIP for a far less sophisticated attack that was allegedly carried out by Uyghurs on a group of PRC security forces in the city of Kashgar just days prior to the opening ceremonies of the Olympics. It remains difficult to assess what really happened in the Kashgar attack and whether it was an organized attack or an impulsive act of violence undertaken by disgruntled citizens. It remains unclear if TIP was involved, and, furthermore, the *New York Times* raised questions about whether it involved Uyghurs at all.[60]

Despite the lack of evidence tying TIP to any terrorist activities during the Olympics, the US Treasury decided to take action against Abdul Haq in 2009, placing him on financial sanctions for his association with al-Qaeda. Interestingly, the press release accompanying this action again repeated almost verbatim claims made by official Chinese documents about TIP, including the allegation that Haq had ordered the military commander of TIP to attack the Olympics.[61] It is also noteworthy that this decision came on the heels of a bilateral meeting between Presidents Obama and Hu on the sidelines of the G20 meetings in London, where they agreed to cooperate on counter-terrorism.[62] Subsequently, Abdul Haq was allegedly killed by a US drone attack in Waziristan, Pakistan in early 2010, although the US military could not confirm his death.[63]

Indeed, between the 2008 Olympics and the alleged assassination of Haq in 2010, TIP continued to use the internet to showcase videos with impressive production values that propagate an image of a well-organized militant organization, but there was little evidence that it was capable of carrying out either militant or terrorist attacks. The fact that Haq was allegedly killed in Waziristan suggests that this is where the organization was based, but my informal discussions with State Department officials serving in Pakistan at the time suggest that they had never heard of a steady stream of Uyghurs coming into Waziristan. According to the US Treasury press release from 2009 when he had been placed on the sanctions list, Abdul Haq had been a member of an important al-Qaeda political council dating from 2005, which had not been revealed previously in PRC documents. If this is true, it may be that TIP was created as nothing more than an al-Qaeda shell propaganda organization in Waziristan led by Haq, but with no, or very few, real Uyghur followers. Contributing to such a theory, most TIP videos during this period only portrayed Abdul Haq, stock footage of training, or clips of Mahsum speaking before his death, and the alleged magazine of TIP, *Islamic Turkistan*, was only published in Arabic. Furthermore, the sleek production values of TIP videos and its magazine add credence to the possibility that they became more solidly connected to al-Qaeda and less Uyghur in composition while headquartered in Waziristan.

While TIP continued either praising or claiming responsibility for various acts of violence in the XUAR after Abdul Haq's presumed death, it is unclear if they really had any capacity to mastermind attacks from abroad. In 2011, they claimed responsibility for violent acts in Kashgar and Khotan, where Uyghurs clashed with Han Chinese and police respectively, but the evidence for their connection to the acts or for the assertion that these were politically motivated terrorist attacks remains unclear.[64] The same is the case for the car that exploded into flames in Tiananmen Square in 2013, discussed at the beginning of this chapter.

It is noteworthy, however, that TIP appeared to be gaining new recruits by 2011. This is evident in a video posted by TIP in 2014 that features Uyghurs who had more recently arrived in Afghanistan and were martyred.[65] Most of these men had joined TIP in Afghanistan after leaving the XUAR in 2010 or 2011. This corresponded to a new exodus of Uyghurs from the XUAR that began in the aftermath of the July 2009 ethnic riots in Urumqi, which will be discussed further below. Although the video does not provide specifics of the routes these men took to get to Pakistan or Afghanistan, it appears that some of them did eventually join TIP in Afghanistan and apparently were engaged in combat. These events obviously bolstered TIP and gave it a fighting force that was now more than just a shell organization and could become useful to al-Qaeda in the field of battle. That said, it is likely that TIP in Afghanistan and Pakistan was still a very small organization. This would only begin to change as they moved to Syria.

TIP in Syria

It is not known exactly when TIP became interested in Syria, but if assumptions about the organization that suggest it has become closely aligned with al-Qaeda are correct, it would make sense that the two organizations' involvement in Syria was approximately co-terminus. Al-Qaeda first became active in Syria with the establishment of the 'Al-Nusra Front to Protect the Levant' in January 2012.[66] Not surprisingly, TIP began publishing articles in its magazines and producing videos for the internet about Syria in late 2012 and early 2013.[67] By June 2013, it reportedly had also distributed a video of Uyghur fighters in Syria, but it only featured one Arabic speaker and a group of masked militants, who were allegedly Uyghurs.[68] However, by 2015, TIP was posting videos of Uyghurs engaged in combat in northern Syria, particularly in the areas around Idlib, Jisr al-Shughur and the Al-Ghab plain.[69] Thus, it appears that TIP had transformed over the course of four years from what was likely a shell organization in Afghanistan with few Uyghurs to a significant fighting force in Syria. How did this happen?

At the same time as TIP was establishing itself in Syria, the flow of Uyghurs fleeing the PRC was only increasing. Although counter-terrorism measures undertaken by the PRC in the XUAR after 2001 proved to be more repressive than those aimed at 'splittism' in the 1990s, it was only after the July 2009 ethnic riots in Urumqi that the regime became a virtual police state, pushing increased numbers of Uyghurs to seek refuge outside China. On 5 July 2009, a group of mostly young Uyghurs organized a street march in Urumqi to protest against the authorities' inaction regarding a case where a group of Han workers killed several Uyghur migrant workers in a southern Chinese factory under the suspicion that the Uyghurs had raped two Han women.[70] Although there are conflicting reports about who initiated the violence, the protest devolved into a bloody conflict between Uyghur protesters, the police and Han citizens. The violence continued for several days as Han vigilante groups began attacking Uyghurs throughout the city in retaliation for Han casualties on the day of the protest. In the end, the unrest was the most violent ethnic conflict in China in decades. Although the Chinese state has been inconsistent in describing this violence as 'terrorism', it has continually maintained that Uyghur groups abroad provoked it. This event increased the anxiety of the PRC with regard to Uyghur dissent and ushered in a new era of policies aimed at even more harshly restricting the political voice and religious observation of Uyghurs within the XUAR.

In the aftermath of the violence, the XUAR government undertook a full-scale effort to hunt down, convict and severely punish Uyghurs who were involved in organizing the original protests or had allegedly been involved in the mass violence. A well-researched report by the Uyghur Human Rights Project documented at least twenty-six instances of death sentences being levied on those involved in the protests and riots, twenty-four of whom were Uyghur and only two of whom were Han Chinese.[71] The number of others who were arrested and given jail terms remains unknown, but the *Financial Times* reported that at least 4,000 Uyghurs had already been arrested within two weeks of the events.[72] According to Human Rights Watch, a large but unknown number of the Uyghurs who were detained in the aftermath of the events, often taken from their homes, have all but disappeared.[73] Although the number of these 'enforced disappearances' is unknown, Human Rights Watch was able to document forty-three cases in depth through interviews with family members.[74] Among those who did not disappear and instead faced criminal charges, many of whom were minors as young as fourteen years of age, human rights groups have documented a large number of breaches of due process in their convictions as well as instances of torture while they were in custody.[75] Finally, in the aftermath of the events, the Chinese government closed access to the internet in the region for ten months.

These events began a crackdown on Uyghur political expression and religious observation as well as an assault on Uyghur culture in the XUAR, the severity of which was only comparable to the Cultural Revolution, but in a context where the state now had much more capacity for surveillance and control. In this context, it is not surprising that Uyghurs have been seeking ways to flee the PRC ever since. Interestingly, in contrast to the 1990s when Uyghurs chose to flee the XUAR via Central Asia, which borders on the region, most of those who have since sought refuge outside China have taken much more difficult routes through South East Asia. These new routes of out-migration reflect just how much cooperation has been forged between the security organs of China and the Central Asian states to prevent Uyghurs of the XUAR from entering its neighbouring states.

However, the new routes have also taken their toll on the Uyghurs who have embarked on them, as is detailed in a recent report from the World

Uyghur Congress (WUC) based on interviews with refugees.[76] Interviews I conducted subsequently in Turkey during June 2016 with refugees who had taken these routes out of the XUAR confirmed much of the information in the WUC report. Entire families of Uyghurs, primarily from rural areas in the regions with the most draconian counter-terrorism campaigns in the XUAR, including Kashgar, Khotan, Aksu and Yarkand, are paying exuberant prices to Han Chinese human traffickers to get them to the border areas of Yunnan province and then to a series of countries including Vietnam, Laos, Thailand, Cambodia and Malaysia. While the routes differ to a certain degree by group of refugees, they are bolstered by a network of safe houses that often keep the refugees hidden for up to a year until they can make their next moves. Many of those who travelled these roads to get to Turkey told me that they had lost family members along the way or had themselves spent time in either Malaysian or Thai prisons. Most of these new refugees are also devoutly religious, and they suggest that their reasons for leaving relate to continual harassment from authorities who have branded them 'extremists' and 'terrorists'. They also note being fined and harassed for having more than two children, wearing beards and praying outside mosques.[77] In addition, many of them had spent time in prison at different points since 2009, under accusation of being 'extremists' or 'terrorists'.

Evidence of this new 'underground railroad' for Uyghurs seeking to escape the PRC emerged almost immediately after the 2009 riots in December of that year, when Cambodia detained and extradited eighteen Uyghurs, including women and children, who had apparently fled the PRC. The Uyghurs were subsequently arrested on return to the PRC, and two of them received life sentences.[78] Likewise, in 2011 and again in 2012, Malaysia extradited eleven and six Uyghurs respectively back to the PRC.[79] While these extraditions drew criticism from international human rights groups, the international community had no idea of the extent of the exodus of Uyghurs that was occurring through South East Asia until Thai authorities arrested some two hundred Uyghur men, women and children who were hiding in a jungle camp in Songkhla province.[80] The Uyghurs claimed to have Turkish citizenship, and Thailand was caught in a diplomatic battle between China and Turkey for the right to have these refugees sent to their country. While Thailand did send approximately 170 of the refugees to Turkey, approximately 100 were extradited to China in July 2015, resulting in large protests outside the Chinese embassy in Turkey after those sent to China were pictured in the media handcuffed and with hoods over their heads on a plane out of Thailand.[81]

My meetings with Uyghur activists in Turkey in June 2016 revealed that much larger transfers of population had been occurring over the last several years.[82] They claimed to have been travelling to South East Asia incessantly over the last several years and had succeeded in getting 10,000 Uyghur refugees transferred to Turkey from a variety of countries, but mostly Malaysia. However, during their travels, they also frequently came into contact with another Uyghur from Turkey who was recruiting people to TIP, promising to bring them to Turkey and onward to Syria. Others were recruited by TIP and perhaps other militant groups upon arriving in Turkey and were escorted to Syria. While this has become a floating population that is difficult to account for, it is conceivable that thousands of them have gone to Syria via Turkey since 2013.

Presumably, this has been a massive opportunity for TIP to reinvent itself from an al-Qaeda-sponsored shell organization into an actual militant force. While most of the refugees I met in Turkey had not been in Syria, they knew many people who had. One of the reasons many Uyghurs are leaving Turkey for Syria is that they have no actual status in Turkey and often struggle to make ends meet. But TIP and other militant groups promise them homes and a livelihood in Syria. Others are going to Syria in order to gain combat experience which they hope to employ eventually in their homeland of 'Eastern Turkestan'. Indeed, the one Uyghur refugee whom I interviewed in Turkey who had been in Syria provided the same justification. As he said, 'My goal was to return to China with knowledge of how to wage war; I came not to stay in Istanbul, not to stay in Syria, but to learn weaponry and return to fight for Eastern Turkistan.' He also noted explicitly that he had been in Syria with TIP, and that there was an entire Uyghur 'neighbourhood' of families with a school, mosque and madrassa. The community he described sounded less like a camp of militants than a Uyghur settlement. He noted that the men would occasionally go to fight battles, but the women and children would stay at home. When asked about the battles in which he had fought, he noted with particular pride that he had fought in the battle of Jisr al-Shughur.

Some of the materials released by TIP appear to reaffirm the statements from this interview, as they highlight the community of Uyghurs in Turkey by showing children in school and women at home. However, these videos also have a particularly militant appearance to them, often portraying children with guns.[83] While such propaganda materials provide an ominous image of TIP in Syria that is certainly more threatening than that which had previously been seen from the organization, there are still questions about its nature as a cohesive organization with long-term members and the capacity to carry out extensive terrorist attacks in China.

In an odd turn of events in 2014, the supposedly dead Abdul Haq re-emerged on a TIP video for the first time since his assumed death by a US drone. Subsequently, he has appeared in several TIP videos, including one condemning Daesh (or the Islamic State) and the Islamic Movement of Uzbekistan, which had changed allegiances from al-Qaeda to Daesh.[84] The fact that Abdul Haq is still influential in the organization and has made such a statement in obvious support of al-Qaeda's conflict with Daesh suggests that TIP is still aligned closely with leaders in al-Qaeda. However, the Uyghur fighters in Syria appear to have little understanding of these connections, nor necessarily any long-term allegiance to TIP. Instead, their primary concern is the future of their homeland. Given that the video footage of TIP in combat in Syria portrays it engaged in conventional warfare and that most of those who go there to gain combat experience are interested in the weapons of warfare rather than the less conventional tactics of terrorists, it is questionable whether these new Uyghur militants can be characterized as terrorists at all per the working definition of the phenomenon provided at the outset of this chapter. For this reason, all the refugees I interviewed in Turkey suggested that the Uyghurs in Syria were not terrorists, but freedom fighters.

The few reliable news reports about the substantial Uyghur community that is presently in Syria also cast doubts on their particular allegiance to TIP. In one article from March 2016 on the website of the Saudi-run Al Arabiya television station, the author describes a substantial community of Uyghur families that have come to Syria, noting that 'a year ago, they were barely hundreds of Uighur fighters, belonging to the Al-Nusra Front-allied Turkistan Islamic Party (TIP); today, according to several sources in the province, there are a few thousand Uighur fighters, and many of them arrived with their families after a long and treacherous journey from China and Central Asia'.[85] The article notes that these people appear more like settlers than international jihadists and are more welcomed than other militants by the local Syrian population because they do not practise rent-seeking locally.[86] Additionally, there has been much speculation that the Uyghurs who have suddenly appeared in large numbers in Syria are being supported mostly by external powers rather than by al-Qaeda. If this is true, it would suggest quite tenuous relations between TIP in Syria and those like Abdul Haq, who presumably remains in Afghanistan or Pakistan. One rather far-fetched theory suggests that China has facilitated their arrival in Syria in order to justify intervention alongside Russia to assist the Syrian government.[87] Another, perhaps more plausible theory is that the Turkish government is facilitating their participation in the civil war as proxies for Turkey's interests.[88] Given that Turkey is already supporting many rebel groups in the same region where Uyghurs are settling, that the Uyghurs going to Syria have come via Turkey, that many of them were allegedly recruited in South East Asia by a Turkish Uyghur, and that TIP allegedly has US-made weapons, there are reasons at least to entertain the possibility of the Turkish government's involvement.

However, regardless of who helped facilitate the allegedly large numbers of Uyghurs who have come to Syria, more than anything else the fate of these Uyghurs reflects the extreme duress under which rural Uyghur communities have come since 2001. These are families from poor rural communities who have given up all they had to flee surreptitiously through extreme conditions and have agreed to live in the middle of a civil war and fight in a battle that has little to do with them. Given that the region where this community allegedly settled was heavily bombed by Russian and Syrian troops in 2017, it is very possible that the community has been all but obliterated. Furthermore, given their apparent lack of dedication to the particular cause they are fighting for, many are probably returning to Turkey. Only time will tell if the substantial expansion of TIP in Syria will translate into an empowered TIP in the future that has the capacity to carry out militant or terrorist acts inside the PRC. However, given that TIP is so reliant on al-Qaeda, it is more likely that the organization will find it disadvantageous to continue aggravating China, which has generally stayed out of international initiatives in GWOT. Regardless, TIP today reflects an active Uyghur militant movement, the likes of which has not existed since the establishment of the PRC. The first potential signs that these new Uyghur militants will pose a threat to China became evident in the summer of 2016, when an alleged Uyghur TIP fighter from Syria was reported to have carried out a suicide bombing at the PRC embassy in Kyrgyzstan. Furthermore, the reports from Kyrgyzstan suggested that this bombing plot was assisted by others from the former Al-Nusra Front in Syria.[89] In many ways, this may be the Uyghur threat that the PRC has long falsely claimed to face, finally come home to roost.

Conclusion: the self-fulfilling prophecy of Uyghur militancy

This chapter has sought to demonstrate how counter-terrorism as a means to suppress a non-militant opposition in an authoritarian state such as China is destined to create militancy. In other words, such states create a self-fulfilling prophecy of terrorism—creating the threat that they had previously and falsely suggested existed. As the sociologist Robert Merton, who is often credited with establishing the term 'self-fulfilling prophecy', notes:

> it is, in the beginning, a *false* definition of the situation evoking a new behavior which makes the original false conception come *true*; this specious validity of the self-fulfilling prophecy perpetuates a reign of error; for the prophet will cite the actual course of events as proof that he was right from the very beginning.[90]

As this brief discussion of the Uyghur case suggests, such a 'reign of error' can also quickly be reproduced by policy-makers and academics around the world, helping to make the imaginary real and the once non-existent suddenly appear. This may become the case with regard to the recent proliferation of Uyghur militancy, whether or not it can be characterized as terrorism. This should be a cautionary tale not only for China, but for Western states who have embraced GWOT without defining its enemy and simultaneously making nefarious allies in the war in order to achieve their objective of obliterating all terrorist organizations with global reach.

While GWOT has arguably created many similar situations around the world where authoritarian states have manipulated the terrorist narrative to suppress local opposition, only to make them terrorists eventually, the Uyghurs who have made the long trip to Syria are certainly one of the most obvious examples of this phenomenon. While many if not most of them will not survive the experience, those who do will likely be much more radicalized and militant than any group of Uyghur nationalists in the modern period. As the head of the Uyghur refugee community whom I met in Turkey stated forcefully when I asked about TIP, 'Why does the Turkistan Islamic Party exist? The Turkistan Islamic Party profited from the Chinese oppression of our homeland; without that, it would not exist; China itself made the Turkistan Islamic Party.'[91]

If one follows the trajectory of the Uyghur terrorist threat since the PRC began its own war on terror in late 2001, one clearly sees the self-fulfilling prophecy that has helped to create TIP as it exists today. It first attempted to brand all Uyghur political organizations internationally as terrorists, but it was only able to convince the international community that one of these organizations, a small under-resourced group of training camps in Afghanistan, was a true terrorist threat. By grossly over-exaggerating this group's capacity, hunting its followers throughout the XUAR, and targeting all religiously inclined Uyghurs as potential terrorists, the PRC eventually brought the few members left in this organization closer to al-Qaeda, for which it served mostly as a shell organization employed for propaganda purposes until it became more useful in Syria. Now, that organization has helped to radicalize a substantial number of Uyghurs and provide them with not just training, but combat experience.

Furthermore, whether or not TIP re-emerges from Syria intact, other Uyghurs fleeing China appear to be seeking military training through other radical Muslim organizations, whether in South East Asia or with the Islamic State of Iraq and al-Sham (ISIS). A recent report released by New America, for example, documents over a hundred Uyghurs fighting with ISIS in Syria, and their profile resembles those who have fought with TIP—impoverished, uneducated, from rural regions (mostly in the regions of Kashgar, Khotan, and Aksu) and accompanied by their families.[92]

Beyond such Uyghurs who have already fled oppression in the XUAR and have been radicalized abroad, there is no reason to believe that more Uyghurs will not flee the PRC to obtain military training in order to return and fight for the liberation of their perceived homeland in the future, or that Uyghurs who remain in the country will not find new ways to launch violent attacks. In fact, given the situation in the country as of 2018, where the surveillance and control of the Uyghur population has reached a pinnacle with few historical precedents, such outcomes are even more likely. As has been well documented in the accounts of investigative journalists and human rights groups and some scholars, the government in the XUAR has been stepping up its counter-terrorism measures in unprecedented ways since early 2017.[93] This has included the use of sophisticated technology employed for surveillance and the tracking of the population, a massive build-up in military and police personnel, the creation of hundreds of checkpoints and small 'convenience' police stations throughout urban areas and, most ominously, the establishment of 're-education' camps that have reportedly detained thousands of Uyghurs and those from other Muslim ethnic groups in the region on the suspicion that they lack loyalty to the PRC.[94]

In the short term, these measures have temporarily succeeded in virtually eliminating Uyghur-initiated violence in the region and in China more generally. However, as the history of the mass suppression of Uyghur voices, religious observation and cultural expression in the aftermath of the 2009 riots in Urumqi demonstrates, such a cessation of violence is probably only temporary and is likely to result in an escalation of violence over the long term. This is all the more the case given that most recent repressive measures inside the XUAR have gone beyond targeting the religious rural populations of the south and now amount to large-scale racial profiling, impacting on even those Uyghurs who have sought to integrate themselves better into PRC society. In this context, the space for Uyghurs seeking to change the conditions in the region from within 'the system' is rapidly shrinking, making the idea of armed struggle a more attractive, if perhaps not the only, option for Uyghurs to have their voices heard. Even if it is possible for the PRC to maintain the present repressive atmosphere in the region indefinitely as a means of preventing internal violent resistance, China's increased interests around the world, especially through the Belt and Road Initiative, will most certainly leave it vulnerable to attack by Uyghurs who have embraced armed resistance as their 'only option' of resistance.

Given the damage done by China's counter-terrorism policies over the last sixteen years, it is difficult to imagine a future scenario where Uyghur militancy is not a factor in the politics of the XUAR and the PRC. Whether such future aspiring militants become 'freedom fighters' or 'terrorists' will likely be a question of who is labelling them, as has long been the case with this dichotomy. Regardless, it appears that the PRC is well on its way to escalating its engagement with its Uyghur population to the armed conflict it has long claimed to be waging. If it remains unclear whether Uyghur terrorism has become a self-fulfilling prophecy for the PRC, Uyghur militancy certainly has.

5

CHINA AND COUNTER-TERRORISM

BEYOND PAKISTAN?

Andrew Small

For the better part of two decades, Pakistan and Afghanistan have provided the main focal points for the overseas terrorist threat facing China. The East Turkestan Islamic Movement (ETIM) had a network of camps in Taliban-run Afghanistan, and after the US invasion, Pakistan's Federally Administered Tribal Areas (FATA) provided the base for ETIM's remnants, which subsequently emerged as the Turkestan Islamic Party (TIP). Their operating environment was heavily conditioned by the central role that Pakistan occupied in the region's terror map. Its sponsorship of the Taliban and other militants gave it a unique capacity to influence how these groups behaved towards China, whether through dissuading them from supporting ETIM / TIP, deterring them from targeting China themselves, or through direct operations on Pakistani soil against ETIM / TIP and its partners. Despite tensions over the issue between China and Pakistan in recent years, in practice this resulted in a highly constrained environment for TIP. While they were able to generate propaganda materials, their capacity to launch attacks in China or on Chinese targets was extremely limited. Small in number, and dependent on larger, more capable groups, such as the Islamic Movement of Uzbekistan (IMU), they had little autonomous space in which to act.

Those conditions have now shifted in several important respects. The Pakistani Army's Zarb-e-Azb operation, in North Waziristan, appears to have displaced TIP from FATA, meaning that, after fifteen years in Pakistan, the group's leadership is now centred in Afghanistan again. The IMU, which was previously TIP's host, has been decimated by the Taliban following its declaration of loyalty to ISIS, to such a degree that some analysts contend that the group no longer meaningfully exists, even if some remnants do. The principal theatre for TIP has also shifted: while the group's emir, Abdul Haq, who was previously believed to have been killed in a US drone strike in 2010, is in Afghanistan, the largest number of fighters are in Syria operating with Jabhat Al-Nusra (now Jabhat Fatah al-Sham).[1] The broader strategic context in which Chinese counter-terrorism policy is operating has seen important changes too. The rise of ISIS introduced a major new actor to the network of global militancy, one that has fewer qualms than al-Qaeda historically exhibited about making China an explicit target. Although more Uyghurs are fighting with Jabhat Al-Nusra than with ISIS, the group's reach poses a different set of problems for Chinese security, exemplified by the fact that it has attracted a small number of non-Uyghur Chinese recruits. The Syria conflict has also reconditioned the pathway to Uyghur militant recruitment: with improvements in security on China's borders with South and Central Asia, the main transit routes to Syria for Uyghurs have generally been through South East Asia and Turkey, with Turkish government support or acquiescence.

Taken together, these changes amount to perhaps the most significant set of shifts in China's external terrorist threat environment since 9/11. While this chapter will be primarily focused on the South Asia dimension, it will also place the situation there in the context of these wider developments. The net effect is that, after many years in which China was able to mediate major elements of its counter-terrorism policy through its closest security partner, Pakistan, Beijing is finally being required to take on a more direct role in addressing the threat across virtually all dimensions of policy—politically, economically and potentially even militarily.

Background

Tensions in Xinjiang between the Chinese government, Han Chinese migrants and the native Uyghur population are long-standing. Grievances over issues ranging from religious and linguistic rights to economic inequities have fed Uyghur aspirations towards greater autonomy or outright independence since the foundation of the People's Republic of China, which absorbed the remnants of the Second East Turkestan Republic into the newly forged state.[2] While much protest has been peaceful, Beijing has also faced small-scale organized militant opposition to its rule, elements of which have had outside support. In the 1960s and 1970s, groups such as the Eastern Turkestan People's Revolutionary Party were largely backed by the KGB, and had a pan-Turkic and Marxist identity.[3] But in the late 1980s and 1990s, the religious revival in the region and the rise of new transnational Islamist movements saw the militant opposition taking on a more explicitly Islamic character. This coincided with heightened Chinese anxieties about separatist sentiment following the establishment of the independent Central Asian republics after the fall of the Soviet Union. Subsequent years saw a particularly harsh cycle of unrest, violence and repression that caused many Uyghurs to flee to neighbouring countries from the 'Strike hard, maximum pressure' campaign, and a spate of deadly bombings and attacks across Xinjiang. A Chinese government document in 1998 listed Uyghur independence movements as the main threat to the stability of the Chinese state.[4]

While the principal focus of Chinese security concerns has been internal, there has also been a substantial foreign policy component, with Beijing seeking to shut down sources of external backing for any political opposition, whether peaceful or violent. These efforts have ranged far afield, including Turkey and Middle Eastern states with influence and reach into Xinjiang. But the preponderance of Beijing's counter-terrorism efforts has been conditioned by local geography. The collapse of the Soviet Union and the opening of cross-border transit routes with Xinjiang made Central Asia the main external concern in the 1990s, motivating the foundation of the 'Shanghai Five' security grouping that subsequently expanded into the Shanghai Cooperation Organization.[5] The Taliban's takeover of Afghanistan and the opportunity they granted to Uyghur militants to set up training camps there turned it into a significant focal point at the turn of the millennium, and drove Chinese efforts to establish ties with the diplomatically isolated Islamic Emirate.[6] After the US invasion displaced many of those fighters into the border areas of Pakistan, FATA became a new centre of attention for Chinese counter-terrorism specialists.

In many ways, this geographical context made the threat relatively manageable. The secular, authoritarian Central Asian governments' counter-terrorism policies were closely aligned with China's own approach. And the state at the centre of the web of many of the region's militant networks, Pakistan, consistently sought to ensure that its 'all-weather friend' did not become a priority target for them. As a result, once they were appropriately discouraged, many of the principal militant and terrorist groups in the region—the Afghan Taliban, al-Qaeda and the Kashmiri groups—rarely concerned themselves with China, nor did they extend significant material support to Uyghur militant groups that sought their backing. Osama bin Laden's few statements about China were notably conciliatory.[7] These conditions have shifted somewhat in recent years, as Pakistan has been drawn into conflict with groups such as the Pakistani Taliban, and Uyghur militants have become better integrated with other jihadi networks. After being expelled from Afghanistan, the weakened TIP were drawn into even greater dependence on the IMU. The IMU facilitated TIP's relationship with al-Qaeda, whose media arm was used to distribute their propaganda materials.[8] But TIP's autonomous capacity to act has remained highly restricted. There is little evidence that it has been directly involved in any attacks on the Chinese mainland from its base in North Waziristan.

This context also informed China's approach to counter-terrorism coordination with Western powers. In the aftermath of 9/11, China was willing to cooperate on issues ranging from sanctions and terrorist financing to the monitoring of shipping containers. It was eager to tie ETIM to the 'Global War on Terror' and won its designation as a terrorist organization.[9] But Beijing was unwilling to assume visible involvement in any broader counter-terrorism coalitions, reluctant to take on a significant counter-terrorism role itself, and averse to being tainted by association with countries that were major targets in their own right. Its approach to counter-terrorism policy outside its borders has been very narrow in scope, almost exclusively focused on Uyghur groups, and otherwise more interested in ensuring that transnational jihadi groups neither support them nor make China an enemy themselves. As a result, broad-based coordination in addressing militancy has been hard to achieve, while certain forms of cooperation that Beijing is keen to see—such as greater intelligence sharing vis-à-vis Chinese targets—are inhibited by Beijing's blurring of the line between terrorists, political activists and ordinary disgruntled citizens.

Syria, ISIS and the new Chinese counter-terrorism landscape

These geographical conditions are now shifting. Much as Afghanistan turned into the jihadis' central focus in the 1980s and 1990s, the war in Syria is redrawing the Chinese threat map. The most capable Uyghur militants are now operating in the north-west of that country, and where TIP propaganda once came out of isolated camps in FATA, it has instead been able to showcase their active military role in—for instance—the Idlib campaign with Jabhat al-Nusra.[10] Assessments from UN counter-terrorism experts place their capabilities—training, combat experience, facility with advanced weapons, access to networks—substantially ahead of anything that TIP exhibited when it was chiefly based in Pakistan and Afghanistan.[11] In smaller numbers, other Uyghurs have joined ISIS itself, which has shown none of al-Qaeda's early inhibitions about targeting China. 'East Turkestan' has featured explicitly in Abu Bakr al Baghdadi's speeches and ISIS propaganda, including Mandarin and Uyghur language material.[12] The killing of a Chinese hostage, Fan Jinghui, in November 2015 was—despite the peculiarities of his personal case—a challenge to a Chinese government that is sensitive to public opinion about the protection of its citizens overseas.[13] Some Chinese experts are also concerned that ISIS's ideological influence is potentially more potent; it is better able to catalyze further 'lone-wolf' attacks, extending its reach to states on China's immediate periphery, and even risks drawing support from China's other Muslim minorities, evidenced by the small number of Hui that have gone to fight in Syria.[14]

One of the biggest challenges facing Beijing is that, unlike in South Asia where Pakistan is an extremely close partner, the country at the nexus of the Syria issue is Turkey. Ankara has long taken an ambivalent position in its handling of the Uyghur issue, providing some support for the political opposition, and a source of refuge for those fleeing Xinjiang, but also placating Beijing for the sake of closer political and commercial relations.[15] Its handling of these matters in the context of the war in Syria has been more problematic from a Chinese perspective. Not only has Turkey allowed Uyghurs ready access to Syria to join anti-Assad forces of various hues, it has actively assisted with a 'pipeline' from South East Asia.[16] In recent years, transit routes for Uyghurs to leave China via Central Asia or Pakistan have become harder to access, due to tighter border controls, leading greater numbers to use people-smuggling networks in Thailand, Malaysia, Indonesia and other states in the region. Ankara has assisted either with the provision of passports or by turning a blind eye to forgeries, enabling a flow of the Uyghurs who are able to make it out to proceed to Turkey, and in some cases onwards to the Syrian battlefields, as well as assisting with arms supplies.[17]

This has posed a number of associated problems for China in South East Asia too. Much as the intermingling of criminal networks and militant transit routes in Central and South Asia saw Uyghurs drawn into groups ranging from the IMU to the Taliban, Uyghurs are developing new connections with militant organizations in South East Asia, reinforced by connections being made in Syria. Two of the men arrested for the Jakarta attacks in January 2016 were Uyghurs connected to the ISIS-affiliated East Indonesia Mujahideen.[18] The Bangkok bombing of August 2015, an attack that appears to have been specifically directed at Chinese targets, has been attributed to Uyghurs seeking revenge for the Thai government's extradition of approximately 100 refugees to China, operating in partnership with Turkish entities.[19] The South East Asian transit routes have also exposed China to more internal dangers than the old Central and South Asian routes: the 2014 attack at Kunming railway station, which killed thirty-one people, was undertaken by Uyghurs who had unsuccessfully tried to flee the country via Vietnam.[20] These changing external conditions couple with a worsening domestic situation. After nearly a decade without any serious terrorist attacks, the period since 2008 saw a marked increase in violent incidents emanating from Xinjiang. The aftermath of the 2009 riots in Urumqi has seen a serious worsening of communal tensions, and of the Chinese state's crackdown, accelerating the number of Uyghurs looking to get out of the country. The salience of terrorism as a major security issue for the Chinese state has increased as a result, particularly as the attacks have moved beyond Urumqi and Southern and Eastern Xinjiang to hit targets in major Chinese cities, including Tiananmen Square itself.[21] Chinese counter-terrorism experts who had previously been skeptical about the involvement of external actors have grown more concerned about the effects of the influence of foreign-produced propaganda, both as inspiration and for improving techniques employed in the attacks, even if not direct material support.

The last two years have also seen a couple of important developments in Afghanistan and Pakistan. The Pakistani Army's Zarb-e-Azb operation addressed a long-standing Chinese concern about the continued presence of Uyghur militants on Pakistani soil. While Pakistan had taken efforts against the ETIM leadership in South Waziristan in the aftermath of 9/11, including killing Hasan Mahsum in 2003, it had been largely unwilling to launch an intervention in North Waziristan. TIP was operating in Haqqani network territory, and while the Pakistani army took steps—at points—to open up targeting windows for US drone strikes, it was reluctant to pursue a larger-scale campaign that might result in blowback in the rest of Pakistan. These considerations changed in 2014. Several factors, including the IMU's attack on Karachi airport, the revised strategy of the new army chief, and even the continued pressure from China itself resulted in the launch of the Zarb-e-Azb campaign in June 2014. While there was much criticism of the campaign's being so widely telegraphed that many fighters were able simply to relocate to the other side of the Afghan border, the net effect—particularly following the Shawal Valley phase—has nonetheless been to deny TIP the operational base in Pakistan that they had enjoyed since 2001.[22] A number of TIP fighters were sent to join the war in Syria ahead of the operation, while the rest of them—including the leadership itself—appear to have established their new headquarters in Eastern Afghanistan.[23]

Ordinarily, this might have been expected to take place in concert with the IMU. The two groups have been closely intertwined since the late 1990s. While there were other factors connecting them, the agreement reached between the Chinese government and the Taliban leadership in 2000 led to ETIM's fighters having to integrate fully with the IMU rather than being allowed to run its own autonomous camps. After the US invasion of Afghanistan, the level of dependency grew further, with Uyghur fighters following the IMU's peregrinations, initially to South Waziristan and then to North Waziristan after the IMU's tensions with Waziri tribal leaders in 2007. But in 2015, the decision by the IMU to declare loyalty to ISIS—which its emir, Usman Ghazi, attributed to the Taliban's deception over the death of Mullah Omar—proved terminal. The Taliban fought with and eliminated the group's fighters and its leader in Zabul province in late 2015, leaving only a small remaining faction.[24] TIP, by contrast, has maintained its affiliation to al-Qaeda (and, therefore, to the Taliban's leadership too), a fact further reinforced by the 'return' of Abdul Haq, who is believed to have a position in al-Qaeda's leadership shura, as emir.[25]

China is also navigating a broader set of counter-terrorism challenges in Pakistan, as a result of its substantial new investment commitments in the country. The China–Pakistan Economic Corridor (CPEC) is a multi-billion-dollar package of energy and infrastructure projects, industrial zones and other economic cooperation schemes between the two sides, adding up to total figures that range from US$ 28 billion (the project list agreed in time for Xi Jinping's visit in April 2015) to $46 billion (a number from the Pakistani government that includes all projects under negotiation; this has even been pushed to $54 billion after new rail and transit projects were agreed in 2016).[26] The Chinese embassy in Pakistan has stated that around $20 billion worth of projects are actually in track on the ground. CPEC projects have already been the subject of attacks, particularly the road-building projects in Balochistan, and in September 2016 the Pakistani army claimed that forty-four Pakistani workers had been killed since the inception of the initiative.[27] Pakistan has put in place a substantial battery of protections for the influx of Chinese personnel working on the projects, establishing a new Special Security Division of over 13,000 security personnel from the army and civilian agencies—which may be increased to closer to 30,000 (a northern and a southern division) as further projects are added.[28] While the concept is not completely new—dedicated protection forces have been established for other overseas Chinese investment projects, such as the Mes Aynak Copper Mine in Afghanistan—the scale, which is larger than many countries' entire combined armed forces, is unprecedented. It also reflects the breadth of China's exposure to terrorist threats targeting the Pakistani state, localized attacks and transnational groups operating in Pakistan. Many of these go back to the early 2000s, when Balochi groups launched attacks on Chinese targets in Gwadar; they expanded after the establishment of the Tehrik-i-Taliban Pakistan (TTP) in 2007, for whom China was an explicit target after its involvement in instigating the crackdown on the Lal Masjid mosque in Islamabad. The threat-list is now even wider, though, including Sindhi groups, al-Qaeda, and ISIS operatives in Pakistan, while China is also vulnerable to the twists and turns of the Pakistani government's relationships with other militant outfits: when they sour, Pakistan's 'all-weather friend' and great economic hope is an obvious focal point for attacks.

China's shifting counter-terrorism strategy

A number of these developments are so recent that it is only possible to reach a very provisional assessment of the implications, while several of them are likely to be subjected to further shifts and reversals. The South East Asian transit routes, for instance, appear to have been somewhat circumscribed since the Erawan Shrine bombing. China has been able to make some progress in improving its cooperation with the Turkish government on the flow of Uyghurs to Syria, and the Turkish government's own strategy in Syria has moved into a new phase. The consolidation of Pakistani state control in North Waziristan is not a given. Neither is TIP's presence in Syria—as the Russian and Western military campaigns intensified, there were already questions about whether a number of fighters were likely to return to locations in Asia.

Nonetheless, there are two clear, intertwined trends that will affect the broad tenor of Chinese policy in this field. The first is that China is no longer able to rely as heavily on its close partner, Pakistan, to navigate the challenge of Uyghur militancy, which is no longer centred in Pakistan. Pakistan is no longer able to exercise the level of influence that it previously enjoyed over the groups composing the TTP, and even the Taliban itself. And many of the relevant groups and actors are now operating in regions entirely outside Pakistan's reach. The result is that Beijing is having to take on a far more direct role than at any other time since post-9/11. It is evidently not starting with a blank slate: in South East Asia, the Middle East and Afghanistan, China has long-standing security and intelligence relationships, and Turkey has long been a centre of support and finance for Uyghur militancy. But none of China's security relationships has the level of depth that has been in place with the Pakistani army and intelligence services for decades.

In South Asia, China's counter-terrorism policy is, already, necessarily less Pakistan-centric. While Pakistan still occupies a critical role for Chinese policy in the region, TIP's location in Afghanistan has pushed Beijing towards closer direct military and intelligence cooperation with the Afghan government. This has been in motion for a number of years, particularly following then-security chief Zhou Yongkang's landmark visit to Kabul in 2012. The State Councillor responsible for public security, Guo Shengkun, visited Afghanistan in November 2014, preceded by Qi Jianguo, the PLA Deputy Chief of the General Staff with responsibility for military intelligence.[29] Efforts by the Afghan government to establish their standing as an alternative security partner for China in the region go back even further. But this has intensified in the last year, with a visit from the PLA Chief of General Staff and Central Military Commission member, Fang Fenghui, in March 2016, followed by the first full-scale package of Chinese military aid.[30] For its part, the Afghan government has extradited a number of Uyghurs to China.

This dovetails with other elements of the rebalancing of Chinese policy in the region, which has largely been focused on ensuring that Afghanistan does not become a safe haven for Uyghur militants after the US drawdown. Following a decade of avoiding any political involvement, Beijing's willingness to take a leading role in the negotiations over Afghanistan's future had seen it pushing forward a reconciliation process with the Taliban, convening an array of bilateral, trilateral and multilateral conclaves, and exerting influence over friends in Pakistan to deliver Taliban representatives for talks.[31] While these have not come to fruition, the process has been notable for Beijing's unusual willingness to take responsibility for facilitating the process, and its close and open coordination with the United States, after years of refusing to collaborate bilaterally on any Afghan initiatives. The recent symbolic package of military aid, to which China has traditionally been averse, also served as a signal to the Taliban of Beijing's continued support for the government in Kabul, and the need for them to join a peace process rather than expecting to be able to secure their goals entirely on the battlefield. Even China's dealings with the Taliban have become more direct, and less subject to Pakistani mediation. While Beijing still takes due care over the sensitivities of its partner, the value of an independent relationship with the group has been clear for some time.

The deployment of Chinese economic instruments in the region has also been portrayed as a long-term means of addressing the terrorist threat. The 'Belt and Road' initiative has partly been framed as a way to provide stability through development across an arc of instability stretching from Xinjiang to the Middle East.[32] China believes that the conditions in which militancy has thrived can really only be addressed through a transformation of the economic situation in these countries. At least in private, Chinese leaders have been explicit in describing plans in these terms—Li Keqiang reportedly characterizes CPEC, a Belt and Road project, as a means of 'weaning the populace from fundamentalism'.[33] It is also intended to function as a large-scale incentive for various actors in the region to prioritize economic and financial rewards over security competition, and the economic rewards that accrue from war.

In a more tentative fashion, there have also been debates in China about whether to take on a more direct military role in counter-terrorism efforts, with the anti-terrorism law of 2015 including provision for the deployment of Chinese security forces overseas.[34] This has focused most strikingly on Syria. The conclusion of those debates has been against intervention, and the terms of the debate appear to have been concerned with the broader value of these missions for the PLA, rather than their specific utility vis-à-vis counter-terrorism goals.[35] Nonetheless, the possibility of serious military missions of this nature was not even being seriously entertained a couple of years ago. The risks, and logistical challenges, are likely to continue to tip the balance against direct intervention but—in the right circumstances—it would be of a piece with a number of other associated developments in the PLA's out of area operations, such as the agreement to build the first Chinese overseas naval facility in Djibouti, the first non-combatant evacuation by PLA-Navy vessels in Yemen, the first deployment of a battalion of combat troops for peacekeeping in South Sudan, and the first confirmed kills by Chinese drones, with the Iraqi army's strikes on ISIS targets in Ramadi. There have been indications that Chinese law enforcement personnel have taken part in joint counter-terrorism operations in Afghanistan's Badakhshan province, though the PLA has denied its own involvement.[36] Chinese counter-terrorism training with Pakistani counterparts since CPEC was established has also opened the door to a more formal role for Chinese security personnel in the protection of projects.[37]

None of this adds up to a fully-articulated strategy to address the new threat environment, and there are evidently many questions in China about what future direction to take. But even these tentative steps are a move beyond the parameters that had guided Chinese counter-terrorism policy for much of the past two decades. Beijing's approach to counter-terrorism outside its borders has traditionally been limited, and risk-averse: Uyghur-centric, unwilling to address broader dynamics of militancy, and focused on ensuring that China remains a low-priority target for transnational jihadi groups. It now involves far greater geographical reach; a wider and more complicated list of partners; a more broad-based approach to addressing the conditions for militancy; and a more direct economic, diplomatic and security role for China, with all the risks that implies. These developments do open up the potential for forms of cooperation on counter-terrorism that have previously been highly constrained. While some inhibitions and disputes about 'double standards' will inevitably persist, there has already been progress in lifting China's sights beyond the narrow focus that traditionally prevailed in counter-terrorism exchanges to more comprehensive forms of coordination, most prominently in Afghanistan. The coming period provides scope to enlarge that further. The shift in the terrorist threat for China beyond its confines in South Asia poses an array of problems for Beijing, but also an opportunity to translate countering violent extremism into one of the main strands of cooperation with powers whose security competition with China is otherwise intensifying.

6

CHINA'S COUNTER-TERRORISM POLICY IN THE MIDDLE EAST

Mordechai Chaziza

This chapter analyzes China's counter-terrorism policy in the Middle East, and the linkage between the threats posed by terrorist groups at home and abroad. Specifically, this is an investigation of China's counter-terrorism policy in response to the growing threat of terrorism and the linkage between Uyghur terrorism in Xinjiang and the increase in Islamist terrorist attacks in the Middle East as it impacts upon China's national security. These terrorist activities and the connections between them show that terrorism and radicalization transcend boundaries and regions, threatening not only countries in the Middle East but also China's homeland security.

The rise in Islamist terror attacks in the Middle East and elsewhere (including Afghanistan and Pakistan) has become an increasing concern for the region and the international community. China, as one of the major investors in the region, is also threatened by these increasing terrorist threats and attacks. The country has become a target for many jihadi organizations, and is currently one of the top recruitment pools for ISIS and al-Qaeda. Like many other large powers and states, China is no longer immune from terrorist attacks and faces both external and internal terrorist threats that feed into each other.

In the post-Cold War era, China is increasingly engaged in the Middle East through broader national interests: namely, to continue its economic growth, preserve its political system ruled by a communist party, defend its sovereignty from foreign threat and other interferences into its internal affairs, and expand its global influence as a rising global economic and political power. Nevertheless, Beijing's engagement with the region has been driven primarily by a search for energy security and a desire to increase its overseas markets and investment opportunities.[1] The core of Chinese Middle East policy is to maintain a stable and peaceful regional environment that facilitates continued domestic reform and development. Consequently, China's counter-terrorism policy in the Middle East seeks to deal with jihadist activities and the threat of terrorism through economic development and aid, peaceful negotiation and conflict management, information exchange and conducting anti-terrorism drills rather than joining the ongoing global war on terror.[2]

Non-interference is a fundamental and generally uncompromising principle of China's foreign policy, though it evolves in accordance with the changes and challenges in the international and regional environment. Given its traditional stance of non-interference, Beijing has firmly resisted greater involvement in the ongoing conflicts by keeping a low and cautious profile, and prefers resolutions through peaceful negotiations. Specifically, China does not involve itself in the internal affairs of other countries, unless to do so is in its own national or economic interests.[3] Chinese leadership considers the Middle East the 'graveyard of great powers', and generally seeks to avoid becoming involved in the region's internal affairs or being perceived as aligning with particular countries or stakeholders.[4]

More importantly, China has gradually begun to play a greater and more diversified role in Middle East trade and investment. While during the Cold War Beijing had maintained economic relations with the Middle East countries, their significance was negligible. Since the end of the Cold War, however, China has had a tremendous economic impact on the Middle East, especially in the energy sector. According to *Xinhua*, over the past decade, China's economic ties with the Middle East increased from US$ 20 billion to $230 billion, and the figure is expected to top $600 billion by 2020.[5] Moreover, China's oil imports have increased dramatically, with the Middle East accounting for just under half of China's crude oil imports in 2016.[6] According to IEA

(International Energy Agency) estimates, the Middle East will provide about half of China's oil supply in 2040, while China will consume about a quarter of the region's oil exports.[7]

However, despite its improved economic growth, diplomatic capabilities and military power, China still shows a lack of desire to become more involved in the affairs of the region. During the Cold War, while on the one hand the complex situation in the region forced Beijing to adhere to non-interference principles, in parallel it aided and supported revolutionary movements of national liberation.[8] But since the end of the Cold War, the changes and challenges in the region have required it to take a more pragmatic approach.[9] At this point in time, Beijing has the capabilities to intervene, but it does not seem to have the appropriate desire. Despite the instability, conflicts and exposure to terrorist risks and attacks in the region, China's formal commitment to the non-intervention principle holds up—at least in its rhetoric—as a basic tenet of Chinese foreign policy.[10]

To date, China has managed to reject involvement in large multinational military coalitions or any military operations against jihadist terrorist organizations in Afghanistan or against the Islamic State. However, the expansion of Islamic terrorism and extremism in the Middle East poses a particularly grave threat to China's national security and a major threat to security and stability in the region.[11] Being a permanent member of the UN Security Council, and also having to manage the world's second largest economy as well as an increasingly powerful military, China is finding such a non-interference policy increasingly untenable.[12]

Meanwhile, China's expanding footprint in the region makes it more vulnerable to terrorism risks and attacks. Beijing is anxious to protect its financial investments overseas, to ensure the safety of Chinese nationals working there, and to secure its energy supply from the Middle East. The trade between China and the region has soared in recent years, rising some 600 per cent in the past decade. Chinese investment between 2005 and 2016 in the Middle East totalled more than $160 billion, while Beijing has also pledged an additional $55 billion in investment and loans to the region.[13]

Additionally, rapid economic growth and the search for energy security have led China to engage increasingly in other regions, including the Middle East. However, since the Middle East is the region most hotly contested by extremist jihadi organizations, this poses a direct threat to the security of Chinese energy investments and the safety of Chinese citizens. In the past decade, eighteen terrorist attacks caused the deaths of forty Chinese nationals living overseas (some of them in the Middle East).[14] Moreover, Chinese nationals, business holdings and military assets abroad have become more vulnerable to terrorist attacks, which in turn could precipitate Chinese nationalist responses at home.[15] For instance, Chinese citizens abroad have become targets for kidnapping and sabotage,[16] and approximately 128 million Chinese travel throughout the world to emigrate, for business opportunities, or for tourism.[17]

Hence, in the foreseeable future, it is likely that China will suffer an increasing number of terrorist attacks at home and abroad perpetrated by Uyghur extremists or by Islamist extremist organizations that assist each other. The terrorist attacks from the Middle East region have the potential to provoke the threat of domestic terrorism, especially from the Muslim Uyghur minority in Xinjiang province, where there are concerns about growing threats from terrorism, extremism and separatism (the 'three evil forces'). The next section presents the domestic terrorism threat in Xinjiang.

The domestic terrorism threat in China

Generally, terror attacks threaten China's core national interests, such as national sovereignty, territorial integrity, national security and unity, i.e. the stability of the society that provides a ground for sustainable economic and social development.[18] The terrorist attacks against China originate primarily from domestic sources, especially from the Xinjiang Uyghur Autonomous Region (XUAR), carried out by Uyghur Muslim ethnic separatists.

Xinjiang province, in the north-west of the country, is of crucial strategic and economic importance to Beijing's national interests. The region serves as a buffer zone against its neighbours, a source of natural resources, a new frontier, a regional springboard and a symbol of Chinese leverage in the region. First, Xinjiang extends China's borders to the Middle East and Central Asia, and acts as a buffer zone between the mainland and its western neighbours. Second, as the region is thinly populated, it protects Beijing from invasion from the Central Asian area by accommodating Chinese military manoeuvres and nuclear testing. More importantly, most of China's nuclear arsenal and strategic missile force are stockpiled here.[19]

Third, Xinjiang region also has vast natural resources (holding up to one-third of China's proven oil resources), and is a key geographic bridge for Beijing's overland pipelines as well as transport corridors for its energy supplies,[20] especially in the event that the US navy cuts off its maritime supply line over conflicts in the Western Pacific.[21] Xinjiang is home to 30 per cent of the country's oil and 40 per cent of the country's coal resources.[22] These natural resources are particularly important to China's energy security, and are essential for continued domestic reform and economic development, as well as key to avoiding future dependence on Middle East petroleum.

In addition, Xinjiang also serves as a regional springboard for Chinese influence. Beijing's position as a Central Asian power enhances its regional leverage, and through its leadership role in the Shanghai Cooperation Organization (SCO), China has strengthened its position vis-à-vis Russia. Moreover, Xinjiang's Muslim population provides China with cultural and ethnic connections to the Middle East, ties which Beijing has historically exploited for commercial and political gain. Finally, Beijing is concerned that if it allows Xinjiang independence, it would set a dangerous precedent for its national integrity. Other similarly situated territories (i.e. Taiwan and Tibet) would increase pressure for similar concessions.[23]

Last, security and social stability in Xinjiang province are very important for the Chinese 'Belt and Road Initiative' (BRI). In 2013, President Xi presented the BRI vision to 'forge closer economic ties, deepen cooperation, and expand development in the Euro-Asia region'.[24] The Chinese BRI is portrayed as an opportunity to reshape the economic and political order in Central Asia and the Asian Pacific region by promoting a network of trade routes, political cooperation and cultural exchange. China intends to place its Xinjiang province at the heart of its engagement with Central and South Asia in an effort to accelerate development and promote stability.[25] Thus, ensuring stability in Xinjiang is both a goal of and prerequisite for the success of Beijing's economic plan ambitions.

China's engagement and integration with Central and South Asia will support development and stability in Xinjiang, as well as prevent the deterioration of the security situation in the region. China sees accelerated development as the most promising cure for the current persistent discontent: by establishing Xinjiang as a gateway to a 'Eurasian Land Bridge' through Central Asia to Europe, Beijing hopes to alleviate one of the greatest terrorist threats to its domestic security.[26]

Since 1949, China's principal approach in Xinjiang had been a policing-oriented strategy that focused on achieving the territorial, political, economic and cultural integration of Xinjiang province and its twelve non-Han ethnic groups into the Chinese state.[27] This strategy was defined by tight political, social and cultural control (via Han Chinese domination of the regional government, regulation of religion and outright suppression of dissent), encouragement of Han Chinese settlement, and state-led economic modernization.[28] Yet China's goal to integrate Xinjiang and the Uyghur population as part of Hanification efforts (i.e. to Sinicize Xinjiang) only sowed mistrust and animosity between the Uyghurs and the Han settlers.

More recently, the Chinese government tried to ameliorate ethnic minority discontent and nurture social stability in the region by driving economic development through hefty investments in mega-projects, such as massive oil and natural gas pipelines and infrastructure developments linking Xinjiang with Central and South Asia.[29] Nevertheless, the Uyghur population identifies less with China and more with its Turkic ethnic and Muslim religious identities. The Uyghur people's origins are with the Turkish peoples, and they share close ethnic, cultural, linguistic, historical and religious ties. They have neither accepted Chinese occupation of their homeland nor their incorporation into the Chinese nation-state and maintain that they are a distinct ethnic group with its own history, geography, language, culture and tradition.[30]

In recent years, the Uyghur population has been seeking to migrate either legally or illegally from China.[31] The Xinjiang Uyghurs represent a wide range of preferences and objectives, ranging from cultural distinction to greater autonomy, either within China or independent of it, with a small minority favouring an Islamic state.[32] Similarly, only a limited segment of the Uyghur population in Xinjiang has participated in significant rebellions or independence movements that advocate violence and terrorist attacks to advance their goals.[33]

The main domestic terrorism threat that Beijing deals with comes from separatist groups belonging to the Turkic-Muslim ethnic minority, most of whom live in China's western Xinjiang province. The militant Uyghur separatists lay claim to a separate state (which they call East Turkestan) or at the least, extensive autonomous authority in Xinjiang province.[34] Notwithstanding, Xinjiang province has experienced periodic outbreaks of ethnic unrest and riots since the founding of the state, but it was only after the 11 September terrorist attacks that Beijing focused public attention on the East Turkestan Islamic Movement (ETIM) as a terrorist group having direct connections to al-Qaeda. According to a Chinese government report, the Uyghur terrorist group ETIM had been responsible for over 200 'terrorist attacks' between 1990 and 2001 that claimed the lives of 162 people and injured 440.[35] However, the number of incidents, deaths and injuries in terrorist attacks is, in fact, substantially lower than the report claims,[36] and there has been little concrete evidence that ETIM mounted successful attacks in Xinjiang during that time.[37]

In addition, another Xinjiang-based terror group, Turkestan Islamic Party (TIP), emerged as a successor organization to ETIM sometime between 2006 and 2008. Believed to consist of hundreds of militants based near Mir Ali in North Waziristan, it is allied with the Pakistani Taliban and the Islamic Movement of Uzbekistan (IMU), one of Central Asia's most resilient Islamist movements.[38] In recent years, there have been a growing number of terrorist attacks in Xinjiang, as well as a string of high-profile terrorist attacks in other major cities, including an attack on the railway station in Kunming and bombing attacks in the Xinjiang city of Urumqi.[39] TIP became more visible and active and raised its profile among al-Qaeda and other jihadi groups, using the internet to call for jihad against Chinese territory.[40]

Beijing's fight against militant terrorist groups in Xinjiang has forced the militant Uyghur separatists into volatile neighbouring countries, such as Pakistan and Afghanistan, where they are forging strategic alliances with, and even leading, jihadist factions affiliated with al-Qaeda and the Taliban.[41] According to Chinese sources, in the past al-Qaeda and the Taliban regime gave direct support to ETIM (i.e. financial and material aid), and the relationship between TIP and al-Qaeda has only grown closer since.[42] Some militant Uyghur separatists found their way to Turkey and onward to Syria to fight alongside Jabhat al-Nusra, until recently al-Qaeda's affiliate in Syria.[43] Beijing's major concern is that the cross-fertilization between jihadi groups leads to the diffusion of tactics and capabilities with potential to increase substantially the sophistication and lethality of terrorist attacks at home.

Moreover, the Uyghur problem is creating tension with the Muslim world about the infringement of religious rights and underprivileged ethnic status in China; Turkey is a case in point.[44] The terrorist attacks in Xinjiang are a major historic source of tension in Sino-Turkish relations, and any deterioration in the situation in Xinjiang has the potential for serious damage to the relations between the two countries.[45] This is because Turkish nationalists see themselves as sharing close ethnic, cultural, linguistic, historical and religious ties with the Uyghur population. Therefore, Turkish governments have offered refuge to Uyghur exiles and activists from Xinjiang, granting most of them Turkish citizenship and providing aid such as housing for their smooth integration into society.[46]

The Uyghur diaspora community in Turkey has also lobbied successive Turkish governments to offer asylum to fleeing activists and to allow Uyghurs to campaign from Turkish territory against Beijing's policies. This community is actively involved in publicizing China's harsh treatment in Xinjiang to the wider international community, and has become one of the most important actors shaping the development of Turkey–China bilateral relations.[47]

In July 2009, Prime Minister Recep Tayyip Erdoğan described the ethnic violence in China's Xinjiang region as 'a kind of genocide'. This caused a crisis in bilateral relations, angered the Chinese government, and turned public opinion in each country against the other.[48] Three years after the crisis, in April 2012, Prime Minister Erdoğan visited China, the first official visit of a Turkish prime minister to China in twenty-seven years. On his first stop, Erdoğan visited Urumqi, capital of China's Xinjiang, to show support and sympathy for the Uyghur people; however, he was careful not to antagonize his Chinese hosts by posturing as the protector of Xinjiang's Uyghurs. Since this visit, Turkey officially emphasizes its support and respect for China's sovereignty and territorial integrity, but still raises the thorny issue of human rights in Xinjiang province.[49]

Both governments try to downplay the dispute over the Uyghurs and highlight trade and infrastructure cooperation, but nonetheless the related conflicts have continued. For example, in July 2015 Turks and Uyghurs protested in the streets of Istanbul and Ankara after hearing that China was forcing Uyghurs in Xinjiang to eat during the Muslim fasting period of Ramadan, and allegedly killed some who resisted.[50] As a result, the Chinese government has issued travel warnings for its citizens travelling to Turkey, and several Chinese companies are freezing their investment projects in Turkey.[51]

China considers the Xinjiang problem part of its internal affairs, and is not likely to let any state, partner or international organization interfere in its minority issues.[52] At the same time, China needs intensive support and close cooperation from Ankara to counter terrorists in Xinjiang.[53] And because Turkey has significant impact on the Turkic and Islamic states in Central Asia, including Azerbaijan, Kazakhstan, Turkmenistan, Uzbekistan and Kyrgyzstan, any imprudent move by China in Xinjiang, if interpreted as anti-Turkic or anti-Islamic, might spark chain reactions in those countries and further complicate the issue.[54]

In summary, China fears that terrorist attacks in Xinjiang by militant Uyghur separatists will harm its continued economic growth and national territorial integrity, and undermine the legitimacy and survival of the Communist regime as well as its core bilateral relationships in the Middle East (i.e. Turkey, Saudi Arabia and Afghanistan). Their fear is that the militant

Uyghur separatists are forging strategic alliances with Islamic terror organizations in the Middle East and becoming increasingly violent and more extreme. This trend is especially troubling to authorities in Beijing, given that many Uyghurs have become jihadists and joined the terrorist groups fighting in Iraq and Syria. It is feared that upon their return to China, they will launch terrorist attacks in the country. The next section presents the external terrorist threats from the Islamist organizations in the Middle East that threaten Chinese national security.

The external terrorism threat in China

The expansion of Islamic terrorism and extremism in the Middle East poses a serious threat to Beijing's overseas interests there, negatively affecting China's economic and social development. Beijing's overseas interests in the Middle East include the security of Chinese citizens, and economic investment and energy supply, essential for long-term economic and social development.[55] Despite the threats, China's large economic footprint in the Middle East in commerce and investments continues to grow. For instance, Chinese investments and contracts in the region during 2005–16 were worth over $115 billion, and Beijing pledged investments and loans of $55 billion in the Middle East region.[56]

This growing presence has exposed China to significant Islamic terrorism and extremism threats. Since the mid-2000s, extremist jihadi organizations in the Middle East have begun to see China as a growing danger, partly because of the perceived US decline as well as China's support for local repressive regimes and its harsh policy against the Uyghur population in Xinjiang.[57] This demonstrates that Chinese assets in the Middle East are both a boon and a liability, and that there is potential for linkage between terrorist groups at home and abroad. This was articulated in 2014 by Wu Sike, China's special envoy to the Middle East, who said that China was a victim of terror whose roots are in the Middle East.[58]

The rise of the Islamic State of Iraq and al-Sham (ISIS), a terrorist group operating across the Middle East, especially in Iraq and Syria, has attracted the attention of the international community for causing insecurity and instability in the region.[59] Although China so far has not been a direct target of ISIS activities, the Islamic State poses potential threats to a wide range of China's national security interests.[60] The terrorist activities of transnational jihadi organizations in the Middle East and the spread into North Africa and Central Asia pose a potential serious challenge to China's national security at both domestic and international levels.

First and foremost, ISIS has openly declared its territorial ambition towards China's Xinjiang province, thus threatening Chinese territorial integrity, and has raised the level of tensions between local Uyghurs and Han people. In July 2014, Islamic State leader Abu Bakr al-Baghdadi condemned China's treatment of the Muslim Uyghur minority in Xinjiang province, asked Chinese Muslims to pledge allegiance to him, and threatened to occupy parts of Xinjiang which appeared on ISIS's caliphate map.[61] Al-Baghdadi also called for jihad against countries that 'seized Muslim rights', ranking China first. ISIS, like al-Qaeda, has become one of the few transnational jihadi organizations in the Middle East that has targeted China so explicitly.[62]

Second, after years in which the most significant Uyghur militant presence was concentrated in the borderlands of Afghanistan and Pakistan, they became jihadists and are now operating with international groups like al-Qaeda and ISIS in Syria and Iraq. The number of Uyghurs fighting with the Islamic State has risen sharply over the past years. Like other countries, Beijing is concerned that Chinese Muslim Uyghur militants who enlist with ISIS will receive training in terrorist techniques, acquire terrorist skills and expand their connections with transnational jihadi organizations.[63] According to the Iraqi Ministry of Defence, Iraqi forces captured what appeared to be a Chinese Uyghur citizen fighting in the ranks of ISIS,[64] and in Indonesia two ethnic Uyghurs were arrested on suspicion of ties to the Islamic State.[65]

Although the exact number of Muslim Uyghurs involved in fighting in the Islamic State remains difficult to determine, it appears to have grown significantly. The Chinese media, newspapers and a large number of websites report that Uyghur militants from Xinjiang were training with ISIS to acquire skills to carry out terrorist attacks at home.[66] According to an Israeli intelligence report, 3,000 Uyghurs are fighting in the ranks of Jabhat Fateh al-Sham, the al-Qaeda branch in Syria (formerly known as the al-Nusra Front), and several hundred fighters in ISIS.[67] However, Syrian and Chinese officials estimate the number of fighters to be around 5,000, most of them with the TIP fighters in northern Syria, who along with their families make about 20,000.[68]

Beijing is also concerned that Afghanistan has the potential to become the new base for the Islamic State,[69] due to the movement's aspirations to extend its self-declared caliphate into Xinjiang. According to Afghan officials, after being battered and beaten in Iraq and Syria, the ISIS terror group is surging fighters into Afghanistan (estimates of 3,000 foreign fighters), rebuilding their presence and perhaps setting up a new base for attacks. They also fear that those numbers are only likely to increase as ISIS fighters from Iraq and Syria leave those countries as part of an effort to regroup.[70]

CHINA'S COUNTER-TERRORISM POLICY IN THE MIDDLE EAST

China is well aware of the threat posed by Islamic jihadist terrorists to the lives of their citizens and financial investments in the Middle East. In recent years, Beijing was caught unprepared for the unexpectedly large presence of Chinese companies, tourists and workers engaged in infrastructure, energy and other projects in the region who found themselves in high-risk zones and conflict areas. For instance, the civil wars in Libya and in Yemen illustrate the emerging vulnerability of Chinese nationals and investments in the region. In both cases, China's navy evacuated Chinese citizens caught up in hostilities.[71]

Moreover, the extremist jihadi activities threaten Beijing's energy security, a primary objective of Chinese foreign policy in the Middle East.[72] The US Energy Information Administration (EIA) reported that China surpassed the US at the end of 2013 as the largest net oil importer and projected that in 2015 Beijing will account for more than one-fourth of the global growth in oil consumption. Beijing would become the world's largest oil consumer by the early 2030s, overtaking the US, and touch 15.5 million barrels per day in 2040.[73] Over the past decade, China's oil imports have increased dramatically, and the Middle East remains the largest source of its crude oil. According to BIMCO's (the Baltic and International Maritime Council) report, the Middle Eastern countries' share of Chinese crude oil imports has declined for three years in a row. China imported 55 per cent from the Middle East in 2015, but 45 per cent from the Middle East during the first ten months of 2017.[74]

For example, from 2005 to 2017 China's investments in Iraq totalled more than $18.5 billion. Beijing is emerging as the largest investor in the nascent Iraqi oil industry, and Chinese energy companies have invested some $16.5 billion there.[75] In 2016, almost half (48 per cent) of Chinese imported crude oil originated from the Middle East, and 9.1 per cent of Chinese imports of oil crude came from Iraq, which become China's fifth-largest oil supplier.[76] The two countries are interested in expanding their cooperation in the energy field, with more investment in exploration and development of oil and gas fields and the construction of infrastructure for storing and transporting energy resources.[77] However, China faces threats from the extremist jihadi activities that led to unrest in Iraq and jeopardized the security of Chinese energy projects and personnel in the country.[78]

More important, the rising Islamist terrorist attacks in the Middle East threaten to destabilize China's efforts at creating East–West linkages through its vision of BRI. The stability of the Middle East, an important link on the BRI, is crucial to the success of this economic initiative and the commerce cooperation between China and the region. Most of the countries in the

Middle East have security concerns and suffer from terrorist attacks that can have a gravely negative impact on the implementation of BRI and make the projects high-risk.[79]

For example, Beijing's desire to promote its vision to connect China with Europe through Central and Western Asia makes Turkey an important and irreplaceable partner in Chinese strategic and economic calculations. Yu Hongyang, the Chinese ambassador to Turkey, stated in April 2015 that Turkey as a major state located on the ancient Silk Road has already welcomed China's Belt and Road Initiative.[80] However, Ankara has suffered huge economic repercussions from its proximity to the Syrian conflict and as the target of attacks from terrorist organizations.[81]

In summary, the rising prominence of jihadi organizations and the frequency of terrorist attacks in the Middle East have exposed Chinese nationals and financial investments overseas to serious threats at home and abroad, which feed into each other. The deterioration of the situation in Xinjiang province might attract the attention of some Islamic terrorist organizations and encourage terrorist activity by the Uyghur Islamist group in Xinjiang or other parts of China. Without minimizing this threat, it seems that extremist jihadi organizations and their terrorist attacks in the Middle East will pose more of a threat to Chinese interests and oil investments overseas rather than in mainland China.

Chinese counter-terrorism policy in the Middle East

The terrorist attacks from the Middle East have the potential to fuel the threat of domestic terrorism, especially from the Muslim Uyghur minority in Xinjiang province. Since 2013, fifteen terrorist attacks in China were closely tied to Islamic terrorist organizations in the Middle East, including the terrorist attack in Kunming, the train station explosion in Urumqi, the Guangzhou railway station blood rampage, and more. These terrorist attacks were all planned and carried out under the direction of overseas Islamic jihadist groups.[82] Although Beijing is not a major target of the Islamic terrorist organizations led by al-Qaeda or ISIS, these terrorist groups have openly expressed their stand against China and posed threats to its national interests.[83]

Generally, Chinese counter-terrorism policy is multifaceted. First, China is against terrorism in all forms. Second, China will spare no effort to eradicate terrorism at the source. Third, China opposes attaching terrorism to any specific ethnic group or religion and is against 'double standards' in the global war on terror. Fourth, China insists that the United Nations and the Security

Council should play a leading role in the global war on terrorism, including military actions. Finally, the international community should adopt a multi-pronged approach, including political, security, economic, financial, intelligence and ideological aspects that target the roots of terrorism as well as its symptoms. It must follow a consistent standard in the global war on terrorism and come up with 'new thinking and new steps' in its response to terrorism.[84] In practice, Chinese counter-terrorism policy in the Middle East includes several measures in different areas: diplomatic, military, political, legislative and economic.

Diplomacy: China joined the global war on terror by participating in the UN counter-terrorism convention and supporting the UN Security Council's anti-terrorism resolutions. Beijing also constructed formal bilateral or multilateral diplomatic mechanisms with some Middle Eastern countries with a view to including counter-terrorism as an essential part of the effort to promote cooperation.[85] For instance, Egypt, Saudi Arabia and Turkey have upgraded their common multilateral or bilateral cooperative relations with China to a strategic cooperative partnership.[86]

Military: China exchanges its information and experience with other countries in the Middle East by joining informal mechanisms, such as anti-terrorism conferences, forums and high-level meetings. Cooperation includes information exchange, economic aid, personnel training, repatriation of Chinese terrorists and jointly conducted anti-terrorism drills.[87] For instance, in October 2016 Special Forces from China and Saudi Arabia held their first joint anti-terrorism combat skills and tactic drills in China.[88]

There is growing evidence that Chinese forces were patrolling in Afghanistan's Little Pamir region, near the Chinese border. To date, China has strongly denied reports that its military is conducting patrols within Afghanistan, but has conceded that 'joint counter-terrorism operations' with Afghan authorities are underway.[89] China is concerned about Uyghur militants who remain active in the region and have professed support for the Islamic State. China has also contributed some funding and combat equipment for the Afghan security forces.[90]

Political: Beijing's counter-terrorism policy in the Middle East is oriented to deal with each case using different measures and policies tailored to specific characteristics. Some examples are Beijing's attempt to mediate between the Afghan government and the Taliban to help secure peace and political reconciliation in Afghanistan,[91] or its hosting of representatives of both the Syrian government and opposition forces as part of its efforts to promote peace talks and the political settlement,[92] as well as influencing Pakistan to refuse to take part in the Saudi campaign against the Houthi rebels in the Yemen civil conflict.[93]

Legislation: In December 2015, the Standing Committee of the National People's Congress passed a new counter-terrorism law that, among other provisions, allows China's armed forces to engage in counter-terrorist missions abroad. The scope of these missions is not precisely defined, to enable maximum flexibility during future crises. Although Beijing has until now shown neither the inclination nor the ability to conduct anti-terrorism operations overseas, this law laid the groundwork for China's armed forces to take part in such operations, thus legalizing China's military actions on behalf of its own citizens and interests in the Middle East.[94]

Economic: China has sought to cultivate cordial relations with all governments and some jihadi groups (i.e. Hamas, the Taliban) through economic development and aid.[95] In January 2016, the Chinese government issued its first Arab Policy Paper,[96] which stopped short of spelling out clearly Chinese strategic interests or intentions in the region. It states Beijing's overall vision for regional relations, but without getting into the complexities of how that vision will be realized, and not adding much to what is already known about China's Middle East foreign policy. The paper reiterates the long-standing principle of non-interference, and emphasizes that Beijing's interactions with the Middle East are largely limited to the economic sphere.[97]

But some foreign media reflected voices in public that called for Beijing to become more involved in fighting the Islamic jihadist terrorists by directly dispatching troops to the Middle East.[98] Nevertheless, China has traditionally refused to interfere with the internal affairs of sovereign states, a foreign policy principle pointedly directed at warning other powers to stay out of Beijing's domestic matters. Hence, China can only share limited participation in counter-terrorism efforts in the Middle East, since it is greatly restrained by a number of factors.

First and foremost, China has a traditional non-interventionist foreign policy and is unlikely to lend active support or participation to multilateral military operations against Islamic jihadist terrorists in the Middle East. At most, Beijing will provide quiet diplomatic support and insist that the military operation take place under UN auspices. The Chinese government is reluctant to become heavily involved in military actions against terrorist organizations in the region, or anywhere else.[99] Second, the divergence between China and its neighbour countries on how to fight against the 'three evil forces' (separatism, religious extremism and terrorism) is another restraining factor. The Middle East is the distribution centre for jihadist terrorist organizations, and many countries there, like Turkey or Afghanistan in particular, readily offer shelter to forces such as key members of ETIM or TIP.[100]

Third, the Western countries are the dominant players in the multilateral military operations against the Islamic jihadist terrorists in the Middle East, but due to diverse opinions on counter-terrorism, these countries adopt entirely different tactics and policy from China. For example, the Obama administration was critical of Beijing's reluctance to get involved in international security issues, given its expanding global interests. Former US President Obama accused China of being a 'free rider for the past thirty years', not doing enough in terms of its responsibility for international security, while importing oil and other resources from places like Iraq.[101]

Fourth, the serious disagreements on terrorism among Middle Eastern countries prevent China from participating in or supporting the military operations against the Islamic terrorists in the region. For example, in the Yemeni civil war, Beijing has been neutral over the Saudi military action against the Houthi rebels (supported by Iran) and avoided antagonizing any of the parties.[102] The Arab countries, Iran, Israel and others are apparently divided on the issue of identifying terrorism, because of the complexity of Middle East core issues, and national, ethnic and religious interests.[103]

Finally, Beijing has traditionally strongly opposed the US approach of using anti-terror operations in the Middle East as an excuse to intervene to serve its own interests. China suspects that efforts by Washington to encourage it to enter into a military campaign against the jihadist terrorist organizations are motivated by a desire to contain China's global ambitions, weaken its military and economic power, and undermine the Communist regime.[104] Moreover, the Chinese government was annoyed and disappointed with the Obama administration's criticism of Beijing's hardline response to ethnic unrest among Muslim Uyghurs in Xinjiang.[105]

In sum, the recent focus of jihadist terrorist organizations on Chinese investments and interests in the Middle East, besides being a threat to China's homeland security, spotlights the questionable sustainability of Beijing's counter-terrorism policy in the region. Nevertheless, for now China is sticking to its policy of non-interference, keeping a low profile and opting to resolve conflict through peaceful negotiations; it seems unlikely to change its stance or participate in any multilateral military operations against jihadist terrorist organizations in the region.

Conclusion

The ethnic minorities issue has been a significant factor in China's foreign relations throughout its history. Since the end of the Cold War in particular, Beijing's stance on the Muslim Uyghur minority in Xinjiang province has been an important pillar in its domestic stability and in shaping its relations with Central Asia.[106] However, in the Middle East, Chinese foreign policy rests on two objectives: promoting economic ties to ensure energy security and a commitment to its policy of non-interference.

Of course, this could change, especially if Islamic jihadist groups such as al-Qaeda and ISIS pose immediate, direct threats to Chinese homeland security. As complexities continue and terrorist attacks increase, Beijing may be forced to re-evaluate its counter-terrorism policy and realize that although it refuses to interfere with the internal affairs of sovereign states, inaction may only exacerbate the problem. Most importantly, Beijing can benefit from gradually changing its counter-terrorism policy, as its overseas interests continue to expand. China's active participation in multilateral military operations against the Islamic terrorist organizations in the Middle East is a positive response to the menace that terrorism poses to its national core interests and domestic security, including a strategic choice to carry out its 'Belt and Road Initiative', as well as a way to shoulder its international responsibility and improve its image.

7

UYGHUR TERRORISM IN A FRACTURED MIDDLE EAST

Raffaello Pantucci[1]

What is the relationship between Uyghur terrorism and the current troubles in the Middle East? The aim of this chapter is to explore this question and attempt to define the impact of Middle Eastern jihadist terrorism on Uyghur terrorism. It will look in particular at what is going on at the moment in Syria and Iraq; it will try to understand the nature of the groups that are there; and, where possible, what activities they appear to be involved in. There are three sections to this chapter: first, a historical study of the links between Middle Eastern jihadis and Uyghurs; second, an investigation of the links between Uyghur extremists and the current conflict in Syria; and finally, some conclusions on how this might all impact on China's future policies.

Uyghur jihadists and al-Qaeda

First, a short history of Uyghur jihadism in the Middle Eastern context will provide useful background. It will be brief because the activity has been fairly limited. Some individuals were indeed involved in Middle Eastern jihadi communities in Afghanistan, but they were never well integrated or prominent. Rather, Uyghur extremists have tended to operate on the fringes of Middle Eastern jihadist groups, and these groups often distance themselves from the Uyghur struggle.[2] More recently this pattern has started to change, but for the most part Uyghur extremists have remained on the fringes of the global jihadist movement.

During the period when the Taliban ruled Afghanistan, a number of Uyghurs moved there and used it as a base to train and plan for incidents back home, or to fight alongside the Taliban. Various reports from jihadist or Taliban leaders at the time indicate that the Chinese Muslims in Afghanistan had pledged allegiance to Mullah Omar and adhered to his ruling that they not use Afghanistan as a base to attack China. At the time, the Taliban were pursuing a relationship with China and did not want to antagonize them.[3] In an interesting contrast, which might help explain why Uyghurs still went to Afghanistan during this period, Jalaluddin Haqqani, the leader of the eponymous Haqqani network, rather championed the Uyghur cause in the early 1990s, boasting of his hosting of Uyghurs at his training camps in the country.[4]

Osama bin Laden and al-Qaeda instead took a different approach to the group. In some narratives bin Laden spoke of China as a power that they could even consider aligning with, since al-Qaeda's focus was almost single-mindedly against the United States and the apostate regimes of the Middle East that they hated, which could possibly correlate with China's position. In a 1999 interview in the Pakistani press, bin Laden said:

> I often hear about Chinese Muslims, but since we have no direct connection with people in China and no member of our organization comes from China, I don't have any detailed knowledge about them. The Chinese government is not fully aware of the intentions of the United States and Israel. These two countries also want to usurp the resources of China ... So I suggest the Chinese government be more careful of the U.S. and the West.[5]

In fact, al-Qaeda's links to China during this period were more focused on using China as a base from which to operate on the internet or to raise money through trading. Al-Qaeda-linked individuals travelled in and out of China, mostly through Guangzhou, transiting to other places or setting down roots to make money in the nascent Chinese boom period. In February 2000, an Egyptian businessman called Sami Ali bought server space and established a website called http://www.maalemaljihad.com (Milestones of Holy War).[6] Ali's relationship with jihadists was not clear, but individuals close to Egyptian

Islamic Jihad (EIJ) were linked to Chinese bank accounts to which he was linked as well. The website established a sister site in Karachi, and the two became a key place for jihadist preachers and ideologues to spread their ideas and ideology in Arabic. The British-based Abu Qatada would publish his speeches through the site, though it was not clear who was ultimately posting the material or where they were based.[7] However, there is little evidence during this period that the various Middle Eastern jihadist groups expressed much interest in what was actually going on in Xinjiang. Certainly, Arabs travelling around the region would have stood out, and the more internationally-minded members of al-Qaeda would not need to travel through the region to get into China.

In the wake of the 11 September 2001 attacks on the United States, there was very little change in the relationship between al-Qaeda and the Uyghurs. Some Uyghurs in Afghanistan then migrated to Pakistan in the wake of the retreat of the Taliban and al-Qaeda from the American military. Abdul Haq al Turkistani in particular appears to have gained considerable trust from al-Qaeda and was a member of the organization's shura committee.[8] At this point we see that the group appears to have been accepted into al-Qaeda's *ummah* (community) of organizations. Under the title of the Turkestan Islamic Party (TIP), it threatened China and the Beijing Olympics in 2008.[9] And whilst there was some evidence of the broader network of Uyghur extremists talking through al-Qaeda-linked networks about planning such attacks,[10] not much actually happened, nor does al-Qaeda seem to have got involved in launching attacks against Chinese interests.

Whilst these first videos from TIP were fairly amateurish, future videos released by the group were issued by the formally al-Qaeda-linked al Fajr media centre. But in the wake of the July 2009 riots in Xinjiang, and the global attention that was suddenly drawn to the plight of the Uyghurs in China, there was clearer and more public evidence of al-Qaeda adopting the Uyghur cause.[11] Senior al-Qaeda ideologue Abu Yahya al Libi spoke publicly about the plight of the Uyghurs, but he was not very clear about whether al-Qaeda and its affiliates should target China.[12] Soon afterwards the group's affiliate in the Maghreb made similar threats, and in many ways this set a pattern for jihadi groups to link themselves to the Uyghur cause.[13] Somalia's al Shabaab put out a video in late 2013 in which they aligned themselves with the cause, and one of the few al-Qaeda ideologues left, Abu Zaid al Kuwaiti, had a posthumous video released in May 2013 (he had died in December 2012) in which he gave advice to the Uyghur cause.[14]

But once again, there was fairly limited evidence of this translating into practical activity directed against China. Whilst at this stage, in contrast to Osama bin Laden's earlier statements, al-Qaeda seems to have designated China as an enemy, this remained a secondary focus, with the group continuing to target almost single-mindedly the West and/or its Middle Eastern allies. Even in the wake of the rioting in Xinjiang in 2009, which sharpened global attention towards the plight of the Uyghurs and brought them more clearly into the pantheon of the global jihadist movement, led by al-Qaeda, there was still little evidence of a strategic effort to support their cause.

Uyghur terrorist plots linked to al-Qaeda

However, there is certainly some evidence of Uyghur presence behind terrorist activity in the Middle East. On 29 June 2010, a court in Dubai found two ethnic Uyghurs guilty of plotting to attack a shopping mall called the Dragon Mart, which consisted of 400 shops selling Chinese-made goods. The pair were hapless Uyghurs whose culpability was questionable, to the point where the judge imposed a lesser sentence because the plotting was still in its 'preliminary stages'.

According to court documents, the ringleader Mayma Ytiming Shalmo, 35, was first recruited by ETIM in Mecca in 2006. While in Saudi Arabia, possibly on Hajj, Shalmo met a man he identified as a deputy leader of ETIM (but who remained nameless in court documents), with whom he discussed the 'premise of jihad in China'. Having agreed that he was interested in doing something for the Uyghur cause, Shalmo reported travelling with the deputy leader to Pakistan's Waziristan region, where he was trained in weapons and how to manufacture explosives from easily available materials. He was then introduced to ETIM's electronics expert, who taught him how to make detonators. Shalmo claims to have spent a year at the mujahideen camps in Pakistan.

After his year of training, Shalmo was given orders from the head of ETIM, relayed through the deputy, to target the Dragon Mart mall in Dubai. He flew from Islamabad to Dubai on 28 July 2007 and spent the autumn in Dubai, twice visiting the mall on what were presumed in court documents to be scouting missions. He then left the country and went back to Saudi Arabia before re-entering the UAE on 22 December 2007 by bus. At this point, his co-conspirator, Wimiyar Ging Kimili, 31, also an ethnic Uyghur, entered the picture, giving Shalmo a place to live on his return to Dubai. At some point during this period, the men entered into discussions about China and jihad, and Kimili agreed to help Shalmo in his operation.

From a practical perspective, Kimili's assistance appears to have been essential. Shalmo apparently spoke neither Arabic nor English, and thus would have been completely reliant on Kimili to go with him to purchase the necessary materials from pharmacies and paint supply shops. When police captured the men, they had in their possession alcohol, potassium permanganate, aluminum, chloride acid, nitric acid, hydrochloric acid, sulphur, acetone and other 'tools to be used in the preparation of explosives'. By June 2008 local authorities started to focus intensively on them, and in July they arrested both. They were quickly convicted and given ten years in prison, in contrast to the usual punishment in Dubai for terrorism which was death. The judge's justification was that the plot was in its 'preliminary stages' and therefore did not warrant the death penalty.[15] An odd plot in many ways, the key aspect for this discussion is that there was little evidence that it was undertaken with any support from al-Qaeda or any other group.

A final plot to mention in this context occurred in July 2010, when police in Oslo disrupted a cell that was part of a broader network of terrorist plots directed by al-Qaeda targeting the north of England and New York.[16] Linked by a common email account in Pakistan, which was sending out orders on behalf of al-Qaeda leader Saleh al Somali, the actual aim and scale of the plot were unclear.[17] In the run-up to arrests, police in Norway noted that the group's activity had declined substantially, and it is possible that the decision to arrest them was driven by an American revelation the day before formally linking the American and British plots and the particular email account. Three men were arrested: Mikael Davud, a 39-year-old ethnic Uyghur with Norwegian citizenship; David Jakobsen, a 31-year-old Uzbek with legal residency in Norway; then German police arrested a third man, Shawan Sadek Saeed Bujak, a 37-year-old Iraqi-Kurd who was on holiday in Duisburg, Germany.[18]

The key figure in the Norwegian plot, Mikael Davud, was apparently in Waziristan at the same time as Najibullah Zazi, the mastermind behind the New York plot to strike at the city's subway system, although it is unclear whether he trained at the same camp. Officials in Norway believe the men were linked to the Turkestan Islamic Party (TIP), with most of these links going through Davud. Reportedly, TIP commander Seyfullah called Davud's phone number in September 2008. Furthermore, Davud was in possession of a passport photograph of missing British extremist Ibrahim Adam (brother of convicted Operation Crevice plotter Anthony Garcia),[19] which Davud claimed he had received from an acquaintance in Turkey in 2009. The connections between the terrorist group and the other two are however confused by the fact that the Uzbek suspect, David Jakobsen, had worked as an informant since November 2009. Jakobsen claimed that he had contacted the police after he realized what he was involved in, and had weekly meetings with them since first providing them with information. Police doubted his word, citing for instance how he had failed to inform them that he had purchased hydrogen peroxide for the purpose of the plot.[20]

This case is more convincing of a link between al-Qaeda and Uyghur jihadis. It appears that al-Qaeda was potentially trying to use this connection to launch a plot in Oslo. The cell were at least trusted enough to be taken into their confidence, though it is unclear how deep or constant this connection was. Part of the difficulty for the Norwegian research was the lengthy periods when the group was not undertaking any activity towards a plot. It is not clear how effective or active the cell was, but it is worth noting the possession of the passport photo, which demonstrated an attempt to use this network to source false documentation to support existing terrorist networks. But whether the plot was to launch an attack on behalf of the Uyghur cause is unclear. Whilst Davud subsequently spoke about planning to attack the Chinese Embassy, and his anger at the Chinese, there was little evidence of preparation in this direction.[21] Instead there was vague evidence of planning an attack against energy installations in Norway.

The key point to draw from these plots is that, despite a clear link between al-Qaeda and broader Uyghur networks linked to ETIM or TIP, there is little evidence of al-Qaeda mobilizing its forces to launch attacks against China through these networks. Instead, at best, there is some evidence that al-Qaeda (through the Norwegian network) saw an opportunity to steer a TIP-linked network to launch an attack on its behalf. Any interest in the Uyghur cause is entirely absent. Similarly, there is little evidence of Uyghur extremists being brought into the mainstream of jihadist groups or narratives through these two plots, though it is worth remembering that Abdul Haq al Turkistani was leader of the group during this period and had close links to al-Qaeda. After he was injured in a drone strike in February 2010, his successor Abdul Shakoor al Turkistani was appointed by al-Qaeda as their leader in Pakistan's tribal areas, showing that Uyghurs were rising into mainstream roles within the organization. But this did not appear to change China's impression of threats from al-Qaeda.[22]

Syria and Iraq

There is some continuity from these individual connections to the current links we see between the international jihadist movement and the Uyghur cause.

Specifically, the group that used to be referred to as ETIM, which is now known as TIP, has reformed substantially on the battlefield in Syria and Iraq, as well as in parts of Afghanistan. These networks have shown a close connection to al-Qaeda-affiliated groups, whilst a few Uyghurs have also identified with the Islamic State of Iraq and Syria (ISIS or Daesh) group. The links between Uyghur jihadis and the main conflicts in the Middle East in Syria and Iraq have been manifest for some time and continue to develop dynamically. There is evidence that Uyghurs have played an active role in fighting and are becoming a more widely accepted and prominent part of the broader jihadist community.

Their participation in the conflict is to some degree simply a reflection of the fact that Sunni Muslims from over 86 countries in 2016—from places as diverse as Australia, Latin America, across the Middle East and Asia—have been drawn to the battlefield.[23] Consequently, it is no surprise that Muslims from China are being drawn in. What is less clear, however, is how much these groups in Syria and Iraq are intent on the Uyghur cause, rather than simply participating in the global jihadist movement. There is some evidence that the Uyghurs involved in the current conflict see this as preparation for a greater struggle against China; but we cannot be sure whether any of the other groups on the ground see a conflict with China as part of their broader goals.

To understand the link between Uyghur extremism and the current conflict in the Levant, three elements stand out: the link to ISIS, the link to other jihadist groups in Syria, and the relationship with Turkey. These three aspects serve as useful lenses through which to analyse Uyghur involvement in Syria and Iraq, and should help reveal how the relationship between Uyghurs and Middle Eastern jihadism has been transformed in the sands of the Levant.

The link to ISIS is frequently questioned. Both Chinese and official sources differ on the numbers concerned, so the link may be rather overstated. But hard data do exist. Some ISIS entry forms have been leaked over the past year, showing that many individuals self-identify as 'East Turkestani' with substantial links to China—through their phone numbers, addresses or other details on the forms. In addition, ISIS has released a few videos specifically addressed to Uyghurs, either in their own language or using Uyghur members of the group to describe their involvement with the purpose of attracting others.

Two reports have been published which detail this information, whilst the author has had access to some other forms. The two public reports, by Nate Rosenblatt for the New America Foundation and Brian Dodwell, Daniel Milton and Don Rassler for the Combating Terrorism Center (CTC) at West Point, both draw on the same data source but with different numbers.[24] The author has further access to the same data, and a third source as well. In other words, the three sources appear to have received different quantitative information, including varying numbers of Uyghurs. The ultimate source of the data appears to be a leak from within ISIS that resurfaces in these different reports. The following paragraphs summarize their key findings and augments these with the author's analysis of a slightly different cluster of ISIS documents.

The New America Foundation report by Rosenblatt identifies 118 individuals from China, of whom 114 were identifiable as specifically from Xinjiang. Of this group, very few were identified as having previous employment: only two reported having a professional job and over 70 per cent had never left China before. Many were married with families, but there was a huge disparity in the age range: from ten to eighty years old. None claimed to have fought jihad previously, and 73 per cent appeared to have joined the group after it took Mosul (the entire dataset covers a period from mid-2013 to mid-2014).[25]

The CTC report instead identifies 138 individuals who were Chinese on the basis of their citizenship response, but 167 on the basis of their residence response.[26] Six individuals are identified as having 'advanced' knowledge of Shariah.[27] The numbers of unemployed seem much lower than those in the Rosenblatt data: between just under 10 per cent and 17 per cent unemployed, with the disparity arising from the fact that not all report on their employment status, sometimes leaving it blank.[28] On age, in contrast to the Rosenblatt report, CTC identifies a 76-year-old Kyrgyzstani as the oldest recruit. Of the 167 CTC numbers, twenty-five identified themselves as willing to be suicide bombers (a relatively high proportion compared to the rest of the overall dataset, in which answers broken down by community varied from 0 to 26.7 per cent, with the Middle East being the source of most of the higher proportions). Finally, seven were identified in exit forms as wanting to leave ISIS territory at some point.[29]

The author's analysis now includes a third cut from a slightly different cluster of ISIS documents, which are likely to come from the same root source. These documents identify 28 individuals in total as having some connection with China, and come in three different formats: entry forms for individuals joining ISIS (nine); exit forms for individuals leaving ISIS to go outside for one reason or another (one); and some Excel sheets which appear to show graduation from training camps (the rest). The Chinese are identified either by describing themselves as 'Turkestani' or as having an address or phone number linked to China. There are believed to be more Uyghur forms amongst this third dataset, but access to the data is somewhat complicated.

In this third dataset, the 28 males had an average age of 24.3, with the oldest being 43 and youngest 16. Seventeen were married, with many saying they had several children. At least one exit form showed an individual who was leaving the country to bring his family to join him from Turkey. Almost all of them came in clusters—as indicated by the dates of entry or the fact that they all seemed to know the same recommender (which was typical of the larger dataset as well, where it was clear that individual recommenders would recruit a cluster of contacts).

The recruits appeared to have a wide range of different former jobs, including a footballer, accountant, mobile phone repairer, road paver, driver, student, trader, sports teacher and surgeon. One claimed to have spent four years in prison previously. One—not the convict—admitted to having 'previously fought jihad in East Turkestan'. None identified as wanting to become suicide bombers, but all declared wanting to become fighters or to train as fighters. A cluster of three (including the footballer) admitted to having previously fought with TIP; and whilst they all had the same 'recommender' into ISIS, they did not seem to have changed sides at the same date: one made the change before the group declared the Caliphate, another just after, and the third didn't specify when.

For the most part, all identified their religious knowledge as fairly limited, though at least one was a *hafiz al koran* (one who had memorized the entire Quran), and a few others admitted to having some depth of religious understanding. One of the most interesting details is their travel patterns, although it is not always clear what the travel question was really asking. On some forms, responders identify their entire life's history of travel, whilst on others it is clear that they are providing a summary of the route they took to Syria. For example, the footballer identifies as having been through Italy–UAE–Russia and Malaysia; whilst another identifies as having been through Laos–Vietnam–Thailand–Malaysia–Turkey. The largest group is ten individuals who went through Malaysia (with nine specifically identifying Kuala Lumpur) to Turkey. One individual lists having left China via Vietnam, then transiting through Thailand and Malaysia before going to Sri Lanka, where he was arrested by authorities. Very few provide any details of next of kin or other points of contact: for example, only four provide telephone numbers for others who could be contacted. In one instance, a camp training form has a special note from an individual who 'does not want to communicate with his parents because the Chinese will take them'. This is interesting in showing the low level of trust that these individuals have for the organization that they are going to fight for, and potentially die for, and its internal security.

At no point in the documents is there evidence of these individuals expressing a desire to launch attacks against China, or of the group having much interest in attacking China. In some ways the most interesting fact is that so many previously had employment and that they used routes through South East Asia to travel to Syria and Iraq. This route for the jihadis reflects a broader trend of Uyghurs fleeing China through South East Asia. In some cases they became involved in local jihadist networks en route, or were deliberately aiming for Syria and Iraq.[30] In other cases the groups seem to be simply migrants fleeing crackdowns in China. A large group was caught in Thailand,[31] while others were shot trying to cross the border into Vietnam.[32] The ISIS dataset shows that during this period when large numbers of Uyghurs appear to have been leaving China through South East Asia, at least some were intending to join the fighting in Syria and Iraq.

The dates when the ISIS dataset shows the Uyghurs to have joined the group are fairly scattered between March and July 2014: i.e. both before and after the taking of Mosul and the declaration of the Caliphate.[33] There is no clear reason why those who left TIP to join ISIS made the shift, though it could be because they all shared a recommender.

One intriguing aspect of the ISIS–Uyghur connection is how little it has emerged in public. Unlike many of the other nationalities that flocked to join ISIS, Uyghurs have not been prominently mentioned: to date only one *nasheed* has been released in Uyghur[34] and two videos.[35] Narratives of prominent Uyghur fighters have also been largely absent. However, indicating the random choice of language for ISIS broadcasts, one *nasheed* has been released in Mandarin.[36] There have been some reports of Uyghurs being executed for trying to leave the group, and there have been reports of Baghdadi mentioning China in his speeches.[37] Most notably, in his Ramadan message of July 2014, he highlighted China as a place where 'Muslims' rights are forcibly seized' and how Muslims in 'East Turkestan' were subjected to 'extreme torture and degradation'.[38] The Chinese press made some protests about the announcement, including references on the cover of the weekly magazine, *Phoenix Weekly*.[39] But the reality was that China was one of a number of locations where Muslims were suffering, and so ISIS treated its Uyghur contingent as simply another of the many different groups of Sunnis who had come to Syria to join up and fight for its self-declared state.

In many ways, the bigger story about Uyghurs and Syria comes from the Turkestan Islamic Party (TIP), which has effectively moved from its old haunt in Pakistan to northern Syria. The degree to which this group has moved towards the Levant is reflected in how it now attributes many of its videos to 'Hizb al Islami al Turkistani in Bilad al Sham', taking its old name and adding 'in the Land of the Levant', thus creating the acronym TIPL (Turkestan Islamic Party in the Levant) for the group's units in Syria. The numbers involved cannot be exact, but a few hundred are believed to be fighting with the group.[40] Some estimates put the number far higher, with Rami Abdurrahman, the head of the independent, British-based Syrian Observatory for Human Rights, estimating about 5,000 Chinese fighters to be in Syria, the majority of whom are fighting alongside TIP.[41] Chinese observers position themselves somewhere between these numbers, with no official figures for those identifying as TIPL or TIP as opposed to ISIS. TIPL's operating location tends to be in the north around Idlib, fighting alongside the jihadi Salafi groups of Jabhat al Nasrah, Hayat-Tahrir al Sham, Ahrar al Sham and the Jaysh al Fath umbrella organization, but it has also shown up in fighting elsewhere around the country.[42] TIPL was involved in breaking the Aleppo siege, releasing a video near the beginning of the assault trumpeting their successes, and in July 2016 it released another video showing them fighting in Latakia.[43] In March 2017 they announced their involvement in the fighting in Hama.[44] The degree to which they are integrated with broader groups is unclear, but not too significant since they tend to fight quite noticeably and regularly alongside the same groups; this suggests a definite preference though not a formal one. But their commitment to the fight is evident from their having deployed at least thirteen suicide bombers in attacks around Syria since May 2014.[45]

There has also been a growing internationalization of TIPL, reflecting its growing prominence amongst the jihadist community in Syria and potentially further afield. It has now released videos highlighting French fighters who have fallen alongside them in Syria, created a French Telegram channel which broadcasts under the name 'Le Parti Islamique Turkistanais', released videos in Russian and Kyrgyz, *nasheeds* in Kazakh and no doubt more.[46] Reflecting the further potential fragmentation and growth of Uyghur groups in Syria, there is now a further group with Uyghur affiliations fighting in Syria, called Katibat al-Ghuraba' al-Turkistaniyyah (KGT). This group emerged in 2017, with its Twitter account opening in February 2017, when it posted a series of pictures of Uyghurs in Xinjiang under Chinese rule; one of its current Telegram accounts opened in August 2017, with a statement of loyalty to al-Qaeda leader Ayman al Zawahiri; then in January 2018 they announced a Palestinian sub-unit.[47] The strength of KGT is unclear, as is its affiliation with TIPL or other groups, but it seems to act in a manner similar to TIPL in that it fights alongside the Salafi-jihadi groups around the country.[48]

The degree to which TIP/TIPL has been embraced by al-Qaeda is made clearer in a 2016 video released by al-Qaeda leader Ayman al Zawahiri as part of his 'Islamic Spring' series of videos. The recorded speeches are delivered over a montage highlighting the unity of the groups that al-Qaeda sees itself leading in the fight against the West. In the particular video which champions the Uyghur cause (it emerged in July 2016 but was likely produced before) we see Zawahiri praising Hassan Mahsum (a founding leader of the organization who had benefited from shelter in Afghanistan when establishing the group) as one of the great leaders of jihad. He compares him with Abdullah Azzam, Osama bin Laden and Abu Musab al Zarqawi, the highest pantheon of jihadist leaders. Zawahiri states that 'East Turkestani' warriors fought alongside al-Qaeda in Tora Bora and were active members of the community of jihadis fighting in Afghanistan. As he puts it, Afghanistan's 'mountains and valleys' know well the 'mujahideen from East Turkistan'. He also talks at some length about the group's activity in Syria, whilst also highlighting how the people of 'East Turkestan' need to rise up against the Chinese. Whilst there is no specific threat of attack to China, this element is fairly implicit. The conclusion of this video embraces the group within the al-Qaeda *ummah*, which is not surprising, but is interesting within the context of its relative novelty—and is in stark contrast to bin Laden's pre-9/11 interview with the Pakistani press.[49]

Probably the most significant data source for TIPL in Syria is the large number of statements, videos and audio clips that the group issues from the battlefield. They are well produced, often with English and Arabic subtitles, and show the group performing much of the classic jihadi activity on a battlefield. They release videos showcasing their role in various operations, including footage of fighters who have been used as suicide bombers. There are videos of fighters using large items of military hardware (showing that they are well equipped), training and marching under banners; children being trained; people cooking; and declamations to camera about how others should come and join them. Interestingly, there is surprisingly little direct threat to China in most of the videos (with some notable exceptions). Rather, many of them could be seen as recruitment instruments, juxtaposing the misery and oppression that Uyghurs face in China with the heroic deeds of TIP on the battlefields of Syria. In addition to highlighting the plight of Uyghurs in China, most of the TIP, TIPL and KGT multimedia output features al-Qaeda-linked imagery and praises their leaders, in a reflection of the outreach that the groups make towards al-Qaeda and their allegiance.

The other consistent element throughout their material is interestingly their anger at ISIS. To provide some examples: TIPL released a statement in

July 2016 deriding the group's supposed links to an attack on the holy shrine in Medina, Saudi Arabia; and in May 2016 an audio message with a video montage purported to be by leader Abdul Haq.[50] In the message he repeatedly attacks ISIS and its leader Abu Bakr al Baghdadi, as well as expressing his displeasure at the Islamic Movement of Uzbekistan (IMU) and its leader, who had pledged allegiance to ISIS. In the video he more explicitly calls for people to attack China, but he prioritizes the conflict in Syria as a context for people to come and train to prepare for the eventual conflict back in China. The allegiance to al-Qaeda is very evident throughout the video, with images praising leaders from all the al-Qaeda networks, as well as prominent sympathetic preachers.

In addition to this rhetorical support, the actual casualties on the battlefield provide evidence of the proximity of al-Qaeda networks to TIP/TIPL groups. On 1 January 2017, an American strike on a convoy of vehicles on the road to Bab al-Hawa near the Turkish border killed Abu Omar al Turkistani, a long-standing TIPL leader, alongside a group of other commanders including Abu Khattab al Qahtani, a senior figure who had fought with Osama bin Laden in Afghanistan as well as with the group in Yemen.[51] More recently, in northern Afghanistan, a US bombing strike in Badakhshan targeted Taliban and East Turkestan Islamic Party (ETIM) training camps. In commenting on the strike, Air Force Major General James B. Hecker said, 'ETIM enjoys support from the Taliban in the mountains of Badakhshan, so hitting these Taliban training facilities and squeezing the Taliban's support networks degrades ETIM capabilities.'[52]

So TIP is undoubtedly active in Syria, is aligned with the jihadi Salafi groups fighting on the battlefield, and has a long-term intention of attacking China. Very little independently verifiable information is available about their numbers, their routes to Syria or much else, but this is the general case with jihadi groups fighting in Syria that are linked to al-Qaeda. In contrast to their ISIS counterparts, they tend to be more controlled in their media output online, with few declaring themselves through Twitter or other social media accounts. The worrying aspect for China is that the group is so clearly aligned with al-Qaeda, which remains a consistent long-term threat in its intent to attack the West (or 'far enemies' more broadly, including potentially China), and is using the conflict in Syria as a way to refresh its brand. Furthermore, in contrast to previous times when the Uyghur community gained only slight international attention from jihadist groups, we now see foreigners fighting alongside TIPL, the group ingratiating itself into ever higher levels of international jihadist networks, and finally gaining more than just rhetorical sympathy from the global Salafi-jihadi community.

In early 2018, reports emerged of the death in Chinese custody of a prominent Uyghur scholar, Sheikh Muhammad Salih Hajim, also known as Sheikh Muhammad Salih al-Kashgari. He was an 82-year-old scholar who had been the first to translate the Quran into the Uyghur language, and unverified reports circulating on social media suggested that he had been detained by Chinese authorities a month earlier. Whatever the case, his death became a cause célèbre amongst the international jihadisphere, with TIPL issuing a statement in Arabic threatening China with retribution for his death.[53] A number of other prominent Salafi-jihadi scholars commented on his death, including Abu Qatada al-Filistini, a prominent cleric linked to al-Qaeda, while pictures were released by TIPL of a ceremony marking his passing in Jisr al Shughour in Syria.[54] While the circumstances of his death remain unclear, the fact the death resonated so widely highlights the degree to which the Uyghur cause has been mainstreamed in the international Salafi-jihadi world.

The final element which should be discussed in this context is the relationship with Turkey. There is evidently some level of connection between the groups fighting in Syria and Turkey itself, though the exact nature is unclear. Turkey is the main conduit for people going to fight in Syria, and it is clear that there has been some complicity within the Turkish system to help Uyghurs leave China. The numbers of people showing up with Turkish travel documents suggest that this is more than an illicit level of collaboration, and there have been repeated comments behind closed doors by Chinese officials about Turkish involvement. The question of whether the Turkish authorities are directing jihadis to fight in Syria through TIPL for their own purposes is unclear. Indeed, one would expect them to be fighting Kurds more prominently if they were so closely aligned with the Turkish state. Any visit to Istanbul confirms the open support for the Uyghur cause. For instance, a restaurant and park near the Blue Mosque in the centre of the city are covered with graffiti directed against China, and the blue East Turkestan flag is often visible at AKP Party rallies. President Erdoğan himself has made inflammatory statements defining Chinese behaviour in Xinjiang as genocide.[55]

But we cannot be sure what this Turkish proximity means in practice—whether a strategic decision has been made to support the Uyghur cause, or any exact motivations for this. Parts of the state may be interpreting their leader's personal support for the Uyghur cause as a green light for them to proceed. It is also possible that the group is seen as an effective proxy to use on the ground in Syria. At the same time, the degree to which the Turkish state would go further to support terrorism is unclear, although there were rumours around the attack on the Erawan Shrine in Thailand.⁵⁶ Whilst the details of the Erawan plot are opaque, the link to a Turkish human smuggling network and the fact of an actual attack were the first explicit targeting of Chinese nationals in a terrorist incident protesting at state activity against Uyghurs.⁵⁷ By contrast, previous terrorist attacks against Chinese targets or citizens tended to be accidental: a case of the wrong place at the wrong time. In some cases, such as the al Shabaab attack in Somalia in July 2015, the China angle was only opportunistically claimed after the fact. In that instance, a Chinese security guard was killed by chance when al Shabaab militants struck a hotel in Mogadishu; the group subsequently claimed that they had purposefully targeted Chinese people, but there was little evidence to support this claim.⁵⁸

Since the attack in Thailand, there was also an assault on the Chinese Embassy in Bishkek in August 2016, when the building was struck by a vehicle driven by a suicide bomber. This attack is significant for the context of this chapter, as it directly targeted Chinese interests and was supposedly undertaken by Uyghurs with fake Central Asian passports who had links to the battlefield in Syria.⁵⁹ The attack appears to be a materialization of China's fears of the potential dangers it could face from the exodus of Uyghurs going to join the Syrian battlefield.

Conclusion

However, the relationship with Turkey is atypical of China's relations in the broader Middle East, where Muslim majority countries ignore the plight of Uyghurs in favour of a strong relationship with Beijing.⁶⁰ Some Middle Eastern countries—Saudi Arabia in particular—have been seen to encourage the growth of Salafism in China, which many commentators see as questionable and likely to exacerbate problems of extremism in the country.⁶¹ But China does not respond to this publicly, and little is known about Middle Eastern support for Muslim communities in China. This 'blind eye' is also characteristic of the jihadist community, in which al-Qaeda, despite occasional statements about the Uyghur, does little to support them or deploy its resources to advance their cause. Instead, Uyghurs are just one of the many groups that jihadists identify within the plight of Muslims globally.

Maybe this perspective is beginning to change following the so-called Arab Spring. As the flames of civil war have spread around the Muslim world and ignited in Syria, the new environment has encouraged Uyghur militancy and jihadism to thrive. It has also strengthened their connection to al-Qaeda, an organization that is also enjoying a renaissance. The key question for Chinese security planners and thinkers is how this threat will mature in the future. Already, the attacks in Bangkok and Bishkek (with additional attempts maybe disrupted) have indicated that Uyghur-related terrorism is becoming a problem outside Xinjiang, and threatens Chinese nationals and interests. Given the growing cadre of trained fighters who will emerge from the conflict in Syria, and the potential training grounds and resources that groups such as TIP will be able to mobilize in the wake of the conflict, it is possible that China will see this problem escalating further. This threat may become hard to contain, given Beijing's relative lack of experience thus far in countering such threats, the growing footprint of Chinese nationals and interests around the world requiring protection, and the newly strengthened community of Uyghur militants with their close links across the global jihadist community.

8

UYGHUR CROSS-BORDER MOVEMENT INTO SOUTH EAST ASIA

BETWEEN RESISTANCE AND SURVIVAL

Stefanie Kam Li Yee

The deadly attack at the Erawan Shrine in Bangkok, Thailand on 17 August 2016 exposed the security threats arising from Uyghurs working in collaboration with regional human trafficking networks in South East Asia. It generated much interest and increasing concern about the potential imminent rise of the Uyghur militant threat in South East Asia. Uyghurs are a Turkic Muslim ethnic minority in Xinjiang, the north-west autonomous region of the People's Republic of China (PRC). Inter-ethnic violence between the Han Chinese and Uyghur Muslims in the restive Xinjiang region has proven to be a serious challenge in China since before the founding of the People's Republic in 1949. To maintain national unity and internal cohesion and to safeguard the Xinjiang region from threats of ethnic separatism and terrorism, China views economic development as key to stability in Xinjiang. China has supplemented its developmental strategy with increased control over Xinjiang in the bid to integrate the region with the rest of China. This integrationist approach to Xinjiang, which relies on state-led modernization efforts to develop the region coupled with securitization of the region,[1] has seen massive migration of Han Chinese into Xinjiang. While many ethnic groups have integrated with Han Chinese culture to various degrees, the Uyghurs, the majority Turkic people of Xinjiang, represent a unique case. Uyghurs perceive their Uyghur identity to be under threat, while outbreaks of violent resistance are increasingly commonplace, as seen in the July 2009 riots in Urumqi. While some Uyghurs have turned to violent resistance, others have sought haven in neighbouring Turkey. China has also attributed a variety of terrorist attacks to the Uyghur-led terrorist East Turkistan Islamic Movement (ETIM) or the Turkistan Islamic Party (TIP). It should be emphasized that the majority of Uyghurs, unlike TIP, are not actively engaged in armed resistance against the state, and may even prefer to adapt to their present living conditions.[2] Nonetheless, there remain some exceptions from segments of the Uyghur community.

Since 2009, the Uyghur struggle for identity has continued in South East Asia, where Turkic-speaking Muslim Uyghurs have fled in transit to Turkey, their ethnic homeland. Uyghurs have transited through countries like Malaysia, Indonesia and Thailand, using fake Turkish passports or claims of Turkish citizenship. Relatively less is understood, however, about why Uyghurs are moving into South East Asia in the context of domestic policies in Xinjiang, and about the nature of this resistance and security implications for South East Asia.

This chapter is presented in four parts. In the first part, I provide an overview of Uyghur separatism and terrorism, viewing the transnational expansion of Uyghur resistance into South East Asia as an expression that cannot be isolated from the larger social resistance of Xinjiang's Uyghurs against Han rule.[3] Uyghur separatism and the perception of threat by the Chinese government can be attributed to a confluence of socio-political factors, which include: a history of tensions between the Central Asian Uyghurs and China, the growing dynamic of radical Islamism in the wider Central and South Asian region, Uyghur linkages with militant movements in the Af-Pak region during the Soviet–Afghan war, and growing agitation for the Uyghur resistance struggle in response to visibly harsh and restrictive Chinese policies.

In the second part, I analyse the development of Uyghur resistance in the twenty-first century by showing how the Chinese government's policy has had an impact on shaping Uyghur perceptions of their identity as under threat.

With some exceptions, China's Xinjiang policies have left Uyghurs with choices either to migrate, to abandon their culture and religious identity in favour of a homogenous Chinese identity, or to give expression to their identity either through violent or non-violent resistance. In the next section, the discussion considers how the broader Uyghur struggle has evolved in ways that are no longer localized, but that intersect with the global forces of Islamist radicalism and pose a challenge to Chinese counter-terrorism policies and objectives.

Uyghur separatism and terrorism

Historically, Xinjiang's north-western frontiers were a source of anxiety for China due to threats from the Central Asian region.[4] The growth of Russian influence and the rise of local Muslim-motivated rebellions began to pose problems for China. One of these rebellions, led by Yaqub Beg, culminated in an East Turkestan government, only to be quelled by the Chinese in 1878. Xinjiang was officially declared a province in 1884 and was immediately taken over by various warlords following the collapse of the Qing Empire in 1911.[5] Chinese control over Central Asia diminished in parallel with the weakening of the Qing dynasty. In the twentieth century, the Soviet Union continued to back Xinjiang's efforts to establish a Kazakh and Uyghur East Turkestan Republic, until Xinjiang was formally reverted to Chinese rule nearing the end of the Civil War. In the continuing struggle for an independent Uyghurstan, some Uyghurs set up a short-lived and independent republic of 'East Turkestan' in 1933 and 1944.[6] In 1955, the Xinjiang Uyghur Autonomous Region (XUAR) was established. At the height of the Cultural Revolution (1966–9), Xinjiang was placed under direct military control.[7] Influenced by external developments, more specifically the Soviet–Afghan war and the rise of Islamic radicalism in the 1960s and 1970s,[8] Uyghur militants formed ties with Pakistani militants as some Uyghurs had fought alongside Filipino Moros, Uzbeks and Arabs, in addition to receiving training in madrassas in Pakistan with the Uzbeks and Tajiks.[9] Commentators have noted that the radicalization of citizens in Afghanistan and Pakistan was likely condoned by China in its assistance of the Taliban forces, who were enlisted to be 'part of the struggle against Soviet hegemonism'.[10] Around the 1980s, as noted by Michael Dillon, Uyghur opposition to Chinese rule became more overtly nationalistic, but only in the 1990s did such opposition expand into political movements, often becoming violent.[11]

With the demise of the Soviet Union in 1991, the newly independent states in Central Asia experienced a broad religious resurgence, which fuelled a rise in ethno-nationalist sentiments in Xinjiang.[12] In 1990, a series of riots and uprisings took place in Baren Township, Akto County, when Afghan-trained Islamists in Xinjiang attacked local police. Rohan Gunaratna notes that the Uyghur connection with al-Qaeda during the Soviet–Afghan war fostered a rise in radical Islam, and separatism in Xinjiang increased in its aftermath.[13] Similarly, as noted by Martin I. Wayne, 'in the Afghan war's wake ... Xinjiang's indigenous insurgency in the 1990s infected society and began severing the state from the people'.[14]

The Islamic Movement of Uzbekistan (IMU) and Islamic Jihad Union (IJU) emerged as the primary terrorist groups in Central Asia in their bid to establish an Islamic state in Uzbekistan. Meanwhile TIP developed close links with the Pakistani Taliban and the Islamic Movement of Uzbekistan (IMU). According to the US State Department, TIP members received training from al-Qaeda in Afghanistan, and the members are linked to the al-Qaeda-affiliate Jabhat al Nusra (newly renamed Jabhat Fatah al-Sham). TIP operates at least two training camps in Syria. One is located in a captured Syrian villa in Idlib or Latakia province. TIP is said to have a training camp used to train child soldiers and has also advertised camps for children and women in the Afghan–Pakistan region.[15] While the US-led war in Afghanistan saw the dismantling of the operational capabilities of these Central Asian militants, they remain persistent in their objectives. These terrorist groups continue to find support and sanctuaries in the tribal areas of Pakistan.

Separatism in Xinjiang also stems from perceived and actual Chinese repression. It derives from the perception that the large Han in-migration has taken over what rightfully belongs to the Uyghurs. China has spared no efforts to prevent and crack down on the three 'forces of evil', namely terrorism, extremism and separatism, in the bid to ensure its internal security and stability. Strict adherence to the rule of law and the subordination of religion to the Chinese regime are some ways that China has sought to further its policies in Xinjiang.[16] During the Second Work Forum on Xinjiang in 2014, Chinese President Xi Jinping called for 'nets spread from the earth to the sky' to defend against terrorist acts in Xinjiang, stressing long-term stability as the main goal for the region. The Party pledged to adhere to the basic principles of 'upholding that which is legal, suppressing that which is unlawful, containing extremism and resisting its penetration, and striking against crime.... [and to] safeguard religious harmony, ethnic unity, and social stability' of the

22 million people of Xinjiang. Against this backdrop, the Uyghur resistance in direct response to China's securitization has become more pronounced.[17] As noted by Sean Roberts, acts of 'violence in the region are more likely in response to the increasingly repressive acts of security organs in the XUAR since the beginning of GWOT than they are to a cohesive separatist movement for Uyghur independence from China'.[18] The growth of the Uyghur diaspora has also seen an overall increase in Uyghur rights organizations who continue to advocate the rights of Uyghurs residing in Xinjiang.

Uyghur resistance in the twenty-first century

The events of 9/11 and the Urumqi riots of 2009 led to more intense and comprehensive state policies in Xinjiang. China made it a priority to fight separatism after 9/11, and put forward a January 2002 report, 'East Turkistan Terrorist Forces Cannot Get Away with Impunity', while 'strike hard' campaigns were re-implemented from late 2001 onwards. These strike hard campaigns were focused on achieving accelerated arrests, trials and sentencing of criminals. They were instituted in conjunction with a system of limited regional autonomy. The Communist Party leader in Xinjiang, Wang Lequan, stressed the fight against ethnic separatists (*minzu fenlie shili*) as one of the Party's most important tasks.[19] The US designation of ETIM as a 'terrorist' organization brought the Uyghur-led group into greater international focus. The ensuing war on terror also increased surveillance and crackdown on militants in the Af-Pak region. The refocusing of efforts on fighting separatists and militants by the CCP, using means of 'indiscriminate suppression in Xinjiang',[20] constrained the Uyghur resistance movement, making it difficult for Uyghurs to carry out violence.

The Urumqi riots of 2009 were the second event in the twenty-first century to signal a development in Uyghur resistance.[21] According to figures released in a PRC State Council white paper, the riots killed 197 people, injured over 1,700, and destroyed or burned 331 shops and 1,325 motor vehicles.[22] In response, the government took decisive and swift economic and security measures to restore order and stability to the region. Joshua Tschantret notes that the timing of the civil unrest during the 2009 Urumqi riots suggests the underlying work of 'collective action' processes by Uyghurs, and notes that 'innovations in terrorism arose in tandem with greater dissent in general'.[23] Around this time, China pressured Turkey to harden its stance towards the Uyghurs, which made it hard for Uyghurs to travel to Turkey. Turkey and

Central Asia have placed restrictions on the entry of Uyghurs, due to security concerns about Uyghur separatists entering the country. Uyghurs have used South East Asia to transit to Turkey, which has contributed to the transnational expansion of the Uyghur resistance.

Since 2013, Uyghur violence has extended beyond Xinjiang, along with the use of tactical innovations such as suicide bombings.[24] This was highlighted by the suicide bombing attack at Beijing's Tiananmen Square in 2013, when Uyghurs mounted a deadly crash using an SUV, killing five bystanders, as well as the Urumqi Railway Station knife stabbing and suicide bombing attack, which left three dead and 79 others injured. Uyghurs have also carried out indiscriminate attacks on civilians, as highlighted in the 1 March 2014 knife stabbing attack at the Kunming Railway Station by Uyghur suspects, which killed 31 and wounded 141 others.

The resurgence of global militant Islam in the 2000s and the Syrian conflict of 2012 have also influenced the nature of Uyghur resistance. Hard-line Uyghurs have adopted a radical Islamist stance in support of their violence. This is reflected in TIP's propaganda videos. In one such video released in the wake of the 2013 Tiananmen Square attack, TIP leader Abdullah Mansour claimed responsibility for the attack, congratulating the 'mujahideen of Turkistan' for carrying out a successful attack which 'caused a strong panic by the haughty Chinese government ... [as a] response to the aggression of the Chinese [government]'. In July 2016, TIP released a few propaganda videos in Russian, calling on Muslims across the world to join the jihad in Khurasan, Syria and Chechnya to 'protect fenceless Muslims in these lands from the aggression of the infidels'. Statements released by TIP highlight the sense of moral outrage caused by perceived injustices experienced by members of their community, and these injustices are frequently portrayed as prompting a war waged on aggressors in defence of Islam. In the aftermath of the Urumqi bomb attacks of April 2014, TIP released a video in which its members 'congratulated the perpetrators of the April 30 attack at the Xinjiang capital Urumqi's South Railway Station as President Xi Jinping wrapped up a visit to the restive region'. Furthermore, the source reported that TIP's head, Abdulheq Damolla, said the attack was 'good news' and would 'fill the suppressed hearts of believers with joy, and fill the apostates and infidels' hearts [a reference to the non-Muslim mujahideen] with fear'. Referring to East Turkestan as 'an integral part of the Muslim *ummah*', the group claimed responsibility for the Urumqi train station attack, referring to it as a 'holy jihadi operation carried out by our mujahideen brothers'. Such propaganda

UYGHUR CROSS-BORDER MOVEMENT INTO SOUTH EAST ASIA

statements released by TIP reflect the growing alignment with radical Islamist rhetoric by hard-line Uyghur resistance movements.

Uyghur cross-border movement into South East Asia

Against the backdrop of tightened borders between Xinjiang and Turkey as well as Central Asia, Uyghurs have been detected in South East Asia. While a majority of Uyghurs travel to South East Asia as peaceful asylum seekers in search of better economic opportunities, first reports of their involvement with militant groups surfaced in 2014, pointing to the possibility that South East Asia might be seen as an attractive staging point for Uyghur violence.[25]

Radical elements in Xinjiang have exploited the same human smuggling and fake documentation networks operating in China and South East Asia to obtain fake passports and reach Turkey on their way to Syria. In January 2015, Chinese police in Shanghai arrested a group of ten Turkish nationals and two Chinese citizens for supplying fake Turkish passports to nine Uyghurs. Allegedly, the Uyghurs were planning to leave China to take part in the Syrian conflict. Despite border controls and crackdown on anti-Chinese activities in Turkey, Uyghurs have entered South East Asia on fake Turkish passports as asylum seekers and successfully travelled to Turkey. The August 2015 attack at the Erawan Shrine in Thailand, which killed twenty and injured 125, thus exposed a network responsible for 'trafficking terrorists from Xinjiang, through Southeast Asia, and onward to Turkey where they are staged, armed, trained, and then sent to fight NATO's proxy war in Syria'.[26] While Syria appears as the preferred final battlefield for radical Uyghur elements, there have also been Uyghurs directly linked to militant groups in South East Asia and to their operations in the region. In 2015, the head of Indonesia's counter-terrorism agency, Saud Usman Nasution, revealed that Uyghur suspects had entered Indonesia's Poso through Medan and had entered South East Asia from Myanmar, followed by southern Thailand and Malaysia, to join a local militant group.[27] On 13 September 2014, Indonesia's Densus 88 police squad foiled a possible terror plot between Uyghurs and Indonesia's militant group, the Eastern Indonesia Mujahideen or Mujahidin Indonesia Timur (MIT), with the arrest of four Uyghurs who had entered Indonesia using forged passports.[28] MIT is one of the few groups in Indonesia that has pledged allegiance to the so-called Islamic State (IS). The Uyghurs, along with the three Indonesians, were travelling in a vehicle in the central Sulawesi district of Poso when authorities stopped them. The authorities found articles with the IS insignia on them in the vehicle. The Uyghurs reportedly had plans to receive military training in bomb-making and weapon-handling with the Indonesian terrorist group, led by Santoso, before returning to their country to launch attacks. In December 2015, Indonesia's elite counter-terrorism unit, Densus 88, arrested eleven militants who were planning to carry out bombing operations in Indonesia. One of the individuals arrested was a Uyghur undergoing training to become a suicide bomber.[29]

Table 1: South East Asian Uyghurs Arrested, Killed or Deported

Date	Place	Incident	Arrest, Killed, Deported or Sentenced
19 December 2009	Cambodia	The Cambodian government repatriated a group of 20 Uyghur asylum seekers.[30]	20 deported
December 2010	Laos	According to Radio Free Asia, Laos deported 7 Muslim Uyghurs. Authorities arrested and deported Memet Eli Rozi, 34, his wife Gulbahar Sadiq, 28, and their 5 children in March 2010.[31]	7 deported
20 August 2011	Malaysia	Amnesty International reported that up to 24 Uyghur refugees were arrested by Malaysian authorities.[32]	24 deported
December 2012	Malaysia	Malaysia repatriated 6 Uyghur men who were using fake passports.[33]	6 deported
14 March 2014	Hat Yai, Thailand	Police rescued about 200 people believed to be Muslim Uyghurs from a human smuggling camp in southern Thailand[34]	200 rescued
18 April 2014	Vietnam	16 Uyghurs were detained by Vietnamese border guards when they were trying to enter Vietnam illegally. They seized the guards' guns and attacked them with knives. 5 Uyghurs and	5 killed, 11 deported

UYGHUR CROSS-BORDER MOVEMENT INTO SOUTH EAST ASIA

		2 guards were killed. The remaining 11 Uyghurs were then repatriated on 21 April.[35]	
21 June 2014	Manila, The Philippines	5 Uyghurs reached the Philippines by using fake Turkish passports.[36]	5 arrested
September 2014	Poso, Central Sulawesi, Indonesia	Police detained 4 Uyghurs for attempting to meet Santoso (Jihadist; the leader of the Mujahideen of Eastern Indonesia).[37]	4 arrested, 3 sentenced for 6 years
1 October 2014	Kuala Lumpur, Malaysia	Malaysian authorities detained 155 Uyghurs, more than half of them children.[38]	155 detained
9 July 2015	Thailand	Thailand repatriated 109 ethnic Uyghurs.[39]	109 deported
17 August 2015	Bangkok, Thailand	A bombing took place close to the Erawan Shrine, killing 20 people (10 Thai, 7 Chinese, 2 Malaysian, 1 Filipino) and injuring 125 people.[40]	Of 17 total suspects, 2 Uyghur suspects were arrested
November 2015	Central Sulawesi, Indonesia	Indonesia security forces shot dead a Uyghur called Farouk (aka Magalasi) when they attacked Santoso's militant group.[41]	1 Uyghur was killed by Indonesian security forces
December 2015	Bekasi, Indonesia	During a raid, Indonesian police found bombing materials, an explosive device and a model of a government building. Ali, the suspect, was a suicide bomber under training. He entered Indonesia via Batam, a small island off Singapore with 2 other Uyghurs. Ali was also suspected of involvement in the Bangkok attack.[42]	1 Uyghur man named Ali was arrested
15 March 2016	Poso, Central Sulawesi, Indonesia	Police shot dead 2 Chinese Uyghurs who were allegedly fighting with Santoso, the leader of MIT.[43] The two men were Nuretin alias Abdul and Magalasi Bahtusan alias Farok.	2 Uyghurs were shot dead

181

| 24 April 2016 | Poso, Central Sulawesi, Indonesia | Police killed a terrorist, who was a member of the East Indonesia Mujahidin (MIT) during crossfire.[44] | 1 Uyghur shot dead |
| 18 May 2016 | Indonesia | Police arrested a Chinese Uyghur when he tried to enter Indonesia via Batam. He was deported to China on 18 May 2016. | 1 Uyghur arrested |

The summary of findings in Table 1 indicates a growing trend of the movement of Uyghurs into South East Asia since 2009, particularly into countries like Cambodia, Laos, Vietnam, Thailand, Malaysia and Indonesia. These reports frequently emerge in light of their arrest for involvement in terrorist activity, deportations or deaths due to a confrontation with the security forces. Such actions may in turn be perceived as signs of increasing heavy-handedness by South East Asian governments towards the Uyghurs—increasing the extent to which Uyghurs see these countries as legitimate targets for terrorist attacks.

The movement into South East Asia can be attributed to a transnational expansion of the Uyghur resistance movement against the backdrop of the Chinese government's crackdown on Uyghur communities following the Urumqi riots of 2009. Thailand and Malaysia have seen the largest number of Uyghur refugees, as evidenced by the numbers from refugee camps being deported. Based on data from Table 1, Uyghur presence in the Philippines was uncovered in 2014, when five Uyghurs were arrested in Manila. According to one commentator, the Uyghurs had entered the Philippines on fake Turkish passports, and 'went to Basilan from Sabah to meet personalities linked with Abu Sayyaf Group (ASG)'. The source added that the Uyghurs also 'visited Cotabato City where they met personalities associated with the Bangsamoro Islamic Freedom Fighters (BIFF) ... [and] also visited Davao City where they met personalities involved in militant activities'.[45]

Uyghur cross-border movement into South East Asia beginning around 2009 can be seen in relation to the broader trend of deadlier attacks in recent years. The discovery of Ali's involvement in training to become a suicide bomber in December 2015 corresponds with the broader trend of suicide bombing attacks carried out by Uyghur separatists in recent years, in Beijing and more recently on the Chinese embassy in the Kyrgyz capital. This reflects continuity in the manifestation of resistance by Uyghur separatists in China and South East Asia and the shift to the use of more innovative methods by the Uyghur resistance so as to circumvent the state's securitization of Xinjiang.[46] Given the fact that suicide bombing attacks are not new to the Uyghur separatists' repertoire, the likelihood of them replicating suicide bombing attacks in South East Asia is high.

The persistence of radical Islamist militant groups and ethno-separatist groups in South East Asia may potentially provide a fertile environment for radicalized Uyghurs to forge alliances with previously isolated movements. During the 1980s, South East Asian Jemaah Islamiyah (JI) and al-Qaeda forged alliances in the form of training and operational collaboration. In the 1990s, JI conducted high-profile attacks before it was finally defeated by the government.[47] Nonetheless, the JI's ideology continues to resonate among the South East Asian groups. A similar strategic alliance between Uyghur militants and these South East Asian militants may lead to a diffusion of tactics and capabilities, increasing the terrorist threat in the region in the medium to long term.[48] Evidence shows that Uyghurs in South East Asia have also formed alliances with South East Asian militants. In 2014, four Uyghurs were found to be linked with the Poso jihadist militant network, the Mujahidin Indonesia Timur (MIT). MIT is believed to be the only 'truly national militant Islamist network currently active in Indonesia',[49] with elements from across Indonesia. In addition, MIT is made up of experienced, well-trained jihadists, many of whom can be traced back to the Darul Islam (DI) anti-colonial Islamist insurgency group fighting the Indonesian republic in the 1950s. Last but not least, MIT operates in Poso, an important site for inter-communal conflict, and local support continues to fuel the grievances of this conflict. Police operations in Poso have been stepped up, and Uyghur militants linked with MIT have also been implicated in the operations, as evidenced by the arrests of four Uyghurs in September 2014 and one Uyghur in December 2015, as well as the deaths of Uyghur militants in two separate crossfire incidents with the police in March and April 2016.

Refugee conditions may also increase the extent to which Uyghurs in South East Asia may form strategic alliances with terrorist groups, either for survival or to increase operational manpower.[50] The cross-border movement of refugees and asylum seekers, whether legal or illegal, is likely to contribute to a large number of them getting housed in refugee camps. This is likely to serve as a breeding ground for radicalization and terrorism. In countries like Thailand, which is home to Rohingya refugees, often the refugee camps are characterized by lack of adequate sanitation, proper shelter and resources, and healthcare infrastructure. Apart from the socio-economic background of the

Uyghur refugees, the existing dwelling spaces of the Uyghurs in South East Asia also have an impact on the refugee experience of the Uyghurs. Geographically isolated and poorly integrated, these Uyghur refugees often leave their homes, their belongings, their family and friends for fear of persecution. While these refugees leave their homes in search of better relief, often the conditions in these refugee camps are inadequate and may fail to provide basic protection for the refugees. The psychological and physical effects of the refugee experience might also lead to Uyghurs staging violent or non-violent protests to demand their basic human rights. This was suggested in the reports of Uyghurs staging hunger strikes in detention centres.[51] The lack of protection measures to pre-empt the process of radicalization and terrorism within such refugee camps could render particular subsets of the refugees sympathetic to the propaganda of terrorist organizations. The repatriation of Uyghurs and the increase in efforts by South East Asian governments to disrupt the human trafficking routes of the Uyghur movement may continue to fuel resentment on the part of Uyghur communities.

Conclusion

Uyghur resistance has expanded to areas beyond the western peripheries of China—Central Asia, Turkey and South Asia—and to locations in South East Asia. This is reflected in the increasing evidence of Uyghur cross-border movement into South East Asia and their involvement in militancy and terrorism. At the same time, the growth of radical Islamism has seen TIP becoming more closely aligned to these influences in their rhetoric. The co-optation of Uyghurs by ethno-separatist militants and radical Islamist groups in South East Asia could lead to further violence. With the defeat of IS, its global decentralized networks may continue to survive by embedding its cause in local grievances. The general conditions of refugee camps in South East Asia may encourage the Uyghurs who are in transit to turn to radicalism. Evidently, Uyghur involvement in militancy in South East Asia, while limited, has raised concerns for China in recent years.

Essentially, the Uyghur cross-border movement into South East Asia should be seen as part of their broader struggle to retain their distinct Uyghur identity. This is due to the perception that state-led integrationist efforts have increasingly restricted the Uyghurs' freedom to practise their culture and religious identity. The Uyghur ethno-nationalist separatist cause (vis-à-vis an independent East Turkestan) and their resistance against the state are not new, but their movement into South East Asia is an unintended consequence of China's domestic policies in Xinjiang. While a majority of the Uyghurs seeking to transit through to South East Asia eventually hope to reach Turkey, their presence in South East Asia has exposed them to the myriad militant and separatist influences indigenous to the region. This has seen Uyghurs linking up with militants, and, furthermore, has made segments of the Uyghurs prone to radicalization and recruitment. At the same time, with the rise in Uyghur diaspora networks and rights groups, this has had the effect of transnationalizing the Uyghur cause. Such developments highlight the mounting challenges for China and South East Asian countries in controlling destabilizing elements beyond their own national borders.

NOTES

INTRODUCTION: TERRORISM AND COUNTER-TERRORISM IN CHINA

1. For a small sample of literature on this subject, see Gardner Bovingdon, *The Uyghurs: Strangers in Their Own Land* (New York: Columbia University Press, 2010); Michael Clarke, *Xinjiang and China's Rise in Central Asia: A History* (London: Routledge, 2011); James A. Millward, *Eurasian Crossroads: A History of Xinjiang* (New York: Columbia University Press, 2007); and Justin Jacobs, *Xinjiang and the Modern Chinese State* (Seattle, WA: University of Washington Press, 2016).
2. For analyses of BRI, see for instance Michael Clarke, 'Belt and Road Initiative: China's New Grand Strategy?', *Asia Policy*, 24, 1 (July 2017), pp. 7–15; Yong Wang, 'Offensive for Defensive: The Belt and Road Initiative and China's New Grand Strategy', *Pacific Review*, 29, 3 (2016), pp. 455–63; and Nadège Rolland, *China's Eurasian Century? Political and Strategic Implications of the Belt and Road Initiative* (Seattle, WA: National Bureau of Asian Research, 2017).
3. William H. Overholt, 'One Belt, One Road, One Pivot', *Global Asia*, 10, 3 (2015), pp. 1–8; and Minjiang Li, 'From Look-West to Act-West: Xinjiang's role in China–Central Asian relations', *Journal of Contemporary China*, 25, 100 (2016), pp. 515–28.
4. Bruce Hoffman, *Inside Terrorism*, 2nd edn (New York: Columbia University Press, 2006).
5. Jeffrey Reeves, 'Ideas and Influence: Scholarship as a Harbinger of Counterterrorism Institutions, Policies, and Laws in the People's Republic of China', *Terrorism and Political Violence*, 28, 5 (2016), p. 833.
6. Ibid., pp. 833–4; Guangcheng Xing, 'China and Central Asia: Towards a New Relationship', in Yongjin Zhang and Rouben Azizian (eds), *Ethnic Challenges Beyond Borders: Chinese and Russian Perspectives on the Central Asian Conundrum* (London: Palgrave Macmillan, 1998), pp. 32–5; and Yizhou Wang, 'Defining Non-Traditional

Security and its Implications for China' (Beijing: Institute for World Economics and Politics Working Paper, 2005).
7. See Shuisheng Zhao, 'China's Periphery Policy and its Asian Neighbors', *Security Dialogue*, 30, 3 (1999), pp. 335–46; and Bates Gill, *Rising Star: China's New Security Diplomacy* (Washington, DC: Brookings Institution Press, 2010).
8. See Chien-peng Chung, 'The Shanghai Cooperation Organization: China's Changing Influence in Central Asia', *China Quarterly*, 180 (2004), pp. 989–1009; Stephen Aris, 'The Shanghai Cooperation Organization: "Tackling the Three Evils"', *Europe–Asia Studies*, 61, 3 (2009), pp. 457–82; and Marc Lanteigne, '"In Medias Res": The Development of the Shanghai Co-operation Organization as a Security Community', *Pacific Affairs*, 79, 4 (2006), pp. 605–22.
9. Russell Ong, 'China's Security Interests in Central Asia', *Central Asian Survey*, 24, 4 (2005), pp. 425–39.
10. Reeves, 'Ideas and Influence', pp. 834–5.
11. See for instance Colin Mackerras, 'Xinjiang at the Turn of the Century: The Causes of Separatism', *Central Asian Survey*, 20, 3 (2001), pp. 294–5.
12. Millward, *Eurasian Crossroads*, pp. 324–5. For incidents of unrest and violence in the 1990s, see Mackerras, 'Xinjiang at the Turn of the Century'; Nicholas Becquelin, 'Xinjiang in the Nineties', *China Journal*, 44 (2000), pp. 65–90; and Brent Hierman, 'The Pacification of Xinjiang: Uighur Protest and the Chinese State, 1988–2002', *Problems of Post-Communism*, 54, 3 (2007), pp. 48–62.
13. See for example Alex P. Schmid, 'Terrorism and Democracy', *Terrorism and Political Violence*, 4, 4 (1992), pp. 14–25; W. L. Eubank and L. Weinberg, 'Does Democracy Encourage Terrorism?', *Terrorism and Political Violence*, 6, 4 (1994), pp. 417–35; J. Eyerman, 'Terrorism and Democratic States: Soft Targets or Accessible Systems', *International Interactions*, 24, 2 (1998), pp. 151–70; Hanne Fjelde, 'Generals, Dictators, and Kings: Authoritarian Regimes and Civil Conflict, 1973–2004', *Conflict Management and Peace Science*, 27, 3 (2010), pp. 195–218; and Quan Li, 'Does Democracy Promote or Reduce Transnational Terrorist Incidents?', *Journal of Conflict Resolution*, 49, 2 (2005), pp. 278–97.
14. Ted R. Gurr, 'Why Minorities Rebel: A Global Analysis of Communal Mobilization and Conflict since 1945', *International Political Science Review*, 14, 2 (1993), pp. 161–201.
15. James A. Piazza, 'Poverty, Minority Economic Discrimination, and Domestic Terrorism', *Journal of Peace Research*, 48, 3 (2011), p. 341. See also Seung-Whan Choi and James A. Piazza, 'Ethnic Groups, Political Exclusion and Domestic Terrorism', *Defence and Peace Economics*, 27, 1 (2016), pp. 37–63.
16. Owen Lattimore, 'Inner Asian Frontiers: Chinese and Russian Margins of Expansion', *Journal of Economic History*, 7, 1 (1947), pp. 24–52.
17. Clarke, *Xinjiang and China's Rise in Central Asia*, pp. 124–40.
18. For critical discussions of the effects of the state-led economic development in

Xinjiang, see Matthew D. Moneyhon, 'China's Great Western Development Project in Xinjiang: Economic Palliative, or Political Trojan Horse?', *Denver Journal of International Law and Policy*, 31, 3 (2002/3), pp. 491–519; Ildikó Bellér-Hann, 'The Bulldozer State: Chinese Socialist Development in Xinjiang', in Madeleine Reeves, Johan Rasanayagam and Judith Beyer (eds), *Ethnographies of the State in Central Asia: Performing Politics* (Bloomington, IN: University of Indiana Press, 2014), pp. 173–97; Alessandra Cappelletti, 'Socio-Economic Disparities and Development Gap in Xinjiang: The Cases of Kashgar and Shihezi', in Michael Clarke and Anna Hayes (eds), *Inside Xinjiang: Space, Place and Power in China's Muslim Far Northwest* (London: Routledge, 2016), pp. 151–82; and Sean Roberts, 'Development with Chinese Characteristics in Xinjiang: A Solution to Ethnic Tension or Part of the Problem?', in Michael Clarke and Douglas Smith (eds), *China's Frontier Regions: Ethnicity, Economic Integration and Foreign Relations* (London: I. B. Tauris, 2016), pp. 22–55.

19. 'Vision and Actions on Jointly Building Silk Road Economic Belt and 21st-Century Maritime Silk Road', National Development and Reform Commission, Ministry of Foreign Affairs and Ministry of Commerce of the People's Republic of China, 28 March, http://en.ndrc.gov.cn/newsrelease/201503/t20150330_669367.html, last accessed 19 May 2015.
20. Roberts, 'Development with Chinese Characteristics in Xinjiang'.
21. Piazza, 'Poverty, Minority Economic Discrimination, and Domestic Terrorism', pp. 38–9.
22. Ibid.
23. For example see Alex P. Schmid, 'Frameworks for Conceptualising Terrorism', *Terrorism and Political Violence*, 16, 2 (2004), pp. 197–221; Arthur H. Garrison, 'Defining Terrorism: Philosophy of the Bomb, Propaganda by the Deed and Change Through Fear and Violence', *Criminal Justice Studies*, 17, 3 (2004), pp. 259–79; Anthony Richards, 'Conceptualizing Terrorism', *Studies in Conflict and Terrorism*, 37, 3 (2014), pp. 213–36.
24. 中华人民共和国反恐怖主义法（2015年12月27日第十二届全国人民代表大会常务委员会第十八次会议通过 [Anti-Terrorism Act adopted at the 12th session of the Standing Committee of the National People's Congress, 18th session], 27 December 2015, http://news.xinhuanet.com/politics/2015-12/27/c_128571798.htm, last accessed 8 March 2017. A translation is also available at the *China Law Translate* website, http://www.chinalawtranslate.com/%e5%8f%8d%e6%81%90%e6%80%96%e4%b8%bb%e4%b9%89%e6%b3%95-%ef%bc%882015%ef%bc%89/?lang=en, last accessed 8 March 2017.
25. Ibid.
26. United States Department of State, *Patterns of Global Terrorism, 2003*, April 2004, p. xii.
27. Bruce Hoffman, *Inside Terrorism*, 2nd edn.

28. Lee Jarvis, 'The Spaces and Faces of Critical Terrorism Studies', *Security Dialogue*, 40, 1 (2009), p. 14.
29. Ibid.
30. Melissa Finn and Bessma Momani, 'Building Foundations for the Comparative Study of State and Non-State Terrorism', *Critical Studies on Terrorism*, 10, 3 (2017), p. 380.
31. Boaz Ganor, 'Defining Terrorism: Is One Man's Terrorist Another Man's Freedom Fighter?', *Police Practice and Research*, 3, 4 (2002), pp. 287–304.
32. Murray Scot Tanner, *China's Response to Terrorism* (Washington, DC: CNA, June 2016), p. 3.
33. A small portion of CCTV footage from the attack can be viewed at https://www.youtube.com/watch?v=saAarcQOtNU, last accessed 8 March 2017. Four attackers were shot dead by police during the attack and four were captured. Of the four captured Uyghurs, three were sentenced to death and one to life imprisonment after a one-day trial in Beijing in September 2014. See 'Four sentenced in China over Kunming Station Attack', BBC News, 12 September 2014, http://www.bbc.com/news/world-asia-china-29170238, last accessed 8 March 2017.
34. 昆明暴恐案始末:8人欲赴境外'圣战'受阻 [Violence in Kunming: 8 attackers attempting to join overseas jihad 'blocked'], 5 March 2014, http://www.ce.cn/xwzx/gnsz/gdxw/201403/05/t20140305_2419638.shtml, last accessed 8 March 2017; and 'Kunming Massacre Gang "Tried to Become Jihadists Overseas" Before Station Attack', *South China Morning Post*, 5 March 2014, http://www.scmp.com/news/china/article/1440951/kunming-massacre-gang-tried-become-jihadists-overseas-station-attack, last accessed 8 March 2017.
35. 'China Train Station Attackers May Have Acted "in Desperation"', Radio Free Asia, http://www.rfa.org/english/news/uyghur/desperate-03032014224353.html
36. For instance, see Richard Bernstein, 'Thailand: From China to Jihad?', *Pulitzer Center*, 9 September 2014, http://pulitzercenter.org/reporting/thailand-china-jihad, last accessed 9 March 2017; Luke Hunt, 'Uyghurs Test ASEAN's Refugee Credentials', *The Diplomat*, 19 March 2014, http://thediplomat.com/2014/03/uyghurs-test-aseans-refugee-credentials/, last accessed 9 March 2017.
37. For TIP's links to Syria, see Michael Clarke, 'Uyghur Militants in Syria: The Turkish Connection', *Terrorism Monitor*, 14, 3 (4 February 2016), https://jamestown.org/program/uyghur-militants-in-syria-the-turkish-connection/, last accessed 9 March 2017.
38. See the data compiled in Mathieu Duchâtel, 'Terror Overseas: Understanding China's Evolving Counter-Terror Strategy', *ECFR Policy Brief* (Brussels: European Council on Foreign Relations, October 2016).
39. Michael Clarke, 'Bangkok Bombing Spotlights Uyghur Woes in Southeast Asia', *The Diplomat*, 28 August 2015, http://thediplomat.com/2015/08/bangkok-bombing-spotlights-uyghur-woes-in-southeast-asia/, last accessed 7 March 2017.

40. Yuwen Wu, 'IS Killing of Chinese Hostage: A Game Changer?', BBC News, 19 November 2015, http://www.bbc.co.uk/news/blogs-china-blog-34865696, last accessed 25 November 2015.
41. 'China Condemns Mali Hotel Attack, Pledges Improved Cooperation to Fight Terrorism', *Xinhua*, 26 November 2015, http://www.focac.org/eng/zjfz/t1318651.htm, last accessed 15 December 2015.
42. Paul J. Smith, 'China's Economic and Political Rise: Implications for Global Terrorism and U.S.-China Cooperation', *Studies in Conflict and Terrorism*, 32, 7 (2009), p. 631.
43. For a sample of some of this literature, see Fareed Zakaria, *The Post-American World, and the Rise of the Rest* (London: Penguin Books, 2008); Stephen M. Walt, 'The End of the American Era', *The National Interest*, 116 (Nov/Dec 2011), pp. 6–16; Christopher M. Layne, 'The Global Power Shift from West to East', *The National Interest*, 119 (May/June 2012), pp. 21–31; Adam Quinn, 'The Art of Declining Politely: Obama's Prudent Presidency and the Waning of American Power', *International Affairs*, 87, 4 (2011), pp. 803–24.
44. Brian Fishman, 'Al-Qaeda and the Rise of China: Jihadi Geopolitics in a Post-Hegemonic World', *Washington Quarterly*, 34, 3 (2011), pp. 47–62.
45. Ibid., p. 47.
46. Ibid., pp. 50–52.
47. Ibid., p. 52.
48. For a discussion of the importance of 'non-interference' for China's foreign policy in the Middle East, see Yitzhak Shichor, 'Fundamentally Unacceptable Yet Occasionally Unavoidable: China's Options on External Interference in the Middle East', *China Report*, 49, 1 (2013), pp. 25–41.
49. Martha Crenshaw, 'Thoughts on Relating Terrorism to Historical Contexts', in Martha Crenshaw (ed.), *Terrorism in Context* (University Park, PA: Pennsylvania State University Press, 1995), p. 3.
50. See for example Josh Chin and Clément Bürge, 'Twelve Days in Xinjiang: How China's Surveillance State Overwhelms Daily Life', *Wall Street Journal*, 19 December 2017, https://www.wsj.com/articles/twelve-days-in-xinjiang-how-chinas-surveillance-state-overwhelms-daily-life-1513700355?mod=fox_australian; and *Trapped in a Virtual Cage: Chinese State Repression of Uyghurs Online* (Washington, DC: Uyghur Human Rights Project, 16 June 2014), http://docs.uyghuramerican.org/Trapped-in-A-Virtual-Cage.pdf
51. See for example 'China Runs Region-wide Re-education Camps in Xinjiang for Uyghurs and Other Muslims', Radio Free Asia, 11 September 2017, https://www.rfa.org/english/news/uyghur/training-camps-09112017154343.html
52. *The Fifth Poison: The Harassment of Uyghurs Overseas* (Washington, DC: Uyghur Human Rights Project, 28 November 2017), https://uhrp.org/docs/The-Fifth-Poison-The-Harrassment-of-Uyghurs-Overseas.pdf

1. CHINA'S 'WAR ON TERRORISM': CONFRONTING THE DILEMMAS OF THE 'INTERNAL–EXTERNAL' SECURITY NEXUS

1. Johan Eriksson and Mark Rhinard, 'The Internal–External Security Nexus: Notes on an Emerging Research Agenda', *Cooperation and Conflict*, 44, 3 (2009), pp. 243–67.
2. Ibid., p. 244.
3. Boaz Ganor, 'Defining Terrorism: Is One Man's Terrorist Another Man's Freedom Fighter?', *Police Practice and Research*, 3, 4 (2002), pp. 287–304.
4. For instance, Dru C. Gladney, *Dislocating China: Muslims, Minorities and Other Subaltern Subjects* (London: Hurst, 2004), pp. 238–57; and Yitzhak Shichor, 'Virtual Transnationalism: Uygur Communities in Europe and the Quest for Eastern Turkestan Independence', in Stefano Allievi and Jørgen S. Nielsen (eds), *Muslim Networks and Transnational Communities in and across Europe* (Leiden: Brill, 2003), pp. 281–311.
5. Eriksson and Rhinard, 'The Internal–External Security Nexus', p. 244.
6. For an example of the latter, see Derek Lutterbeck, 'Blurring the Dividing Line: The Convergence of Internal and External Security in Western Europe', *European Security*, 14, 2 (2005), pp. 231–53.
7. Eriksson and Rhinard, 'The Internal–External Security Nexus', p. 252.
8. Fiona Adamson, for instance, characterizes globalization as 'marked by an increased mobility of people, capital and goods, and ideas and information across national borders'. Fiona Adamson, 'Globalisation, Transnational Political Mobilisation, and Networks of Violence', *Cambridge Review of International Affairs*, 18, 1 (2005), p. 33.
9. Paul J. Smith, 'Transnational Security Threats and State Survival: A Role for the Military?', *Parameters*, 30, 3 (2000), p. 79.
10. James N. Rosenau mapped the distinctions between 'sovereignty-bound' and 'sovereignty-free' actors and phenomena in James N. Rosenau, *Along the Domestic–Foreign Frontier: Exploring Governance in a Turbulent World* (Cambridge: Cambridge University Press, 1997); and *Distant Proximities: Dynamics Beyond Globalization*, (Princeton, NJ: Princeton University Press, 2003).
11. For various interpretations of 9/11 as a point of rupture for international order, see for example Barry Buzan, 'Will the "global war on terrorism" be the new Cold War?' *International Affairs*, 82, 6 (2006), pp. 1101–18; and Audrey Kurth Cronin,

'Behind the Curve: Globalization and International Terrorism', *International Security*, 27, 3 (2002/3), pp. 30–58.
12. Joseph Nye, 'The New Rome Meets the New Barbarians', *The Economist*, 21 March 2002, http://www.economist.com/node/1045181, last accessed 30 June 2015.
13. For Cerny's initial iteration of this position, see Philip G. Cerny, 'Neomedievalism, Civil War and the New Security Dilemma: Globalisation as Durable Disorder, *Civil Wars*, 1, 1 (1998), pp. 36–64. For a revised post-9/11 version, see Philip G. Cerny, 'Terrorism and the New Security Dilemma', *Naval War College Review*, 58, 1 (2002), pp. 10–33.
14. Cerny, 'Neomedievalism', p. 40.
15. For a representative sample of literature that traces the development of this consensus, see Walter Laqueur, 'Postmodern Terrorism', *Foreign Affairs*, 75, 5 (1996), pp. 24–36; Steven Simon and Daniel Benjamin, 'America and the New Terrorism', *Survival*, 42, 1 (2000), pp. 59–75; Bruce Hoffman, 'Al-Qaeda, Trends in Terrorism, and Future Potentialities: An Assessment', *Studies in Conflict and Terrorism*, 26, 6 (2003), pp. 429–42; Bruce Hoffman, *Inside Terrorism*, 2nd edn (New York: Columbia University Press, 2006), pp. 63–80; James A. Piazza, 'Incubators of Terror: Do Failed and Failing States Promote Transnational Terrorism?', *International Studies Quarterly*, 52, 3 (2008), pp. 469–88; and Fawaz Gerges, 'ISIS and the Third Wave of Jihadism', *Current History*, 113, 767 (2014), pp. 339–43.
16. The concept of a 'fourth wave' has been elucidated in David C. Rapoport, 'The Four Waves of Rebel Terror and September 11', *Anthropoetics*, 8, 1 (2002), http://www.anthropoetics.ucla.edu/ap0801/terror.htm, last accessed 10 March 2017.
17. Eriksson and Rhinard, 'The Internal–External Security Nexus', p. 247.
18. Ibid., p. 248.
19. Ibid.
20. For example, see Gladney, *Dislocating China*, pp. 238–57; Shichor, 'Virtual Transnationalism'; Isik Kuşçu, 'The Origins of Uyghur Long-Distance Nationalism: The First Generation Uyghur Diaspora in Turkey', *OAKA*, 8, 16 (2013), pp. 73–94; and Tian Guang and Mahesh Ranjan Debata, 'Identity and Mobilization in Transnational Societies: A Case Study of Uyghur Diasporic Nationalism', *China and Eurasia Forum Quarterly*, 8, 4 (2010), pp. 59–78.
21. Adamson, 'Globalisation, Transnational Political Mobilisation, and Networks of Violence', p. 37.
22. Margaret Keck and Kathryn Sikkink have described this, in the context of a general examination of the emergence and dynamics of transnational advocacy networks, as a 'boomerang pattern'. See Margaret Keck and Kathryn Sikkink, *Activists beyond Borders: Advocacy Networks in International Politics* (Ithaca, NY: Cornell University Press, 1998).
23. See James A. Millward, *Eurasian Crossroads: A History of Xinjiang* (New York:

Columbia University Press, 2007); and Peter C. Perdue, *China Marches West: The Qing Conquest of Central Eurasia* (Cambridge, MA: Belknap Press, 2005).

24. See for example June Teufel Dreyer, 'China's Vulnerability to Minority Separatism', *Asian Affairs: An American Review*, 32, 2 (2005), pp. 69–86; and Michael Clarke, 'China's "War on Terror" in Xinjiang: Human Security and the Causes of Violent Uighur Separatism', *Terrorism and Political Violence*, 20, 2 (2008), pp. 271–301.

25. Enze Han, 'From Domestic to International: The Politics of Ethnic Identity in Xinjiang and Inner Mongolia', *Nationalities Papers*, 39, 6 (2011), pp. 941–62.

26. See Yitzhak Shichor, 'Pawns in Central Asia's Playground: Uyghurs between Moscow and Beijing', *East Asia*, 32, 2 (2015), p. 103; and Ablet Kamalov, 'Uyghurs in the Central Asian Republics: Past and Present', in Michael Clarke and Colin Mackerras (eds), *China, Xinjiang and Central Asia: History, Transition and Crossborder Interaction into the 21st Century* (London: Routledge, 2009), pp. 117–21.

27. See for example Gardner Bovingdon, *The Uyghurs: Strangers in Their Own Land* (New York: Columbia University Press, 2010), pp. 133–5; Melvyn C. Goldstein, 'The United States, Tibet, and the Cold War', *Journal of Cold War Studies*, 8, 3 (2006), pp. 145–64; and Han, 'From Domestic to International'.

28. This extends to the era of the great Turkic–Muslim rebellion in Xinjiang against the Manchus led by the Koqandi adventurer Yaqub Beg between 1864 and 1876. The Ottoman Sultan not only provided his prospective state in Kashgar with weaponry and military advisers, but also bestowed the title of *emir* on Yaqub. For the most comprehensive English-language account of the Yaqub Beg rebellion, see Hodong Kim, *Holy War in China: The Muslim Rebellion and State in Chinese Central Asia, 1864–1877* (Stanford, CA: Stanford University Press, 2004).

29. Alptekin's activities in this context focused on the publication of books and journals on the history of 'East Turkestan' (i.e. Xinjiang) and advocacy of the Uyghur cause within Turkey. In this latter regard, as Isik Kuscu has detailed, Apltekin (and also Bugra) emphasized 'Islam and Turkicness' as 'central components' of Uyghur identity as a means of underscoring (a) ethnic difference between Uyghurs and the Han Chinese and (b) the 'imperialist' divide-and-rule tactics underpinning the Soviet and Chinese classification and demarcation of separate Turkic ethnic groups (e.g. Uyghurs, Kazakhs, Uzbeks etc.). Internationally, Alptekin attempted to enlist support for Uyghur nationalist claims through a broad appeal to anti-communist sentiment in the Muslim world, the non-aligned developing world, and Taiwan. See Yitzhak Shichor, 'Limping on Two Legs: Uyghur Diaspora Organizations and the Prospects for Eastern Turkestan Independence', *Central Asia and the Caucasus*, 6, 48 (2007), pp. 117–25; and Kusçu, 'The Origins of Uyghur Long-Distance Nationalism', pp. 86–9.

30. It should be recalled here that Turkish military forces had fought against the 'Chinese People's Volunteers' during the Korean War.

31. Kilic Bugra Kanat, 'The Securitization of the Uyghur Question and its Challenges', *Insight Turkey*, 18, 1 (2016), p. 195.
32. See Bovingdon, *The Uyghurs*; and Kamalov, 'Uyghurs in the Central Asian Republics', pp. 121–5.
33. See Michael Dillon, 'Central Asia: The View from Beijing, Urumqi and Kashghar', in Mehdi Mozaffari (ed.), *Security Politics in the Commonwealth of Independent States: The Southern Belt* (London: Macmillan, 1997), p. 140.
34. For Turkey's post-Cold War activism in Central Asia, see Shireen Hunter, 'Bridge or Frontier? Turkey's Post–Cold War Geopolitical Posture', *International Spectator*, 34, 1 (1999), pp. 71–2. See also Hakan Fidan, 'Turkish Foreign Policy towards Central Asia', *Journal of Balkan and Near Eastern Studies*, 12, 1 (2010), pp. 109–21.
35. A high point of Turkish rhetorical support for Uyghur aspirations in this period came in July 1995 when Istanbul's then mayor, Recep Tayyip Erdoğan, named a section of the Sultan Ahmet (Blue Mosque) Park in honour of Uyghur diaspora leader, Isa Yusuf Alptekin. Erdoğan asserted at the opening of the park that: 'Eastern Turkestan is not only the home of the Turkic peoples but also the cradle of Turkic history, civilization and culture. To forget that would lead to the ignorance of our own history, civilization and culture. The martyrs of Eastern Turkestan are our own martyrs.' Erdoğan's statement was reproduced in 'Istanbul Names Park for Isa Yusuf Alptekin', *East Turkistan Information Bulletin*, 5, 4 (1995), http://caccp.freedomsherald.org/et/etib/etib5_4.html#4, last accessed 19 November 2016.
36. See Michael Clarke, 'Xinjiang in the "Reform" Era, 1978–91: The Political and Economic Dynamics of Dengist Integration', *Issues and Studies*, 43, 2 (2007), pp. 50–54; and David Winchester, 'Beijing vs. Islam', *Asiaweek*, 23, 42 (24 October 1997), p. 37. For contemporary media reports on this incident, both Chinese and non-Chinese, see 'Rebellion Quelling Detailed', *Urumqi Xinjiang Television Network*, 22 April 1990, in FBIS-CHI 90–078, 23 April, pp. 62–5; David Chen, 'Killings Reported in Riot Suppression', *South China Morning Post*, 11 April 1990, in FBIS-CHI 90–070, 11 April 1990, p. 48; and Robert MacPherson, 'Traveller Reports Unrest in Xinjiang Region', *AFP*, 20 April 1990, in FBIS-CHI 90–077, 20 April 1990, p. 52.
37. Adapted from Dillon, 'Central Asia; The View from Beijing, Urumqi and Kashghar', pp. 140–41; and James Millward, 'Violent Separatism in Xinjiang: A Critical Assessment', *Policy Studies*, 6 (Washington, DC: East-West Center, 2004).
38. See, for instance, 'Song Hanliang Blames "Separatists"', *AFP*, 25 April 1990, in FBIS-CHI 90–080, 25 April 1990, p. 67; and 'Turkish Press on Developments', *Istanbul Milliyet*, 21 April 1990, in FBIS-CHI 90–080, 25 April 1990, pp. 69–70. Song Hanliang was then Xinjiang's CCP First Secretary.
39. See Sean Roberts, 'A "Land of Borderlands": Implications of Xinjiang's Trans-

border Interactions', in S. Frederick Starr (ed.), *Xinjiang: China's Muslim Borderland* (Armonk, NY: M. E. Sharpe, 2004); and Ziad Haider, 'Sino-Pakistan Relations and Xinjiang's Uighurs: Politics, Trade and Islam along the Karakoram Highway', *Asian Survey*, 45, 4 (2005), pp. 522–45.

40. Michael Clarke, 'China, Xinjiang and the Internationalisation of the Uyghur Issue', *Global Change, Peace and Security*, 22, 2 (2010), pp. 213–29.
41. Information Office of State Council, '"East Turkistan" Terrorist Forces Cannot Get Away With Impunity', 21 January 2002, http://www.china.org.cn/english/2002/Jan/25582.htm, last accessed 21 February 2017.
42. The WUC and ETIC were incorrectly identified by the MPS as 'terrorist' organizations, with both organizations being much more akin to what Adamson and Keck and Sikkink would describe as 'transnational mobilisation' or 'advocacy' networks. Both groups are NGOs based in Germany and are primarily engaged in publication of Xinjiang and Uyghur related news and information as a means of publicizing the cause of greater Uyghur autonomy in Xinjiang.
43. See for instance Millward, 'Violent Separatism in Xinjiang'; Clarke, 'China's "War on Terror" in Xinjiang'; and Sean Roberts, 'Imaginary Terrorism: The Global War on Terror and the Uyghur Terrorist Threat', *PONARS Eurasia Working Paper* (Washington, DC: Elliot School of International Affairs, March 2012), http://www.ponarseurasia.org/sites/default/files/Roberts_WorkingPaper_March2012.pdf, last accessed 7 June 2018.
44. See Andrew Small, *The China-Pakistan Axis: Asia's New Geopolitics* (London: Hurst & Co., 2015), pp. 145–50; Jacob Zenn, 'Jihad in China? Marketing the Turkistan Islamic Party', *Terrorism Monitor*, 9, 11 (2011), https://www.jamestown.org/program/jihad-in-china-marketing-the-turkistan-islamic-party/, last accessed 7 June 2018. Jacob Zenn, 'Turkistan Islamic Party Increases its Media Profile', *Central Asia-Caucasus Analyst*, 5 February 2014, http://www.cacianalyst.org/publications/analytical-articles/item/12909-turkistan-islamic-party-increases-its-media-profile.html, last accessed 1 June 2018.
45. Adapted from Murray Scot Tanner, *China's Response to Terrorism* (Washington, DC: CNA, March 2016), pp. 31–2.
46. See Michael Clarke, 'China and the Uyghurs: The "Palestinization" of Xinjiang?', *Middle East Policy*, 22, 3 (2015), pp. 127–46.
47. 金一南: 美想推翻巴沙尔政权 或将陷入困局, China National Radio, 1 November 2012, http://mil.cnr.cn/jmhdd/gfsk/wgf/201211/t20121101_511278541.html, last accessed 7 June 2018.
48. Lin Meilian, 'Xinjiang Terrorists Finding Training, Support in Syria, Turkey', *Global Times*, 7 January 2013, http://www.globaltimes.cn/content/792959.shtml#.UdLRkpxn1t1, last accessed 19 June 2016.
49. Metin Gurcan, 'How Islamic State is Exploiting Asian Unrest to Recruit Fighters', *Al-Monitor*, 9 September 2015, http://www.al-monitor.com/pulse/origi-

nals/2015/09/turkey-china-xinjiang-uighurs-isis-prevent-extremism.html#, last accessed 1 October 2016.

50. 'Uyghur Families Colonize Syrian Village', *Al Mayadeen*, 3 September 2015, http://www.memritv.org/clip/en/5089.htm, last accessed 25 June 2016.
51. See for example 'Kazakh Child Soldier Executes Russian Spies', *Foreign Policy*, 13 January 2015, http://foreignpolicy.com/2015/01/13/kazakh-child-soldier-executes-russian-spies-in-islamic-state-video/, last accessed 1 October 2016.
52. See Thomas Joscelyn, 'New al Nusrah Front Video Shows Moments Before Mass Execution of Syrian Soldiers', *Long War Journal*, 25 November 2015, http://www.longwarjournal.org/archives/2015/11/new-al-nusrah-front-video-shows-moment-before-mass-execution-of-syrian-soldiers.php, last accessed 11 March 2016; and Caleb Weiss, 'Turkistan Islamic Party Shows Fighters on Frontlines in Northwestern Syria', *Long War Journal*, 14 October 2015, http://www.longwarjournal.org/archives/2015/10/turkistan-islamic-party-shows-fighters-on-frontlines-in-northwestern-syria.php, last accessed 11 March 2016.
53. Leith Aboufadel, 'Uyghur Terrorist Killed by the Syrian Army in Northwest Hama', *Al-Masdar News*, 26 October 2015, http://www.almasdarnews.com/article/uyghur-terrorist-killed-by-the-syrian-army-in-northwest-hama/, last accessed 11 February 2017.
54. See Zachary Abuza, 'Uyghurs Look to Indonesia for Terror Guidance', *Asia Times*, 10 October 2014, http://www.atimes.com/atimes/Southeast_Asia/SEA-01–101014.html, last accessed 20 June 2016; and Zahara Tiba, 'Uyghurs on Trial in Indonesia are Turkish Citizens, Lawyer Says', *Benar News*, 4 September 2015, http://www.benarnews.org/english/news/indonesian/indonesia-uyghurs-04092015161611.html, last accessed 20 June 2016.
55. Catherine Putz, 'Thailand Deports 100 Uyghurs to China', *The Diplomat*, 11 July 2015, http://thediplomat.com/2015/07/thailand-deports-100-uyghurs-to-china/, last accessed 20 June 2016.
56. Seymour Hersh, 'Military to Military', *London Review of Books*, 38, 1 (2016), https://www.lrb.co.uk/v38/n01/seymour-m-hersh/military-to-military, last accessed 11 February 2017.
57. See Michael Clarke, 'Uyghur Militants in Syria: The Turkish Connection', *Terrorism Monitor*, 14, 3 (2016), https://jamestown.org/program/uyghur-militants-in-syria-the-turkish-connection/, last accessed 15 March 2017.
58. 'Illegal migrants' failed dreams of "heavenly life"', *Xinhua*, 18 July 2015, http://news.xinhuanet.com/english/2015–07/18/c_134424601.htm, last accessed 15 March 2017.
59. Edward Wong, 'Turks Are Held in Plot to Help Uighurs Leave China', *New York Times*, 14 January 2015, http://www.nytimes.com/2015/01/15/world/asia/10-turks-said-to-be-under-arrest-for-aiding-terrorist-suspects-in-china.html?_r=0, last accessed 15 March 2017.
60. Liu Chang, 'Turks, Uyghurs held in Smuggling, Terrorism Scheme', *Global Times*,

14 January 2015, http://www.globaltimes.cn/content/901866.shtml, last accessed 15 March 2017.
61. Eriksson and Rhinard, 'The Internal–External Security Nexus', p. 253.
62. Ibid.
63. Matt McDonald defines securitization 'as a process in which an actor declares a particular issue, dynamic or actor to be an "existential threat" to a particular referent object. If accepted as such by a relevant audience, this enables the suspension of normal politics and the use of emergency measures in responding to that perceived crisis.' Matt McDonald, 'Constructivism', in Paul D. Williams (ed.), *Security Studies: An Introduction* (London: Routledge, 2008), p. 69. See also Ole Waever, 'Securitization and Desecuritization', in Ronnie D. Lipschutz (ed.), *On Security* (New York: Columbia University Press, 1995), pp. 46–86.
64. See for example Michael Clarke, 'The Problematic Progress of "Integration" in the Chinese State's Approach to Xinjiang, 1759–2005', *Asian Ethnicity*, 8, 3 (2007), pp. 261–89.
65. See Clarke, *Xinjiang and China's Rise in Central Asia*, pp. 125–9.
66. Nicolas Becquelin, 'Staged Development in Xinjiang', *China Quarterly*, 178 (June 2004), pp. 358–78.
67. Raffaello Pantucci and Alexandros Petersen, 'China's Inadvertent Empire', *The National Interest*, 122 (November/December 2012), pp. 31–3.
68. 'Xi Suggests China, CA Build Silk Road Economic Belt', *Xinhua*, 7 September 2013, http://news.xinhuanet.com/english/china/2013–09/07/c_132700695.htm, last accessed 1 February 2017.
69. For detailed discussion, see Becquelin, 'Staged Development in Xinjiang'; Matthew D. Moneyhon, 'China's Great Western Development Project in Xinjiang: Economic Palliative, or Political Trojan Horse?', *Denver Journal of International Law and Policy*, 31, 3 (2002/3), pp. 491–519; Elena Barabantseva, 'Development as Localization: Ethnic Minorities in China's Official Discourse on the Western Development Project', *Critical Asian Studies*, 41, 2 (2009), pp. 225–54; and Carla Freeman, 'From "Blood Transfusion" to "Harmonious Development": The Political Economy of Fiscal Allocations to China's Ethnic Regions', *Journal of Current Chinese Affairs*, 41, 4 (2012), pp. 11–44.
70. For example, the 'renovation' of much of the old city of Kashgar, one of southern Xinjiang's centres of traditional Uyghur culture and the hub of the famed Silk Road, through the $500 million 'Kashgar Dangerous House Reform' programme, has displaced thousands of Uyghur residents and brought an influx of Han migrants to the region. Such dynamics ultimately contribute to long-standing perceptions among Uyghurs of demographic dilution and economic disenfranchisement. See Ildikó Bellér-Hann, 'The Bulldozer State: Chinese Socialist Development in Xinjiang', in Madeleine Reeves, Johan Rasanayagam and Judith Beyer (eds), *Ethnographies of the State in Central Asia: Performing Politics* (Bloomington, IN: University of Indiana Press, 2014), pp. 173–97.

71. For a good overview of core economic drivers of Uyghur grievance, see Debasish Chaudhuri, 'Minority Economy in Xinjiang—A Source of Uyghur Resentment', *China Report*, 46, 1 (2010), pp. 9–27; Sean Roberts and Kilic Bugra Kanat, 'China's Wild West: A Cautionary Tale of Ethnic Conflict and Development', *The Diplomat*, 15 July 2013, http://thediplomat.com/2013/07/chinas-wild-west/?allpages=yes, last accessed 1 February 2017; and Yan Sun, 'The Roots of China's Ethnic Conflicts', *Current History* 113, 764 (September 2014), pp. 233–4.
72. See for example Loveday Wright, 'Xinjiang: Restrictions on Religion May Lead to "Uighur Radicalization"', *Deutsche Welle*, 8 August 2014, http://www.dw.de/xinjiang-restrictions-on-religion-may-lead-to-uighur-radicalization/a-17841070, last accessed 17 March 2016; and 'Ban in Public Buses Targets Muslims in Xinjiang', *The National*, 6 August 2014, http://www.thenational.ae/world/east-asia/ban-in-public-buses-targets-muslims-in-xinjiang, last accessed 17 March 2016.
73. Cao Siqi, 'Xinjiang Counties Identify 75 Forms of Religious Extremism', *Global Times*, 25 December 2014, http://www.globaltimes.cn/content/898563.shtml, last accessed 19 March 2016.
74. Ma Rong, 'A New Perspective in Guiding Ethnic Relations in the Twenty-first Century: "De-politicization" of Ethnicity in China', *Asian Ethnicity*, 8, 3 (2007), p. 214. For excellent discussions of how this debate has evolved, see James Leibold, 'Ethnic Policy in China: Is Reform Inevitable?', *Policy* Studies, 68 (Washington, DC: East–West Center, 2013), pp. 14–21; Barry Sautman, 'Scaling Back Minority Rights? The Debate About China's Ethnic Policies', *Stanford Journal of International Law*, 46 (2010), pp. 51–120; and David Tobin, 'Worrying About Ethnicity: A New Generation of China Dreams?', in David Kerr (ed.), *China's Many Dreams: Comparative Perspectives on China's Search for National Rejuvenation* (London: Palgrave Macmillan, 2015), pp. 65–93.
75. Rong, 'A New Perspective in Guiding Ethnic Relations', p. 214.
76. Leibold, 'Ethnic Policy in China', p. 18.
77. James Leibold and Timothy Grose, 'Islamic Veiling in Xinjiang: The Political and Societal Struggle to Define Uyghur Female Adornment', *China Journal*, 76 (July 2016), pp. 80, 88.
78. Ibid., pp. 88–90.
79. 'Xinjiang nüxing "liangli gongcheng" yu xiandai wenhua' [Modern culture and 'Project Beauty' for Xinjiang women], *Tianshan Net*, 9 May 2012, http://www.ts.cn/special/2011_Beautiful/2012–05/09/content_6814977.htm, last accessed 9 February 2017.
80. Leibold and Grose, 'Islamic Veiling in Xinjiang', p. 93.
81. James Millward, 'China's Two Problems with the Uyghurs', *Los Angeles Review of Books*, 28 May 2014, https://lareviewofbooks.org/essay/chinas-two-problems-uyghurs, last accessed 21 April 2016.
82. Brandon Barbour and Reece Jones, 'Criminals, Terrorists, and Outside Agitators:

Representational Tropes of the "Other" in the 5 July Xinjiang, China Riots', *Geopolitics*, 18, 1 (2013), p. 112.
83. Keith Martin, 'China and Central Asia: Between Seduction and Suspicion', *RFE/RL Research Report* 3, 25 (24 June 1994), pp. 30–32.
84. '"Shanghai Five" Nations Sign Joint Statement', *People's Daily*, 6 July 2000, http://en.people.cn/200007/06/eng20000706_44803.html, last accessed 4 October 2016. On the rise of radical Islamism in Central Asia, see Ahmed Rashid, *Jihad: The Rise of Militant Islam in Central Asia* (New Haven, CT: Yale University Press, 2002).
85. Marc Lanteigne, '"In Medias Res": The Development of the Shanghai Co-operation Organization as a Security Community', *Pacific Affairs* 79, 4 (2006/7), p. 616.
86. Flemming Splidsboel Hansen, 'The Shanghai Cooperation Organisation', *Asian Affairs*, 39, 2 (2008), p. 220.
87. Boris Rumer, 'The Powers in Central Asia', *Survival*, 44, 3 (2002), pp. 59–60.
88. Thomas Ambrosio, 'Catching the "Shanghai Spirit": How the Shanghai Cooperation Organization Promotes Authoritarian Norms in Central Asia', *Europe–Asia Studies*, 60, 8 (2008), pp. 1321–44.
89. Suzanna Farizova, 'Allies Let Him Down', *Kommersant*, 29 August 2008, http://www.kommersant.com/p1017558/SCO_refused_to_support_russia/, last accessed 1 June 2018; and Stephen Blank, 'The Shanghai Cooperation Organization and the Georgian Crisis', *China Brief*, 8, 17 (2008).
90. Michael Clarke, 'Widening the Net: China's Anti-Terror Laws and Human Rights in the Xinjiang Uyghur Autonomous Region', *The International Journal of Human Rights* 14, 4 (2010), pp. 542–58.
91. Zhao Huasheng, 'China's Views of and Expectations from the Shanghai Cooperation Organization', *Asian Survey*, 53, 3 (2013), p. 440.
92. Richard Weitz, 'Shanghai Cooperation Organization: A New Force in Asian Security?', *Korean Journal of Defense Analysis*, 23, 1 (2011), p. 133.
93. Zhao, 'China's Views of and Expectations from the Shanghai Cooperation Organization', p. 441.
94. Nicole J. Jackson, 'Trans-Regional Security Organisations and Statist Multilateralism in Eurasia', *Europe–Asia Studies*, 66, 2 (2014), p. 185.
95. Cui Jia and Gao Bo, 'Xinjiang Doubles Terror Fight Budget', *China Daily*, 17 January 2014, http://www.chinadaily.com.cn/china/2014-01/17/content_17240295.htm, last accessed 23 January 2017.
96. Julia Famularo, 'How Xinjiang has Transformed China's Counterterrorism Policies', *National Interest*, 26 August 2015, http://nationalinterest.org/feature/how-xinjiang-has-transformed-china%E2%80%99s-counterterrorism-13699, last accessed 5 March 2017.
97. Adrian Zenz and James Leibold, 'Xinjiang's Rapidly Evolving Security State', *China Brief*, 17, 4 (14 March 2017), https://jamestown.org/program/xinjiangs-rapidly-evolving-security-state/, last accessed 1 June 2018.

98. Weixing Hu, 'Xi Jinping's "Big Power Diplomacy" and China's Central National Security Commission', *Journal of Contemporary China*, 25, 98 (2016), p. 167.
99. Shen Dingli, 'Framing China's National Security', *China–US Focus*, 23 April 2014, http://www.chinausfocus.com/peace-security/framing-chinas-national-security/#sthash.of0a7dBc.dpuf, last accessed 16 June 2016.
100. David M. Lampton, 'Xi Jinping and the National Security Commission: Policy Coordination and Political Power', *Journal of Contemporary China*, 24, 95 (2015), p. 763.
101. See for example Shi Lan, 'Pride and Prejudice in Anti-Terror Fight', *China Daily*, 4 January 2016, http://www.chinadaily.com.cn/opinion/2016–01/04/content_22917814.htm, last accessed 25 February 2016; and Shen Dingli, 'US' Accusation about Anti-Terror Law', *China Daily*, 30 December 2015, http://www.chinadaily.com.cn/opinion/2015-12/30/content_22863020.htm, last accessed 7 February 2017.
102. Peter Mattis, 'New Law Reshapes Chinese Counterterrorism Policy and Operations', *China Brief*, 16, 2 (25 January 2016).
103. 'Counter Terrorism Law of the People's Republic of China, Passed by the 18th Session of the Standing Committee of the 12th National People's Congress on December 27, 2015', *China Law Translate*, https://www.chinalawtranslate.com/反恐怖主义法-(2015)/?lang=en, last accessed 3 February 2017; and for the Chinese text, see http://news.xinhuanet.com/politics/2015–12/27/c_128571798.htm, last accessed 3 February 2017.
104. See for instance Susan Trevaskes, 'Rationalising Stability Preservation through Mao's Not So Invisible Hand', *Journal of Current Chinese Affairs*, 42, 2 (2013), pp. 51–77.
105. Shannon Tiezzi, 'Suicide Bombings in China: Beyond Terrorism', *The Diplomat*, 22 July 2015, http://thediplomat.com/2015/07/suicide-bombings-in-china-beyond-terrorism/, last accessed 7 November 2016.
106. Counter Terrorism Law of the People's Republic of China.
107. 'Suspect of Guangxi mail bomb confirmed dead in blast', *South China Morning Post*, 2 October 2015, http://www.scmp.com/news/china/policies-politics/article/1863584/suspect-chinese-parcel-bomb-attacks-confirmed-dead, last accessed 11 July 2016.
108. Tho Cliff, 'The "Terror" Angle in China's Domestic "Stability Maintenance"', *China Policy Institute Blog*, 18 March 2016, http://blogs.nottingham.ac.uk/chinapolicyinstitute/2016/03/18/the-terror-angle-in-chinas-domestic-stability-maintenance,/ last accessed 8 May 2016.
109. See Norrin Ripsman and T. V. Paul, 'Globalization and the National Security State: A Framework for Analysis', *International Studies Review*, 7, 2 (2005), pp. 199–227.

2. 'FIGHTING THE ENEMY WITH FISTS AND DAGGERS': THE CHINESE COMMUNIST PARTY'S COUNTER-TERRORISM POLICY IN THE XINJIANG UYGHUR AUTONOMOUS REGION

1. For a fascinating discussion of the challenges which scholars confront when using ancient texts—such as the Commentary of Zuo—to decipher and interpret Chinese views on ethnicity, see Tamara Chin, 'Antiquarian as Ethnographer: Han Ethnicity in Early China Studies', in Thomas Mullaney, James Patrick Leibold, Stéphane Gros and Eric Armand Vanden Bussche (eds), *Critical Han Studies: The History, Representation, and Identity of China's Majority* (Berkeley, CA: University of California Press, 2012), pp. 128–46, 287–99.
2. Christopher K. Johnson, 'Thoughts from the Chairman: Xi Jinping Unveils his Foreign Policy Vision', *Center for Strategic and International Studies*, 8 December 2014, https://www.csis.org/analysis/thoughts-chairman-xi-jinping-unveils-his-foreign-policy-vision, last accessed 5 March 2017.
3. Leaders since Deng Xiaoping have pledged to create a *xiaokang*, or 'moderately well-off' society in China. See 'All About "*Xiaokang*"', *Xinhua News Agency*, 10 November 2002, http://www.china.org.cn/english/features/48531.htm, last accessed 5 March 2017; An Baijie, 'Xi pledges "new era" in building moderately prosperous society', *China Daily*, 19 October 2017, http://www.chinadaily.com.cn/china/2017-10/19/content_33428169_2.htm, last accessed 27 January 2018; Christopher K. Johnson and Scott Kennedy, 'Xi Jinping Opens 19th Party Congress Proclaiming a New Era—His', Center for Strategic and International Studies, 18 October 2017, https://www.csis.org/analysis/xi-jinping-opens-19th-party-congress-proclaiming-new-era-his, last accessed 27 January 2018.
4. Xi Jinping, 'Full text of Xi Jinping's report at 19th CPC National Congress', *China Daily*, 4 November 2017, http://www.chinadaily.com.cn/china/19thcpcnationalcongress/2017-11/04/content_34115212.htm, last accessed 27 January 2018; Shannon Tiezzi, 'Why 2020 is a Make-or-Break Year for China', *The Diplomat*, 13 February 2015, http://thediplomat.com/2015/02/why-2020-is-a-make-or-break-year-for-china/, last accessed 5 March 2017. For more information on how the Chinese government conceptualizes the 'China Dream', see Zhang Zhouxiang, 'Chinese Dream to benefit entire world', *China Daily*, 23 November 2017, http://www.chinadaily.com.cn/opinion/2017-11/23/content_34881148.htm, last accessed 27 January 2018; 'Chinese Dream', *Xinhua*, http://www.xinhuanet.com/english/special/chinesedream/, last accessed 27 January 2018; and 'Chinese Dream', *China Daily*, http://www.chinadaily.com.cn/china/Chinese-dream.html, last accessed 27 January 2018.
5. For an introduction to Turkic Muslim peoples as well as Xinjiang [East Turkestan] society and history, see the following: Gardner Bovingdon, *The Uyghurs: strangers in their own land* (New York: Columbia University Press, 2010); David Brophy, *Uyghur Nation: Reform and Revolution on the Russia–China Frontier* (Cambridge,

MA: Harvard University Press, 2016); Trine Brox and Ildikó Bellér-Hann (eds), *On the Fringes of the Harmonious Society: Tibetans and Uyghurs in Socialist China* (Copenhagen: NIAS Press, 2014); Michael Clarke and Anna Hayes (eds), *Inside Xinjiang: space, place, and power in China's Muslim Far Northwest* (New York: Routledge, 2016); Tom Cliff, *Oil and Water: Being Han in Xinjiang* (Chicago, IL: University of Chicago Press, 2016); Ben Hillman and Gray Tuttle (eds), *Ethnic Conflict and Protest in Tibet and Xinjiang: Unrest in China's West* (New York: Columbia University Press, 2016); Justin Jacobs, *Xinjiang and the Modern Chinese State* (Seattle, WA: University of Washington Press, 2016); James Leibold and Chen Yangbin, *Minority Education in China: Balancing unity and diversity in an era of critical pluralism* (Hong Kong: Hong Kong University Press, 2014); James Millward, *Eurasian Crossroads: A History of Xinjiang* (New York: Columbia University Press, 2007); Joanne Smith Finley, *The Art of Symbolic Resistance: Uyghur identities and Uyghur–Han relations in contemporary Xinjiang* (Boston, MA: Brill, 2013); Joanne Smith Finley and Xiaowei Zang (eds), *Language, Education and Uyghur Identity in Urban Xinjiang* (New York: Routledge, 2015); and Rian Richard Thum, *The Sacred Routes of Uyghur History* (Cambridge, MA: Harvard University Press, 2014).

6. Stanley Toops, 'Spatial Results of the 2010 Census in Xinjiang', University of Nottingham, China Policy Institute: *Analysis blog*, 7 March 2016, https://cpianalysis.org/2016/03/07/spatial-results-of-the-2010-census-in-xinjiang/, last accessed 5 March 2017.

7. For example, see Emily Feng and Edward Wong, 'Q. and A.: Ben Hillman and Gray Tuttle on Ethnic Unrest in Xinjiang and Tibet', *New York Times*, 26 May 2016, http://www.nytimes.com/2016/05/27/world/asia/china-xinjiang-tibet-ethnic-unrest.html, last accessed 5 March 2017; 'Settlers in Xinjiang: Circling the wagons', *The Economist*, 25 May 2013, http://www.economist.com/news/china/21578433-region-plagued-ethnic-strife-growth-immigrant-dominated-settlements-adding, last accessed 5 March 2017; "China's drive to settle new wave of migrants in restive Xinjiang", South China Morning Post, http://www.scmp.com/news/china/society/article/1789160/chinas-drive-settle-new-wave-migrants-restive-xinjiang, last accessed 7 June 2018; and Tom Mitchell, 'China's Great Game: New frontier, old foes', *Financial Times*, 13 October 2015, https://www.ft.com/content/60f33cf8-6dae-11e5-8171-ba1968cf791a, last accessed 5 March 2017.

8. Tom Cliff, 'Oil and Water: Being Han in Xinjiang', *Chinoiresie*, 25 July 2016, http://www.chinoiresie.info/oil-and-water-being-han-in-xinjiang/, last accessed 5 March 2017.

9. Michael Clarke, 'Beijing redoubles counter-terrorism efforts in Xinjiang', *East Asia Forum*, 26 February 2014, http://www.eastasiaforum.org/2014/02/26/beijing-redoubles-counter-terrorism-efforts-in-xinjiang/, last accessed 5 March 2017. Some observers question why Xi Jinping failed to launch a strike-hard campaign at the beginning of his tenure; it is possible that he desired to consolidate greater power before beginning to implement his bold vision for strengthening the Party-state.

10. 'Xinjiang's Party chief wages "people's war" against terrorism', *China Daily*, 26 May 2014, http://europe.chinadaily.com.cn/china/2014-05/26/content_17541353.htm, last accessed 5 March 2017.
11. Ibid.
12. Adrian Zenz and James Leibold, 'Chen Quanguo: The Strongman Behind Beijing's Securitization Strategy in Tibet and Xinjiang', *China Brief*, 21 September 2017, https://jamestown.org/program/chen-quanguo-the-strongman-behind-beijings-securitization-strategy-in-tibet-and-xinjiang/, last accessed 27 January 2018.
13. See 'Statement by H.E. Mr. Tang Jiaxuan, Minister of Foreign Affairs and Head of Delegation of The People's Republic of China, At the 56th Session of the UN General Assembly', Permanent Mission of the People's Republic of China to the UN, 11 November 2001, http://www.china-un.org/eng/zt/fk/t28933.htm, last accessed 5 March 2017; Shirley A. Kan, 'U.S.-China Counterterrorism Cooperation: Issues for U.S. Policy', Congressional Research Service, 15 July 2010, https://fas.org/sgp/crs/terror/RL33001.pdf, last accessed 5 March 2017; 'Counter-Terrorism and Human Rights: The Impact of the Shanghai Cooperation Organization', *Human Rights in China*, March 2011, http://www.hrichina.org/en/publications/hric-report/counter-terrorism-and-human-rights-impact-shanghai-cooperation-organization, last accessed 5 March 2017; and Eleanor Albert, 'The Shanghai Cooperation Organization', *Council on Foreign Relations*, 14 October 2015, http://www.cfr.org/china/shanghai-cooperation-organization/p10883, last accessed 5 March 2017.
14. Xi Jinping, 'Speech at the Meeting Marking the 65th Anniversary of the Founding of the Chinese People's Political Consultative Conference', *Guangming Daily*, 22 September 2014, as cited in *Theory China*, 13 November 2014, http://en.theorychina.org/xsqy_2477/201411/t20141113_314382.shtml, last accessed 5 March 2017.
15. James Leibold, 'China's Minority Report: When Racial Harmony Means Homogenization', *Foreign Affairs*, 23 March 2016, https://www.foreignaffairs.com/articles/china/2016-03-23/chinas-minority-report, last accessed 5 March 2017.
16. James Leibold, 'China's Ethnic Policy Under Xi Jinping', *China Brief*, 19 October 2015, https://jamestown.org/program/chinas-ethnic-policy-under-xi-jinping/, last accessed 5 March 2017.
17. Losang Jamcan (Losang Gyaltsen), 'Handling Ethnic Issues the Chinese Way', *Seeking Truth (Qiushi Journal)*, 7, 3, 24 (July–September 2015), http://english.qstheory.cn/2015-08/19/c_1116183251.htm, last accessed 5 March 2017.
18. 'Document 9: A ChinaFile Translation', *Asia Society, ChinaFile* blog, 8 November 2013, https://www.chinafile.com/document-9-chinafile-translation, last accessed 5 March 2017.
19. Ibid. Party leaders have subsequently placed great emphasis on the study and imple-

mentation of the 'spirit' of the Nineteenth Party Congress, which took place 18–24 October 2017. See '19th National Congress of the Communist Party of China', www.gov.cn, http://english.gov.cn/19thcpccongress/, last accessed 8 February 2018.

20. Ibid.
21. Ibid. For further analysis of this issue, see Julia Famularo, 'The China–Russia NGO Crackdown', *The Diplomat*, 23 February 2015, http://thediplomat.com/2015/02/the-china-russia-ngo-crackdown/, last accessed 5 March 2017.
22. 'Document 9: A ChinaFile Translation'.
23. See 'The Belt and Road Initiative', State Council of the People's Republic of China, http://english.gov.cn/beltAndRoad/, last accessed 8 February 2018; and Michael Clarke, 'Cracks in China's New Silk Road', *China Policy Institute: Analysis* blog, 15 March 2016, https://cpianalysis.org/2016/03/15/cracks-on-chinas-new-silk-road-xinjiang-one-belt-one-road-and-the-trans-nationalization-of-uyghur-terrorism/, last accessed 5 March 2017.
24. 古丽燕 [Gu Liyan], '新时期'东突'恐怖活动新动向及对策研究 [A New Era for the 'East Turkestan' Terrorist Movements: New Trends and Countermeasures]', 新疆警官高等专科学校学报 [*Journal of Xinjiang Police Officers' Academy*] 33, 1 (June 2013), p. 7.
25. 王秀丽 [Wang Xiuli], '新疆网络安全领域意识形态建设之思想 [Xinjiang Internet Security: Reflecting on and Constructing an Ideological Sphere]', 新疆警官高等专科学校学报 [*Journal of Xinjiang Police Officers' Academy*] 32, 1 (January 2012), p. 27.
26. 陈全成 [Chen Quancheng], '中国梦理论维度下维护新疆高校安全稳定的路径思考 [Research on the Way to Maintain Security and Stability at Xinjiang Universities Based on the 'China Dream' Theory], 喀什大学学报/喀什师范学院学报 [*Journal of Kashgar University/Journal of Kashgar Teachers College*] 36, 4 (July/August 2015), pp. 10–13.
27. While serving as Tibet Autonomous Region Party Secretary, current Xinjiang Party Secretary Chen Quanguo published an article on Tibet ideological work in the CCP journal *Seeking Truth*, entitled 'Ensuring the Security of Tibet's Ideological Realm with the Spirit of Daring to Show the Sword—Conscientiously Studying and Implementing the Important Essence of the Speech Made by General Secretary Xi Jinping at the National Propaganda and Ideology Word Conference'. For those seeking greater insight into his political, ideological and security priorities, see 陈全国 [Chen Quanguo], '以敢于亮剑的精神确保西藏意识形态领域安全—认真学习贯彻习近平总书记在全国宣传思想工作会议上的重要讲话精神 [Ensuring the Security of Tibet's Ideological Realm with the Spirit of Daring to Show the Sword—Conscientiously Studying and Implementing the Important Essence of the Speech Made by General Secretary Xi Jinping at the National Propaganda and Ideology Word Conference]', 求实 [*Seeking Truth*], 1 November 2013, http://www.qstheory.cn/zxdk/2013/201321/201310/t20131030_284158.htm, last accessed

5 March 2017. For an English translation of the article, see 'TAR Party Secretary Chen Quanguo on New Propaganda and Control of Social Media Strategy', *High Peaks Pure Earth*, 11 November 2013, http://highpeakspureearth.com/2013/tar-party-secretary-chen-quanguo-on-new-propaganda-and-control-of-social-media-strategy/, last accessed 5 March 2017.

28. 张弛 [Zhang Chi], '新疆维吾尔自治区文化厅党组中心组迅速学习贯彻中央、自治区党委文件精神 [The XUAR Department of Culture seeks to rapidly study and implement the spirit of Document 9]', 中华人民共和国文化部 [Ministry of Culture of the People's Republic of China], 24 May 2013, http://www.mcprc.gov.cn/whzx/qgwhxxlb/xinjiang/201305/t20130524_422932.html, last accessed 5 March 2017.
29. See Zhang, 'The XUAR Department of Culture seeks to rapidly study and implement the spirit of Document 9'.
30. See the following section of China's 1997 White Paper on Freedom of Religious Belief: 'Legal Protection of the Freedom of Religious Belief', Information Office of the State Council of the People's Republic of China, http://china.org.cn/e-white/Freedom/f-2.htm, last accessed 5 March 2017.
31. 'Regulations on Religious Affairs (Chinese and English Text)', Congressional-Executive Commission on China, http://www.cecc.gov/resources/legal-provisions/regulations-on-religious-affairs, last accessed 5 March 2017.
32. Ibid.
33. Ibid.
34. Tian Shaohui, 'China Focus: Xi calls for improved religious work', *Xinhua*, 23 April 2016, http://news.xinhuanet.com/english/2016–04/23/c_135306131.htm, last accessed 28 January 2018.
35. See Appendix I of 'Devastating Blows: Religious Repression of Uighurs in Xinjiang', *Human Rights Watch*, 17, 2(C) (April 2005), https://www.hrw.org/reports/2005/china0405/china0405.pdf, last accessed 5 March 2017, to read the entire text of the 2001 Xinjiang Uyghur Autonomous Region Regulations on the Management of Religious Affairs.
36. Ibid.
37. US Department of State, Bureau of Democracy, Human Rights, and Labor, '2016 International Religious Freedom Report: China (Includes Tibet, Hong Kong, and Macau)', *US Department of State*, 15 August 2017, http://www.state.gov/j/drl/rls/irf/religiousfreedom/index.htm?year=2016&dlid=268722, last accessed 27 January 2018.
38. Ibid.
39. For further information, see '2016 International Religious Freedom Report: China'.
40. General Secretary Xi was likely the first CCP leader since Jiang Zemin to chair a national religious affairs conference. Normally, the head of the State Administration for Religious Affairs chairs such meetings. See Jessica Batke, 'PRC Religious Policy: Serving the Gods of the CCP', *China Leadership Monitor*, 52 14 February 2017,

https://www.hoover.org/sites/default/files/research/docs/clm52jb.pdf, last accessed 28 January 2018.

41. See James Leibold, 'Xinjiang Work Forum Marks New Policy of "Ethnic Mingling"', *China Brief*, 19 June 2014, https://jamestown.org/program/xinjiang-work-forum-marks-new-policy-of-ethnic-mingling/, last accessed 5 March 2017.

42. '精心做好宗教工作: 三论学习贯彻习近平总书记新疆工作座谈会重要讲话精神 [Do Religious Work Meticulously Well: Three Theories on the Study and Implementation of General Secretary Xi Jinping's Important Speech at the Xinjiang Work Forum]', 人民日报 [*People's Daily*], 4 June 2014, sec. A1, http://opinion.people.com.cn/n/2014/0604/c1003–25099303.html, last accessed 5 March 2017.

43. Leibold, 'Xinjiang Work Forum Marks New Policy of "Ethnic Mingling"'.
44. 'Do Religious Work Meticulously Well'.
45. Ibid.
46. Ibid.
47. Ibid.
48. Ibid.
49. Ibid.
50. Ibid.
51. Tian Shaohui, 'China Focus: Xi calls for improved religious work'.
52. Ibid.
53. 'Do Religious Work Meticulously Well'.
54. Cui Jia, 'Curbs on Religious Extremism Beefed up in Xinjiang', *China Daily*, 29 November 2014, www.chinadaily.com.cn/china/2014–11/29/content_18996900.htm, last accessed 5 March 2017.
55. Ibid.; Julia Famularo, 'The Latest from the Shanghai Cooperation Organization', *National Interest*, 24 September 2013, http://nationalinterest.org/commentary/the-latest-the-shanghai-cooperation-organization-9118, last accessed 5 March 2017; and 'Regulations on Religious Affairs (Chinese and English Text)', Congressional-Executive Commission on China.
56. Mao Weihua and Cui Jia, 'New Xinjiang regulation aims to prevent extremism', *China Daily*, 31 March 2017, http://www.chinadaily.com.cn/china/2017–03/31/content_28747922.htm, last accessed 3 February 2018. Even before the legislation was passed, various initiatives sought to root out 'extremist' practices from society. For example, as part of the 'Three Illegals and One Item' campaign, authorities banned 'illegal' religious publications, activities and teachings, as well as items perceived as potential 'tools of terrorism', such as 'knives, flammable objects, remote-controlled toys, and objects sporting symbols related to Islam'. Officials began to confiscate Qurans published prior to 2012, claiming that they also contained 'extremist' content. See Qiao Long, Wong Lok-to and Luisetta Mudie, 'Chinese Police Order Xinjiang's Muslims to Hand in All Copies of the Quran', Radio Free Asia, 27 September 2017, https://www.rfa.org/english/news/uyghur/

chinese-police-order-xinjiangs-muslims-to-hand-in-all-copies-of-the-quran-0927 2017113203.html, last accessed 8 February 2018.

57. 《新疆维吾尔自治区去极端化条例》公布实施 [Xinjiang Uyghur Autonomous Region Regulation on De-extremification, Implementation Announcement], 国家宗教事务局 [State Administration for Religious Affairs], 1 April 2017, http://www.sara.gov.cn/old/dfgz/395966.htm, last accessed 3 February 2018. For an unofficial English translation, see 'Xinjiang Uyghur Autonomous Region Regulation on De-extremification', *China Law Translate*, 30 March 2017, http://www.chinalawtranslate.com/新疆维吾尔自治区去极端化条例/?lang=en, last accessed 3 February 2018.
58. Mao Weihua and Cui Jia, 'New Xinjiang regulation aims to prevent extremism'.
59. 'China Uighurs: Ban on long beards, veils in Xinjiang', *Al Jazeera*, 1 April 2017, http://www.aljazeera.com/news/2017/04/china-uighurs-ban-long-beards-veils-xinjiang-170401050336713.html, last accessed 4 February 2018. For more information on the purported '75 signs of religious extremism', see Simon Denyer, 'From burqas to boxing gloves, China's 75 tips for spotting extremist Muslims', *Washington Post*, 12 December 2014, https://www.washingtonpost.com/news/worldviews/wp/2014/12/12/from-burqas-to-boxing-gloves-chinas-75-tips-for-spotting-extremist-muslims/, last accessed 6 February 2018; Cao Siqi, 'Xinjiang counties identify 75 forms of religious extremism', *Global Times*, 25 December 2014, http://www.globaltimes.cn/content/898563.shtml, last accessed 6 February 2018; '新疆部分地区学习识别75种宗教极端活动 遇到可报警 [Some parts of Xinjiang learn to recognize 75 types of religious extremist activities: report them to police upon encountering them]', 中国社会科学院 [Chinese Academy of Social Sciences], 24 December 2014, http://www.cssn.cn/zjx/zjx_zjsj/201412/t20141224_1454905.shtml, last accessed 6 February 2018.
60. Cui Jia, 'Rule of Law is "Key to Xinjiang Terror Fight"', *China Daily*, 26 November 2014, http://www.chinadaily.com.cn/china/2014-11/26/content_18980203.htm, last accessed 5 March 2017.
61. Leibold, 'Xinjiang Work Forum Marks New Policy of "Ethnic Mingling"'.
62. Peter Ford, 'China Targets "Hostile Foreign Forces" in Crescendo of Accusations', *Christian Science Monitor*, 9 November 2014, www.csmonitor.com/World/Asia-Pacific/2014/1109/China-targets-hostile-foreign-forces-in-crescendo-of-accusations?cmpid, last accessed 5 March 2017; 王秀丽 [Wang Xiuli], '新疆网络安全领域意识形态建设之思考 [Reflecting on Building a Xinjiang Network Security Ideological Sphere]', 新疆警官高等专科学校学报 [*Journal of Xinjiang Police Officers' Academy*], 1 (2012), mall.cnki.net/magazine/Article/JGXJ201201009.htm, last accessed 5 March 2017; and Andrew Browne, 'Patriot Blogger Embodies Beijing's Web Vision', *Wall Street Journal*, 2 December 2014, http://www.wsj.com/articles/patriot-blogger-embodies-beijings-web-vision-1417515371, last accessed 5 March 2017.

63. 'Anti-Terror Cooperation', *China Daily*, 3 July 2013, www.chinadaily.com.cn/opinion/2013−07/03/content_16712493.htm, last accessed 5 March 2017; Phillip Wen, 'Internet behind Terrorism in China, Including Kunming Railway Massacre: Xinjiang Leader', *Sydney Morning Herald*, 7 March 2014, www.smh.com.au/world/internet-behind-terrorism-in-china-including-kunming-railway-massacre-xinjiang-leader-20140306-hvghi.html, last accessed 5 March 2017; 'China's Xinjiang Problem: The Net is Cast', *The Economist*, 1 July 2014, http://www.economist.com/blogs/analects/2014/07/chinas-xinjiang-problem, last accessed 5 March 2017; and David Wertime, 'An Internet Where Nobody Says Anything', *Foreign Policy*, 25 September 2014, foreignpolicy.com/2014/09/25/an-internet-where-nobody-says-anything/, last accessed 5 March 2017.

64. For background information and Chinese perspectives on the recent Hong Kong protests as well as the 2008–9 unrest in ethnographic Tibet and Xinjiang, see the following articles: 'HK Students at Risk of Anti-China Scheming', *Global Times*, 22 October 2014, http://www.globaltimes.cn/content/887550.shtml, last accessed 5 March 2017; 'China Publishes Evidences of Dalai Clique's Masterminding of Riots', *Xinhuanet*, 2 April 2008, http://news.xinhuanet.com/english/2008−04/02/content_7901044.htm, last accessed 5 March 2017; and 'The Riots in Xinjiang: Is China Fraying?', *The Economist*, 9 July 2009, www.economist.com/node/13988479, last accessed 5 March 2017.

65. 'Xinjiang Government Issues Internet Regulation, Keeps Strict Controls on Information', Congressional-Executive Commission on China, 8 December 2009, www.cecc.gov/publications/commission-analysis/xinjiang-government-issues-internet-regulation-keeps-strict, last accessed 5 March 2017; and 'Xinjiang Uyghur Autonomous Region Informatization Promotion Regulation (Chinese Text)', Congressional-Executive Commission on China, 25 September 2009, http://www.cecc.gov/resources/legal-provisions/xinjiang-uyghur-autonomous-region-informatization-promotion-regulation, last accessed 27 January 2018; 杨涛 [Yang Tao], '新疆维吾尔自治区人民政府关于加强互联网信息安全管理的通告 [Xinjiang Uyghur Autonomous Region People's Government Notice on Strengthening the Management of Internet Information Security]', 新疆日报 *Xinjiang Daily*, 7 January 2015, http://www.xjdaily.com.cn:8090/jryw/1167822.shtml, last accessed 5 March 2017.

66. 'Xinjiang Government Issues Internet Regulation, Keeps Strict Controls on Information'; 'Xinjiang Uyghur Autonomous Region Informatization Promotion Regulation (Chinese Text)'; 杨涛 [Yang Tao], '新疆维吾尔自治区人民政府关于加强互联网信息安全管理的通告 [Xinjiang Uyghur Autonomous Region People's Government Notice on Strengthening the Management of Internet Information Security]'.

67. Chris Mirasola, 'Understanding China's Cybersecurity Law', Brookings Institution, *Lawfare blog*, 8 November 2016, https://www.lawfareblog.com/understanding-

chinas-cybersecurity-law, last accessed 5 March 2017; Josh Chin and Eva Dou, 'China's New Cybersecurity Law Rattles Foreign Tech Firms', *Wall Street Journal*, 6 November 2016, https://www.wsj.com/articles/china-approves-cybersecurity-law-1478491064, last accessed 5 March 2017.

68. Josh Chin and Eva Dou, 'China's New Cybersecurity Law Rattles Foreign Tech Firms.'
69. 'China: Abusive Cybersecurity Law Set to be Passed', *Human Rights Watch*, 6 November 2016, https://www.hrw.org/news/2016/11/06/china-abusive-cybersecurity-law-set-be-passed, last accessed 5 March 2017.
70. For more information on the evolution of Chinese cybersecurity policies, see Samm Sacks, 'China's Cybersecurity Law Takes Effect: What to Expect', Brookings Institution, *Lawfare blog*, 1 June 2017, https://www.lawfareblog.com/chinas-cybersecurity-law-takes-effect-what-expect, last accessed 27 January 2018.
71. Sophie Beach, 'The Perils of Going Online in Xinjiang', *China Digital Times*, 22 April 2014, http://chinadigitaltimes.net/2014/04/perils-going-online-xinjiang/, last accessed 5 March 2017.
72. Henryk Szadziewski and Greg Fay, 'How China Dismantled the Uyghur Internet', *The Diplomat*, 22 July 2014, thediplomat.com/2014/07/how-china-dismantled-the-uyghur-internet, last accessed 5 March 2017.
73. Julia Famularo, 'Beijing's Self-Defeating Arrest of Ilham Tohti', *National Interest*, 23 January 2014, nationalinterest.org/commentary/beijings-self-defeating-arrest-ilham-tohti-9756, last accessed 5 March 2017; and Wertime, 'An Internet Where Nobody Says Anything'.
74. 'China Jails Students of Uighur Scholar Ilham Tohti', BBC, 9 December 2014, www.bbc.com/news/world-asia-china-30390801, last accessed 5 March 2017; and Bai Tiantian, 'Ilham Tohti Students Sentenced', *Global Times*, 9 December 2014, http://www.globaltimes.cn/content/895665.shtml, last accessed 5 March 2017.
75. '[Section] II. Human Rights: Freedom of Religion', in '2017 Annual Report', Congressional-Executive Commission on China, 5 October 2017, https://www.cecc.gov/publications/annual-reports/2017-annual-report, last accessed 27 January 2018. See also Xin Lin, Hai Nan, Wong Lok-to and Luisetta Mudie, 'China Tightens Controls on Religious Activity, Targets Ethnic Groups', Radio Free Asia, 14 September 2017, https://www.rfa.org/english/news/china/religion-crackdown-09142017155745.html, last accessed 27 January 2018.
76. Li Ruohan, 'Xinjiang to be a key focus of revised religious regulation', *Global Times*, 30 January 2018, http://www.globaltimes.cn/content/1087333.shtml, last accessed 6 February 2018.
77. State Council, People's Republic of China, 'China revises regulation on religious affairs', State Council, 7 September 2017, http://english.gov.cn/policies/latest_releases/2017/09/07/content_281475842719170.htm, last accessed 27 January

2018. For the full text of the revised religious regulations, see 中华人民共和国国务院令第686号, 宗教事务条例 [State Council, People's Republic of China, Order No. 686, Religious Affairs Regulations], 中华人民共和国中央人民政府 [Central People's Government of People's Republic of China], 7 September 2017, http://www.gov.cn/zhengce/content/2017-09/07/content_5223282.htm, last accessed 27 January 2018. For an unofficial English translation, see 'Religious Affairs Regulations 2017', *China Law Translate*, 7 September 2017, https://www.chinalawtranslate.com/宗教事务条例-2017/?lang=en, last accessed 27 January 2018.

78. Cui Jia, 'State Council amends rules governing religion', *China Daily*, 8 September 2017, http://www.chinadaily.com.cn/china/2017-09/08/content_31717459.htm, last accessed 27 January 2018; 'China's revised religious regulations threaten survival of Tibetan Buddhism', *International Campaign for Tibet*, 18 September 2017, https://www.savetibet.org/chinas-revised-religious-regulations-threaten-survival-of-tibetan-buddhism/, accessed 27 January 2018. See also 中华人民共和国国务院令 第686号, 宗教事务条例 [State Council, People's Republic of China, Order No. 686, Religious Affairs Regulations] or 'Religious Affairs Regulations 2017', *China Law Translate*.

79. Jessica Batke, 'PRC Religious Policy: Serving the Gods of the CCP'; '[Section] II. Human Rights: Freedom of Religion', in '2017 Annual Report', Congressional-Executive Commission on China.

80. Yang Sheng, 'China's revised regulations on religion fend off foreign influences', *Global Times*, 11 September 2017, http://www.globaltimes.cn/content/1065935.shtml, last accessed 27 January 2018; Cui Jia, 'State Council amends rules governing religion'.

81. Xin Lin, Hai Nan, Wong Lok-to and Luisetta Mudie, 'China Tightens Controls on Religious Activity, Targets Ethnic Groups'.

82. Jessica Batke, 'PRC Religious Policy: Serving the Gods of the CCP'.

83. '[Section] II. Human Rights: Freedom of Religion', in '2017 Annual Report', Congressional-Executive Commission on China; Yang Sheng, 'China's revised regulations on religion fend off foreign influences'.

84. Tian Shaohui, 'China Focus: Xi calls for improved religious work'.

85. 'China's revised religious regulations threaten survival of Tibetan Buddhism', *International Campaign for Tibet*.

86. Fu Yiqin, 'What Will China's National Security Commission Actually Do?', *Foreign Policy, Tea Leaf Nation* blog, 8 May 2014, foreignpolicy.com/2014/05/08/what-will-chinas-national-security-commission-actually-do/, last accessed 5 March 2017.

87. Jane Perlez, 'New Chinese Panel Said to Oversee Domestic Security and Foreign Policy', *New York Times*, 13 November 2013, http://www.nytimes.com/2013/11/14/world/asia/national-security-committee-china.html?_r=0, last accessed 5 March 2017.

88. Ibid.
89. David M. Lampton, 'Xi Jinping's High-Risk Policy Needs a National Security Commission', *YaleGlobal*, 5 May 2015, http://yaleglobal.yale.edu/content/xi-jinpings-high-risk-policy-needs-national-security-commission, last accessed 5 March 2017.
90. Ibid.
91. Joel Wuthnow, 'China's Much-Heralded NSC has Disappeared', *Foreign Policy*, 30 June 2016, http://foreignpolicy.com/2016/06/30/chinas-much-heralded-national-security-council-has-disappeared-nsc-xi-jinping/, last accessed 5 March 2017.
92. Charles Hutzler, 'China's Police Ministry Orders Campaign Against Terrorism', *Wall Street Journal*, 25 May 2014, http://www.wsj.com/articles/SB10001424052702304811904579584010905901476, last accessed 5 March 2017.
93. Cao Yuwei, 'China Sets up Anti-terror Groups Nationwide', *CRI English*, 28 May 2014, http://english.cri.cn/7146/2014/05/28/191s828792.htm, last accessed 5 March 2017.
94. For example, see 桂田田 [Gui Tiantian], 揭秘'反恐工作领导小组' [Secret 'Counter-terrorism Work Leading Small Groups'], 北京青年报 [*Beijing Youth Daily*], 26 May 2014, http://epaper.ynet.com/html/2014-05/26/content_60884.htm?div=-1, last accessed 5 March 2017; '县局领导参加嵩县社会信息资源整合暨反恐工作会议 [Leaders of Song County Bureau Attend Work Meeting to Integrate Social Communication Resources with Counter-terrorism Efforts]', 9 December 2016, 中共嵩县县委政法委 [Central Song County County Political and Legal Affairs Commission], http://www.sxxwzfw.com/plus/view.php?aid=504, last accessed 5 March 2017; '我县召开全县反恐处突工作会议 [My County Initiated a County-wide Counter-terrorism Emergency Response Work Meeting]', 远安县公安局 [Yan'an County Public Security Bureau], 6 July 2016, http://www.yuanan.gov.cn/html/yagaj/html/tpxw/2016/0706/346282.html, last accessed 5 March 2017; '花溪区召开行业重点目标摸底梳理、评定推进会 [Huaxi District Convenes Meeting to Thoroughly Assess and Advance Key Industrial Objectives]', Guiyang Municipality Public Security Bureau, Huaxi Branch Website, 13 October 2016, http://hxfj.gyga.gov.cn/templet/yyfj/ShowArticle.jsp?id=126040&siteId=fj_hx, last accessed 5 March 2017; '天津市2016-1号反恐演习圆满完成 [January 2016 Tianjin City Counter-terrorism Exercise Successfully Completed]', 天津市卫生和计划生育委员会 [Tianjin Health and Family Planning Commission], 16 February 2016, http://www.tjwsj.gov.cn/html/wsjn/QXWSXX22914/2016-02-16/Detail_643425.htm, last accessed 5 March 2017; '上海市法学会反恐研究中心成立 [Shanghai Law Society Establishes Counter-terrorism Research Center]', 上海市法学会 [Shanghai Law Society], 7 September 2012, http://www.sls.org.cn/Pages/Detail.aspx?id=3604, last accessed 5 March 2017; '构建具有海南特色的反恐机制 [Building Counter-terrorism Mechanisms with Hainan Characteristics]', 海南日报 [*Hainan*

Daily], 25 December 2015, http://hnrb.hinews.cn/html/2015-12/25/content_2_5.htm, last accessed 5 March 2017.

95. For example, see Moritz Rudolf, Marc Julienne and Johannes Buckow, 'China's Counterterrorism Campaign Goes Global', *The Diplomat*, 3 June 2015, http://thediplomat.com/2015/06/chinas-counterterrorism-campaign-goes-global/, last accessed 5 March 2017; Sophie Richardson, 'Dispatches: China–US Dialogue—Counterterrorism or Counter-Productive?', *Human Rights Watch*, 6 August 2015, https://www.hrw.org/news/2015/08/06/dispatches-china-us-dialogue-counterterrorism-or-counter-productive, last accessed 5 March 2017; 'U.S. holds counterterrorism talks with China, calls for deeper cooperation', CBS News, 25 October 2016, http://www.cbsnews.com/news/us-holds-counterterrorism-talks-with-china-calls-for-deeper-cooperation/, last accessed 5 March 2017; 'China's policies on Asia-Pacific security cooperation', *China Daily*, 12 January 2016, http://www.chinadaily.com.cn/opinion/2017-01/12/content_27931422_11.htm, last accessed 5 March 2017; and 'Measures to eliminate international terrorism (Agenda item 107)', General Assembly of the United Nations, Legal: Sixth Committee, 69th Session, http://www.un.org/en/ga/sixth/69/int_terrorism.shtml, last accessed 5 March 2017.

96. Tom Porter, 'China appoints first anti-terror chief paving way for controversial cybersecurity bill', *International Business Times*, 21 December 2015, http://www.ibtimes.co.uk/china-appoints-first-anti-terror-chief-paving-way-controversial-cybersecurity-bill-1534366, last accessed 5 March 2017.

97. 桂田田 [Gui Tiantian], 揭秘'反恐工作领导小组' [Secret 'Counter-terrorism Work Leading Small Groups'].

98. For original text of regulations, see 张雨、李楠楠 [Zhang Yu, Li Nannan], '新疆维吾尔自治区实施《中华人民共和国反恐怖主义法》办法 [XUAR Implementation Measures for the PRC Counter-terrorism Law]', 人大新闻网 [*National People's Congress News*], 1 August 2016, http://npc.people.com.cn/n1/2016/0801/c14576-28601824.html, last accessed 5 March 2017; 桂田田 [Gui Tiantian], 揭秘'反恐工作领导小组' [Secret 'Counter-terrorism Work Leading Small Groups'].

99. 张, 李, [Zhang, Li], '新疆维吾尔自治区实施《中华人民共和国反恐怖主义法》办法 [XUAR Implementation Measures for the PRC Counterterrorism Law]'. See also the working English translation of the regulations on the *China Law Translate* website, available at http://chinalawtranslate.com/xjcounter-terror/?tpedit=1&lang=en, last accessed 5 March 2017.

100. Nectar Gan, 'Chinese media shine light on little-known "counterterrorism leading group" in Xinjiang,' *South China Morning Post*, 17 November 2015, http://www.scmp.com/news/china/policies-politics/article/1879667/chinese-media-shine-light-little-known-counterterrorism, last accessed 5 March 2017; 张, 李, [Zhang, Li], '新疆维吾尔自治区实施《中华人民共和国反恐怖主义法》办法 [XUAR Implementation Measures for the PRC Counterterrorism Law]'. See also the

working English translation of the regulations on the *China Law Translate* website, available at http://chinalawtranslate.com/xjcounter-terror/?tpedit=1& lang=en, last accessed 5 March 2017.

101. 张、李, [Zhang, Li], '新疆维吾尔自治区实施《中华人民共和国反恐怖主义法》办法 [XUAR Implementation Measures for the PRC Counterterrorism Law]'. See also the working English translation of the regulations on the *China Law Translate* website, available at http://chinalawtranslate.com/xjcounter-terror/?tpedit=1& lang=en, last accessed 5 March 2017.

102. 陈孟、李镭 [Chen Meng and Li Lei], '郭声琨：坚决打赢反恐人民战争 切实维护社会安全稳定 [Guo Shengkun: Resolutely Win the People's Battle Against Terrorism, Effectively Ensure Social Security and Stability]', 人民网 [People.cn], 13 April 2017, http://politics.people.com.cn/n1/2017/0413/c1001-29209353.html, last accessed 28 January 2018. See also Xinhua, 'China maintains tough crackdown on terrorism', English.gov.gn, 14 April 2017, http://english.gov.cn/state_council/state_councilors/2017/04/14/content_281475626547296.htm, last accessed 28 January 2018.

103. Sophie Richardson, 'China Poised to Repeat Tibet Mistakes', *Human Rights Watch*, 20 January 2017, https://www.hrw.org/news/2017/01/20/china-poised-repeat-tibet-mistakes, last accessed 5 March 2017.

104. Adrian Zenz and James Leibold, 'Xinjiang's Rapidly Evolving Security State', *China Brief*, 14 March 2017, https://jamestown.org/program/xinjiangs-rapidly-evolving-security-state/, last accessed 28 January 2018.

105. Ibid.

106. See Adrian Zenz and James Leibold, 'Xinjiang's Rapidly Evolving Security State', as well as Adrian Zenz and James Leibold, 'Chen Quanguo: The Strongman Behind Beijing's Securitization Strategy in Tibet and Xinjiang'. For more information on grid-style social management, see Wu Qiang, 'Urban Grid Management and Police State in China: A Brief Overview', *China Change*, 12 August 2014, https://chinachange.org/2013/08/08/the-urban-grid-management-and-police-state-in-china-a-brief-overview/, last accessed 29 January 2018; Lucy Hornby, 'China reverts to "grid management" to monitor citizens' lives', *Financial Times*, 3 April 2016, https://www.ft.com/content/bf6a67c6-940e-11e5-bd82-c1fb-87bef7af, last accessed 29 January 2018.

107. Adrian Zenz and James Leibold, 'Xinjiang's Rapidly Evolving Security State'.

108. Adrian Zenz and James Leibold, 'Xinjiang's Rapidly Evolving Security State'.

109. James Leibold and Adrian Zenz, 'Beijing's Eyes and Ears Grow Sharper in Xinjiang', *Foreign Affairs*, 23 December 2016, https://www.foreignaffairs.com/articles/china/2016-12-23/beijings-eyes-and-ears-grow-sharper-xinjiang, last accessed 29 January 2018.

110. '武警副司令：国内暴恐活动向热兵器有组织转变 [PAP Deputy Commander: Domestic Terrorists Moving Towards Hot Weapons]', 解放军报 [*Military News Online*],

8 March 2015, http://mil.news.sina.com.cn/2015-03-08/1209823571.html, last accessed 28 January 2018.
111. Ibid.
112. '武警副司令：国内暴恐活动向热兵器有组织转变 [PAP Deputy Commander: Domestic Terrorists Moving Toward Hot Weapons]', 罗铮 张华婧 [Luo Zheng and Zhang Huajing], '王永生：武警部队已经成为国家反恐核心力量 [Wang Yongsheng: The People's Armed Police Already Represent a Key Force in the National Fight Against Terror]', 中国军网 [*China Military Online*], 7 March 2015, http://www.81.cn/jwgz/2015-03/07/content_6384705.htm, last accessed 5 March 2017.
113. 罗铮 张华婧 [Luo Zheng and Zhang Huajing], '王永生：武警部队已经成为国家反恐核心力量 [Wang Yongsheng: The People's Armed Police Already Represent a Key Force in the National Fight Against Terror]'.
114. '武警副司令：暴恐向热兵器有组织转变 武警成反恐核心 [PAP Deputy Commander: Violent Terrorism is Moving Toward Hot Weapons, Organizational Change: PAP Will Become Core of Fight Against Terror]', *Xinhua*, 8 March 2015, http://news.xinhuanet.com/mil/2015-03/08/c_127557352_2.htm, last accessed 5 March 2017.
115. Cui Jia, 'Xinjiang security funding increased by 90 percent', *China Daily*, 13 January 2010, http://www.chinadaily.com.cn/china/2010-01/13/content_9311035.htm, last accessed 5 March 2017.
116. Cui Jia and Gao Bo, 'Xinjiang doubles terror fight budget', *China Daily*, 17 January 2014, http://www.chinadaily.com.cn/bizchina/2014-01/17/content_17240577.htm, last accessed 5 March 2017.
117. Josh Chin and Clément Bürge, '12 Days in Xinjiang: How China's Surveillance State Overwhelms Daily Life', *Wall Street Journal*, 17 December 2017, https://www.wsj.com/articles/twelve-days-in-xinjiang-how-chinas-surveillance-state-overwhelms-daily-life-1513700355, last accessed 2 February 2018.
118. 关于2017年中央本级支出预算的说明 [A Description of the Central Government's Expenditures in 2017], 中华人民共和国财政部 [People's Republic of China, Ministry of Finance], 28 January 2018, http://yss.mof.gov.cn/2017zyys/201703/t20170324_2565768.html, last accessed 28 January 2018. Officials attributed the 2017 PAP budget increase to salary adjustments, and the public security budget increase to a rise in the number of cases investigated.
119. David Shambaugh, *China Goes Global: The Partial Power* (New York: Oxford University Press, 2013), p. 328.
120. 'China passes new national security law extending control over internet', *Guardian*, 1 July 2015, https://www.theguardian.com/world/2015/jul/01/china-national-security-law-internet-regulation-cyberspace-xi-jinping, last accessed 5 March 2017.
121. Frank Langfitt, 'In China, Beware: A Camera May Be Watching You', *NPR*, 29 January 2013, http://www.npr.org/2013/01/29/170469038/in-china-beware-a-camera-may-be-watching-you%250A, last accessed 5 March 2017.

122. 陈树琛 [Chen Shusen], '织智能'天网'保一方平安 [Weaving a Smart "Skynet" Preserves the Peace]', 安徽日报 [*Anhui Daily News*], 7 July 2015, http://epaper.anhuinews.com/html/ahrb/20150707/article_3330281.shtml, last accessed 5 March 2017.
123. Du Guodong, 'Video security cameras zoom in on privacy issues', *China Daily*, 26 April 2010, http://www.chinadaily.com.cn/cndy/2010–04/26/content_9772995.htm, last accessed 5 March 2017.
124. Langfitt, 'In China, Beware: A Camera May Be Watching You'.
125. Du Guodong, 'Video security cameras zoom in on privacy issues'.
126. Langfitt, 'In China, Beware: A Camera May Be Watching You'.
127. Malcom Moore, 'China installs 40,000 CCTV cameras in Xinjiang ahead of anniversary of deadly riots', *Daily Telegraph*, 2 July 2010, http://www.telegraph.co.uk/news/worldnews/asia/china/7867536/China-installs-40000-CCTV-cameras-in-Xinjiang-ahead-of-anniversary-of-deadly-riots.html, last accessed 5 March 2017.
128. Josh Chin and Clément Bürge, '12 Days in Xinjiang: How China's Surveillance State Overwhelms Daily Life'. See also James Millward, 'What It's Like to Live in a Surveillance State', *New York Times*, 3 February 2018, https://www.nytimes.com/2018/02/03/opinion/sunday/china-surveillance-state-uighurs.html, last accessed 4 February 2018; Clément Bürge, 'Life Inside China's Total Surveillance State', *Wall Street Journal*, 19 December 2017, http://www.wsj.com/video/life-inside-chinas-total-surveillance-state/CE86DA19-D55D-4F12-AC6A-3B2A573492CF.html, last accessed 4 February 2018.
129. Ibid.
130. 'China Uses Facial Recognition to Fence in Villagers in Far West', *Bloomberg*, 17 January 2018, https://www.bloomberg.com/news/articles/2018–01–17/china-said-to-test-facial-recognition-fence-in-muslim-heavy-area, last accessed 2 February 2018.
131. 'China: Minority Region Collects DNA from Millions', *Human Rights Watch*, 13 December 2017, https://www.hrw.org/news/2017/12/13/china-minority-region-collects-dna-millions, last accessed 2 February 2018.
132. Ibid.
133. Ibid. Chinese authorities publicly rebutted claims that the programme constitutes a human rights violation. 'China's government has the right to take measures it deems as proper to protect national security', argued Turgunjan Tursun, a PRC academic. He added that 'the collection of such information is not harmful to the residents, nor does it affect people's rights'. See Li Ruohan, 'China slams HRW's report on alleged Xinjiang human rights violations', *Global Times*, 13 December 2017, http://www.globaltimes.cn/content/1080190.shtml, last accessed 2 February 2018.
134. Ben Blanchard, 'China to increase video surveillance in security push', Reuters, 13 May 2015, http://www.reuters.com/article/us-china-security-idUSKBN-0NY1F420150513, last accessed 5 March 2017.

135. 'China: Police "Big Data" Systems Violate Privacy, Target Dissent', *Human Rights Watch*, 19 November 2017, https://www.hrw.org/news/2017/11/19/china-police-big-data-systems-violate-privacy-target-dissent, last accessed 4 February 2018.
136. Cara McGoogan, '"Minority Report"-style technology to predict crime in China', *Daily Telegraph*, 9 March 2016, http://www.telegraph.co.uk/technology/2016/03/09/minority-report-style-technology-to-predict-crime-in-china/, last accessed 5 March 2017.
137. Ibid.; Tom Phillips, 'China testing facial-recognition surveillance system in Xinjiang—report', *Guardian*, 18 January 2018, https://www.theguardian.com/world/2018/jan/18/china-testing-facial-recognition-surveillance-system-in-xinjiang-report, last accessed 2 February 2018.
138. Ibid.
139. Samantha Hoffman, 'Managing the State: Social Credit, Surveillance and the CCP's Plan for China', *China Brief*, 17 August 2017, https://jamestown.org/program/managing-the-state-social-credit-surveillance-and-the-ccps-plan-for-china/, last accessed 2 February 2018.
140. 'China invents the digital totalitarian state', *The Economist*, 17 December 2016, http://www.economist.com/news/briefing/21711902-worrying-implications-its-social-credit-project-china-invents-digital-totalitarian, last accessed 5 March 2017; Charles Clover, 'China: When big data meets big brother', *Financial Times*, 19 January 2016, https://www.ft.com/content/b5b13a5e-b847-11e5-b151-8e15c9a029fb, last accessed 5 March 2017. For more information on China's emerging social credit system, see also Samuel Wade, 'Jeremy Daum on China's Social Credit System', *China Digital Times*, 18 January 2018, https://chinadigitaltimes.net/2018/01/giving-credit-jeremy-daum-chinas-social-credit-system/, last accessed 2 February 2018; Mareike Ohlberg, Shazeda Ahmed and Bertram Lang, 'Central Planning, Local Experiments: The complex implementation of China's Social Credit System', *MERICS China Monitor*, 12 December 2017, https://www.merics.org/sites/default/files/2017-12/171212_China_Monitor_43_Social_Credit_System_Implementation.pdf, last accessed 2 February 2018; and Mirjam Meissner, 'China's Social Credit System: A big-data enabled approach to market regulation with broad implications for doing business in China', *MERICS China Monitor*, 24 May 2017, https://www.merics.org/sites/default/files/2017-09/China%20Monitor_39_SOCS_EN.pdf, last accessed 2 February 2018.
141. Paul Mozur, 'China Cuts Mobile Service of Xinjiang Residents Evading Internet Filters', *New York Times*, 23 November 2015, http://www.nytimes.com/2015/11/24/business/international/china-cuts-mobile-service-of-xinjiang-residents-evading-internet-filters.html?_r=3, last accessed 5 March 2017; Mary-Ann Russon, 'China cuts phone service of Xinjiang citizens using WhatsApp and VPNs', *International Business Times*, 24 November 2015, http://www.ibtimes.

co.uk/china-cuts-phone-service-xinjiang-citizens-using-whatsapp-vpns-1530266, last accessed 5 March 2017.
142. Oiwan Lam, 'Leaked Xinjiang police report describes circumvention tools as "terrorist software"', *Global Voices*, 29 October 2016, https://www.hongkongfp.com/2016/10/29/leaked-xinjiang-police-report-describes-circumvention-tools-terrorist-software/, last accessed 5 March 2017; Qiao Long and Luisetta Mudie, 'Man Held in China's Xinjiang for Downloading "Terrorist" Circumvention Software', Radio Free Asia, 28 October 2016, http://www.rfa.org/english/news/uyghur/software-10282016121811.html, last accessed 5 March 2017.
143. Manya Koetse, 'Chinese Internet Users Concerned About Crack Down on VPNs', *What's On Weibo*, 23 January 2017, http://www.whatsonweibo.com/chinese-internet-users-concerned-crack-vpns/, last accessed 5 March 2017.
144. Qiao Long, Ghulchehra Hoja, Alim Seytoff, Mamatjan Juma, Luisetta Mudie and Joshua Lipes, 'Xinjiang Authorities Take Further Steps Towards Total Digital Surveillance', Radio Free Asia, 29 June 2017, https://www.rfa.org/english/news/uyghur/surveillance-06292017134132.html, last accessed 30 January 2018.
145. Qiao Long, Xi Wang and Luisetta Mudie, 'China Orders Xinjiang's Android Users to Install App That Deletes "Terrorist" Content', Radio Free Asia, 14 July 2017, https://www.rfa.org/english/news/china/china-orders-xinjiangs-android-users-to-install-app-that-deletes-terrorist-content-07142017102032.html, last accessed 30 January 2018; Oiwan Lam, 'China's Xinjiang Residents are Being Forced to Install Surveillance Apps on Mobile Phones', *Global Voices*, 19 July 2017, https://globalvoices.org/2017/07/19/chinas-xinjiang-residents-are-being-forced-to-install-surveillance-apps-on-mobile-phones/#, last accessed 30 January 2018.
146. Ibid.
147. Oiwan Lam, 'China's Xinjiang Residents are Being Forced to Install Surveillance Apps on Mobile Phones'.
148. 乔龙 [Qiao Long], '新疆少数民族使用苹果手机受阻 [Xinjiang Ethnic Minorities Detained Over iPhone Usage]', 自由亚洲电台普通话 [Radio Free Asia Mandarin Service], 18 January 2018, https://www.rfa.org/mandarin/yataibaodao/shaoshu-minzu/ql1–01182018105108.html, last accessed 3 February 2018.
149. Ibid.
150. At the same time, however, Apple continues to submit to Chinese demands in order to maintain access to the domestic market as a whole. Apple agreed to remove VPN tools from its app store in August 2017. It also began to store domestic users' iCloud data at a centre it built in Guizhou on 28 February 2018, where its local partner (a Chinese company with government linkages) will run the data centre. Apple will open a second data centre in Inner Mongolia in 2020. For more information, see Paul Mozur, Daisuke Wakabayashi and Nick Wingfield, 'Apple Opening Data Center in China to Comply with Cybersecurity Law', *New York*

Times, 12 July 2017, https://www.nytimes.com/2017/07/12/business/apple-china-data-center-cybersecurity.html, last accessed 8 February 2018; 'RSF urges journalists to quit Apple iCloud China by 28 February', *Reporters without Borders*, 5 February 2018, https://rsf.org/en/news/rsf-urges-journalists-quit-apple-icloud-china-28-february, last accessed 8 February 2018; 'Apple to build another data center', *Global Times*, 7 February 2018, http://www.globaltimes.cn/content/1088664.shtml, last accessed 8 February 2018.

151. 工信部张峰：企业和用户正常跨境访问互联网不受影响 [Ministry of Industry and Information Technology Zhang Feng: cross-border access to the Internet by enterprises and users is unaffected], 新浪科技 [Sina Technology], 30 January 2018, http://tech.sina.com.cn/t/2018-01-30/doc-ifyqyuhy7600608.shtml, last accessed 4 February 2018; Wen Yuqing, Lin Ping and Luisetta Mudie, 'China to Block Overseas VPN Services From End of March', Radio Free Asia, 31 January 2018, https://www.rfa.org/english/news/china/china-to-block-overseas-vpn-services-from-end-of-march-01312018102313.html, last accessed 4 February 2018.

152. Nithin Coca, 'The slow creep and chilling effect of China's censorship', *Daily Dot*, 20 August 2016, http://www.dailydot.com/layer8/china-tibet-xinjiang-censorship/, last accessed 5 March 2017.

153. Mozur, 'China Cuts Mobile Service of Xinjiang Residents Evading Internet Filters'.

154. Szadziewski and Fay, 'How China Dismantled the Uyghur Internet'.

155. Zhao Lei, 'High-tech lookout keeps eye on border', *China Daily*, 6 November 2015, http://usa.chinadaily.com.cn/china/2015-11/06/content_22383753.htm, last accessed 5 March 2017. For examples of some of the technologies available, see 边防检查站无线视频监控系统方案 [Border Checkpoint Wireless Video Surveillance Programme], 腾远智拓 [Suntor Electronics], 15 November 2016, http://www.4008075595.com/content_3_5_128.html, last accessed 30 January 2018; 'UAV Border Inspection in Xinjiang China', Suntor Electronics, 9 September 2017, http://www.cofdm-transmitter.com/news/uav-border-inspection-in-xinjiang-china-27609.html, last accessed 30 January 2018; 高清数字化边海防昼夜远程监控系统 [High-definition Digital Coastal Defense Round-the-Clock Remote Monitoring System], 秀歌科技 [Xiuge Tech], 26 December 2016, http://www.xiugetech.com/news/8.html, last accessed 30 January 2018.

156. Elsa Kania, 'China's Employment of Unmanned Systems: Across the Spectrum from Peacetime to Wartime', Brookings Institution, *Lawfare blog*, 22 May 2017, https://lawfareblog.com/chinas-employment-unmanned-systems-across-spectrum-peacetime-wartime, last accessed 30 January 2018; Cui Jia, 'Drones will help Xinjiang fight terror', *China Daily*, 2 May 2017, http://www.chinadaily.com.cn/china/2017-05/02/content_29158788.htm, last accessed 30 January 2018; Zhao Lei, 'High-tech lookout keeps eye on border'; 訾豪、徐嘉宁 [Zi Hao

and Xu Jianing], '北疆巡逻，无人机很了不起！[Drones are Great for Patrolling Northern Xinjiang!]', 新华 [*Xinhua*], 20 March 2017, http://www.xinhuanet.com/mil/2017–03/20/c_129513220.htm, last accessed 30 January 2018.
157. Zhao Lei, 'High-tech lookout keeps eye on border'.
158. Shannon Tiezzi, 'China and the Lethal Drone Option', *The Diplomat*, 15 January 2015, http://thediplomat.com/2015/01/china-and-the-lethal-drone-option/, last accessed 5 March 2017; Daniel Medina, 'China is now using drones to catch "terrorists" in Xinjiang', *Quartz*, 29 August 2014, http://qz.com/256104/china-is-now-using-drones-to-catch-terrorists-in-xinjiang/, last accessed 5 March 2017.
159. Mu Xuequan, 'China's drone blasts off missile in SCO anti-terror drill', *Xinhua*, 26 August 2014, http://news.xinhuanet.com/english/china/2014-08/26/c_126921067.htm, last accessed 5 March 2017.
160. Shannon Tiezzi, 'China and the Lethal Drone Option'; Elsa Kania, 'China's Employment of Unmanned Systems: Across the Spectrum from Peacetime to Wartime'.
161. Josh Chin and Clément Bürge, '12 Days in Xinjiang: How China's Surveillance State Overwhelms Daily Life'.
162. For example, see 乔龙 [Qiao Long], '何平公安部称新疆暴恐仍有发生 阿克苏地区戒备巡逻加强 [Public Security Bureau states violence still occurring in Xinjiang, alerts Aksu that it will strengthen patrols]', Radio Free Asia (Mandarin Service), 27 February 2016, http://www.rfa.org/mandarin/yataibaodao/shaoshuminzu/ql2–02272016111106.html, last accessed 5 March 2017; and '中国官员下令在新疆进行昼夜巡逻 [Chinese officials order 24 hour patrols in Xinjiang]', Voice of America (Mandarin Service), 1 July 2013, http://www.voachinese.com/a/xinjiang-patrol/1692304.html, last accessed 5 March 2017; and Zhang Hui, 'Police street patrols in Beijing at maximum level to counter terrorism', *Global Times*, 29 June 2015, http://www.globaltimes.cn/content/929517.shtml, last accessed 5 March 2017.
163. Searching for images of PAP and SWAT patrols in Xinjiang (i.e. 新疆武警巡逻图片 or 新疆特警巡逻图片) yields a large number of results on Chinese websites. See also '利剑出鞘 雷霆万钧——自治区举行反恐维稳誓师大会 [Unsheathing a sharp sword as powerful as a thunderbolt: the autonomous region holds a meeting to pledge mass efforts in counterterrorism and stability maintenance]', 天山网 [*Tianshan Net*], 28 February 2017, http://news.ts.cn/content/2017–02/28/content_12532953_all.htm#content_1, last accessed 5 March 2017; and Graham Adams, 'The Xinjiang Perspective: In Photos', *The Diplomat*, 17 April 2013, http://thediplomat.com/2013/04/by-graham-adams/, last accessed 5 March 2017.
164. Tom Phillips, 'China launches massive rural "surveillance" project to watch over Uighurs', *Daily Telegraph*, 20 October 2014, http://www.telegraph.co.uk/news/worldnews/asia/china/11150577/China-launches-massive-rural-surveillance-project-to-watch-over-Uighurs.html, last accessed 31 January 2018. A more for-

mal translation for the name of the campaign (访民情惠民生聚民心) is 'Visit the People, Care for the People's Livelihoods, Win People's Hearts'.

165. For example, see 访民情惠民生聚民心 [Visit the People, Care for the People's Livelihoods, Win People's Hearts], 新疆维吾尔自治区教育厅 [Xinjiang Uyghur Autonomous Region Education Bureau], http://www.xjedu.gov.cn/xjjyt/jyzt/fhj/12440.htm, last accessed 31 January 2018; '访惠聚'专题 [Special Topic: 'Visit, Benefit, Come Together'], 中国科学院新疆分院 [Chinese Academy of Social Sciences, Xinjiang Branch], http://www.xjb.cas.cn/ztlm/fhjzt/, last accessed 31 January 2018.

166. '我区持续接力开展"访惠聚"驻村工作: 7.6万名驻村工作队队员开启驻村新生活 [Our Region Continued to Carry Out "Visit, Benefit, Come Together" Work by Residing in Villages: 76,000 Village Team Members Initiate New Life by Living in Villages]', 新疆日报 [*Xinjiang Daily*], 31 January 2018, http://wap.xjdaily.com/xjrb/20180131/98019.html, last accessed 3 February 2018.

167. 于富春 [Yu Fuchun], '自治区高院机关举办新一轮"访惠聚" 驻村工作队成员培训班 [Authorities from the XUAR High Court held a new round of training for team members participating in "Visit, Benefit, Come Together"]', *XUAR High Court*, 31 January 2018, http://www.xjcourt.org/public/detail.php?id=30907, last accessed 31 January 2018.

168. Ibid.

169. Sophie Richardson, 'China Poised to Repeat Tibet Mistakes', *Human Rights Watch*, 20 January 2017, https://www.hrw.org/news/2017/01/20/china-poised-repeat-tibet-mistakes, last accessed 5 March 2017.

170. Irade, Mamatjan Juma and Brooks Boliek, 'Chinese Government Sends Religious Monitors to Xinjiang's Hotan', Radio Free Asia, 24 October 2016, http://www.rfa.org/english/news/uyghur/the-chinese-government-sends-10242016142604.html, last accessed 5 March 2017.

171. Gulchehra Hoja, Mamatjan Juma, Alim Seytoff and Joshua Lipes, 'China Embeds Cadres in Uyghur Homes During Ramadan', Radio Free Asia, 8 June 2017, https://www.rfa.org/english/news/uyghur/cadres-06082017164658.html, last accessed 31 January 2018.

172. Ibid.

173. Zhang Hui, 'Xinjiang officials assigned as relatives to Uyghur villagers for ethnic unity campaign', *Global Times*, 11 January 2018, http://www.globaltimes.cn/content/1084401.shtml, last accessed 31 January 2018.

174. Zhao Yusha, 'Xinjiang sets up local committees to better serve religious activities', *Global Times*, 22 November 2016, http://www.globaltimes.cn/content/1019614.shtml, last accessed 5 March 2017; see also Richardson, 'China Poised to Repeat Tibet Mistakes'.

175. James Leibold and Adrian Zenz, 'Beijing's Eyes and Ears Grow Sharper in Xinjiang'.

176. For example, see 2017年新疆巴州第二批便民警务站招聘2373人简章 [2017 Xinjiang Bayingol Prefecture General Regulations on Efforts to Recruit Second Round of 2373 Individuals for Convenience Police Stations], 学宝公务员考试网 [Xuebao Civil Service Examination Network], 11 January 2017, http://www.chinagwy.org/html/gdzk/xinjiang/201701/87_183658.html, last accessed 5 March 2017; 2017年新疆和静县便民警务站事业性岗位人员资格审查通知(第二批) [2017 Xinjiang (Bayingol Prefecture) Hejing County Notice on Qualifications for Convenience Police Station Job Positions (Second Round)], 华图教育网: 公安招警考试 [China Education Network: Police Recruitment and Examinations], 18 January 2017, http://zhaojing.huatu.com/news/xinjiang/2017/0118/1543587.html, last accessed 5 March 2017; 新疆塔城市公安局便民警务站招聘公告 [Xinjiang Tacheng City Public Security Bureau Convenience Police Service Stations Recruitment Notice], 公务员考试网 [Civil Service Examination Network], 14 December 2016, http://www.gjgwy.net/zkzx/zjks/120533.html, last accessed 5 March 2017; and 2016年新疆洛浦县便民警务服务站招聘工作人员360人 [2016 Xinjiang (Hotan Prefecture) Lop County Convenience Police Service Stations to Recruit 360 Personnel] 华图教育网: 公安招警考试 [China Education Network: Police Recruitment and Examinations], 9 October 2016, http://zhaojing.huatu.com/news/xinjiang/2016/1009/1520377.html, last accessed 5 March 2017. See also Leibold and Zenz, 'Beijing's Eyes and Ears Grow Sharper in Xinjiang'; Wu Qiang, 'Urban Grid Management and Police State in China: A Brief Overview'; 5, 2017; and 'China: Alarming New Surveillance, Security in Tibet', *Human Rights Watch*, 20 March 2013, https://www.hrw.org/news/2013/03/20/china-alarming-new-surveillance-security-tibet, last accessed 5 March 2017.

177. 便民警务站：密织安全网 便民零距离 [Convenience Police Service Stations: Closely Woven Security Nets, Convenient and Face-to-Face], 亚心网 [Heart of Asia Network], 27 October 2016, http://news.iyaxin.com/content/2016–10/27/content_10148180.htm, last accessed 5 March 2017.

178. 新疆特检院为'便民警务站建设'保驾护航 [Xinjiang Special Equipment Testing Institute Completes Convenience Police Service Station Construction] 国家质量监督检验检疫总局 [General Administration of Quality Supervision, Inspection and Quarantine of the People's Republic of China], 29 November 2016, http://www.aqsiq.gov.cn/xxgk_13386/zxxxgk/201611/t20161129_478237.htm, last accessed 5 March 2017.

179. See Leibold and Zenz, 'Beijing's Eyes and Ears Grow Sharper in Xinjiang'; 便民警务站便民更安民 [Convenience Police Service Stations are Convenient and Reassure the Public], 新疆网 [*Xinjiang Net*], 18 October 2016, http://www.xinjiangnet.com.cn/2016/1018/1665071.shtml, last accessed 5 March 2017; 便民警务站：密织安全网 便民零距离 [Convenience Police Service Stations: Closely Woven Security Nets, Convenient and Face-to-Face].

180. Leibold and Zenz, 'Beijing's Eyes and Ears Grow Sharper in Xinjiang'; Wu Qiang, 'Urban Grid Management and Police State in China: A Brief Overview'.

181. Zhang Hui, 'Police street patrols in Beijing at maximum level to counter terrorism', *Global Times*, 29 June 2015, http://www.globaltimes.cn/content/929517.shtml, last accessed 5 March 2017.

182. Jilili Musa and Brooks Boliek, 'Chinese Offer Reward for Information on Terrorism, Religion in Xinjiang', Radio Free Asia, 12 April 2016, http://www.rfa.org/english/news/uyghur/chinese-offer-reward-04122016164714.html, last accessed 5 March 2017; Anna Lipscomb, 'Culture Clash: Ethnic Unrest In Xinjiang', USC US–China Institute, *US–China Today*, 19 September 2016, http://uschina.usc.edu/article@usct?culture_clash_ethnic_unrest_in_xinjiang_20291.aspx, last accessed 5 March 2017.

183. Eset Sulaiman, Alim Seytoff and Joshua Lipes, 'Xinjiang Authorities Reward Residents for "Tips on Terrorism"', Radio Free Asia, 17 March 2017, https://www.rfa.org/english/news/uyghur/reward-03172017152706.html, last accessed 30 January 2018; Shohret Hoshur and Joshua Lipes, 'China Dangles Huge Payouts For Tips on "Terrorists" in Largely Uyghur Hotan Prefecture', Radio Free Asia, 20 December 2017, https://www.rfa.org/english/news/uyghur/tips-12202017172516.html, last accessed 30 January 2018.

184. Shohret Hoshur, Alim Seytoff and Joshua Lipes, 'China to Punish "Two-Faced" Uyghur Officials in New Reward Scheme', Radio Free Asia, 26 December 2017, https://www.rfa.org/english/news/uyghur/rewards-12262017144824.html, last accessed 6 February 2018.

185. Deng Xiaoci, 'Xinjiang launches app to receive security tip-offs', *Global Times*, 27 April 2017, http://www.globaltimes.cn/content/1044528.shtml, last accessed 30 January 2018. See also 李龙, 韩婷 [Li Long and Han Ting], '乌鲁木齐警方推广应用"百姓安全" APP [Urumqi Police Promote Usage of "Safety for the Public" App]', 人民网 [People.cn], 26 April 2017, http://xj.people.com.cn/n2/2017/0426/c186332-30096322.html, last accessed 30 January 2018.

186. '"百姓安全"APP首批线索人获现金奖励, [First Batch of People Submitting Tips to the "Safety for the Public" App Received Rewards]', 新疆日报 [*Xinjiang Daily*], 30 July 2017, http://wap.xjdaily.com/xjrb/20170730/74212.html, last accessed 30 January 2018. 'WeChat red envelopes' enable smartphone users to send funds through the WeChat Pay mobile payment service. For more information, see Catherine Shu, 'Traditional Red Envelopes are Going Digital Thanks to China's Largest Internet Companies', *TechCrunch*, 8 February 2016, https://techcrunch.com/2016/02/08/smartphone-hongbao/, last accessed 30 January 2018.

187. Eset Sulaiman and Richard Finney, 'New Xinjiang Party Boss Boosts Surveillance, Police Patrols', Radio Free Asia, 16 December 2016, https://www.rfa.org/english/news/uyghur/boosts-12162016145709.html, last accessed 5 March 2017.

188. Wong Siu-san, Sing Man and Luisetta Mudie, 'Vehicles to Get Compulsory GPS Tracking in Xinjiang', Radio Free Asia, 20 February 2017, https://www.rfa.org/english/news/uyghur/xinjiang-gps-02202017145155.html, last accessed 30 Jan-

uary 2018. See also Tom Phillips, 'China orders GPS tracking of every car in troubled region', *Guardian*, 21 February 2017, https://www.theguardian.com/world/2017/feb/21/china-orders-gps-tracking-of-every-car-in-troubled-region, last accessed 2 February 2018.
189. Nectar Gan, 'Passports taken, more police ... new party boss Chen Quanguo acts to tame Xinjiang with methods used in Tibet', *South China Morning Post*, 12 December 2016, http://www.scmp.com/news/china/policies-politics/article/2053739/party-high-flier-uses-his-tibet-model-bid-tame-xinjiang, last accessed 5 March 2017.
190. Eset Sulaiman, Xin Lin, Pan Jiaqing, Ho Shan, Mamatjan Juma and Luisetta Mudie, 'Passports in Xinjiang's Ili to be Handed into Police Stations: China', Radio Free Asia, 13 May 2015, https://www.rfa.org/english/news/uyghur/uyghur-yili-05132015140829.html, last accessed 1 February 2018.
191. Ng Yik-tung, Sing Man, Yang Fan, Irade, Mamatjan Juma and Luisetta Mudie, 'China Recalls Passports Across Xinjiang Amid Ongoing Security Crackdown', Radio Free Asia, 20 October 2016, https://www.rfa.org/english/news/uyghur/xinjiang-passports-10202016144107.html, last accessed 1 February 2018.
192. Edward Wong, 'Police Confiscate Passports in Parts of Xinjiang, in Western China', *New York Times*, 1 December 2016, https://www.nytimes.com/2016/12/01/world/asia/passports-confiscated-xinjiang-china-uighur.html, last accessed 5 March 2017. According to Radio Free Asia, 'Since October 2016, the Public Security Bureau (PSB) in Xinjiang has issued a series of notices ordering Uyghur residents of Changji Hui (in Chinese, Changji Huizu) Autonomous Prefecture's Manas (Manasi) county, the seat of Kumul (Hami) prefecture, the capital Urumqi's Midong district, and the Xinjiang Production and Construction Corps administrated city of Shihezi to hand over their passports. According to the notices, if the passports were not submitted by a specific deadline, they would become "invalid," and "further action will be taken" against the holder. In no circumstance was a timetable provided for how long the passports would be held by the authorities and, according to information from local PSBs, the campaign to recall the travel documents was limited to residents of Xinjiang.' See Gulchehra Hoja and Joshua Lipes, 'China Expands Recall of Passports to Uyghurs Outside of Xinjiang', Radio Free Asia, 8 December 2017, https://www.rfa.org/english/news/uyghur/passports-12082017152527.html, last accessed 1 February 2018.
193. 'China: Passports Arbitrarily Recalled in Xinjiang', *Human Rights Watch*, 21 November 2016, https://www.hrw.org/news/2016/11/21/china-passports-arbitrarily-recalled-xinjiang, last accessed 5 March 2017.
194. Zhao Yusha and Cui Meng, 'Xinjiang officials deny holding ordinary citizens' passports', *Global Times*, 25 November 2016, http://www.globaltimes.cn/content/1020272.shtml, last accessed 5 March 2017.
195. Gulchehra Hoja and Joshua Lipes, 'China Expands Recall of Passports to Uyghurs Outside of Xinjiang'.

196. Emily Feng, 'China targets Muslim Uighurs studying abroad', *Financial Times*, August 1 2017, https://www.ft.com/content/0ecec4fa-7276-11e7-aca6-c6bd07df1a3c, last accessed 4 February 2018; Jilil Kashgary, Alim Seytoff and Joshua Lipes, 'Uyghur Student in Cairo Narrowly Avoids Arrest by Chinese, Egyptian Agents', Radio Free Asia, 25 July 2017, https://www.rfa.org/english/news/uyghur/student-07252017162120.html, last accessed 4 February 2018; Gulchehra Hoja, Alim Seytoff and Roseanne Gerin, 'Egyptian Authorities Forcibly Disappear 16 Uyghur Students from Notorious Prison', Radio Free Asia, 25 September 2017, https://www.rfa.org/english/news/uyghur/egyptian-authorities-forcibly-disappear-16-uyghur-students-from-notorious-prison-09252017124938.html, last accessed 4 February 2017. See also Nour Youssef, 'Egyptian Police Detain Uighurs and Deport them to China', *New York Times*, 6 July 2017, https://www.nytimes.com/2017/07/06/world/asia/egypt-muslims-uighurs-deportations-xinjiang-china.html, last accessed 4 February 2018.
197. Abduweli Ayup, Mamatjan Juma, Alim Seytoff and Joshua Lipes, 'Nearly 20 Uyghur Students Unaccounted for Four Months After Egypt Raids', Radio Free Asia, 30 October 2017, https://www.rfa.org/english/news/uyghur/students-10302017162612.html, last accessed 4 February 2018.
198. Shohret Hoshur, Alim Seytoff and Joshua Lipes, 'Uyghurs in Xinjiang Re-Education Camps Forced to Express Remorse Over Travel Abroad', Radio Free Asia, 13 October 2017, https://www.rfa.org/english/news/uyghur/camps-10132017150431.html, last accessed 3 February 2018.
199. Ibid.
200. Ibid.
201. Tom Phillips, 'China holding at least 120,000 Uighurs in re-education camps', *Guardian*, 25 January 2018, https://www.theguardian.com/world/2018/jan/25/at-least-120000-muslim-uighurs-held-in-chinese-re-education-camps-report, last accessed 6 February 2018; Megha Rajagopalan, 'This is what a 21st-Century Police State Really Looks Like', *BuzzFeed News*, 18 October 2017, https://www.buzzfeed.com/meghara/the-police-state-of-the-future-is-already-here, last accessed 6 February 2018; Eset Sulaiman and Paul Eckert, 'China Runs Region-wide Re-education Camps in Xinjiang for Uyghurs and Other Muslims', Radio Free Asia, 11 September 2017, https://www.rfa.org/english/news/uyghur/training-camps-09112017154343.html, last accessed 6 February 2018; Shohret Hoshur, Alim Seytoff and Joshua Lipes, 'Nearly Half of Uyghurs in Xinjiang's Hotan Targeted for Re-Education Camps', Radio Free Asia, 9 October 2017, https://www.rfa.org/english/news/uyghur/camps-10092017164000.html, last accessed 6 February 2018; Shohret Hoshur, Alim Seytoff, Mamatjan Juma and Joshua Lipes, 'Elderly Among Thousands of Uyghurs Held in Xinjiang Re-Education Camps', Radio Free Asia, 26 October 2017, https://www.rfa.org/

english/news/uyghur/elderly-10262017150900.html, last accessed 4 February 2018; Shohret Hoshur, Alim Seytoff and Joshua Lipes, 'Re-Education Camps in Two Xinjiang Counties Hold Thousands of Uyghurs: Officials', Radio Free Asia, 29 September 2017, https://www.rfa.org/english/news/uyghur/camps-09292017160826.html, last accessed 6 February 2018.

202. Shohret Hoshur and Joshua Lipes, 'New Guidelines on Uyghur "Signs of Extremism" Issued to Xinjiang Authorities', Radio Free Asia, 7 November 2017, https://www.rfa.org/english/news/uyghur/guidelines-11072017153331.html, last accessed February 6, 2018. See also Simon Denyer, 'From burqas to boxing gloves, China's 75 tips for spotting extremist Muslims'; Cao Siqi, 'Xinjiang counties identify 75 forms of religious extremism'; and '新疆部分地区学习识别75种宗教极端活动 遇到可报警 [Some parts of Xinjiang learn to recognize 75 types of religious extremist activities: report them to police upon encountering them]'.

203. Shohret Hoshur and Joshua Lipes, 'Uyghur Detentions Continue in Xinjiang, Despite Pledge to End with Party Congress', Radio Free Asia, 8 January 2018, https://www.rfa.org/english/news/uyghur/detentions-01082018164453.html, last accessed 6 February 2018; Qiao Long and Luisetta Mudie, 'China's Mass Detention of Xinjiang's Ethnic Minorities Shows No Sign of Let-up', Radio Free Asia, 1 November 2017, https://www.rfa.org/english/news/uyghur/detention-11012017120255.html, last accessed 6 February 2018.

204. Shohret Hoshur, Alim Seytoff and Joshua Lipes, 'Re-Education Camps in Two Xinjiang Counties Hold Thousands of Uyghurs: Officials'.

205. Maya Wang, 'China: Free Xinjiang "Political Education" Detainees', *Human Rights Watch*, 10 September 2017, https://www.hrw.org/news/2017/09/10/china-free-xinjiang-political-education-detainees, last accessed 3 February 2018.

206. Ibid.

207. Shohret Hoshur and Joshua Lipes, 'Around 120,000 Uyghurs Detained for Political Re-Education in Xinjiang's Kashgar Prefecture', Radio Free Asia, 22 January 2018, https://www.rfa.org/english/news/uyghur/detentions-01222018171657.html, last accessed 6 February 2018; Shohret Hoshur and Joshua Lipes, 'Uyghur Inmates in Xinjiang's Korla City Endure Overcrowded Re-Education Camps', Radio Free Asia, 3 January 2018, https://www.rfa.org/english/news/uyghur/camps-01032018155622.html, last accessed 4 February 2018; Shohret Hoshur and Joshua Lipes, 'Overcrowded Political Re-Education Camps in Hotan Relocate Hundreds of Uyghur Detainees', Radio Free Asia, 26 January 2018, https://www.rfa.org/english/news/uyghur/camps-01262018140920.html, last accessed 6 February 2018.

208. Shohret Hoshur and Joshua Lipes, 'Uyghur Inmates Suffer Health Complications Due to Neglect in Xinjiang Detention Centers', Radio Free Asia, 18 January 2018, https://www.rfa.org/english/news/uyghur/health-01182018171513.html, last accessed 4 February 2018; Shohret Hoshur, Alim Seytoff, Mamatjan

Juma and Joshua Lipes, 'Elderly Among Thousands of Uyghurs Held in Xinjiang Re-Education Camps', Radio Free Asia, 26 October 2017, https://www.rfa.org/english/news/uyghur/elderly-10262017150900.html, last accessed 4 February 2018.

209. Shohret Hoshur and Joshua Lipes, 'Uyghur Inmates in Xinjiang's Korla City Endure Overcrowded Re-Education Camps'.

210. Shohret Hoshur and Joshua Lipes, 'Nearly 10 Percent of Residents of a Xinjiang Township Detained by Chinese Authorities', Radio Free Asia, 14 December 2017, https://www.rfa.org/english/news/uyghur/detained-12142017140125.html, last accessed 4 February 2018.

211. Shohret Hoshur and Joshua Lipes, 'Threat of Re-Education Camp Drives Uyghur Who Failed Anthem Recitation to Suicide', Radio Free Asia, 5 February 2018, https://www.rfa.org/english/news/uyghur/suicide-02052018165305.html, last accessed 8 February 2018.

212. Overcrowding and 'terrible' conditions in orphanages across Xinjiang is reportedly a growing problem as more and more parents are sent to re-education camps. A Uyghur police officer in Kashgar prefecture similarly reported that the government has placed a number of children in orphanages because their parents were sent to re-education camps. XUAR authorities have reportedly sent some of these children to other regions of China for care. See Gulchehra Hoja, Shohret Hoshur, Mamatjan Juma, Alim Seytoff and Joshua Lipes, 'Children of Detained Uyghurs Face "Terrible" Conditions in Overcrowded Xinjiang Orphanages', Radio Free Asia, 18 October 2017, https://www.rfa.org/english/news/uyghur/children-10182017144425.html, last accessed 4 February 2018. For more on overcrowded facilities in Hotan, see Shohret Hoshur and Joshua Lipes, 'Overcrowded Political Re-Education Camps in Hotan Relocate Hundreds of Uyghur Detainees', Radio Free Asia, 26 January 2018, https://www.rfa.org/english/news/uyghur/camps-01262018140920.html, last accessed 4 February 2018.

213. Shohret Hoshur, Alim Seytoff and Joshua Lipes, 'Nearly Half of Uyghurs in Xinjiang's Hotan Targeted for Re-Education Camps', Radio Free Asia, 9 October 2017, https://www.rfa.org/english/news/uyghur/camps-10092017164000.html, last accessed 6 February 2018.

214. Qiao Long and Luisetta Mudie, 'China's Mass Detention of Xinjiang's Ethnic Minorities Shows No Sign of Let-up', Radio Free Asia, 1 November 2017, https://www.rfa.org/english/news/uyghur/detention-11012017120255.html, last accessed 4 February 2018. See also Qiao Long and Luisetta Mudie, 'China Carries Out "Mass Detentions" of Ethnic Kazakhs in Xinjiang', Radio Free Asia, 13 November 2017, https://www.rfa.org/english/news/uyghur/kazaks-arrests-11132017130345.html, last accessed 4 February 2018.

215. Shohret Hoshur, Alim Seytoff, Mamatjan Juma and Joshua Lipes, 'Chinese Authorities Jail Four Wealthiest Uyghurs in Xinjiang's Kashgar in New Purge',

Radio Free Asia, 5 January 2018, https://www.rfa.org/english/news/uyghur/wealthiest-01052018144327.html, last accessed 6 February 2018.
216. Ibid.
217. Radio Free Asia Uyghur and Cantonese services, Mamatjan Juma, Vivian Kwan and Roseanne Gerin, 'Xinjiang Regional Government Passes New Counter-terrorism Law', Radio Free Asia, 5 August 2016, http://www.rfa.org/english/news/uyghur/xinjiang-regional-government-passes-new-counterterrorism-law-08052016160441.html, last accessed 5 March 2017.
218. Cui Jia, 'Xinjiang toughens anti-terror stance', *China Daily*, 3 August 2016, http://usa.chinadaily.com.cn/china/2016–08/03/content_26324682.htm, last accessed 5 March 2017; Cui Jia and Mao Weihua, 'Regulation targets root of terrorism', *China Daily*, 6 August 2016, http://www.chinadaily.com.cn/china/2016–08/06/content_26366056.htm, last accessed 5 March 2017.
219. 'Xinjiang issues China's first local counterterrorism law', *China Daily*, 5 August 2016, http://usa.chinadaily.com.cn/china/2016–08/05/content_26364290.htm, last accessed 5 March 2017.
220. 张, 李 [Zhang, Li], '新疆维吾尔自治区实施《中华人民共和国反恐怖主义法》办法 [XUAR Implementation Measures for the PRC Counterterrorism Law]'. See also the unofficial English translation of the regulations on the *China Law Translate* website.
221. Cui Jia, 'Xinjiang toughens anti-terror stance'.
222. Chun Han Wong, 'China Adopts Sweeping National-Security Law', *Wall Street Journal*, 1 July 2015, http://www.wsj.com/articles/china-adopts-sweeping-national-security-law-1435757589, last accessed 5 March 2017; Carl Minzner, 'What Direction for Legal Reform under Xi Jinping', Jamestown Foundation, *China Brief*, 4 January 2013, https://jamestown.org/program/what-direction-for-legal-reform-under-xi-jinping/, last accessed 5 March 2017.
223. Chun Han Wong, 'China Adopts Sweeping National Security Law'.
224. Stanley Lubman, 'China's New Law on International NGOs—and Questions about Legal Reform', *Wall Street Journal*, 25 May 2016, http://blogs.wsj.com/chinarealtime/2016/05/25/chinas-new-law-on-international-ngos-and-questions-about-legal-reform/, last accessed 5 March 2017.
225. Ibid. See also Chris Mirasola, 'Understanding China's Foreign NGO Activities Law', 16 May 2016, Brookings Institution, *Lawfare* blog, https://www.lawfareblog.com/understanding-chinas-foreign-ngo-activities-law, last accessed 5 March 2017; and Julia Famularo, 'Chinese Religious Regulations in the Xinjiang Uyghur Autonomous Region: A Veiled Threat to Turkic Muslims?', *Project 2049 Institute*, 8 April 2015, http://www.project2049.net/documents/Famularo_PRC_Religious_Regulations_Xinjiang.pdf, last accessed 5 March 2017.
226. Chun Han Wong, 'China Adopts Sweeping National-Security Law'.
227. Radio Free Asia Uyghur and Cantonese services, Mamatjan Juma, Vivian Kwan

and Roseanne Gerin, 'Xinjiang Regional Government Passes New Counter-terrorism Law', Radio Free Asia, 5 August 2016, http://www.rfa.org/english/news/uyghur/xinjiang-regional-government-passes-new-counterterrorism-law-08052016160441.html, last accessed 5 March 2017.

228. Barbara Demick, 'China imposes intrusive rules on Uighurs in Xinjiang', *Los Angeles Times*, 5 August 2014, http://www.latimes.com/world/asia/la-fg-china-privacy-20140805-story.html, last accessed 5 March 2017.
229. Chun Han Wong, 'China Adopts Sweeping National Security Law'.
230. '习近平: 全面提高新形势下宗教工作水平 [Xi Jinping: Comprehensively Promote the New Status of Religious Work under New Circumstances],' 新华 [*Xinhua*], 23 April 2016, http://news.xinhuanet.com/politics/2016-04/23/c_111871 6540.htm, last accessed 5 March 2017.
231. '新疆维吾尔自治区第九次代表大会隆重开幕 [The XUAR Opens its 9th Representative Congress with Great Ceremony', 天山网 [*Tianshan Net*], 29 October 2016, http://news.ts.cn/content/2016-10/29/content_12356505.htm, last accessed 5 March 2017.
232. '精心做好宗教工作: 三论学习贯彻习近平总书记新疆工作座谈会重要讲话精神 [Do Religious Work Meticulously Well: Three Theories on the Study and Implementation of General Secretary Xi Jinping's Important Speech at the Xinjiang Work Forum]'.
233. In addition to purportedly stimulating economic development, 'Project Beauty' was also meant as a direct support to China's religious policies in the XUAR. A stated goal of the programme is to 'strengthen quality education for women' by organizing a campaign to 'allow beautiful hair to float freely [remove headscarves] and expose one's pretty face [remove veils]. All kinds of organizations should guide and hold demonstrations for women from all ethnic groups, at all levels of education and training, through propaganda and mobilization [efforts] in order to change old ideas.' The goal is to 'help them establish healthy, civilized philosophy on life' and 'lead women of every ethnic group in Xinjiang to highlight the "Xinjiang Spirit" of loving the nation and Xinjiang.' Another 'Project Beauty' initiative seeks to 'standardize' ethnic minority garb in Xinjiang. Its stated purpose is to 'preserve and enhance ethnic minority traditional clothing culture and to promote the healthy development of Xinjiang's modern clothing industry'. Yet, an article by a state-sponsored media outlet also reveals that 'as a result of the negative influence of the "three evil forces", a minority of the public in Xinjiang has blindly adopted foreign clothing with an extremist religious character. This has had a negative influence on Xinjiang's traditional culture and clothing.' A number of bureaus are thus working together to 'systemize and standardize the traditional clothing of each ethnic group in Xinjiang'. Chinese authorities wish to 'standardize' ethnic minority clothing in order to define which types of clothing are 'traditional' and which types of clothing are effectively 'foreign'. Given that they have perceived a link between religious extremism and conservative

women's dress in Xinjiang, they aim to target Islamic garb as 'foreign' and thus not part of the 'traditional' Uyghur culture. This type of official thinking has already permeated the XUAR. For more information, see 朱凯莉 [Zhu Ruili], '[天山访谈录]'靓丽工程'让新疆女性更自立自强自信 [Tianshan Interview, 'Project Beauty' Enables Xinjiang Women to Become More Independent and Self-Confident]', 靓丽工程: 做靓丽女性 展大美新疆 [Project Beauty: Making Beautiful Women, Developing a Beautiful Xinjiang], 天山网 [*Tianshan Net*], 5 September 2012, http://news.ts.cn/content/2012-09/05/content_7209909.htm, last accessed 5 March 2017; 朱凯莉 [Zhu Ruili], '化妆品业 化妆品饰品专家献计新疆女性'靓丽工程' [Cosmetics, Accessories Experts Offer Advice to Xinjiang Women through "Project Beauty"]', 靓丽工程: 做靓丽女性 展大美新疆 [Project Beauty: Making Beautiful Women, Developing a Beautiful Xinjiang], 天山网 [*Tianshan Net*], 8 September 2011, http://www.ts.cn/special/2011_Beautiful/2011-09/08/content_6154485.htm, last accessed 5 March 2017.

234. See, for example, Brent Crane, 'A Tale of Two Chinese Muslim Minorities', *The Diplomat*, 22 August 2014, http://thediplomat.com/2014/08/a-tale-of-two-chinese-muslim-minorities/, last accessed 5 March 2017; Hannah Beech, 'If China is Anti-Islam, Why are These Chinese Muslims Enjoying a Faith Revival?', *Time*, 12 August 2014, http://time.com/3099950/china-muslim-hui-xinjiang-uighur-islam/, last accessed 5 March 2017; and Rukiye Turdush, Mamatjan Juma and Rachel Vandenbrink, 'A Muslim Divide in China', Radio Free Asia, 30 November 2012, http://www.rfa.org/english/news/uyghur/hui-11302012 172354.html, last accessed 5 March 2017.

235. James Leibold, 'Creeping Islamophobia: China's Hui Muslims in the Firing Line', *China Brief*, 20 June 2016, https://jamestown.org/program/creeping-islamophobia-chinas-hui-muslims-in-the-firing-line/, last accessed 5 March 2017; Viola Zhou, 'Why China's Hui Muslims Fear They're Next to Face Crackdown on Religion', *South China Morning Post*, 11 March 2017, http://www.scmp.com/week-asia/society/article/2078121/why-chinas-hui-muslims-fear-theyre-next-face-crackdown-religion, last accessed 2 February 2018. See also Christian Shepherd, 'Muslim county in China bans children from religious events over break', Reuters, 17 January 2018, https://www.reuters.com/article/us-china-religion/muslim-county-in-china-bans-children-from-religious-events-over-break-idUSKBN1F60PI, last accessed 2 February 2018.

236. Frank Dikotter, *The Discourse of Race in Modern China* (Hong Kong: Hong Kong University Press, 1992), p. 9.

237. 'Efforts to Boost "Leapfrog Development" in Xinjiang', *China Daily*, 5 July 2010, http://www.chinadaily.com.cn/china/2010-07/05/content_10058467.htm, last accessed 5 March 2017.

238. Leibold, 'Xinjiang Work Forum Marks New Policy of "Ethnic Mingling"', pp. 3–4.

239. Ibid.
240. Ilham Tohti, 'My Ideals and the Career Path I Have Chosen', trans. Uighur Human Rights Project, Julia Famularo and Yaxue Cao, *China Change*, 6 April 2014, www.chinachange.org/2014/04/06/my-ideals-and-the-career-path-i-have-chosen/, last accessed 5 March 2017.

3. 'FIGHTING TERRORISM ACCORDING TO LAW': CHINA'S LEGAL EFFORTS AGAINST TERRORISM

1. Fu Hualing, 'Responses to terrorism in China', in Victor V. Ramraj, Michael Hor, Kent Roach and George Williams (eds), *Global Anti-terrorism Law and Policy*, 2nd edn (Cambridge: Cambridge University Press, 2012), pp. 344–5.
2. James Millward, 'Violent separatism in Xinjiang: a critical assessment', *Policy Studies*, 6 (Washington, DC: East–West Center, 2004), http://www.eastwestcenter.org/fileadmin/stored/pdfs/PS006.pdf, last accessed 20 January 2018, pp. 2–10.
3. See Information Office of State Council, '"East Turkistan" terrorist forces cannot get away with impunity', 21 January 2002, http://www.china.org.cn/english/2002/Jan/25582.htm, last accessed 20 January 2018.
4. Jeremy Page and Emre Peker, 'As Muslim Uighurs flee, China sees Jihad risk', *Wall Street Journal*, 1 February 2015, http://www.wsj.com/articles/as-muslim-uighurs-flee-china-sees-jihad-risk-1422666280, last accessed 20 January 2018. See also Marc Julienne, Moritz Rudolf and Johannes Buckow, 'Beyond doubt: the changing face of terrorism in China', *The Diplomat*, 28 May 2015, http://thediplomat.com/2015/05/beyond-doubt-the-changing-face-of-terrorism-in-china, last accessed 20 January 2018.
5. Jeremy Page, 'Over 100 Chinese fighters have joined Islamic State in Syria', *Wall Street Journal*, 25 July 2016, http://www.wsj.com/articles/china-terror-claims-bolstered-by-new-evidence-1469435872, last accessed 20 January 2018.
6. 'Ruling the country according to law' is China's interpretation of the Western concept 'the rule of law'.
7. Zhang Chunxian, 'Quanmian tuijin yifa zhi jiang [Fully promote the efforts of ruling Xinjiang according to law]', *Renmin Ribao [People's Daily]*, 7 January 2015, http://politics.people.com.cn/n/2015/0107/c1001-26337939.html, last accessed 20 January 2018.
8. In Chinese law, both the NPC and its Standing Committee are competent legislative organs.
9. Ng Tze-Wei, 'First anti-terror draft now under NPC scrutiny', *South China Morning Post*, 26 October 2011, http://www.scmp.com/article/982897/first-anti-terror-draft-now-under-npc-scrutiny, last accessed 20 January 2018.
10. For a full text of the 'Counter-Terrorism Law' (in Chinese), see *Xinhua*, 27 December 2015, http://news.xinhuanet.com/politics/2015-12/27/c_128571798.htm, last accessed 20 January 2018.

11. See Bingzhi Zhao, 'Lüetan fan kongbu fa de lifa dingwei [A brief discussion about the legislative orientation of the Counter-Terrorism Law]', *Fazhi Ribao* [*Legal Daily*], 2 July 2014, http://www.legaldaily.com.cn/zbzk/content/2014–07/02/content_5643358.htm, last accessed 20 January 2018; also Jia Yu, 'Zhongguo fazhi fankong de lichengbei [China's landmark law on countering terrorism: an introduction to the Counter-Terrorism Law]', *Renmin Fazhi* [Rule of Law for the People], 8, 2016, pp. 18–19.
12. While the 'Coordination Group' was only responsible for coordinating efforts, the 'Leading Group' has the power to give orders. See Zhang Xiaobo, 'Govt sets up national anti-terror team', *Global Times*, 28 August 2013, http://www.globaltimes.cn/content/807172.shtml, last accessed 20 January 2018.
13. Cui Xiaosu, 'Guo Shengkun jianren guojia fankongbu gongzuo lingdao xiaozu zuzhang [Guo Shengkun holds a concurrent post as chief of the National Counter-Terrorism Leading Group]', *Renmin Ribao* [*People's Daily*], 28 August 2013, http://politics.people.com.cn/n/2013/0828/c1001–22722118.html, last accessed 20 January 2018.
14. Apart from this sole provision, many other ordinary, although not terrorism-specific, provisions may also be used for anti-terrorism purposes. See Du Miao, 'Fankong lifa xingfa yanjiu [On anti-terrorism criminal legislation]' (Beijing: Law Press China, 2009), pp. 244–8; also Bingzhi Zhao and Jianfeng Yin, 'Zhongguo xingfa zhong de kongbu huodong fanzui [Terrorism crimes in Chinese criminal law]', in Bingzhi Zhao (ed.),*Guoji kongbuzhuyi fanzui jiqi fangzhi duice zhuanlun* [*Issues on international terrorism and its prevention and suppression*] (Beijing: China People's Public Security University Press, 2005), pp. 147–65.
15. See Du, 'Fankong lifa xingfa yanjiu', pp. 220–21.
16. Wang Xiumei, 'Lun kongbuzhuyi fanzui de chengzhi ji woguo lifa de fazhan wanshan [On the suppression of terrorism crimes and the improvements to the legislation in China]', *Zhongguo Faxue* [*Journal of Chinese Law*], 3 (2002), pp. 139–40; also Taiyun Huang, 'Xingfa xiuzheng'an jiedu quanbian [A collection of all interpretations on Criminal Law amendments]' (Beijing: People's Court Press, 2011), pp. 245–61.
17. For a full text of the amendment, see *Xinhua*, 30 August 2015, http://news.xinhuanet.com/legal/2015–08/30/c_1116414724.htm, last accessed 20 January 2018). See also Zunyou Zhou, 'China's Draft Counter-Terrorism Law', *China Brief*, 17 July 2015, https://jamestown.org/program/chinas-draft-counter-terrorism-law, last accessed 20 January 2018.
18. Bingzhi Zhao, Bing Yuan and Jing Guo, 'Fankong xingshi fazhi de lixing goujian [Rational making of counter-terrorism criminal law]', *Fazhi Ribao* [*Legal Daily*], 25 March 2015, http://epaper.legaldaily.com.cn/fzrb/content/20150325/Articel12002GN.htm, last accessed 20 January 2018.
19. See Du Miao, 'Zhongguo fankong lifa de lishi yanjin [Historical development of

the Chinese anti-terrorism legislation]', in Liu Renwen (ed.), *Xingshi fazhi shiye xia de shehui wending yu fankong* [*Social stability and anti-terrorism from the perspective of criminal law*] (Beijing: Social Sciences Academic Press, 2013), p. 101; also Liu Renwen, 'Zhongguo fankong xingshi lifa de miaoshu yu pingxi [Analysis of anti-terrorism legislation in China]', *Faxuejia* [*Jurists' Review*], 4 (2013), pp. 48–9.

20. See Sharon La Franiere, 'Beijing expands safeguards for criminal suspects', *New York Times*, 14 March 2012, http://www.nytimes.com/2012/03/15/world/asia/china-passes-new-safeguards-for-criminal-suspects-though-secret-detentions-by-police-are-still-allowed.html, last accessed 20 January 2018; also Dui Hua Foundation, 'China's new Criminal Procedure Law: Death Penalty Procedures', 3 April 2012, http://www.duihuahrjournal.org/2012/04/chinas-new-criminal-procedure-law-death_03.html, last accessed 20 January 2018.

21. See Stanley Lubman, 'China's Criminal Procedure Law: good, bad and ugly', *Wall Street Journal*, 21 March 2012, http://blogs.wsj.com/chinarealtime/2012/03/21/chinas-criminal-procedure-law-good-bad-and-ugly/, last accessed 20 January 2018); also Dui Hua Foundation, 'China's new Criminal Procedure Law'.

22. See Jerome Cohen and Yu Han, 'Seeking Shelter', *South China Morning Post*, 28 September 2011, http://www.cfr.org/china/seeking-shelter/p26064, last accessed 20 January 2018; and La Franiere, 'Beijing expands safeguards'.

23. Jianfu Chen, *Criminal Law and Criminal Procedure Law in the People's Republic of China: commentary and legislation* (Leiden/Boston: Nijhoff, 2013), p. 92.

24. Susan Trevaskes, 'Severe and swift justice in China', *British Journal of Criminology*, 47, 1 (2007), pp. 23–4.

25. Wanhuai Sun, 'Kuanyanxiangji de xingshi zhengce ying huigui wei sifa zhengce [The criminal policy of "balancing severity and leniency" should return to a judicial policy]', *Faxue Yanjiu* [*Chinese Journal of Law*], 4 (2014), p. 175.

26. Tania Branigan, 'China launches "strike hard" crackdown in Xinjiang', *Guardian*, 3 November 2009, https://www.theguardian.com/world/2009/nov/03/china-strike-hard-crackdown-xinjiang, last accessed 20 January 2018.

27. See 'Xinjiang starts campaign against terror', *Xinhua*, 23 May 2014, http://news.xinhuanet.com/english/china/2014–05/23/c_133356740.htm, last accessed 20 January 2018.

28. Cui Jia and Gao Bo, 'Report outlines regional terror crackdown', *China Daily*, 25 November 2014, http://www.chinadaily.com.cn/china/2014–11/25/content_18971501.htm, last accessed 20 January 2018.

29. For a general discussion of the old definition in the CTD, see Li Zhe, 'China', in Kent Roach (ed.), *Comparative Counter-Terrorism Law* (Cambridge: Cambridge University Press, 2015), pp. 582–4.

30. Zunyou Zhou, 'China's Comprehensive Counter-Terrorism Law', *The Diplomat*, 23 January 2016, http://thediplomat.com/2016/01/chinas-comprehensive-counter-terrorism-law, last accessed 20 January 2018.

31. Zhou, 'China's Draft Counter-Terrorism Law'.
32. Zunyou Zhou, 'In defining terrorism, China should heed global practices', *South China Morning Post*, 9 March 2015, http://www.scmp.com/comment/insight-opinion/article/1731061/defining-terrorism-china-should-heed-global-practices, last accessed 20 January 2018.
33. Du Miao, 'Zhongguo kongbu huodong zuzhi he renyuan rending "shuangguizhi" yanjiu [On the "double-track" listing of terrorist organizations and individuals in China]', *Zhongguo Renmin Gong'an Daxue Xuebao* (Shehui Kexue Ban) [*Journal of People's Public Security University of China* (Social Sciences Edition)], 1 (2016), pp. 67–9.
34. Anna Oehmichen, 'UN-EU-Terrorist Listings—Legal Foundations and Impacts', *Zeitschrift für Internationale Strafrechtsdogmatik (ZIS)*, 9 (2014), p. 419.
35. Gavin Sullivan, 'Rethinking terrorist blacklisting', *Guardian*, 10 December 2010, https://www.theguardian.com/commentisfree/libertycentral/2010/dec/10/terrorist-blacklisting-un-report-human-rights, last accessed 20 January 2018.
36. See 'Combating terrorism, we have no choice', *People's Daily*, 18 December 2003, http://en.people.cn/200312/18/eng20031218_130652.shtml, last accessed 20 January 2018.
37. See 'China identifies alleged "Eastern Turkistan" terrorists', *Xinhua*, 21 October 2008, http://news.xinhuanet.com/english/2008-10/21/content_10229518.htm, last accessed 20 January 2018.
38. See Yan Zhang, 'Authorities name six as terrorists', *China Daily*, 7 April 2012, http://usa.chinadaily.com.cn/china/2012-04-07/content_14996384.htm, last accessed 7 June 2018.
39. See 'Chinese militant "shot dead"', BBC, 23 December 2003, http://news.bbc.co.uk/2/hi/asia-pacific/3343241.stm, last accessed 20 January 2018.
40. Shirley A. Kan, 'U.S.–China counterterrorism cooperation: issues for U.S. policy' (Washington, DC: Congressional Research Service, 15 July 2010), https://fas.org/sgp/crs/terror/RL33001.pdf, pp. 9–10.
41. 'Uyghur Exile Leadership Passes to "Younger Generation" in Munich Election', Radio Free Asia, 13 November 2017, http://www.rfa.org/english/news/uyghur/election-11132017152921.html, last accessed 20 January 2018.
42. For further information about the WUC, visit its website, http://www.uyghurcongress.org/en/.
43. Zunyou Zhou, *Balancing Security and Liberty: Counter-Terrorism Legislation in Germany and China* (Berlin: Duncker & Humblot, 2014), p. 155.
44. See 'Eliminating online terror is a war China must win', *Xinhua*, 24 June 2014, http://news.xinhuanet.com/english/indepth/2014-06/24/c_133434243.htm, last accessed 20 January 2018.
45. See Lucy Hornby, 'Xinjiang leader says online videos spark China separatist attacks', *Financial Times*, 6 March 2014, https://www.ft.com/content/984a7346-a51f-

11e3-a7b4-00144feab7de, last accessed 7 April 2015; and Teddy Ng, 'Xinjiang to work with National Security Commission to curb violence, Zhang Chunxian says', *South China Morning Post*, 7 March 2014, http://www.scmp.com/news/china/article/1442255/xinjiang-work-national-security-commission-curb-violence-zhang-chunxian, last accessed 20 January 2018.

46. Beina Xu and Eleanor Albert, 'Media censorship in China', *Council on Foreign Relations*, 17 February 2017, http://www.cfr.org/china/media-censorship-china/p11515, last accessed 20 January 2018.
47. See Michael Martina and Ben Blanchard, 'China says 28 foreign-led "terrorists" killed after attack on mine', Reuters, 20 November 2015, http://www.reuters.com/article/us-china-security-xinjiang-idUSKCN0T909920151120, last accessed 20 January 2018; and Javier C. Hernandez, 'China acknowledges killing 28 people; accuses them of role in mine attack', *New York Times*, 20 November 2015, https://www.nytimes.com/2015/11/21/world/asia/china-xinjiang-uighurs-raid-coal-mine-attack.html, last accessed 20 January 2018.
48. Zunyou Zhou, 'In cyberspace, China's aim is to control and censor, no matter what it says', *South China Morning Post*, 23 December 2015, http://www.scmp.com/comment/insight-opinion/article/1893924/cyberspace-chinas-aim-control-and-censor-no-matter-what-it, last accessed 20 January 2018.
49. In fact, before the adoption of the CSL, China had announced regulations that require internet users to register with their real names for an array of internet services. See Josh Chin, 'China is requiring people to register real names for some internet services', *Wall Street Journal*, 4 February 2015, https://www.wsj.com/articles/china-to-enforce-real-name-registration-for-internet-users-1423033973, last accessed 20 January 2018.
50. For example, China has a massive internet surveillance and censorship apparatus, known as the 'Great Firewall', to block access to information that the government deems harmful. Internet users in China are banned from popular Western social media sites such as Facebook, Twitter and YouTube. See Kristie Lu Stout, 'China's Great Firewall: fortune at the expense of freedom?', CNN, 25 March 2015, http://edition.cnn.com/2015/03/25/asia/china-internet-censorship-kristie-lu-stout, last accessed 20 January 2018.
51. Zhuang Pinghui, 'China pushes through cybersecurity law despite foreign business fears', *South China Morning Post*, 7 November 2016, http://www.scmp.com/news/china/policies-politics/article/2043646/china-pushes-through-cybersecurity-legislation-heavily, last accessed 20 January 2018.
52. Jennifer Zhang, 'China to codify internet control measures', *The Diplomat*, 16 July 2015, http://thediplomat.com/2015/07/china-to-codify-internet-control-measures, last accessed 20 January 2018.
53. Cao Bin, 'A year without internet in Xinjiang', *Xinhua*, 20 April 2014, http://news.xinhuanet.com/english/indepth/2014-04/20/c_133276600.htm, last accessed 20 January 2018.

54. Edward Wong, 'After long ban, western China is back online', *New York Times*, 14 May 2010, http://www.nytimes.com/2010/05/15/world/asia/15china.html, last accessed 20 January 2018.
55. Ben Blanchard, 'China tells banks to report terror suspicions', Reuters, 17 January 2014, http://www.reuters.com/article/us-china-banks-terror-idUSBREA0G07 920140117, last accessed 20 January 2018.
56. For a full text of the law, see *Xinhua*, 7 September 2017, http://news.xinhuanet.com/politics/2017-09/07/c_1121624896.htm, last accessed 20 January 2018.
57. See 'Central govt pledges better governance in Xinjiang', *Xinhua*, 30 May 2014, http://www.chinadaily.com.cn/china/2014-05/30/content_17552753.htm, last accessed 20 January 2018.
58. For further information on the amended law, see Jianxin Li, '"Xinjiang weiwuer zizhiqu zongjiao shiwu tiaoli" xiuding dansheng ji [The birth of the revised Regulation on Religious Affairs of XUAR]', *Xinjiang Ribao* [*Xinjiang Daily*], 30 December 2014, http://news.ts.cn/content/2014-12/30/content_10868075_all.htm, last accessed 20 January 2018; and Cui Jia, 'Curbs on religious extremism beefed up in Xinjiang', *China Daily*, 29 November 2014, http://www.chinadaily.com.cn/china/2014-11/29/content_18996900.htm, last accessed 20 January 2018.
59. Li Ya'nan, 'Wulumuqi shi gonggong changsuo jiang jinzhi chuandai mengmian zhaopao [Urumqi city will ban the wearing of burqas]', *Renmin Ribao* [*People's Daily*], 17 January 2015, http://politics.people.com.cn/n/2015/0117/c1001-26403482.html, last accessed 20 January 2018.
60. Fang Chen, 'Xinjiang qu jiduanhua diaocha [An investigation of de-radicalization efforts in Xinjiang]', *Fenghuang Wang* [*iFeng*], 2015, http://news.ifeng.com/mainland/special/xjqjdh, last accessed 20 January 2018.
61. Liu Hangying, 'Fan kongbuzhuyi fa zhong "anzhi jiaoyu" zhidu tanxi [A tentative analysis of the "placement and education" regime in the Counter-Terrorism Law]', *Liaoning Jingcha Xueyuan Xuebao* [*Journal of Liaoning Police College*], 4 (2016), pp. 9–11.
62. Zunyou Zhou, 'Abolition of re-education through labor a milestone', *China Daily*, 5 December 2013, http://www.chinadaily.com.cn/opinion/2013-12/05/content_17152734.htm, last accessed 20 January 2018.
63. Ni, Chunle, *Kongbuzhuyi fanzui teshu susong chengxu bijiao yanjiu* [*Comparative study of special judicial procedures for terrorism crime*] (Beijing: Qunzhong Press, 2013), p. 196.
64. See 'China signs extradition treaties with 39 nations', *China Daily*, 20 March 2015, http://www.chinadaily.com.cn/china/2015-03/20/content_19865295.htm, last accessed 20 January 2018.
65. Margaret K. Lewis, 'Mutual legal assistance and extradition: human rights implications', *China Rights Forum*, 2, 2007, pp. 89–93, http://www.hrichina.org/sites/

default/files/PDFs/CRF.2.2007/CRF-2007–2_Extradition.pdf, last accessed 20 January 2018; and Steven Chase and Robert Fife, 'Justin Trudeau defends extradition treaty talks with China', *Globe and Mail*, 21 September 2016, http://www.theglobeandmail.com/news/politics/justin-trudeau-defends-extradition-treaty-talks-with-china/article31997509, last accessed 20 January 2018.

66. Charlie Savage, 'U.S. frees last of the Chinese Uighur detainees from Guantánamo Bay', *New York Times*, 31 December 2013, https://www.nytimes.com/2014/01/01/us/us-frees-last-of-uighur-detainees-from-guantanamo.html, last accessed 20 January 2018.
67. See Paul J. Smith, 'China's economic and political rise: implications for global terrorism and U.S.–China cooperation', *Studies in Conflict and Terrorism*, 32, 7 (2009), p. 638.
68. Tom Phillips, 'China accuses US of human rights "double-standards"', *Daily Telegraph*, 9 December 2014, http://www.telegraph.co.uk/news/worldnews/asia/china/11282190/China-accuses-US-of-human-rights-double-standards.html, last accessed 20 January 2018.
69. Zunyou Zhou, 'America's double standards on terrorism', *South China Morning Post*, 6 January 2014, http://www.scmp.com/comment/insight-opinion/article/1399064/americas-double-standards-terrorism, last accessed 20 January 2018.
70. Michael Clarke, 'Widening the net: China's anti-terror laws and human rights in the Xinjiang Uyghur Autonomous Region', *International Journal of Human Rights*, 14, 4 (2010), p. 554.
71. Michael Clarke, 'Bangkok bombing spotlights Uyghur woes in Southeast Asia', *The Diplomat*, 28 August 2015, http://thediplomat.com/2015/08/bangkok-bombing-spotlights-uyghur-woes-in-southeast-asia, last accessed 20 January 2018.
72. See 'China defends Thailand's repatriation of illegal Uygur immigrants', *Xinhua*, 10 July 2015, http://news.xinhuanet.com/english/2015–07/10/c_134401871.htm, last accessed 20 January 2018.
73. See 'Commentary: Thailand's repatriation of illegal immigrants just a legal issue', *Xinhua*, 12 July 2015, http://news.xinhuanet.com/english/2015-07/12/c_134405288.htm, last accessed 20 January 2018.
74. Michael Martina, 'Draft Chinese law paves way for counter-terror operations abroad', Reuters, 27 February 2015, http://www.reuters.com/article/us-china-military-idUSKBN0LV0PN20150227, last accessed 20 January 2018.
75. Smith, 'China's economic and political rise', p. 640.
76. Mathieu Duchâtel, 'Terror overseas: understanding China's evolving counter-terror strategy', *European Council on Foreign Relations Policy Brief* (October 2016), p. 6, http://www.ecfr.eu/page/-/ECFR_193_-_TERROR_OVERSEAS_UNDERSTANDING_CHINAS_EVOLVING_COUNTER_TERROR_STRATEGY.pdf, last accessed 20 January 2018.
77. See 'China: Draft Counterterrorism Law a Recipe for Abuses', Human Rights

Watch, 20 January 2015, https://www.hrw.org/news/2015/01/20/china-draft-counterterrorism-law-recipe-abuses, last accessed 20 January 2018.
78. Zhang Jinping, 'Zhongguo fankongbu fa zhong jingwai wuli fankongbu xingdong de liangge yuanzexing guiding [Two principal provisions regarding overseas military counter-terrorism operations provided by China's Counter-Terrorism Law]', *Dangdai Shijie* [*Modern World*], 3 (2016), pp. 55–6.
79. For further information, see Christina Lin, 'If Assad asks, China can deploy troops to Syria', *Times of Israel*, 19 September 2015, http://blogs.timesofisrael.com/if-assad-asks-china-can-deploy-troops-to-syria, last accessed 20 January 2018; and Kian Beng Kor, 'Time for China to do more to fight global terror', *Straits Times*, 27 November 2015, http://www.straitstimes.com/asia/east-asia/time-for-china-to-do-more-to-fight-global-terror, last accessed 20 January 2018.
80. See Zhou, *Balancing Security and Liberty*, p. 1; also Clarke, 'Widening the net', p. 546.
81. Cui Jia, 'Terrorists strike, but progress made', *China Daily*, 30 December 2016, http://www.chinadaily.com.cn/china/2016-12/30/content_27820409.htm, last accessed 20 January 2018.
82. Wang Yong and Mei Jianming, 'Dangqian fankong douzheng de tedian, tiaozhan ji yingdui celüe [Characteristics, challenges and response strategies of the present counter-terrorism battle]', *Zhongguo Renmin Gong'an Daxue Xuebao* (Shehui Kexue Ban) [*Journal of People's University of Public Security of China* (Social Sciences Edition)], 1 (2016), p. 23.

4. THE NARRATIVE OF UYGHUR TERRORISM AND THE SELF-FULFILLING PROPHECY OF UYGHUR MILITANCY

1. Megha Rajagopalan, 'China security chief blames Uighur Islamists for Tiananmen attack', Reuters, 1 November 2013, https://www.reuters.com/article/us-china-tiananmen/china-security-chief-blames-uighur-islamists-for-tiananmen-attack-idUSBRE9A003L20131101, last accessed 7 June 2018.
2. Numerous media sources suggested that TIP had claimed responsibility for the attack; see Jonathan Kaiman, 'Islamist Group Claims Responsibility for Attack on China's Tiananmen Square', 25 November 2013, https://www.theguardian.com/world/2013/nov/25/islamist-china-tiananmen-beijing-attack. However, Rafaello Pantucci is more precise in his assertion that TIP praised the attack rather than claimed responsibility, and this important distinction is suggestive of the degree to which TIP actually is able to carry out attacks in China. See Raffaello Pantucci, 'Tiananmen Attack: Islamist Terror or Chinese Protest?', *China Brief*, 14, 1 (9 January 2014), http://www.jamestown.org/single/?tx_ttnews%5Btt_news%5D=41798&no_cache=1#.V6fYGVch6-Q, last accessed 1 March 2015.
3. Katie Hunt, 'China Executes Tiananmen Square Attack "Masterminds"',

CNN.com, 24 August 2014, http://www.cnn.com/2014/08/24/world/asia/china-tiananmen-executions/, last accessed 15 March 2016.
4. Walter Laqueur, *Terrorism* (London: Weidenfeld & Nicolson, 1977), p. 179.
5. Gerald Seymour, *Harry's Game: A Thriller* (New York: Random House, 1975).
6. Boaz Ganor, 'Defining Terrorism: Is One Man's Terrorist Another Man's Freedom Fighter?', *Police Practice and Research*, 3, 4 (2002), pp. 287–304.
7. United States Department of State, *Patterns of Global Terrorism, 2003*, April 2004, p. xii.
8. Ganor, 'Defining Terrorism', p. 289.
9. Ganor, 'Defining Terrorism', pp. 294–5.
10. See Pantucci, 'Tiananmen Attack'.
11. Paul Mooney, 'The Tiananmen Square Car Crash: Terrorism Or Accident?', *Forbes*, 31 October 2013, http://www.forbes.com/sites/paulmooney/2013/10/31/the-tiananmen-square-car-crash-terrorism-or-accident/#75d8caf87935, last accessed 11 November 2014.
12. When speaking historically about states that controlled the present territory of China, it is not useful to call these states 'Chinese'. Many of the empires that emanated from what is today China were not ruled by ethnic Chinese, or Han. This is true, for example, about the Qing Dynasty, which was ruled by ethnic Manchus. In this context, it is more accurate to talk about 'states based in China' than about 'China' when referring to periods prior to 1911.
13. 'China mass stabbing: Deadly knife attack in Kunming,' BBC, 2 March 2014, http://www.bbc.com/news/world-asia-china-26402367, last accessed 1 March 2015.
14. 'Urumqi attack kills 31 in China's Xinjiang region', BBC, 23 May 2014, http://www.bbc.com/news/world-asia-china-27502652, last accessed 17 June 2014; and 'Militant Islamist Group Says Deadly Xinjiang Bomb Attack "Good News"', Radio Free Asia, 15 May 2014, http://www.rfa.org/english/news/uyghur/attack-05152014171933.html, last accessed 17 June 2014.
15. 'At least 50 reported to have died in attack on coalmine in Xinjiang in September', *Guardian*, 1 October 2015, https://www.theguardian.com/world/2015/oct/01/at-least-50-reported-dead-in-september-attack-as-china-celebrates-xinjiang, last accessed 1 December 2015.
16. Sean R. Roberts, *Self-Fulfilling Prophecy: How the War on Terror and China Created Uyghur Militancy*, forthcoming.
17. 'Text: President Bush Addresses the Nation', *Washington Post*, 20 September 2001, http://www.washingtonpost.com/wp-srv/nation/specials/attacked/transcripts/bushaddress_092001.html, last accessed 29 January 2017.
18. Ibid.
19. 'Terrorist Activities Perpetrated by "Eastern Turkistan" Organizations and their Ties with Osama bin Laden and the Taliban', 29 November 2001, website of the

Permanent Mission of the People's Republic of China to the United Nations, http://www.china-un.org/eng/zt/fk/t28937.htm, last accessed 22 January 2017.
20. Ibid.
21. Information Office of State Council, '"East Turkistan" Terrorist Forces Cannot Get Away with Impunity', China.org.cn, http://www.china.org.cn/english/2002/Jan/25582.htm, last accessed 5 February 2017.
22. Ibid.
23. However, it was also intended for a domestic audience, and in July of the same year an accompanying video documentary making many of the same points was broadcast on national television. See Yitzhak Shichor, 'Fact and Fiction: A Chinese Documentary on Eastern Turkestan Terrorism', *China and Eurasia Forum Quarterly*, 4, 2 (2006), pp. 89–108.
24. The original Executive Order 13224, which was adopted twelve days after the 11 September attacks, can be found on the website of the US Department of State, https://www.state.gov/j/ct/rls/other/des/122570.htm, last accessed 29 January 2017. ETIM was added to the list of organizations to which this order applied only a year later, in September 2002. It should be noted that ETIM does not feature on the US Foreign Terrorist Organizations (FTO) list, which is subject to the strictest sanctions. Rather, it is on both the Other Terrorist Organizations and the Terrorist Exclusion lists, which call for less strict sanctions. The original UN Security Council Resolution sanctioning al-Qaeda was passed in 1999: see UN Security Council website, http://www.un.org/en/ga/search/view_doc.asp?symbol=S/RES/1267(1999), last accessed 29 January 2017. The sanctions laid out in this resolution were expanded in 2002 through Resolution 1390, http://www.un.org/en/ga/search/view_doc.asp?symbol=S/RES/1390(2002), last accessed 1 February 2017. Only in September 2002, however, was ETIM added to the list of organizations to which these sanctions were applied.
25. See House of Representatives Committee on Foreign Affairs, 16 June 2009, pp. 93–6.
26. Beina Xu, Holly Fletcher and Jayshree Bajoria, *A Backgrounder: The East Turkestan Islamic Movement (ETIM)*, Council on Foreign Relations Publication 9179, last updated 4 September 2014, http://www.cfr.org/china/east-turkestan-islamic-movement-etim/p9179, last accessed 7 April 2016.
27. See 'In the Spotlight: East Turkestan Islamic Movement (ETIM)', Center for Defense Information, 9 December 2002, http://www.che.ntu.edu.tw/ntuche/safety/upload/browse.php?u=Oi8vd2ViLmFyY2hpdmUub3JnL3dlYi8yMDEyMDExNDE3NTAxNy9odHRwOi8vd3d3LmNkaS5vcmcvdGVycm9yaXNtL2V0aW0uY2Zt&b=13, last accessed 8 September 2015.
28. See IntelCenter, *About Us*, http://www.intelcenter.com/aboutus.html, last accessed 8 September 2015; and IntelCenter, *Wall Charts*, https://store.intelcenter.com/collections/wall-charts/products/turkistan-islamic-party-tip-threat-awareness-

44-36-wc#gs.CpbpCC4, last accessed 8 September 2015. It should be noted here that the Turkistan Islamic Party (TIP) has more recently replaced ETIM as a threat among those who believe such a threat exists. This shift is discussed further later in this chapter.

29. See IPT, 'About the Investigative Project on Terrorism', http://www.investigative-project.org/about.php, last accessed 19 August 2015; and IPT, 'Terrorist Organizations and Other Groups of Concern: East Turkistan Islamic Movement (ETIM)', last updated 24 August 2007, http://www.investigativeproject.org/profile/146, last accessed 19 August 2015

30. Most of the secondary literature on ETIM cites as primary sources internet communications that are assumed to originate from the organization itself. Some of these communications have allegedly appeared on bulletin boards and other interactive sites assumed to be frequented by militant Muslim groups. Others, which claim to be video messages from the organization, appear to originate from YouTube (www.youtube.com). Given the many ways that information can be manipulated on the internet, the authenticity of all of these sources is difficult to verify.

31. See Rohan Gunaratna, 'SourceWatch: Your Guide to the Names Behind the News', http://www.sourcewatch.org/index.php?title=Rohan_Gunaratna, last accessed 19 August 2015.

32. The direct citations are from Rohan Gunaratna and Kenneth George Pereire, 'An Al-Qaeda Associate Group Operating in China?', *China and Eurasia Forum Quarterly*, 4, 2 (2006), pp. 55–61. Additionally, see Gunaratna, 'Xinjiang: China's Flashpoint?', Site Monitoring Service Jihadist Threat, 1 July 2009, http://news.siteintelgroup.com/component/content/article/121-rohan-0709, last accessed 13 September 2015; and Rohan Gunaratna, *Inside Al Qaeda: Global Network of Terror* (New York: Columbia University Press, 2002).

33. For examples, see John Wang, 'Eastern Turkistan Islamic Movement: A Case Study of a New Terrorist Organization in China', *International Journal of Offender Therapy and Comparative Criminology*, 47, 5 (2003), pp. 568–84; Major Shawn M. Patrick, *The Uyghur Movement: China's Insurgency in Xinjiang* (Leavenworth, KA: Monograph of the School of Advanced Military Studies, 2010); and Martin I. Wayne, 'Understanding China's War on Terror: Top-Down vs. Bottom-up Approaches (A Case Study of Counter-insurgency)', Doctoral Dissertation in International Studies, University of Denver, CO, 2006.

34. J. Todd Reed and Diana Raschke, *The ETIM: China's Islamic Militants and the Global Terrorist Threat* (Santa Barbara, CA: Praeger, 2010).

35. Ibid., p. vii.

36. For all of the publicly available files from the Combatant Status Review Board and Administrative Review Board hearings of Uyghur detainees, see the China citizen category in the *New York Times* 'Guantanamo Docket', http://projects.nytimes.

com/guantanamo/country/china, last accessed 27 November 2016. My interviews with former detainees in Albania took place in Tirana, Albania during July 2009.
37. '"East Turkistan" Terrorist Forces Cannot Get Away with Impunity'.
38. Ibid.
39. Wikipedia cites an Arabic source as noting that he had initially come to Mecca, likely on the hajj, following his departure from China. See Wikipedia, 'Hasan Mahsum', https://en.wikipedia.org/wiki/Hasan_Mahsum#cite_note-5, last accessed 6 August 2016.
40. See David S. Cloud and Ian Johnson, 'In Post-9/11 World, Chinese Dissidents Pose U.S. Dilemma', *Wall Street Journal* (Eastern Edition), 3 August 2004, pp. A1–A6.
41. Several of the detainees do acknowledge that Hasan Mahsum and Abdul Haq were associated with the 'camp' in Jalalabad where they stayed. See, for example, *Summary of Administrative Review Board Proceedings for ISN 277*, pp. 3–4; *Summary of Unsworn Detainee Statement, ISN 281*, p. 4; *Summary of Unsworn Detainee Statement, ISN 328*, pp. 7–8.
42. *Summary of Unsworn Detainee Statement, ISN 281*, p. 4.
43. *Summary of Unsworn Detainee Statement, ISN 276*, p. 3.
44. See Sean R. Roberts, 'The Uighurs of the Kazakstan Borderlands: Migration and the Nation', *Nationalities Papers*, 26, 3 (1998), pp. 511–30.
45. The name of this region is a contentious issue. The name 'Xinjiang', or 'New Frontier', is generally associated with Beijing's control of the region, first under the Qing and subsequently under Chinese states. The Uyghur independence movement therefore categorically refutes this name, which they view as a colonial moniker denying their right to sovereignty over the region. Uyghur activists instead tend to refer to the region as Eastern Turkistan or, less frequently, as Uyghurstan. The name 'Eastern Turkistan' was likewise created by outsiders to reflect the eastern areas of a general cultural region seen as the 'land of the Turks'. Using either 'Xinjiang' or 'Eastern Turkistan' to refer to this region therefore positions oneself on one side or the other of the Uyghur–PRC conflict over the region. For this reason, I have chosen here to refer to the region by its present legal name, the Xinjiang Uyghur Autonomous Region or XUAR.
46. Sean R. Roberts, 'A "Land of Borderlands": Implications of Xinjiang's Trans-Border Interactions', in S. Frederick Starr (ed.), *Xinjiang: China's Muslim Borderland* (Armonk, NY: M. E. Sharpe, 2004), pp. 216–37.
47. By the late 1990s and early 2000s when these men came to Kazakhstan and Kyrgyzstan, it was increasingly difficult for individual Uyghur entrepreneurs to make a profit in former Soviet Central Asia as this trade was increasingly becoming the domain of organized networks of Central Asian retailers and Han Chinese manufacturers or wholesalers. I have documented this elsewhere; see Roberts, 'A "Land of Borderlands"'.

48. Abu Bakker Qassim, 'The View from Guantanamo', *New York Times*, 17 September 2006, http://www.nytimes.com/2006/09/17/opinion/17qassim.html, last accessed 20 April 2016.
49. For a detailed survey of this litigation, see Jason S. Pinney, 'The Uighurs at Guantanamo: "Sometimes We Just Didn't Get the Right Folks"', *Northeastern University Law Journal*, 1, 1 (2009), pp. 139–56.
50. Ibid.
51. Eastern Turkistan" Terrorist Killed', *China Daily*, 24 December 2003, http://www.chinadaily.com.cn/en/doc/2003-12/24/content_293163.htm, last accessed 3 June 2015.
52. 'Uyghur Separatist Denies Links to Taliban, Al-Qaeda', Radio Free Asia, 27 January 2002, http://www.rfa.org/english/news/politics/85871-20020127.html, last accessed 3 June 2015.
53. 'Hasan Mahsum', https://www.youtube.com/watch?v=UqFZohw7Qak, last accessed 3 July 2016.
54. Ibid.
55. Cloud and Johnson, 'In Post-9/11 World, Chinese Dissidents Pose U.S. Dilemma'.
56. 'China Identifies Alleged East Turkistan Terrorists', *Xinhua*, 21 October 2008, http://news.xinhuanet.com/english/2008-10/21/content_10229518.htm, last accessed 3 July 2016.
57. Ibid.
58. This video, which opened with animation of a burning Beijing Olympics flag, portrayed a single masked Uyghur commander brandishing an AK-47 automatic rifle and making threats to undertake substantial bombing attacks inside China during the Olympics. See 'Turkistan Islamic Party', http://www.youtube.com/watch?v=pwO_wX5olNQ&feature=related, last accessed 11 April 2014.
59. 'China Says Deadly Bomb Blasts, Olympics not Linked', Agence Presse France, 22 July 2008.
60. Edward Wong, 'Doubt Arises in Account of an Attack in China', *New York Times*, 28 September 2008, http://www.nytimes.com/2008/09/29/world/asia/29kashgar.html, last accessed 15 June 2015.
61. US Department of Treasury, 'Treasury Targets Leader of Group Tied to Al Qaida', 20 April 2009, https://www.treasury.gov/press-center/press-releases/Pages/tg92.aspx, last accessed 19 October 2015. Compare the language of this press release to the official wording of the PRC document accusing Haq of terrorism: 'China Identifies Alleged East Turkistan Terrorists', *Xinhua*, 21 October 2008, http://news.xinhuanet.com/english/2008-10/21/content_10229518.htm, last accessed 19 October 2015.
62. White House, 'Statement on Bilateral Meeting with President Hu of China', 1 April 2009, https://obamawhitehouse.archives.gov/the-press-office/statement-bilateral-meeting-with-president-hu-china, last accessed 17 October 2015.

63. Andrew McGregor, 'Will Xinjiang's Turkistani Islamic Party Survive the Drone Missile Death of its Leader?', *Terrorism Monitor*, 8, 10 (12 March 2010), http://www.jamestown.org/single/?no_cache=1&tx_ttnews%5Btt_news%5D=36144, last accessed 8 March 2017.
64. Michael Wines, 'Militant Band Claims Role in Western China Attacks', *New York Times*, 8 September 2011, http://www.nytimes.com/2011/09/09/world/asia/09china.html, last accessed 7 March 2017.
65. *Jannat Ashikliri*, posted on Archive.org, 18 March 2014, https://archive.org/details/jennet_ashikliri_10, last accessed 17 June 2014
66. Al-Arabiya, 'Islamist group claims Syria bombs "to avenge Sunnis"', 21 March 2012.
67. Jacob Zenn, 'An Overview of Chinese Fighters and Anti-Chinese Militant Groups in Syria and Iraq', *China Brief*, 14, 19 (10 October 2014).
68. Ibid.
69. See 'Turkistan Islamic Party in Sahl Al-Ghab', Archive.org, posted 29 October 2015, https://archive.org/details/TIPInSahlAlGhab, last accessed 5 November 2015; and 'Conquest of Jisr al-Shughur', Jihadology.net, http://jihadology.net/2015/05/01/ṣawt-al-islam-presents-a-new-video-message-from-ḥizb-al-islami-al-turkistani-turkistan-islamic-party-in-bilad-al-sham-conquest-of-jisr-al-shaghur/, last accessed 20 March 2016.
70. *'Justice, Justice', The July 2009 Protests in Xinjiang, China* (Amnesty International Publications, 2010), https://www.amnesty.org/en/documents/ASA17/027/2010/en/, last accessed 7 March 2017.
71. 'Can Anyone Hear Us? Voices from the 2009 Unrest in Urumchi', Uyghur Human Rights Project, July 2010, p. 52, http://docs.uyghuramerican.org/Can-Anyone-Hear-Us.pdf, last accessed 14 September 2015. It should be noted that UHRP thus far has only been able to verify that nine of the executions have been carried out (eight Uyghurs and one Han Chinese). No public information has been available on the other cases. In addition to these death sentences, courts convicted an additional nine people (eight of whom are Uyghurs) to death sentences with a two-year reprieve.
72. Kathrin Hille, 'Xinjiang Widens Crackdown on Uighurs', *Financial Times*, 19 July 2009, https://www.ft.com/content/5aa932ee-747c-11de-8ad5-00144feabdc0, last accessed 8 June 2018.
73. Human Rights Watch, '"We Are Afraid to Even Look for Them": Enforced Disappearances in the Wake of Xinjiang's Protests', October 2009.
74. Ibid., p. 5.
75. See *'Justice, Justice'*, pp. 21–5; 'Can Anyone Hear Us?', pp. 42–52; and Human Rights Watch, 2009, pp. 18–20.
76. 'Seeking a Place to Breathe Freely: Current Challenges Faced by Uyghur Refugees and Asylum Seekers', Munich: World Uyghur Congress, June 2016, http://www.uyghurcongress.org/en/wp-content/uploads/dlm_uploads/WUC-Seeking-a-Place-to-Breathe-Freely-June–2016.pdf, last accessed 17 July 2016.

77. Although there has long been a limit of two children imposed on China's minorities, many rural Uyghurs who had larger families in the 1990s were able to escape detection by authorities by not registering all of their children. In the XUAR today, however, the surveillance of local communities is so intense that such deception is no longer possible. This policy was relaxed throughout China beginning in late 2015, when it was announced that Han could now have two children, but local authorities in the XUAR simultaneously began a variety of measures to put pressure on Uyghurs to limit new births, articulating these policies as part of the region's counter-terrorism strategy. See 'Remote Control: The Government in Xinjiang is Trying to Limit Muslim Births', *The Economist*, 7 November 2015, http://www.economist.com/news/china/21678007-government-xinjiang-trying-limit-muslim-births-remote-control, last accessed 1 December 2015.
78. 'Life in Prison for Asylum Seekers', Radio Free Asia, 26 January 2012, http://www.rfa.org/english/news/uyghur/life-in-prison-01262012205722.html, last accessed 1 December 2015.
79. 'Malaysia Hit for Deporting Uyghurs', Radio Free Asia, 4 February 2013, http://www.rfa.org/english/news/uyghur/deport-02042013020002.html, last accessed 1 March 2017.
80. Catherine Putz, 'Thailand Deports 100 Uyghurs to China', *The Diplomat*, 11 July 2015, http://thediplomat.com/2015/07/thailand-deports-100-uyghurs-to-china/, last accessed 1 March 2017.
81. Ibid.
82. Given the sensitivity of this issue, the names of the activists with whom I met in Turkey are left anonymous.
83. 'Uyghur Turkistan Islamic Party and Jabhat Al Nusra (Al-Qaeda) getting liquidated by Hezbollah, Syrian Army and Russians in the Turkman Mountains', Liveleak.com, http://www.liveleak.com/view?i=d97_1448670254, last accessed 1 March 2017.
84. Bill Roggio and Thomas Jocelyn, 'Turkistan Islamic Party leader criticizes the Islamic State's "illegitimate" caliphate', *Long War Journal*, 11 June 2016, http://www.longwarjournal.org/archives/2016/06/turkistan-islamic-party-leader-remains-loyal-to-al-qaeda-criticizes-islamic-states-illegitimate-caliphate.php, last accessed 3 March 2017.
85. Mohanad Hage Ali, 'China's proxy war in Syria: Revealing the role of Uighur fighters', Al-Arabiya, 2 March 2016.
86. See also John Hayward, 'Chinese Uighur Settlers Flow into Syria, Replacing War Refugees', *Breitbart*, 4 March 2016.
87. Ali, 'China's proxy war in Syria'.
88. See Charles Paul Freund, 'Syria: Chinese Uyghurs Killing Russian Spies According to Turkey's Plan. It's a Zionist conspiracy, of course', *Reason*, 3 October 2015, https://reason.com/archives/2015/10/03/syria-chinese-uyghurs-killing-russian-

sp, last accessed 7 November 2015. A less conspiratorial version of these allegations was also published in an editorial of *Zaman* newspaper in Turkey, but I have been unable to retrieve it due to the Turkish government's closing of *Zaman*.
89. Olga Dzyubenko, 'Kyrgyzstan says Uighur militant groups behind attack on China's Embassy', Reuters, 6 September 2016, http://www.reuters.com/article/us-kyrgyzstan-blast-china-idUSKCN11C1DK, last accessed 8 December 2016.
90. Robert K. Merton, 'The Self-fulfilling Prophecy', *Antioch Review*, 8, 2 (1948), p. 185.
91. Author interview in Turkey, June 2016.
92. Nate Rosenblatt, *All Jihad is Local: What ISIS' Files Tell Us about Its Fighters* (Washington, DC: New America Foundation, August 2016).
93. For more detail, see James Leibold and Adrian Zenz, 'Xinjiang's Rapidly Evolving Security State', *Jamestown Foundation China Brief*, 17, 4 (14 March 2017), https://jamestown.org/program/xinjiangs-rapidly-evolving-security-state/, last accessed 1 June 2018; James Leibold and Adrian Zenz, 'Beijing's Eyes and Ears Grow Sharper in Xinjiang', *Foreign Affairs*, (23 December 2016), https://www.foreignaffairs.com/articles/china/2016-12-23/beijings-eyes-and-ears-grow-sharper-xinjiang, last accessed 1 June 2018; 'The Bullies of Urumqi: The Extraordinary Ways in Which China Humiliates Muslims', *The Economist*, 4 May 2017, http://www.economist.com/news/china/21721680-bans-abnormal-beards-and-even-name-muhammad-extraordinary-ways-which-china-humiliates?cid1=cust/ddnew/n/n/n/2017054n/owned/n/n/nwl/n/n/na/Daily_Dispatch/email), last accessed 1 June 2018; Massoud Hayoun, 'Surrealism Abounds in China's Uyghur Crackdown', *Pacific Standard*, 3 May 2017, https://psmag.com/news/surrealism-abounds-in-chinas-uyghur-crackdown, last accessed 1 June 2018; Katie Hunt, Chieu Luu and Steven Jiang, 'Why is China Banning Beards and Veils in Xinjiang?', CNN, 31 March 2017, http://www.cnn.com/2017/03/31/asia/china-xinjiang-new-rules/, last accessed 1 June 2018; Human Rights Watch, 'Free Xinjiang "Political Education" Detainees: Muslim Minorities Held for Months in Unlawful Facilities', 10 September 2017, https://www.hrw.org/news/2017/09/10/china-free-xinjiang-political-education-detainees, last accessed 1 June 2018; Nathan Vanderklippe, 'China Probes Deeper into the Lives of Uyghur Minority', *Globe and Mail*, 29 December 2017, https://www.theglobeandmail.com///news/world/scholars-shocked-by-changes-in-chinas-xinjiang-comparing-it-to-north-korea-and-apartheid-era-southafrica/article37455333/?click=sf_globe, last accessed 1 June 2018.
94. It is particularly noteworthy that these 're-education' camps have detained people formerly not suspected of terrorism, such as those with relatives studying or living abroad.

5. CHINA AND COUNTER-TERRORISM: BEYOND PAKISTAN?

1. Jacob Zenn, 'Al-Qaeda-Aligned Central Asian Militants in Syria Separate from Islamic State-Aligned IMU in Afghanistan', *Terrorism Monitor*, 13, 11 (May 2015), https://jamestown.org/program/al-qaeda-aligned-central-asian-militants-in-syria-separate-from-islamic-state-aligned-imu-in-afghanistan/, last accessed 5 August 2016.
2. Michael Dillon, *Xinjiang: China's Muslim Far Northwest* (London: Routledge, 2009), p. 77.
3. James Millward, 'Violent Separatism in Xinjiang: A Critical Assessment', *Policy Studies*, 6 (Washington, DC: East–West Center, 2004), p. 7, http://www.eastwestcenter.org/fileadmin/stored/pdfs/PS006.pdf, last accessed 5 August 2016.
4. Brent Hierman, 'The Pacification of Xinjiang: Uighur Protest and the Chinese State, 1988–2002', *Problems of Post-Communism*, 54, 3 (2007), pp. 48–62.
5. Rebecca Louise Nadin, 'China and the Shanghai 5 / Shanghai Cooperation Organization: 1996–2006, A Decade on a New Diplomatic Frontier', PhD Dissertation, University of Sheffield, 2007, http://ethos.bl.uk/OrderDetails.do?uin=uk.bl.ethos.443900, last accessed 5 August 2016.
6. Ahmed Rashid, *Jihad: The Rise of Militant Islam in Central Asia* (New York: Penguin, 2003), p. 204.
7. 'Bin Ladin Charges U.S. involvement in China Bombings', *Islamabad, The Muslim in English*, 15 March 1997, pp. 1–11; 'New Analysis: Bin Ladin: Dissident Turns Pan-Islamist', *The Observer* in 'Compilation of Usama Bin Ladin Statements 1994–January 2004', FBIS Report, January 2004, p. 39, http://www.fas.org/irp/world/para/ubl-fbis.pdf, last accessed 5 August 2016.
8. Raffaello Pantucci, 'A Post-Mortem Analysis of Turkistani Amir Emeti Yakuf: A Death that Sparked More Questions than Answers', *Terrorism Monitor*, 3, 10 (1 November 2012), https://jamestown.org/program/a-post-mortem-analysis-of-turkistani-amir-emeti-yakuf-a-death-that-sparked-more-questions-than-answers/, last accessed 5 August 2016.
9. 'China: Uighur Group Added to U.S. List of Terrorist Organizations', Eurasianet, 31 August 2002, https://eurasianet.org/s/china-uighur-group-added-to-us-list-of-terrorist-organizations, last accessed 5 August 2016.
10. Caleb Weiss, 'Turkistan Islamic Party had significant role in recent Idlib offensive', *Long War Journal*, 30 April 2015, http://www.longwarjournal.org/archives/2015/04/turkistan-islamic-party-had-significant-role-recent-idlib-offensive.php, last accessed 5 August 2016.
11. Private exchange with author, January 2016.
12. Alexa Olesen, 'China Sees Islamic State Inching Closer to Home', *Foreign Policy*, 11 August 2014, http://foreignpolicy.com/2014/08/11/china-sees-islamic-state-inching-closer-to-home/, last accessed 5 August 2016.
13. Yuwen Wu, 'IS killing of Chinese hostage: A game changer?', BBC News,

19 November 2015, http://www.bbc.com/news/blogs-china-blog-34865696, last accessed 5 August 2016.
14. Private exchanges with author, Washington, DC, May 2015.
15. Hugh Pope, *Sons of the Conquerors: The Rise of the Turkic World* (Overlook TP, 2006), ch. 9.
16. Michael Kaplan, 'China's Uighurs look towards Turkey for help', Al Jazeera, 7 March 2015, http://www.aljazeera.com/news/2015/03/china-uighurs-turkey-150306121246048.html, last accessed 5 August 2016.
17. Lucy Hornby, 'China accuses Turkey of aiding Uighurs', *Financial Times*, 12 July 2015, https://www.ft.com/content/93607210-285c-11e5-8613-e7aedbb7bdb7, last accessed 5 August 2016.
18. Randy Fabi and Agustinus Beo Da Costa, 'Indonesia turns to China as ethnic Uighurs join would-be jihadis', Reuters, 6 January 2016, http://www.reuters.com/article/us-indonesia-security-idUSKBN0UK0SE20160106, last accessed 5 August 2016.
19. 'Bangkok bomb trial of Chinese Uighurs begins after delays', Reuters, 15 November 2016, http://www.reuters.com/article/us-thailand-blast-idUSKBN13A0FR, last accessed 25 November 2016.
20. 'Kunming knife gang "tried to leave China" before attack', Agence France Presse, 5 March 2014, http://www.telegraph.co.uk/news/worldnews/asia/china/1067 7244/Kunming-knife-gang-tried-to-leave-China-before-attack.html, last accessed 5 August 2016.
21. Megha Rajagopalan, 'China security chief blames Uighur Islamists for Tiananmen attack', Reuters, 1 November 2013, http://www.reuters.com/article/us-china-tiananmen-idUSBRE9A003L20131101, last accessed 5 August 2016.
22. Aymen Ijaz, 'Zarb-e-Azb: Strengthening Pak-China Relations', IPRI, 3 November 2015, http://www.ipripak.org/zarb-e-azb-strengthening-pak-china-relations/, last accessed 5 August 2016.
23. Carlotta Gall, 'Pakistan's Hand in the Rise of International Jihad', *New York Times*, 6 February 2016, http://www.nytimes.com/2016/02/07/opinion/sunday/pakistans-hand-in-the-rise-of-international-jihad.html, last accessed 5 August 2016.
24. Jacob Zenn, 'The IMU is extinct: what next for Central Asia's jihadis?', *Central Asia-Caucasus Analyst*, 3 May 2016, http://www.cacianalyst.org/publications/analytical-articles/item/13357-the-imu-is-extinct-what-new-for-central-asias-jihadis?.html, last accessed 5 August 2016.
25. Bill Roggio, 'Turkistan Islamic Party emir thought killed in 2010 reemerged to lead group in 2014', *Long War Journal*, 11 June 2015, http://www.longwarjournal.org/archives/2015/06/turkistan-islamic-party-emir-thought-killed-in-2010-reemerged-to-lead-group-in-2014.php, last accessed 5 August 2016.
26. Shahbaz Rana, 'Four new schemes to be part of CPEC', *Express Tribune*, 23 December 2016, https://tribune.com.pk/story/1272267/four-new-schemes-part-cpec/, last accessed 27 February 2017.

27. Syed Raza Hassan, 'Attacks have killed 44 Pakistanis working on China corridor since 2014', Reuters, 8 September 2016, http://www.reuters.com/article/us-pakistan-china-idUSKCN11E1EP, last accessed 27 February 2017.
28. 'Interior ministry releases notification for CPEC's Special Security Division', PCI, 21 January 2017, http://www.cpecinfo.com/cpec-news-detail?id=MTAzNQ==, last accessed 27 February 2017; larger figures from interviews in Islamabad, Karachi, Gwadar, September, November and December 2016.
29. Zhao Huasheng, 'What Is Behind China's Growing Attention to Afghanistan?', Carnegie Endowment for International Peace, 8 March 2015, http://carnegieendowment.org/2015/03/08/what-is-behind-china-s-growing-attention-to-afghanistan-pub-59286, last accessed 5 August 2016.
30. Jessica Donati and Ehsanullah Amiri, 'China Offers Afghanistan Army Expanded Military Aid', *Wall Street Journal*, 9 March 2016, http://www.wsj.com/articles/china-offers-afghanistan-army-expanded-military-aid-1457517153, last accessed 5 August 2016.
31. For more detailed background, see Andrew Small, 'From Bystander to Peacemaker', *Berlin Policy Journal*, 27 April 2015, http://berlinpolicyjournal.com/from-bystander-to-peacemaker/, last accessed 5 August 2016.
32. Wang Jisi, 'Westward: China's Rebalancing Geopolitical Strategy', International and Strategic Studies Report 73, Center for International and Strategic Studies at Peking University, 2012, pp. 6–7.
33. Shishir Gupta, 'Govt makes it clear: India has not forgotten Pakistan-occupied Kashmir', *Hindustan Times*, 24 May 2015, http://www.hindustantimes.com/india-news/nsa-makes-it-clear-india-has-not-forgotten-pakistan-occupied-kashmir/article1-1350639.aspx, last accessed 5 August 2016.
34. Ben Blanchard, 'China passes controversial counter-terrorism law', Reuters, 28 December 2015, http://www.reuters.com/article/us-china-security-idUSKBN0UA07220151228, last accessed 5 August 2016.
35. Interviews in Beijing, Shanghai and Washington, DC, January–June 2016.
36. Charles Clover, 'Mystery deepens over Chinese forces in Afghanistan', *Financial Times*, 26 February 2017, https://www.ft.com/content/0c8a5a2a-f9b7-11e6-9516-2d969e0d3b65, last accessed 27 February 2017.
37. Interviews in Islamabad, Karachi, September, November 2016.

6. CHINA'S COUNTER-TERRORISM POLICY IN THE MIDDLE EAST

1. Jon B. Alterman, *China's Balancing Act in the Gulf* (Washington, DC: Center for Strategic and International Studies, 2013); Dawn Murphy, *Rising Revisionist? China's Relations with the Middle East and Sub-Saharan Africa in the Post-Cold War Era* (Washington, DC: George Washington University, 2012).
2. Mordechai Chaziza, 'China's Middle East foreign policy and the Yemen crisis:

Challenges and implications', *Middle East Review of International Affairs*, 19, 2 (2015), pp. 18–25; Mordechai Chaziza, 'The Arab Spring: Implications for Chinese Policy', *Middle East Review of International Affairs*, 17, 2 (2013), pp. 73–83.
3. Mordechai Chaziza and Ogen S. Goldman, 'What factors increase the probability of Chinese interventions in intrastate wars?', *Asian Journal of Political Science*, 24, 1 (2016), pp. 1–20; Mordechai Chaziza and Ogen S. Goldman, 'Revisiting China's Non-Interference Policy towards Intrastate Wars', *Chinese Journal of International Politics*, 7, 1 (2014), pp. 89–115.
4. Jon B. Alterman and John Garver, *The Vital Triangle: China, the United States, and the Middle East* (Washington, DC: Center for Strategic and International Studies, 2008).
5. Wang Jian, 'One Belt One Road: A Vision for the Future of China-Middle East Relations', Al Jazeera, 9 May 2017, http://studies.aljazeera.net/en/reports/2017/05/belt-road-vision-future-china-middle-east-relations-170509102227548.htmlm, last accessed 9 January 2018.
6. 'China looks beyond the Middle East for its crude oil fix', *Tanker Shipping and Trade*, 29 August 2017, http://www.tankershipping.com/news/view,china-looks-beyond-the-middle-east-for-its-crude-oil-fix_48954.htm, last accessed 9 January 2018.
7. Michael Lelyveld, 'China's Oil Import Dependence Climbs as Output Falls', Radio Free Asia, 4 December 2017, http://www.rfa.org/english/commentaries/energy_watch/chinas-oil-import-dependence-climbs-as-output-falls-12042017102429.html, last accessed 9 January 2018.
8. Yitzhak Shichor, *The Middle East in China's Foreign Policy, 1949–1977* (Cambridge: Cambridge University Press, 1979).
9. Nadine Godehardt and David Shim, 'Post-2014 Afghanistan and its Impact on Northeast Asia', *Asian Perspective*, 38, 4 (2014), pp. 497–517; Mathieu Duchâtel, Oliver Bräuner and Zhou Hang, 'Protecting China's Overseas Interests: The Slow Shift Away from Non-interference', *Policy Paper* 41 (Stockholm: Stockholm International Peace Research Institute, 2014), https://www.sipri.org/publications/2014/sipri-policy-papers/protecting-chinas-overseas-interests-slow-shift-away-non-interference, last accessed 5 March 2017.
10. Yitzhak Shichor, 'Fundamentally Unacceptable Yet Occasionally Unavoidable: China's Options on External Interference in the Middle East', *China Report*, 49, 1 (2013), pp. 25–41.
11. Mathieu Duchâtel, 'Terror Overseas: Understanding China's Evolving Counter-Terror Strategy', *European Council on Foreign Relations (ECFR)*, 26 October 2016, http://www.ecfr.eu/publications/summary/terror_overseas_understanding_chinas_evolving_counter_terror_strategy7160, last accessed 5 March 2017.
12. Ivan Campbell, Thomas Wheeler, Larry Attree, Dell Marie Butler and Bernardo

Mariani, *China and Conflict-Affected States: Between Principle and Pragmatism* (London: Saferworld, 2012); Mike Bird, 'China Just Overtook the U.S. as the World's Largest Economy', *Business Insider*, 8 October 2014, http://www.businessinsider.com/china-overtakes-us-as-worlds-largest-economy-2014–10, last accessed 5 March 2017.

13. Richard Fontaine and Michael Singh, 'Middle Kingdom Meets Middle East', Washington Institute for Near East Policy, 3 April 2017, http://www.washingtoninstitute.org/policy-analysis/view/middle-kingdom-meets-middle-east, last accessed 9 January 2018.
14. Duchâtel, 'Terror Overseas'.
15. Philip B. K. Potter, 'Terrorism in China: Growing Threats with Global Implications', *Strategic Studies Quarterly*, 7, 4 (2013), pp. 70–92.
16. Wang Jin, 'Selective Engagement: China's Middle East Policy after the Arab Spring', *Strategic Assessment*, 19, 2 (2016), pp. 105–17.
17. 'Overall Situation of Consular Protection and Assistance Outside China', Consular Protection Service of the Chinese Foreign Ministry, 5 May 2016, http://www.immd.gov.hk/pdforms/id907e.pdf, last accessed 5 March 2017.
18. 'White Paper on China's Peaceful Development', China's Information Office of State Council, 6 September 2011, http://politics.people.com.cn/GB/1026/15598619.html, last accessed 5 March 2017.
19. Mark A. Stokes, 'China's Nuclear Warhead Storage and Handling Systems', Project 2049 monograph, 12 March 2010, https://project2049.net/documents/chinas_nuclear_warhead_storage_and_handling_system.pdf, last accessed 5 March 2017; William Wan, 'Georgetown Students Shed Light on China's Tunnel System for Nuclear Weapons', *Washington Post*, 29 November 2011, https://www.washingtonpost.com/world/national-security/georgetown-students-shed-light-on-chinas-tunnel-system-for-nuclear-weapons/2011/11/16/gIQA6AmKAO_story.html?utm_term=.c9c992f64281, last accessed 5 March 2017.
20. Raphael Israeli, 'China's Uyghur Problem', *Israel Journal of Foreign Affairs*, 4, 1 (2010), pp. 89–101.
21. Christina Lin, 'A New Eurasian Embrace: Turkey Pivots East While China Marches West', *Transatlantic Academy Paper Series*, 3 (2014), http://www.transatlanticacademy.org/sites/default/files/publications/Lin_NewEurasianEmbrace_May14_web.pdf, last accessed 5 March 2017.
22. Li Jingrong, 'Xinjiang to Forge Overland Channel for Energy Transmission', China.Org.CN, 7 February 2007, http://china.org.cn/english/environment/199295.htm, last accessed 5 March 2017.
23. Dana Carver Boehm, 'China's Failed War on Terror: Fanning the Flames of Uighur Separatist Violence', *Berkeley Journal of Middle Eastern and Islamic Law*, 2 (2009), pp. 61–124.
24. 'President Xi Jinping Delivers Important Speech and Proposes to Build a Silk Road

Economic Belt with Central Asian Countries', Ministry of Foreign Affairs, People's Republic of China, 7 September 2013, http://www.fmprc.gov.cn/mfa_eng/topics_665678/xjpfwzysiesgjtfhshzzfh_665686/t1076334.shtml, last accessed 5 March 2017.
25. Mingjiang Li, 'From Look-West to Act-West: Xinjiang's role in China-Central Asian relations', *Journal of Contemporary China*, 25, 100 (2016), pp. 515–28.
26. Thomas Zimmerman, 'The New Silk Roads: China, the U.S., and the Future of Central Asia', Center on International Cooperation, October 2015, http://cic.nyu.edu/sites/default/files/zimmerman_new_silk_road_final_2.pdf, last accessed 5 March 2017.
27. Anna Hayes and Michael Clarke (eds), *Inside Xinjiang: Space, Place and Power in China's Muslim Far Northwest* (London: Routledge, 2016).
28. Michael Clarke, 'China's Terrorist Problem Goes Global', *The Diplomat*, 7 September 2016, http://thediplomat.com/2016/09/chinas-terrorist-problem-goes-global/, last accessed 5 March 2017; and Guy Burton, 'China and the Jihadi Threat', Middle East Institute, 9 August 2016, http://www.mei.edu/content/map/china-and-jihadi-threat, last accessed 5 March 2017.
29. Michael Clarke, 'China and the Uyghurs: The "Palestinization" of Xinjiang?', *Middle East Policy*, 22, 3 (2015), pp. 127–46.
30. Clarke, 'China's Terrorist Problem Goes Global'.
31. Jeremy Page and Emre Peker, 'As Muslim Uighurs Flee, China Sees Jihad Risk', *Wall Street Journal*, 1 February 2015, http://www.wsj.com/articles/as-muslim-uighurs-flee-china-sees-jihad-risk-1422666280, last accessed 5 March 2017.
32. Elizabeth Van Wie Davis, 'Uighur Muslim Ethnic Separatism in Xinjiang, China', *Asian Affairs: An American Review*, 35, 1 (2008), pp. 15–30.
33. Andrew D. W. Forbes, *Warlords and Muslims in Chinese Central Asia: A Political History of Republican Sinkiang, 1911–1949* (Cambridge: Cambridge University Press, 1986).
34. Yoram Evron, 'China's Anti-Terrorism Policy', *Strategic Assessment*, 10, 3 (2007), pp. 76–83.
35. Information Office of the State Council of the PRC, 'East Turkistan Terrorist Forces Cannot Get Away with Impunity', *People's Daily*, 21 January 2002, http://www.china.org.cn/english/2002/Jan/25582.htm, last accessed 5 March 2017.
36. Clarke, 'China and the Uyghurs'.
37. Michael Clarke, 'China's "War on Terror" in Xinjiang: Human Security and the Causes of Violent Uighur Separatism', *Terrorism and Political Violence*, 20, 2 (2008), pp. 271–301; James M. Millward, 'Violent Separatism in Xinjiang: A Critical Assessment', *Policy Studies*, 6 (Washington, DC: East-West Center, 2004), http://www.eastwestcenter.org/system/tdf/private/PS006.pdf?file=1&type=node&id=32006, last accessed 5 March 2017.
38. Jacob Zenn, 'Jihad in China? Marketing the Turkistan Islamic Party', *Terrorism Monitor*, 9, 11 (2011), http://www.jamestown.org/single/?tx_ttnews[tt_news]=

37662&no, last accessed 5 March 2017; Brian Fishman, 'Al-Qaeda and the Rise of China: Jihadi Geopolitics in a Post-Hegemonic World', *Washington Quarterly*, 34, 3 (2011), pp. 47–62.
39. Burton, 'China and the Jihadi Threat'.
40. Shannon Tiezzi, 'Turkestan Islamic Party Expresses Support for Kunming Attack', *The Diplomat*, 20 March 2014, http://thediplomat.com/2014/03/turkestan-islamic-party-expresses-support-for-kunming-attack/, last accessed 5 March 2017.
41. Siegfried O. Wolf, 'Why China's Uighurs are joining jihadists in Afghanistan', *Deutsche Welle*, 24 July 2015, http://www.dw.com/en/why-chinas-uighurs-are-joining-jihadists-in-afghanistan/a-18605630, last accessed 5 March 2017.
42. Evron, 'China's Anti-Terrorism Policy'.
43. Michael Clarke and Raffaello Pantucci, 'China is Supporting Syria's Regime. What Changed?', *National Interest*, 17 September 2016, http://nationalinterest.org/feature/china-supporting-syrias-regime-what-changed-17738, last accessed 5 March 2017.
44. Raymond Lee, 'Muslims in China and their Relations with the State', Al Jazeera Centre for Studies, 26 August 2015, http://studies.aljazeera.net/mritems/Documents/2015/8/26/2015826105410922580China.pdf, last accessed 5 March 2017.
45. Yitzhak Shichor, 'See No Evil, Hear No Evil, Speak No Evil: Middle Eastern Reactions to Rising China's Uyghur Crackdown', *Griffith Asia Quarterly*, 3, 1 (2015), pp. 62–85; and Israeli, 'China's Uyghur Problem'.
46. Yitzhak Shichor, 'Virtual Transnationalism: Uyghur Communities in Europe and the Quest for Eastern Turkestan Independence', in Stefano Allievi and Jørgen S. Nielsen (eds), *Muslim Networks and Transnational Communities in and across Europe* (Leiden, Boston: Brill, 2003), pp. 281–311.
47. Mordechai Chaziza, 'Sino-Turkish Solid Strategic Partnership: China's Dream or a Reality?', *China Report*, 52, 4 (2016), pp. 265–83.
48. 'Turkey Attacks China Genocide', BBC, 10 July 2009, http://news.bbc.co.uk/1/hi/8145451.stm, last accessed 5 March 2017; and 'China Demands Turkish Retraction', BBC, 14 July 2009, http://news.bbc.co.uk/2/hi/8149379.stm, last accessed 5 March 2017.
49. Cheng Guangjin and Zhou Wa, 'Erdogan's Visit Boosts Relations', *China Daily*, 10 April 2012, http://europe.chinadaily.com.cn/europe/2012–04/10/content_15011189.htm, last accessed 5 March 2017.
50. 'Anti-China Protests in Turkey Take Toll on Economic Ties', *Turkish Digest*, 6 July 2015, http://turkishdigest.blogspot.co.il/2015/07/anti-china-protests-in-turkey-take-toll.html, last accessed 5 March 2017.
51. 'Foreign Ministry Spokesperson Hua Chunying's Regular Press Conference on July 6, 2015', Ministry of Foreign Affairs, People's Republic of China, 6 July 2015, http://www.fmprc.gov.cn/mfa_eng/xwfw_665399/s2510_665401/t1278960.shtml, last accessed 5 March 2017.

52. 'Don't Twist Facts', *China Daily*, 14 July 2009, http://www.chinadaily.com.cn/opinion/2009-07/14/content_8424256.htm, last accessed 5 March 2017.
53. Zan Tao, 'An Alternative Partner to the West? Turkey's Growing Relations with China', Middle East Institute, 25 October 2013, http://www.mei.edu/content/alternative-partner-west-turkey%E2%80%99s-growing-relations-china, last accessed 5 March 2017.
54. Shan Wei and Weng Cuifen, 'China's New Policy in Xinjiang and its Challenges', *East Asian Policy*, 2, 3 (2010), pp. 58–66.
55. Zhao Jun and Hu Yu, 'On China's New Era Anti-Terrorism Governance in the Middle East', *International Affairs Studies*, 4 (2013), pp. 57–68.
56. Jennine Liu, 'China's ISIS Woes', *The Diplomat*, 26 February 2016, http://thediplomat.com/2016/02/chinas-isis-woes/, last accessed 5 March 2017.
57. Fishman, 'Al-Qaeda and the Rise of China'.
58. Bai Tiantian, 'China at Risk from Syria Spillover', *Global Times*, 29 July 2014, http://www.globaltimes.cn/content/873090.shtml, last accessed 5 March 2017.
59. Zana Khasraw Gulmohamad, 'The Rise and Fall of the Islamic State of Iraq and Al-Sham (Levant) ISIS', *Global Security Studies*, 5, 2 (2014), pp. 1–11.
60. Mordechai Chaziza, 'ISIS risks, prospects and opportunities to Chinese foreign policy in the Middle East', *Middle East Policy Council*, XXIII, 1 (2016), pp. 25–33.
61. Colleen Curry, 'See the Terrifying ISIS Map Showing its 5-Year Expansion Plan', ABC News, 3 July 2014, http://abcnews.go.com/International/terrifying-isis-map-showing-year-expansion-plan/story?id=24366850, last accessed 5 March 2017; Sushmita Dhekne, 'ISIS Plans to Take Holy War to China, occupy Xinjiang', *Thatsmags*, 11 August 2014, http://www.thatsmags.com/china/post/6282/isis-targets-xinjiang-to-take-the-holy-war-further, last accessed 5 March 2017.
62. Duchâtel, 'Terror Overseas'.
63. Jack Moore, 'Xinjiang's Uighur Muslims Receiving "Terrorist Training" from Isis Fighters for Attacks in China', *International Business Times*, 22 September 2014, http://www.ibtimes.co.uk/xinjiangs-uighur-muslims-receiving-terrorist-training-isis-fighters-attacks-china-1466594, last accessed 5 March 2017.
64. Jaime A. FlorCruz, 'Capture of Chinese National Fighting with ISIS Gives China Jitters', CNN, 5 September 2014, http://edition.cnn.com/2014/09/05/world/asia/china-isis, last accessed 5 March 2017.
65. 'Islamic State Suspects are Chinese Uygurs', *South China Morning Post*, 15 September 2014, http://www.scmp.com/news/asia/article/1593082/indonesia-says-4-chinese-uygurs-caught-suspected-islamic-state-ties, last accessed 5 March 2017.
66. 'ISIS Training Xinjiang Militants: Chinese Media', *Hindustan Times*, 23 September 2014, http://www.hindustantimes.com/world-news/isis-training-xinjiang-militants-chinese-media/article1-1267296.aspx, last accessed 5 March 2017.
67. Itamar Eichner, 'Israeli report: thousands of Chinese jihadists are fighting in Syria',

Ynet, 27 March 2017, http://www.ynetnews.com/articles/0,7340,L-4941411,00. html, last accessed 9 January 2018.

68. Gerry Shih, 'AP Exclusive: Uighurs fighting in Syria take aim at China', Associated Press, 23 December 2017, https://apnews.com/79d6a427b26f4eeab226571956 dd256e/AP-Exclusive:-Anger-with-China-drives-Uighurs-to-Syrian-war, last accessed 9 January 2018.

69. Richard Weitz, 'China and Afghanistan after the NATO Withdrawal', Jamestown Foundation, 17 November 2015, http://jamestown.org/uploads/tx_jamquickstore/China_and_Afghanistan_After_the_NATO_Withdrawal.pdf, last accessed 9 January 2018.

70. Jeff Seldin, 'Afghan Officials: Islamic State Fighters Finding Sanctuary in Afghanistan', Voice of America News, 18 November 2017, https://www.voanews.com/a/afghan-officials-islamic-state-finds-sanctuary-in-afghanistan/4122270.html, last accessed 9 January 2018.

71. Chaziza, 'China's Middle East foreign policy and the Yemen crisis'.

72. Erica S. Downs, *China's Quest for Energy Security* (Santa Monica, CA: RAND Corporation, 2000), http://www.rand.org/pubs/monograph_reports/MR1244.html, last accessed 5 March 2017.

73. 'China's oil demand to reach 15.5 million b/d in 2040: IEA', *S&P Global Platts*, 13 November 2017, https://www.platts.com/latest-news/oil/singapore/chinas-oil-demand-to-reach-155-million-bd-in-27888325, last accessed 9 January 2018.

74. 'U.S. Crude Exports Exceed Oil Products Exports', *Maritime Executive*, 12 December 2017, https://maritime-executive.com/article/us-crude-exports-exceed-oil-products-exports, last accessed 9 January 2018.

75. 'Chinese Investments and Contracts in Iraq 2005–2016', *China Global Investment Tracker*, 2017, https://www.aei.org/china-global-investment-tracker/, last accessed 5 March 2017.

76. Daniel Workman, 'Top 15 Crude Oil Suppliers to China', *World's Top Exports*, 22 December 2017, http://www.worldstopexports.com/top-15-crude-oil-suppliers-to-china/, last accessed 9 January 2018.

77. Shannon Tiezzi, 'China and Iraq Announce Strategic Partnership', *The Diplomat*, 23 December 2015, http://thediplomat.com/2015/12/china-and-iraq-announce-strategic-partnership/, last accessed 5 March 2017.

78. Dexter Roberts, 'Iraq Crisis Threatens Chinese Oil Investments', *Business Week*, 18 June 2014, http://www.businessweek.com/articles/2014–06–17/iraq-crisis-could-threaten-chinese-oil-investments, last accessed 5 March 2017); Du Juan, 'Iraq Crisis May Change China's Oil Suppliers', *China Daily*, 17 June 2014, http://usa.chinadaily.com.cn/2014–06/17/content_17595493.htm, last accessed 5 March 2017.

79. Christina Lin, 'ISIS Caliphate Meets China's Silk Road Economic Belt', *Middle East Review of International Affairs*, 18, 4 (2014), http://www.rubincenter.

org/2015/02/isis-caliphate-meets-chinas-silk-road-economic-belt/, last accessed 5 March 2017.
80. 'Belt and Road Initiative to Boost China–Turkey Cooperation', Central People's Government of the People's Republic of China, 21 April 2015, http://english.gov.cn/news/international_exchanges/2015/04/22/content_281475093929218.htm, last accessed 5 March 2017.
81. Chaziza, 'Sino-Turkish Solid Strategic Partnership'.
82. Jacob Zenn, 'Beijing, Kunming, Urumqi and Guangzhou: The Changing Landscape of Anti-Chinese Jihadists', *China Brief*, 14, 10 (2014), https://jamestown.org/program/beijing-kunming-urumqi-and-guangzhou-the-changing-landscape-of-anti-chinese-jihadists/, last accessed 5 March 2017.
83. Zachary Keck, 'Al-Qaeda Declares War on China, Too', *The Diplomat*, 22 October 2014, http://thediplomat.com/2014/10/Al-Qaeda-declares-war-on-china-too/, last accessed 5 March 2017.
84. 'Spotlight: China Backs UN's Leading Role as Security Council OKs Anti-Terror Resolution', *Xinhua*, 25 September 2014, http://news.xinhuanet.com/english/china/2014–09/25/c_133671747.htm, last accessed 5 March 2017.
85. Zhao and Hu, 'On China's New Anti-Terrorism Governance in the Middle East'.
86. Mordechai Chaziza, 'Comprehensive Strategic Partnership: A New Stage in China–Egypt Relations', *Middle East Review of International Affairs*, 20, 3 (2016), pp. 41–50.
87. Zhao and Hu, 'On China's New Anti-Terrorism Governance in the Middle East'.
88. Michael Martina, 'China holds first anti-terror drills with Saudi Arabia', Reuters, 27 October 2016, http://www.reuters.com/article/us-china-saudi-security-idUSKCN12R0FD, last accessed 5 March 2017.
89. Arushi Kumar, 'Way China's One Belt, One Road Matters for Afghanistan', South Asian Voices, 12 May 2017, https://southasianvoices.org/why-china-one-belt-one-road-matters-afghanistan/, last accessed 9 January 2018.
90. Andrew deGrandpre, 'Three countries undermining Afghanistan progress that President Trump didn't call out', *Washington Post*, 22 August 2017, https://www.washingtonpost.com/news/worldviews/wp/2017/08/22/russia-iran-and-china-are-undermining-afghanistans-progress-but-president-trump-didnt-call-them-out/?utm_term=.b3e4f162e601, last accessed 9 January 2018.
91. James Dobbins and Carter Malkasian, 'Time to Negotiate in Afghanistan: How to Talk to the Taliban', *Foreign Affairs*, July/August 2015, https://www.foreignaffairs.com/articles/afghanistan/2015–06–16/time-negotiate-afghanistan, last accessed 5 March 2017.
92. 'China to invite Syria factions to talks', *Global Times*, 21 December 2015, http://www.globaltimes.cn/content/959610.shtml, last accessed 5 March 2017.
93. Mordechai Chaziza, 'China–Pakistan Relationship: A Game-changer for the Middle East?', *Contemporary Review of the Middle East* 3, 2 (2016), pp. 147–61.

94. 'China Says Overseas Anti-Terror Missions must Respect Host Nation', Reuters, 31 December 2015, http://www.reuters.com/article/us-china-security-idUSK-BN0UE0NE20151231, last accessed 5 March 2017.
95. 'China Urges Hamas to Recognize Israel, Invites al-Zahar to Summit', *Haaretz*, 17 May 2006, http://www.haaretz.com/news/china-urges-hamas-to-recognize-israel-invites-al-zahar-to-summit-1.187878, last accessed 5 March 2017.
96. 'Full text of China's Arab Policy Paper', *Xinhua*, 13 January 2016, http://news.xinhuanet.com/english/china/2016–01/13/c_135006619.htm, last accessed 5 March 2017.
97. Shannon Tiezzi, 'Revealed: China's Blueprint for Building Middle East Relations', *The Diplomat*, 14 January 2016, http://thediplomat.com/2016/01/revealed-chinas-blueprint-for-building-middle-east-relations, alst accessed 5 March 2017.
98. Dingding Chen, 'China Should Send Troops to Flight ISIS', *The Diplomat*, 12 September 2014, http://thediplomat.com/2014/09/china-should-send-troops-to-fight-isis/, last accessed 5 March 2017.
99. Chaziza, 'ISIS risks, prospects and opportunities to Chinese foreign policy in the Middle East'.
100. Clarke and Pantucci, 'China is Supporting Syria's Regime'; and Wolf, 'Why China's Uighurs are joining jihadists in Afghanistan'.
101. Bree Feng, 'Obama's "Free Rider" Comment Draws Chinese Criticism', *Sinosphere*, 13 August 2014, http://sinosphere.blogs.nytimes.com/2014/08/13/obamas-free-rider-comment-draws-chinese-criticism/?_, last accessed 5 March 2017.
102. Chaziza, 'China's Middle East foreign policy and the Yemen crisis'.
103. Zhao Jun, 'The Current Situations and Prospects of Anti-terrorism Governance in the Middle East', *Arab World Studies*, 3 (2013), pp. 54–5.
104. John Irish, 'China rules out joining anti-terrorism coalitions, says helping Iraq', Reuters, 12 February 2016, http://www.reuters.com/article/us-mideast-crisis-china-idUSKCN0VL1SV, last accessed 5 March 2017.
105. 'Country Reports on Terrorism 2013', United States Department of State Bureau of Counterterrorism, 30 April 2014, http://www.state.gov/documents/organization/225050.pdf, last accessed 5 March 2017.
106. Michael Clarke, 'The Impact of Ethnic Minorities on China's Foreign Policy: The Case of Xinjiang and the Uyghur', *China Report*, 53, 1 (2017), pp. 1–25.

7. UYGHUR TERRORISM IN A FRACTURED MIDDLE EAST

1. The author is grateful to Amy Younger for her support in researching and footnoting this chapter.
2. Andrew Small, 'China's Man in the Taliban', *Foreign Policy*, 3 August 2015, http://foreignpolicy.com/2015/08/03/chinas-man-in-the-taliban-mullah-omar/, last accessed 1 June 2018.

3. Brynjar Lia, *Architect of Global Jihad* (London: Hurst & Co., 2007); and Mullah Abdul Salam Zaeef, *My Life with the Taliban* (London: Hurst & Co., 2010).
4. Vahid Brown and Don Rassler, *Fountainhead of Jihad: The Haqqani Nexus 1973–2012* (London: Hurst & Co., 2013), p. 111.
5. Cited in Brian Fishman, 'Al Qaeda and the Rise of China: Jihadi Geopolitics in a Post-Hegemonic World', *Washington Quarterly*, 34, 3 (2011), p. 49.
6. Guatanamo Testimonials Project, 'Testimonies of the Defense Department', Center for the Study of Human Rights in the Americas, p. 4080, http://humanrights.ucdavis.edu/projects/the-guantanamo-testimonials-project/testimonies/testimonies-of-the-defense-department/csrts/csrt_isn_905.pdf, last accessed 1 June 2018.
7. Andrew Higgins, Karby Leggett and Alan Cullison, 'How Al Qaeda Put the Internet in Service of Global Jihad', *Wall Street Journal*, 11 November 2002, https://www.wsj.com/articles/SB1036967366463939428, last accessed 1 June 2018.
8. Bill Roggio, 'Turkistan Islamic Party emir thought killed in 2010 re-emerged to lead group in 2014', *Long War Journal*, 11 June 2015, https://www.longwarjournal.org/archives/2015/06/turkistan-islamic-party-emir-thought-killed-in-2010-reemerged-to-lead-group-in-2014.php, last accessed 1 June 2018.
9. Tania Branigan, 'Olympics threatened by Islamic separatists', *Guardian*, 27 July 2008, https://www.theguardian.com/sport/2008/jul/27/olympicgames2008.terrorism, last accessed 1 June 2018.
10. This information was included in a State Department cable leaked by WikiLeaks which was reprinted by Norwegian daily *Aftenposten*, 12 October 2011, https://www.aftenposten.no/norge/i/Kyp64/882008-BEIJING-2008-SUMMER-OLYMPICS-USG-SITUATION-REPORT-8, last accessed 1 June 2018.
11. Tania Branigan, 'Al-Qaida threatens to target Chinese over Muslim deaths in Urumqi', *Guardian*, 14 July 2009, https://www.theguardian.com/world/2009/jul/14/al-qaida-threat-china-urumqi, last accessed 1 June 2018.
12. Inal Ersan, 'Prepare to fight China, Qaeda figure tells Uyghurs', Reuters, 7 October 2009, http://www.reuters.com/article/us-qaeda-china-xinjiang-idUSTRE5961AJ20091007, last accessed 1 June 2018.
13. Malcolm Moore, 'Al Qaeda vows revenge on China over Uyghur deaths', *Daily Telegraph*, 14 July 2009, http://www.telegraph.co.uk/news/worldnews/asia/china/5822791/Al-Qaeda-vows-revenge-on-China-over-Uighur-deaths.html, last accessed 1 June 2018.
14. Raffaello Pantucci, 'China and the Middle East', ASU Center for Strategic Communication, 5 June 2014.
15. Raffaello Pantucci, 'Uyghurs convicted in East Turkestan Islamic Movement Plot in Dubai', *Terrorism Monitor*, 8, 29 (22 July 2010), https://jamestown.org/program/uyghurs-convicted-in-east-turkestan-islamic-movement-plot-in-dubai/. The information cited in this article draws on court documents the author has in his

possession which are translated from Arabic, which might help explain some problematic transliterations of names.
16. Scott Shane and Eric Schmitt, 'Norway Announces Three Arrests in Terrorist Plot', *New York Times*, 8 July 2010, http://www.nytimes.com/2010/07/09/world/europe/09norway.html, last accessed 1 June 2018.
17. Petter Nesser and Brynjar Lia, 'Lessons Learned from the July 2010 Norwegian Terrorist Plot', *CTC Sentinel*, 1 August 2010, https://ctc.usma.edu/posts/lessons-learned-from-the-july-2010-norwegian-terrorist-plot, last accessed 1 June 2018.
18. Ibid.
19. Operation Crevice refers to a large al-Qaeda-linked plot uncovered in the UK in 2004. Chris Summers and Dominic Casciani, 'Fertiliser bomb plot: the story', BBC News, 30 April 2007, http://news.bbc.co.uk/1/hi/6153884.stm, last accessed 1 June 2018.
20. Raffaello Pantucci, 'Manchester, New York and Oslo: Three Centrally directed Al-Qa'ida plots', *CTC Sentinel*, 1 August 2010, https://ctc.usma.edu/posts/manchester-new-york-and-oslo-three-centrally-directed-al-qaida-plots, last accessed 1 June 2018.
21. 'Suspects confess to terror plan', *NewsinEnglish*, 29 September 2010, http://www.newsinenglish.no/2010/09/29/suspect-confesses-to-terror-plan/, last accessed 1 June 2018.
22. Bill Roggio, 'Al Qaeda appoints new leader of forces in Pakistan's tribal areas', *Long War Journal*, 9 May 2011, https://www.longwarjournal.org/archives/2011/05/al_qaeda_appoints_ne_2.php, last accessed 1 June 2018.
23. There have been many reports about the number and origin of foreigners drawn to fight alongside ISIS. In June 2014, a report by Richard Barrett published by the Soufan Group identified some 81 countries—though this number is higher in other reports. Richard Barrett, *Foreign Fighters in Syria*, June 2014, http://www.soufangroup.com/foreign-fighters-in-syria/, last accessed 1 June 2018.
24. Nate Rosenblatt, 'All Jihad is Local: What ISIS' files tell us about its fighters', New America Foundation, July 2016, https://www.newamerica.org/international-security/policy-papers/all-jihad-is-local/; and Brian Dodwell, Daniel Milton and Don Rassler, 'The Caliphate's Global Workforce: An inside look at the Islamic States' foreign fighter paper trail', Combating Terrorism Center, West Point, April 2016, https://ctc.usma.edu/postsl, last accessed 1 June 2018 the-caliphates-global-workforce-an-inside-look-at-the-islamic-states-foreign-fighter-paper-trail
25. Rosenblatt, 'All Jihad is Local', pp. 26–8.
26. Dodwell, Milton and Rassler, 'The Caliphate's Global Workforce', pp. 9–11.
27. Ibid., p. 20.
28. Ibid., p. 22.
29. Ibid., pp. 31, 36.
30. Nodirbek Soliev, 'The Rise of Uyghur Militancy in and beyond Southeast Asia:

An Assessment', *Counter Terrorist Trends and Analyses*, 9, 1 (February 2017), pp. 14–19; and Bilveer Singh, 'Southeast Asian Terrorism: The Rise of the Uyghur Factor', *RSIS Commentary*, 4 January 2016, https://www.rsis.edu.sg/wp-content/uploads/2016/01/CO16001.pdf, last accessed 1 June 2018.

31. Ron Corben, 'Thailand facing dilemma over fate of ethnic Uyghurs', Voice of America, 14 July 2017, https://www.voanews.com/a/thailand-facing-dilema-over-fate-of-ethnic-uighurs/3944075.html, last accessed 1 June 2018.
32. 'China police "shoot two Uyghurs trying to enter Vietnam"', BBC News, 19 January 2015, http://www.bbc.com/news/world-asia-china-30875969, last accessed 1 June 2018.
33. 'Sunni rebels declare new "Islamic Caliphate"', Al Jazeera, 30 June 2014, http://www.aljazeera.com/news/middleeast/2014/06/isil-declares-new-islamic-caliphate-201462917326669749.html, last accessed 1 June 2018.
34. http://jihadology.net/2015/07/07/al-ḥayat-media-center-presents-a-new-video-nashid-from-the-islamic-state-come-my-friend/, last accessed 1 June 2018.
35. Michael Martina and Ben Blanchard, 'Uyghur IS fighters vow blood will "flow in rivers" in China', Reuters, 1 March 2017, https://www.reuters.com/article/us-mideast-crisis-iraq-china/uighur-is-fighters-vow-blood-will-flow-in-rivers-in-china-idUSKBN16848H, last accessed 1 June 2018; and subsequently in October 2017 a short seven-minute video was released in Uyghur and Arabic. Earlier in June 2015 the group published a video showcasing an 81-year-old Uyghur who was fighting for them, alongside some Uyghur children who shouted threatening statements to China when asked about what they were being taught in ISIS schools.
36. Josh Chin, 'ISIS releases slickly-produced Mandarin song seeking Chinese recruits', *Wall Street Journal*, 7 December 2015, https://blogs.wsj.com/chinarealtime/2015/12/07/isis-releases-slickly-produced-mandarin-song-seeking-chinese-recruits/, last accessed 1 June 2018.
37. Gianluca Mezzofiore, 'Isis: Three Chinese Uyghur militants "executed" after escape attempt', *International Business Times*, 5 February 2015, http://www.ibtimes.co.uk/isis-three-chinese-uighur-militants-executed-after-escape-attempt-1486766, last accessed 8 June 2018; Alexa Olesen, 'China Sees Islamic State Inching Closer to Home', *Foreign Policy*, 11 August 2014, http://foreignpolicy.com/2014/08/11/china-sees-islamic-state-inching-closer-to-home/, last accessed 1 June 2018.
38. 'A Message to the Mujahidin and the Muslim Ummah in the Month of Ramadan', speech by Abu Bakr al Baghdadi, released by the al-Hayat media center, 1 July 2014.
39. http://www.ifengweekly.com/CoverDetil.php?id=3, last accessed 1 June 2018.
40. Antoine Vagneur-Jones, 'War and opportunity: the Turkistan Islamic Party and the Syrian conflict', Fondation pour la Recherche Stratégique, 2 March 2017, https://www.frstrategie.org/publications/notes/war-and-opportunity-the-

turkistan-islamic-party-and-the-syrian-conflict-07–2017, last accessed 1 June 2018. The ECFR report cites 200, while the New America Foundation cites up to 300.

41. Catherine Wong, 'Concerns grow over rise in Chinese jihadis in Syria', Associated Press, 22 April 2017, http://www.scmp.com/news/china/diplomacy-defence/article/2089808/inside-shadowy-world-chinese-militants-fighting-syria, last accessed 1 June 2018.

42. Thomas Joscelyn, 'Jihadists and other rebels claim to have broken through siege of Aleppo', *Long War Journal*, 7 August 2016, https://www.longwarjournal.org/archives/2016/08/jihadists-and-other-rebels-claim-to-have-broken-through-siege-of-aleppo.php, last accessed 1 June 2018.

43. 'Rise of Chinese extremists fighting in Syria raises concerns at home', *The National*, 22 April 2017, https://www.thenational.ae/world/rise-of-chinese-extremists-fighting-in-syria-raises-concerns-at-home-1.25584, last accessed 1 June 2018.

44. Thomas Joscelyn, 'Analysis: Insurgents launch major offensive against Assad regime in Hama province', *Long War Journal*, 24 March 2017, https://www.longwarjournal.org/archives/2017/03/analysis-insurgents-launch-major-offensive-against-assad-regime-in-hama-province.php, last accessed 1 June 2018.

45. Caleb Weiss, 'Suicide bombings detail Turkistan Islamic Party's role in Syria', *Long War Journal*, 3 May 2017, https://www.longwarjournal.org/archives/2017/05/suicide-bombings-detail-turkistan-islamic-partys-role-in-syria.php, last accessed 1 June 2018.

46. Much of this material is in the author's possession through applications like Telegram or Twitter, and Caleb Weiss at *Long War Journal* has published on some aspects of this, a subject he has tracked for some time. For example, Caleb Weiss, 'Turkistan Islamic Party in Syria confirms death of French-born fighter', *Long War Journal*, 19 February 2017, https://www.longwarjournal.org/archives/2017/02/turkistan-islamic-party-in-syria-confirms-death-of-french-born-fighter.php, last accessed 1 June 2018.

47. Caleb Weiss, 'Uighur group in Syria creates Palestinian sub-unit', *Long War Journal*, 25 January 2018, https://www.longwarjournal.org/archives/2018/01/uighur-group-in-syria-creates-palestinian-sub-unit.php, last accessed 1 June 2018.

48. For an insight into their activity in January 2018 in Aleppo, see this Twitter chain: https://twitter.com/ibnnabih1/status/953685642910846977?lang=en, last accessed 8 June 2018.

49. Thomas Joscelyn, 'Zawahiri praises Uyghur jihadists in ninth episode of "Islamic Spring" series', *Long War Journal*, 7 July 2016, https://www.longwarjournal.org/archives/2016/07/zawahiri-praises-uighur-jihadists-in-ninth-episode-of-islamic-spring-series.php, last accessed 1 June 2018.

50. Thomas Joscelyn and Bill Roggio, 'Turkistan Islamic Party leader criticises the Islamic State's "illegitimate caliphate"', *Long War Journal*, 11 June 2016, https://

www.longwarjournal.org/archives/2016/06/turkistan-islamic-party-leader-remains-loyal-to-al-qaeda-criticizes-islamic-states-illegitimate-caliphate.php, last accessed 1 June 2018.

51. '8 militants and commanders killed by the airstrikes on Sermada road', Syrian Observatory for Human Rights, 2 January 2017, http://www.syriahr.com/en/?p=58266, last accessed 1 June 2018.

52. Terri Moon Cronk, 'US Forces Strike Taliban, East Turkestan Islamic Movement Training Sites', *DoD News*, 7 February 2018, http://www.centcom.mil/MEDIA/NEWS-ARTICLES/News-Article-View/Article/1435570/us-forces-strike-taliban-east-turkestan-islamic-movement-training-sites/, last accessed 1 June 2018.

53. Issued by Islam Awazi, copy in author's possession.

54. References in author's possession.

55. 'Turkish leader calls Xinjiang killings "genocide"', Reuters, 11 July 2009, http://uk.reuters.com/article/us-turkey-china-sb/turkish-leader-calls-xinjiang-killings-genocide-idUKTRE56957D20090711, last accessed 1 June 2018.

56. 'Thai police believe Bangkok bombing suspect is in Turkey', *Deutsche Welle*, 15 September 2015, http://www.dw.com/en/thai-police-believe-bangkok-bombing-suspect-is-in-turkey/a-18714540, last accessed 1 June 2018.

57. Amy Sawitta Lefevre and Andrew R. C. Marshall, 'Bangkok shrine bombers first targeted pier for Chinese tourists', Reuters, 25 February 2016, http://www.reuters.com/article/us-thailand-blast-china/bangkok-shrine-bombers-first-targeted-pier-for-chinese-tourists-idUSKCN0VY2XP, last accessed 1 June 2018.

58. 'Funeral for Chinese guard killed in Somalia', *Xinhuanet*, 2 August 2015, http://news.xinhuanet.com/english/2015–08/02/c_134472268.htm, last accessed 1 June 2018.

59. Catherine Putz, '3 convicted for Chinese Embassy attack in Bishkek', *The Diplomat*, 30 June 2017, http://thediplomat.com/2017/06/3-convicted-for-chinese-embassy-attack-in-bishkek/, last accessed 1 June 2018.

60. This point is made in Andrew Scobell and Alireza Nader, *China in the Middle East: The Wary Dragon*, (RAND, 2016), https://www.rand.org/content/dam/rand/pubs/research_reports/RR1200/RR1229/RAND_RR1229.pdf, last accessed 1 June 2018. It is also illustrated by such media reporting as Abigail Hauslohner, 'In the Middle East, little outcry over China's Uyghurs', *Time*, 17 July 2009, http://content.time.com/time/world/article/0,8599,1911002,00.html, last accessed 1 June 2018. This article is significant as it was published in the wake of the July 2009 rioting in Xinjiang, which captured international headlines about the plight of Uyghurs.

61. Alice Su, 'China doesn't mind Islamic extremists: as long as they are not Uyghur', *Foreign Policy*, 16 December 2016, http://foreignpolicy.com/2016/12/16/china-doesnt-mind-islamic-extremists/, last accessed 1 June 2018; and Mohammed al Sudairi, 'Chinese Salafism and the Saudi Connection', *The Diplomat*, 23 October

2014, https://thediplomat.com/2014/10/chinese-salafism-and-the-saudi-connection/, last accessed 1 June 2018.

8. UYGHUR CROSS-BORDER MOVEMENT INTO SOUTH EAST ASIA: BETWEEN RESISTANCE AND SURVIVAL

1. For a detailed study on China's integrationist approach to Tibet, see Tsering Topgyal, *China and Tibet: The Perils of Insecurity* (London: Hurst & Co., 2016).
2. Nimrod Baranovitch, 'From Resistance to Adaptation: Uyghur Popular Music and Changing Attitudes among Uyghur Youth', *China Journal*, 58 (July 2007), pp. 5–82.
3. Joshua Tschantret, 'Repression, Opportunity, and Innovation: The Evolution of Terrorism in Xinjiang, China', *Terrorism and Political Violence* (2016), p. 3.
4. David Kang, *East Asia before the West: Five Centuries of Trade and Tribute* (New York: Columbia University Press, 2010).
5. Andrew D. W. Forbes, *Warlords and Muslims in Chinese Central Asia: A Political History of Republican Sinkiang, 1911–1949* (Cambridge: Cambridge University Press, 1986).
6. Michael Clarke, 'China's "War on Terror" in Xinjiang: Human Security and the Causes of Violent Uighur Separatism', *Terrorism and Political Violence*, 20, 2 (2008), p. 274; Joseph F. Fletcher, 'Ch'ing Inner Asia c.1800', in Denis Twitchett and John K. Fairbank (eds), *The Cambridge History of China*, Vol. 10, Late Ch'ing, 1800–1911, Pt 1 (Cambridge: Cambridge University Press, 1978), pp. 35–106; James A. Millward, *Beyond the Pass: Economy, Ethnicity and Empire in Chinese Central Asia, 1759–1864* (Stanford, CA: Stanford University Press, 1998); Forbes, *Warlords and Muslims*; and David Brophy, *Uyghur Nation: Reform and Revolution on the Russia–China Frontier* (Cambridge, MA: Harvard University Press, 2016), pp. 240–64.
7. Donald H. McMillen, 'The Urumqi Military Region: Defense and Security in China's West', *Asian Survey*, 22, 8 (1982), pp. 709–10.
8. Yitzhak Shichor, 'Blow up: Internal and External Challenges of Uyghur Separatism and Islamic Radicalism to Chinese Rule in Xinjiang', *Asian Affairs: An American Review*, 32, 2 (2005), p. 127.
9. Zia Ur Rehman, 'ETIM's Presence in Pakistan and China's Growing Pressure', Norwegian Peacebuilding Resource Centre (2014).
10. Chung Chien-peng, 'China's "War on Terror": September 11 and Uyghur Separatism', *Foreign Affairs*, 81, 4 (2002), pp. 8–12.
11. Michael Dillon, *Xinjiang: China's Muslim Far Northwest* (London and New York: Routledge, 2004), p. 59.
12. Gaye Christoffersen, 'Xinjiang and the Great Islamic Circle: The Impact of Transnational Forces on Chinese Regional Economic Planning', *China Quarterly*, 133 (1993), p. 134.

13. Rohan Gunaratna, *Inside Al Qaeda: Global Network of Terror* (New York: Columbia University Press, 2002), p. 173.
14. Martin I. Wayne, 'Inside China's War on Terrorism', *Journal of Contemporary China*, 18, 59 (2009), p. 252.
15. Caleb Weiss, 'Turkistan Islamic Party had significant role in recent Idlib offensive', *Long War Journal*, 30 April 2015, http://www.longwarjournal.org/archives/2015/04/turkistan-islamic-party-had-significant-role-recent-idlib-offensive.php, last accessed 16 September 2016.
16. Cui Jia, 'Rule of law is "key to Xinjiang terror fight"', *China Daily*, 26 November 2014, http://www.chinadaily.com.cn/china/2014-11/26/content_18980203.htm, last accessed 16 September 2016.
17. June Teufel Dreyer, 'China's Vulnerability to Minority Separatism', *Asian Affairs: An American Review*, 32, 2 (2005), pp. 69–86; and Clarke, 'China's "War on Terror" in Xinjiang'.
18. Sean Roberts, 'Imaginary Terrorism? The Global War on Terror and the Narrative of the Uyghur Terrorist Threat', *PONARS Eurasia Working Paper* (Washington, DC: Elliot School of International Affairs, 2012), p. 24.
19. Ibid.
20. Tschantret, 'Repression, Opportunity, and Innovation', p. 10.
21. See James M. Millward, 'Introduction: Does the 2009 Urumchi Violence Mark a Turning Point?', *Central Asian Survey*, 28, 4 (2009), pp. 347–60.
22. 'People's Republic of China, Development and progress in Xinjiang, Section VII', Office of the State Council, 21 September 2009, http://news.xinhuanet.com/english/2009-09/21/content_12090477.htm, last accessed 5 August 2016.
23. See Tschantret, 'Repression, Opportunity, and Innovation', p. 14.
24. Ibid.
25. Jeremy Page and Emre Peker, 'As Muslim Uighurs Flee, China Sees Jihad Risk', *Wall Street Journal*, 1 February 2015, https://www.wsj.com/articles/as-muslim-uighurs-flee-china-sees-jihad-risk-1422666280, last accessed 16 September 2016.
26. Tony Cartalucci, 'Turkish-Uyghur Terror Inc.—America's Other Al Qaeda', *New Eastern Outlook*, 23 September 2015, http://journal-neo.org/2015/09/23/turkish-uyghur-terror-inc-americas-other-al-qaeda/, last accessed 19 September 2016.
27. 'RI, China Hunting Down Xinjiang Terrorism Suspects in Poso', *Jakarta Post*, 10 February 2015, http://www.thejakartapost.com/news/2015/02/10/ri-china-hunting-down-xinjiang-terrorism-suspects-poso.html, last accessed 16 September 2016.
28. Zachary Abuza, 'Uyghurs look to Indonesia for terror guidance', *Asia Times*, 10 October 2014, http://www.atimes.com/atimes/Southeast_Asia/SEA-01-101014.html, last accessed 19 September 2016.
29. 'Nabbed Indonesian Militants "groomed suicide bombers"', *Straits Times*, 25 December 2015, http://www.straitstimes.com/world/nabbed-indonesian-militants-groomed-suicide-bombers last accessed 19 September 2016.

30. 'China: Account for Uyghur Refugees Forcibly Repatriated to China', *Human Rights Watch*, 28 January 2010, https://www.hrw.org/news/2010/01/28/china-account-uighur-refugees-forcibly-repatriated-china, last accessed 19 September 2016.
31. 'Laos Deports Seven Uyghurs', Radio Free Asia, 15 December 2010, http://www.rfa.org/english/news/uyghur/deport-12152010183037.html last accessed 19 September 2016.
32. 'Uyghur Arrests and Deportation Heighten Concern over Malaysia Deal', Amnesty International, 20 August 2011, http://www.amnesty.org.au/news/comments/26538/, last accessed 19 September 2016.
33. Kendrick Kuo and Kyle Springer, 'Illegal Uyghur Immigration in Southeast Asia', *CogitASIA*, 24 April 2014, https://www.cogitasia.com/illegal-uighur-immigration-in-southeast-asia/, last accessed 8 June 2018; 'Malaysia accused over deporting Uighur asylum seekers to China', 5 February 2013, https://www.theguardian.com/world/2013/feb/05/malaysia-uighur-asylum-seekers-china, last accessed 8 June 2018.
34. Andrew R. C. Marshall, 'Suspected Uighurs rescued from Thai trafficking camp', Reuters, 14 March 2014, http://www.reuters.com/article/us-thailand-UyghuridUSBREA2D0A920140314, last accessed 19 September 2016.
35. Edward Wong, 'Deadly Clash Reported on Border of China and Vietnam', *New York Times*, 19 April 2014, http://www.nytimes.com/2014/04/20/world/asia/deadly-clash-between-vietnamese-border-guards-and-chinese-migrants-reported.html?_r=1, last accessed 19 September 2016.
36. Rommel C. Banlaoi, 'Uyghur militants in Southeast Asia: Should PH be worried?', *Rappler*, 7 January 2016, http://www.rappler.com/thought-leaders/118137-uyghur-militants-southeast-asia-philippines, last accessed 19 September 2016.
37. Yenni Kwok, 'Is there a Uyghur Terrorist Buildup Taking Place in Southeast Asia?', *Time*, 28 December 2015, http://time.com/4161906/Uyghur-terrorism-indonesia-thailand-islam-isis/, last accessed 19 September 2016.
38. '155 Uighur immigrants found in Malaysia apartments', *Straits Times*, 3 October 2014, http://www.straitstimes.com/asia/se-asia/155-uighur-immigrants-found-in-malaysia-apartments, last accessed 19 September 2016.
39. '中国从东南亚遣返企图参加'圣战'的偷渡人员 [Illegal immigrants who attempt to participate in "jihad" are repatriated from South East Asia to China]', *Xinhua Net*, China, 11 July 2015, http://www.xinhuanet.com/legal/2015-07/11/c_1115892366.htm, last accessed 19 September 2016.
40. 'Bangkok Bomb: Deadly blast rocks Thailand capital', BBC News, UK, 17 August 2015, http://www.bbc.com/news/world-asia-33963280, last accessed 19 September 2016.
41. Yenni Kwok, 'Is there a Uyghur Terrorist Buildup Taking Place in Southeast Asia?'
42. Farouk Arnaz, 'Uighur arrested by Densus 88 suspected to be preparing for sui-

cide bombing', *Jakarta Globe*, 24 December 2015, http://jakartaglobe.beritasatu.com/news/Uighur-arrested-densus-88-suspected-preparing-suicide-bombing/, last accessed 19 September 2016.

43. 'Two Chinese Uyghur radicals killed in Indonesia: Police', *Daily Mail*, UK, 16 March 2016, http://www.dailymail.co.uk/wires/afp/article-3494627/Two-Chinese-Uyghur-radicals-killed-Indonesia-police.html, last accessed 19 September 2016; 'Anggota Kelompok Teroris Santoso yang Tewas Ditembak Berasal dari China', *Kompas*, 16 March 2016, http://regional.kompas.com/read/2016/03/16/12412401/Anggota.Kelompok.Teroris.Santoso.yang.Tewas.Ditembak.Berasal.dari.China, last accessed 19 September 2016; Rinaldy Sofwan, 'WNA Uyghur Gabung Kelompok Teroris Santoso Sejak 2014', CNN Indonesia, 16 March 2016, https://www.cnnindonesia.com/nasional/20160316164921-20-117865/wna-uighur-gabung-kelompok-teroris-santoso-sejak-2014, last accessed 19 September 2016; 'Indonesian Forces Kill 2 Ethnic Uyghur Militants', *Straits Times*, 17 March 2016, https://www.straitstimes.com/asia/se-asia/indonesian-forces-kill-2-ethnic-uighur-militants, last accessed 19 September 2016; Agustinus Beo Da Costa and Kanupriya Kapoor, 'Indonesia Security Forces Kill Two Chinese Uyghur Militants in Sulawesi Shootout', Reuters, 16 March 2016, https://uk.reuters.com/article/uk-indonesia-security-idUKKCN0WI0Q0, last accessed 19 September 2016; and 'More Uyghur Militants Infiltrating Indonesia: China', *Straits Times*, 18 March 2016, https://www.straitstimes.com/asia/east-asia/more-uighur-militants-infiltrating-indonesia-china, last accessed 19 September 2016.

44. Ruslan Sangadji, 'Police believe killed terrorist may be Uyghur fugitive', *Jakarta News*, 27 April 2016, http://www.thejakartapost.com/news/2016/04/27/police-believe-killed-terrorist-may-be-uighur-fugitive.html, last accessed 19 September 2016.

45. Rommel C. Banlaoi, 'Uyghur militants in Southeast Asia: Should PH be worried?', *Rappler*, 7 January 2016, http://www.rappler.com/thought-leaders/118137-uyghur-militants-southeast-asia-philippines, last accessed 23 September 2016.

46. Tschantret notes that the use of suicide bombings is a violent tactic which Uyghurs have used to circumvent repression by the state. See Tschantret, 'Repression, Opportunity, and Innovation', p. 16.

47. See Michael C. Horowitz and Philip B. K. Potter, 'Allying to Kill: Terrorist Intergroup Cooperation and the Consequences for Lethality', *Journal of Conflict Resolution*, 58, 2 (2012), p. 209.

48. See Philip B. K. Potter, 'Terrorism in China: Growing Threats with Global Implications', *Strategic Studies Quarterly* 7, 4 (2013), p. 71; M. C. Horowitz, 'Nonstate Actors and the Diffusion of Innovations: The Case of Suicide Terrorism', *International Organization*, 64, 1 (2010), pp. 39–40.

49. Sidney Jones, 'Poso's Jihadist Network', *Jane's Terrorism and Insurgency Monitor*, 7 February 2013, p. 18.

50. Jeff Crisp, 'Refugees and the Global Politics of Asylum', Evaluation and Policy Analysis Unit, UNHCR, Geneva (2003).
51. 'Uyghur Refugees go on Hunger Strike in Thai Detention Centre', Radio Free Asia, 22 January 2015, http://www.rfa.org/english/news/uyghur/refugee-hunger-strike-01222015152248.html, last accessed 19 September 2016.

INDEX

Abu Sayyaf Group (ASG): 182
Adam, Ibrahim: 161
Adamson, Fiona: theory of 'transnational political mobilisation networks', 21
Administrative Measures for Financial Institutions on Reporting Suspicious Transactions for Terrorist Financing (Reporting Regulation)(2007): 89; provisions of, 89–90
Administrative Measures on the Freezing of Terrorism-Related Assets (Asset Freezing Regulation)(2014): 89
Afghanistan: 12, 18–19, 21, 25, 34, 108, 111, 113–14, 118, 123, 125, 129–30, 141, 147–8, 153–4, 158–9, 177; Badakhshan Province, 139, 169; Jalalabad, 112, 114, 116; Kabul, 137–8; Little Pamir region, 153; Mes Aynak Copper Mine, 136; Operation Enduring Freedom (2001–14), 22, 25, 95, 104, 113, 129, 176; Soviet Invasion of (1979–89), 75–6, 132–3, 174; Zabul Province, 135
Ahrar al Sham: 167
Albania: 113–14; Tirana, 113–14
Ali, Sami: background of, 158–9
Alptekin, Isa Yusuf: 23–4

Amnesty International: personnel of, 61–2
Anti-Money Laundering Law (AML Law)(2006): 77; provisions of, 89
Arab Policy Paper (2016): 154
Arab Spring: Syrian Civil War (2011–), 27–8, 95, 111, 122, 124, 132–3, 157, 171
Arabic (language): 119
Asia-Pacific Economic Cooperation (APEC): 94
Asian Infrastructure and Investment Bank (AIIB): 3
al-Assad, Bashar: regime of, 133
Association of Southeast Asian Nations (ASEAN) Plus Three: 94
Australia: 1, 33, 163
Azerbaijan: 148
Al-Azhar Islamic University: students of, 66
Azzam, Abdullah: 168

al Baghdadi, Abu Bakr: 150, 169; speeches of, 133, 166
Baicheng Attack (2015): 87
Balochi: 136
Baltic and International Maritime Council (BIMCO): 151

INDEX

Bangsamoro Islamic Freedom Fighters (BIFF): 182
Baren Incident (1990): 24
Beg, Yaqub: 175
Beijing Car Attack (2013): 25, 73, 99, 101, 118, 178
Belt and Road Initiative (BRI): 3, 11, 42–3, 145, 151–2, 156; aims of, 14, 127; projects, 138
Bequelin, Nicholas: 61–2
Bujak, Shawan Sadek Saeed: arrest of (2010), 161
Burma: 95
Bush, George W.: 8; foreign policy of, 103

Cambodia: 95, 121, 182
Canada: 94
Center for Defense Information (CDI): 107
Central Military Commission (CMC): 37, 95–6; personnel of, 137
Central Religious Affairs Conference (2016): 45–6, 48, 52
Cerny, Philip G.: 23
Chaziza, Mordechai: 12–13
Chechnya: 178
Chen Quancheng: 43
Chen Quanguo: 41; XUAR Party Chairman, 55, 63–4, 70
China, Imperial (221BC–1912AD): Qing Dynasty (1636–1912), 102, 175
China, People's Republic of (PRC): 1–5, 12, 17–18, 23, 27–9, 31, 42, 47, 55–6, 72, 85–6, 90–1, 94, 97, 100, 107, 109–10, 123–5, 127, 129–30, 136–7, 141–2, 160, 163, 165, 171, 182–3; Aksu, 121, 126; Akto County, 176; as member of S-5, 33; Bachu, 47; Baren Township, 176; Beijing, 2, 4–5, 11, 13–15, 22–3, 25–6, 32, 34, 36–8, 45–6, 51–2, 54, 57–8, 61, 64, 66, 70–1, 76, 99, 101, 131, 137–9, 142–4, 146, 148–52, 154, 172; borders of, 130, 153; Bortala Mongol Autonomous Prefecture, 61, 67; Changji City, 60; crude oil imports of, 142, 151; Cultural Revolution (1966–76), 111, 120, 175; economy of, 29, 57; founding of (1949), 173; Guangdong, 26; Guangxi, 37; Guangzhou, 51; Hotan, 24; Ili Kazakh Autonomous Prefecture, 61, 66; Kashgar, 24, 47, 67–8, 111, 121, 126; Khotan, 117, 121, 126; Korla, 67–8; Kunming, 10–11; Lukqun, 25; Ministry of Foreign Affairs (MFA), 84; Ministry of Public Security (MPS), 25, 59, 78, 84, 90; Ministry of State Security (MSS), 57, 84; National Security Commission (NSC), 36–8; Public Security Ministry, 54; Qara Yulghun, 67; Shanghai, 28, 179; Tibet Autonomous Region, 41; Urumqi, 12, 24–6, 47, 54, 61, 64, 147; Xinjiang Province, 3–7, 10–14, 17–18, 21–31, 35–6, 38–9, 51, 53, 56, 58–60, 62–3, 65–7, 76–7, 83, 87, 107, 130–1, 134, 141, 144–5, 147–9, 152, 159, 172–4, 179, 183, 185; Xinjiang Uyghur Autonomous Region (XUAR), 2, 6, 17, 40–1, 43, 45–7, 50, 54–5, 57–8, 62–3, 69–71, 75, 99, 105, 108, 111, 113, 118, 120, 125, 144, 175; XUAR Department of Culture, 44; Yarkand, 121; Yining, 24; Yunnan Province, 11, 25, 121
China-Pakistan Economic Corridor (CPEC): 138–9; funding of, 135–6

INDEX

Chinese Civil War (1927–36/1946–50): 175
Chinese Communist Party (CCP): 6–7, 22, 37, 43, 45, 47–52, 58, 63, 69, 72, 76, 177; ethnic policies of, 41; founding of (1921), 40; General Office, 42; members of, 39–40, 42, 46, 48, 53; Third Plenum (2013), 53
von Clausewitz, Carl: 20
CleanWebGuard: 61
Cliff, Thomas: 37–8, 40
Cohen, Nick: 69
Cold War: 9, 18–19, 22, 32, 38, 142–3; end of, 20, 28, 156
Columbia University Press: 109
Combatant Status Review and Administrative Review Boards: 110
Combating Terrorism Center (CTC): personnel of, 163; report on Uyghur presence in ISIS, 164
Constitution of China: 45, 91
Council for Foreign Relations (CFR): 107
Counter-Terrorism Decision (CTD) (2011): 77, 83, 85; replaced with CTL (2015), 77
Counter-Terrorism Law (CTL): 6, 77–8, 84–9, 94, 96–7; adoption of (2015), 77; de-radicalization provisions of, 92–3; provisions of, 84, 87–8, 92, 95
counter-terrorism legislation: 8; Article III, 8; provisions of, 69
Crenshaw, Martha: 13
Criminal Law: 77; amending of (1997), 78–9; Article 120, 78–9
Criminal Procedure Law (CPL)(2012): 77; Article 73, 80–1; Article 83, 81; designated residential surveillance (DRS), 81; ordinary residential surveillance (ORS), 81; Technical Investigation Measures (TIMs), 81–3
Cuba: Guantanamo Bay, 95, 112–16
Cybersecurity Law (CSL)(2016): 77; provisions of, 87–8
Cyberspace Administration of China (CAC): 87

Damolla, Abdulheq: leader of TIP, 178
Davud, Mikael: arrest of (2010), 161
Decision on Amending the Criminal Procedure Law (2012): 77
Demirel, Süleyman: 23
Deng Xiaoping: funeral of, 24; 'reform and opening' policy of, 29
Dillon, Michael: 175
Djibouti: 138
Document 9: 44, 46; provisions of, 42
Dodwell, Brian: 163

East Turkestan: 75–6, 146, 184; independence movement, 95
East Turkestan Information Center (ETIC): 25, 85
East Turkestan Islamic Movement (ETIM): 24–5, 85, 99–100, 107, 109, 111, 115–16, 129, 146, 163, 169, 174, 177; allegiance to, 101–2; members of, 134, 155; recognition as terrorist organization, 106–7; terrorist attacks attributed to, 146; training camps, 169
East Turkestan Liberation Organization (ETLO): 25, 85
East Turkestan Republic: proposals for, 24
'East Turkestan' Terrorist Forces Cannot Get Away with Impunity (2002): 105
Eastern Indonesia Mujahideen: 179
Eastern Turkestan People's Revolutionary Party: KGB support for, 131

271

Egypt: 153; Cairo, 66
Egyptian Islamic Jihad (EIJ): 158–9
Eighteenth Party Congress (2012): 42
Erdoğan, Recep Tayyip: political rhetoric of, 148, 170; visit to China (2012), 148
Erikson, Johan: 28, 35–6; theory of 'internal-external security nexus', 18–19
ETIM: China's Islamic Militants and the Global Terrorist Threat, The: 109
European Union (EU): Framework Decision of June 2, 2002 on Combating Terrorism, 84

Falun Gong: members of, 3
Famularo, Julia: 6, 36
Fan Jinghui: death of (2015), 133
Fang Fenghui: PLA Chief of General Staff, 137
Ferghana Valley: 33
Financial Action Task Force (FATF): 89
Financial Times: 120
First Xinjiang Work Forum (2010): 72
Fishman, Brian: observations of jihadist terrorism, 12
Fourth Plenum (2014): 50
France: Paris, 89
Free Uyghurstan: 23
Freedom House: 86

Ganor, Boaz: 10, 101
Garcia, Anthony: 161
Georgia: 34
Germany: 88, 94; Duisburg, 161; Munich, 85
Ghazi, Usman: 135
Global Times: 28, 52–3
Global War on Terror (GWOT): 100–1, 104–5, 108, 114, 124–5, 132, 153, 177; political use of narrative, 104
globalization: 19–20
Great Firewall: use of VPNs to bypass, 60, 86
Great Western Development (2000): launch of, 29
Grose, Timothy: 31–2
Group of Twenty (G20): London Summit (2009), 117
Gu Liyan: 43
Gunaratna, Rohan: 108–9
Guo Shengkun: 55; Minister of Public Security, 54; visit to Afghanistan (2014), 137
Gurcan, Metin: 26
Gurr, Ted: 7

Hamas: 154
Han (ethnic group): 7, 26, 30, 37, 51, 119, 130–1, 150, 173; colonization/settlement of, 22, 145–6; culture of, 28, 174
Haq, Abdul: 111–12, 115, 123, 135; alleged leader of TIP, 116; death of (2010), 117–18, 130
Haqqani, Jalaluddin: leader of Haqqani Network, 158
Haqqani Network: 158
Harvard Law School: 69
Hayat-Tahrir al Sham: 167
Hersh, Seymour: 27
Hoffman, Bruce: definitions of terrorism, 9; *Inside Terrorism*, 4
Hong Kong Protests (2008): 51
Houthis: 153
Hu Jintao: 72, 117; national security policies of, 58
Hui (ethnic group): 40
Human Rights Watch: 59, 96

Indonesia: 11, 27, 133, 174, 179; Den-

sus 88 (police squad), 179–80; Poso, 179–80, 183
International Energy Agency (IEA): 142–3
International Uyghur Union: formation of (1992), 23
Investigative Project on Terrorism (IPT): 108
Iran: 155
Iraq: 11, 26, 149, 166; Chinese financial investment in, 151; crude oil exports of, 151; military of, 138; Ministry of Defence, 150; Mosul, 164, 166; Operation Iraqi Freedom (2003–11), 106; Ramadi, 138
Islam: 6, 23, 32, 53, 71, 108; Hajj, 160, 178; Qu'ran, 47–8, 165, 170; radical, 23, 34, 175–6; Ramadan, 46, 63, 148; Shariah, 164; Sunni, 163; symbols of, 30
Islamic Jihad Union (IJU): 176
Islamic Movement of Uzbekistan (IMU): 25, 33, 130, 132, 147, 169, 176; Attack on Karachi Airport (2014), 134–5
Islamic Party of East Turkestan: members of, 24
Islamic State (IS/Daesh): 76, 96, 123, 153, 163, 184; Fall of Mosul (2014), 164, 166; pledges of allegiance to, 179
Islamic States of Iraq and al-Sham (ISIS): 11–12, 18, 26–7, 96, 126, 130, 138, 141, 149, 156, 163–4; ideology of, 150; members of, 27, 136, 141–2, 150, 165–6; propaganda of, 133; supporters of, 27–8
Islamism: 2, 13, 25, 131, 141, 144, 149, 176; radical, 21, 24, 178, 184; Uyghur, 152
Israel: 155

Italy: 165

Jabhat Fatah al-Sham: 150, 176; formerly Jabhat Al-Nusra, 130
Jabhat Al-Nusra: 133, 147, 167; as Jabhat Fatah al-Sham, 130, 176
Jakobsen, David: activity as informant, 161–2; arrest of (2010), 161
Jarvis, Lee: 9
Jaysh al Fath: 167
Jemaah Islamiyah (JI): attacks conducted by, 183
Jiang Zemin: launch of Great Western Development (2000), 29
jihadism: 11–12, 26, 28, 32, 96, 108, 123, 132–3, 142–3, 147, 149, 162–3, 172; global, 104; Islamic, 154; social media, 27; Uyghur, 76, 157–8, 162
Jin Yinan, General: 26
Journal of Kashgar University: 43
Journal of Xinjiang Police Officers' Academy: 43
Justice and Development Party (AKP): 170

Kadeer, Rebiya: 85, 88, 95
Kam, Stefanie: 11
Kariaji, Abudula: 111
al-Kashgari, Sheikh Muhammad Salih (Sheikh Muhammad Salih Hajim): death of (2018), 170
Katibat al-Ghuraba' al-Turkistaniyyah (KGT): 168; emergence of, 167
Kazakhs (ethnic group): 40
Kazakhstan: 5, 23, 33–4, 66, 94, 108, 113, 148; Almaty, 23; as member of S-5, 33; Uyghur population of, 22
Kunming Train Station Knife Attack (2014): 26, 37, 152, 178–9; perpetrators of, 10–11, 102, 178; victims of, 102, 178

INDEX

Kurds (ethnic group): 161
al Kuwaiti, Abu Zaid: posthumous video released by (2013), 159
Kyrgyzstan: 5, 33–4, 94, 108, 113, 124, 148; as member of S-5, 33

bin Laden, Osama: 112, 158–60, 168–9; political rhetoric of, 132
Laqueur, Walter: 100
Lampton, David: 36, 53
Laos: 11, 95, 121, 182
Lebanon: 26
Leibold, James: 31–2, 36, 47, 55
Li Keqiang: view of CPEC, 138
Li Peng: diplomatic tour of (1994), 33
Li Wei: 97
al Libi, Abu Yahya: 159
Liu Hangying: 93
Long War Journal: 27
Losang Gyaltsen: Tibet Autonomous Region Chairman, 41
Lubman, Stanley: 69

Ma Mingcheng: Xinjiang People's Congress Deputy Director and Legislative Affairs Committee Director, 49
Ma Rong: 31
Mahsum, Hasan: 112, 115–16, 168; background of, 111; death of (2003), 25, 117, 134; founder of ETIM, 85, 106, 111; phone interview with Radio Free Asia (2002), 116
Malaysia: 27, 95, 121, 133, 165, 174, 179, 182
Mali: Bamako, 12
Mandarin (language): 67, 133, 166
Mansour, Abdullah: leader of TIP, 178
Mao Zedong: 47, 60
Al Mayadeen TV: 26–7
Medvedev, Dmitry: 34

Memeti, Memetiming: leader of TIP, 85
Merton, Robert: concept of 'self-fulfilling prophecy', 125
Milton, Daniel: 163
Minzner, Carl: 50
Mongolia, Inner: 22
Moros, Filipino: 175
Moustapha, Imad: Syrian Foreign Minister, 26
mujahideen: factions of, 23
Mujahidin Indonesia Timur (MIT): 11, 179, 183; allegiance to IS, 179
al-Murabitoun: Bamako Hotel Attack (2015), 12
Myanmar: 179

Nasution, Saud Usman: 179
National Counter-Terrorism Coordination Group: upgraded to National CTLG (2013), 78
National Counter-Terrorism Leading Group (National CTLG): 78, 84, 86
National Development and Reform Commission: 59
National Endowment for Democracy: 43
National People's Congress: 51; Standing Committee, 77, 154
nationalism: 175; Chinese, 144; ethno-, 4, 176, 184; Turkic, 23; Uyghur, 23
neoliberalism: 42
New America Foundation: personnel of, 163; report on Uyghur presence in ISIS, 164
new security diplomacy (NSD): development of, 4–5
New York Times: 114, 119
Nineteenth Party Congress (2016): 52, 63–4, 66–7; use in unity week campaign (2017), 63–4

INDEX

Ninth Criminal Law Amendment (2015): 77, 79–80
Nye, Joseph: 20
non-governmental organisation (NGO): legislation, 69–70
North Atlantic Treaty Organization (NATO): 179; member states of, 23
Northwest University of Political Science and Law: faculty of, 96
Norway: 162; Oslo, 161–2
al-Nusra Front: 27, 123–4, 150; establishment of (2012), 119

Obama, Barack: 117, 155
Olympic Games (2008): 76, 83, 117
Omar, Mullah: 158; death of, 135
One Belt, One Road initiative: 7
Operation Crevice: personnel involved in, 161
Özal, Turgut: 23

Pakistan: 12–13, 18–19, 24, 108, 113, 117–18, 123, 141, 147, 158, 160, 166, 177; Federally Administered Tribal Areas (FATA), 129–30, 133; Islamabad, 136, 160; Lal Masjid Mosque, 136; military of, 85, 130, 134; North Waziristan, 25, 132, 135, 147; South Waziristan, 25, 85, 134–5; Special Security Division, 136
Pantucci, Raffaello: 11
Paul, T.V.: 38
People's Armed Militia: 57
People's Armed Police (PAP): 37, 57, 62–3; personnel of, 56
People's Bank of China (PBC): 84, 89; Anti-Money Laundering Bureau (AMLB), 84, 88; China Anti-Money Laundering Monitoring and Analysis Centre (China ALMAC), 90; efforts to combat terrorist financing, 88
People's Daily: 46–7
People's Liberation Army (PLA): 2–3, 17, 37, 138; General Staff, 137; Navy (PLA-Navy), 138
People's Liberation Army Air Force (PLAAF): personnel of, 62
Philippines: 182; Manila, 182
Piazza, James: 7–8
Project Beauty campaign (2011–): 32

al-Qaeda: 5, 32, 85, 106, 108–9, 112–13, 115–16, 118, 122, 124, 130, 132, 136, 150, 156, 162, 168–9, 183; affiliates of, 18, 25, 146; branches of, 150; focus on China, 158–9; members of, 141–2, 159, 161–2; *ummah* of, 159, 168
al-Qaeda in the Islamic Maghreb (AQIM): affiliates of, 12
al Qahtani, Abu Khattab: 169
Qassim, Abu Bakker: 114
Qatada, Abu: 159
Qi Jianguo: PLA Deputy Chief of the General Staff, 137

Radio Free Asia: 87, 116
Radio Frequency Identification (RFID): 65
Rassler, Don: 163
re-education through labour (RTL): abolition of (2013), 93
Regional Anti-Terrorist Structure (RATS SCO): 94
Regional Ethnic Autonomy Law (REAL): provisions of, 71
Regulation on Religious Affairs (RRA): 90–1
Reeves, Jeffrey: 4–5
Rhinard, Mark: 28, 35–6; theory of

'internal-external security nexus', 18–19
Ripsman, Norrin: 38
Roberts, Sean: 9, 177
Rosenblatt, Nate: 163–4
Russian Federation: 5, 94, 124, 165; as member of S-5, 33; Yekaterinburg, 35
Russo-Georgian War (2008): 34

Salafism: 167, 170
Santoso: 180
Saudi Arabia: 148, 153; Mecca, 160; Medina, 169
Second East Turkestan Republic: 131
Second Work Conference (2014): 91
Second Xinjiang Work Forum (2014): 46, 176
Several Guiding Opinions on Further Suppressing Illegal Religious Activities and Combating the Infiltration of Religious Extremism in Accordance with Law (Counter-Extremism Document)(2014): 91–2
Several Guiding Opinions on Further Suppressing Illegal Religious Activities and Combating the Infiltration of Religious Extremism in Accordance with Law (Counter-Extremism Document)(2014): 91–2
Several Opinions on Further Strengthening and Improving the Work with regard to Islam (Islamic Religion Management Document): 92
Seymour, Gerald: *Harry's Game* (1975), 100
al-Shabaab: 159, 171
Shalmo, Mayma Ytiming: recruited by ETIM (2006), 160–1
Shambaugh, David: *China Goes Global: The Partial Power*, 57

Shanghai Cooperation Organization (SCO): 34, 54, 94–5, 131, 145; Counter-Terrorism Convention, 35; formerly S-5, 5, 33; member states of, 11, 35; Regional Anti-Terrorism Center, 34; Regional Anti-Terrorism Structure (RATS), 34–5; Shanghai Covenant on the Suppression of Terrorism, Separatism and Religious Extremism, 33–4
Shanghai Five (S-5): 33; as SCO, 5, 33
Shen Dingli: 36
Shen Jinke: 62
Silk Road: 152
Silk Road Economic Belt: proposed development of, 30
Silk Road Fund (SRF): 3
Singapore: 108
Skynet: 36; development of, 58
Small, Andrew: 12–13
Smith, Paul J.: 12
al Somali, Saleh: 161
Somalia: 159, 171
Soviet Union (USSR): 31, 75–6; collapse of (1991), 4, 21, 23, 29, 131, 176; Committee for State Security (KGB), 131; Moscow, 23
Special Police Units: 55
Sri Lanka: 165
State Administration for Religious Affairs: 52
State Council: 177
Strike Hard (campaign): 30
Studies in Conflict and Terrorism: 4
Syria: 11–12, 19, 26, 96, 110, 118–19, 122, 124, 126, 147, 149–50, 153–4, 166, 168, 170, 172, 178; Civil War (2011–), 27–8, 95, 111, 122, 124, 132–3, 157, 171; Al-Ghab plain, 119; Idlib Province, 27, 119, 133, 176; Jisr Al-Shughur, 26, 119, 170; Latakia Province, 176

INDEX

Tajikistan: 5, 94; as member of S-5, 33; Dushanbe, 34
Taliban: 33, 104, 106, 112–13, 115–16, 132, 134, 154; Bab al-Hawa, 169; members of, 135; Pakistani, 25, 132, 147; regime of (1996–2001), 131, 158; supporters of, 104; territory controlled by, 25
Tehrik-i-Taliban Pakistan (TTP): establishment of (2007), 136
Teng Biao: 69
terrorism: 1, 3–4, 6, 10–13, 19, 30, 36, 38, 52, 75–6, 107, 117, 120, 155, 161; criminalization of, 78–80; definitions of, 9, 83–4, 100–1; domestic, 144; ethno-religious, 45; financing of, 86–90; international, 24; Islamic, 143, 149; Islamist, 141; jihadist, 12, 157; Uyghur, 5–6, 17–18, 21, 25–9, 33, 75–6, 103, 109–10, 117, 125, 127, 157, 174
Terrorism and Political Violence: 4
Terrorist Activities Perpetrated by 'Eastern Turkistan' Organizations and their Links with Osama bin Laden and the Taliban (2001): 104
Thailand: 27, 121, 133, 174, 182; Bangkok, 12, 27, 172; Bishkek, 171–2; deporting of Uyghurs to China, 95; Erawan Shrine Bombing (2015), 12, 27, 134, 136, 171, 173, 179; Rohingya refugees in, 183
Third Criminal Law Amendment (2001): 77; provisions of, 79
Tianjin Airlines Hijack Attempt (2012): 25
Tibet: 22–3, 51, 55, 58, 71; Lhasa, 31
Tibetan Work Forum: 41
Tohti, Ilham: 40, 52, 72–3
Tschantret, Joshua: 177
Turkestan Islamic Party (TIP): 11, 25, 96, 99, 103, 108, 110, 125, 129, 132, 137, 147, 159, 161, 163, 165–6, 169, 174, 178; alleged participation in Syrian Civil War, 27, 119–20, 122–3, 136; attacks attributed to, 25–7; *Islamic* Turkistan, 118; members of, 85, 111, 116–19, 122–3, 135, 155, 178; use of social media, 117
Turkestan Islamic Party in the Levant (TIPL): 167–70
Turkey: 22–4, 26, 32, 66, 94, 114, 121, 124, 130, 136, 148, 153, 165, 174, 177–9; Ankara, 26, 133, 148, 152; borders of, 169; Istanbul, 148; National Intelligence Agency (MIT), 27; Uyghur diaspora in, 147–8; Uyghur seeking asylum in, 95
Turkic (ethno-linguistic group): 71, 146, 173–4; detention of, 67; efforts to restrict movement of, 65–7; Uyghur activism in, 122
Al-Turkistani, Abbas: 27
al Turkistani, Abdul Shakoor: al-Qaeda leader in Pakistani tribal areas, 162
al Turkistani, Abu Omar: death of (2017), 169
Turkmenistan: 34, 148
Twitter: 167, 169

United Arab Emirates (UAE): Dragon Mart Mall Attack Plot (2007), 160; Dubai, 160–1
United Kingdom (UK): 2, 33
United Nations (UN): 54, 94, 152, 154; Draft Comprehensive Convention on International Terrorism, 84; Refugee Agency, 95; resolution 1267, 106; Resolution 1360, 106; Security Council (UNSC), 90, 106, 152–3
United States Code: Section 2656f(d), 9

INDEX

United States of America (USA): 2, 12, 34, 43, 94, 108, 114; 9/11 Attacks, 1–2, 4–5, 18, 20, 22, 30, 33–4, 38, 41, 49, 76, 78–9, 94, 103–6, 116, 132, 134, 137, 146, 159, 168, 177; Central Intelligence Agency (CIA), 95; Executive Order 13224, 106; military of, 105, 117; National Security Act (1947), 38; Navy of, 144; New York, 161; State Department, 106, 118, 176; Treasury Department, 117–18; United States Military Academy at West Point, 163; Washington DC, 23, 155
unmanned aerial vehicles (UAVs): 62
Urumqi Market Bombing (2014): 147; political impact of, 54
Urumqi Public Security Bureau: 65
Urumqi Regulation on Banning the Wearing of Burqas in Public Places (2015): 77, 91
Urumqi Riots (2009): 51, 126–7, 134, 160, 177–8, 182; casualties of, 76, 119
US Energy Information Agency (EIA): 151
Uyghur (ethnic group): 7–8, 12, 18, 31–3, 51, 58, 63–4, 68, 95, 99–100, 105, 107, 110, 112–16, 120, 125–7, 133–4, 136, 146–7, 149, 155–6, 158, 162–4, 168, 170–1, 173–5, 178–9, 182; diaspora of, 5, 22–3, 109, 147–8, 185; language of, 64, 170; migration of, 11; militancy, 6, 12–13, 19, 21, 26, 37, 100, 103, 110, 123, 127, 130, 148, 150, 153, 172, 183; online communities, 51–2; overseas students, 66; radicalization of, 15, 18; recruitment into ISIS, 27–8; refugees, 120–2, 183–4; separatism, 18, 21–2, 24, 27–9, 34–5, 75, 104, 106, 147–8, 174, 176–8, 182; state targeting of cultural identity of, 31–2; territory inhabited by, 2
Uyghur American Association: 43
Uyghur Human Rights Project: 120
Uyghur Liberation Organization: 23
Uzbekistan: 5, 94, 108, 148; Tashkent, 34
Uzbeks (ethnic group): 175

Vietnam: 95, 121, 134, 165, 182
virtual private networks (VPNs): efforts to block overseas providers, 61; use to bypass Great Firewall, 60, 86

Wall Street Journal: 58, 111, 116
Wang Lequan: 177
Wang Xiuli: 43
Wang Yongsheng: PAP Deputy Commander, 56
War on Terror: political impact of, 3, 24
Wayne, Martin I.: 176
Weber, Max: theory of 'monopoly of legitimate violence', 20
Weiss, Caleb: 26
Wimiyar Ging Kimili: 160
Woeser, Tsering: 72
World Uyghur Congress (WUC): 21, 25, 85, 88; report on Uyghur refugee routes, 120–1
Wu Sike: 149

Xi Jinping: 40–1, 45–8, 53–4, 69, 71–2, 176, 178; foreign policy of, 3, 7, 14; General Secretary of CCP, 39–40, 46, 70; ideological education policies of, 44–5; national security policies of, 36–7, 52, 60
Xinhua: 142
Xinjiang Daily: 65

INDEX

Xinjiang Production and Construction Corps (XPCC): 54
Xinjiang Uyghur Autonomous Region Regulation on De-extremification (2017): 49–50
Xinjiang Uyghur Autonomous Region Regulations on the Management of Religious Affairs: 45
Xinjiang Work Forum: 70
XUAR Implementing Rules on the Counter-Terrorism Law (Xinjiang IRCTL)(2016): 92–3
XUAR People's Congress: 49; Standing Committee, 68–9
XUAR Regulation on De-Radicalization (2017): 77, 93–4
XUAR Regulations on Religious Affairs and Anti-Extremist Regulations: 50
XUAR Religious Affairs Regulations (2015): 49–51, 77

Yang Huanning: Vice Public Security Minister, 54
Yemen: 138; Civil War (2015–), 153–5
Yessen, Nayim: 49; Director of XUAR People's Congress Standing Committee, 69
YouTube: 117
Yu Hongyang: Chinese Ambassador to Turkey, 152
Yusuf, Zahideen: background of, 24

al-Zawahiri, Ayman: 'Islamic Spring' (video series), 168
Zazi, Najibullah: 161
Zenz, Adrian: 36, 55
Zhang Chunxian: XUAR Party Secretary, 40, 86
Zhang Feng: Minister of Industry and Information Technology, 61
Zhang Jinping: 96
Zhao Huasheng: 34–5
Zhou Yongkang: visit to Kabul (2012), 137
Zhu Shengwu: 62
Zunyou Zhou: 6